Thickening Fat

Thickening Fat: Fat Bodies, Intersectionality, and Social Justice seeks to explore the multiple, variable, and embodied experiences of fat oppression and fat activisms. Moving beyond an analysis of fat oppression as singular, this book will aim to unpack the volatility of fat—the mutability of fat embodiments as they correlate with other embodied subjectivities, and the threshold where fat begins to be reviled, celebrated, or amended. In addition, *Thickening Fat* explores the full range of intersectional and liminal analyses that push beyond the simple addition of two or more subjectivities, looking instead at the complex alchemy of layered and unstable markers of difference and privilege.

Cognizant that the concept of intersectionality has been filled out in a plurality of ways, *Thickening Fat* poses critical questions around how to render analysis of fatness intersectional and to thicken up intersectionality, where intersectionality is attenuated to the shifting and composite and material dimensions to identity, rather than reduced to an "add difference and stir" approach. The chapters in this collection ask what happens when we operationalize intersectionality in fat scholarship and politics, and we position difference at the center and start of inquiry.

May Friedman is an Associate Professor in the Ryerson University School of Social Work and Ryerson/York graduate program in Communication and Culture, and she holds a PhD in Women's Studies from York University. Dr. Friedman has a long publication history including the award-winning monograph *Mommyblogs and the Changing Face of Motherhood* (2013), as well as several edited collections.

Carla Rice is Professor and Canada Research Chair specializing in Embodiment/Subjectivity Studies and in Arts-based/Research Creation Methodologies at the University of Guelph, and she holds a PhD from York University in Gender and Women's Studies. She founded *Re•Vision: The Centre for Art and Social Justice* as a leading-edge creative research center with a mandate to foster inclusive communities, well-being, equity, and justice. She has received numerous awards for advocacy, research, and mentorship including the Feminist Mentorship Award and the Mary McEwen Award for Outstanding Gender Studies Scholarship, and she was recently inducted into the Royal Society of Canada, College of New Scholars, Artists and Scientists. She has published numerous books and articles, and directs multiple research grants.

Jen Rinaldi is an Assistant Professor in the Legal Studies program at Ontario Tech University. She earned a doctoral degree in Critical Disability Studies at York University, and a master's degree in Philosophy at the University of Guelph. She and Kate Rossiter authored *Institutional Violence & Disability: Punishing Conditions* (2018).

Thickening Fat

Fat Bodies, Intersectionality, and Social Justice

Edited by May Friedman, Carla Rice, and Jen Rinaldi

Routledge
Taylor & Francis Group

NEW YORK AND LONDON

First published 2020
by Routledge
52 Vanderbilt Avenue, New York, NY 10017

and by Routledge
2 Park Square, Milton Park, Abingdon, Oxon, OX14 4RN

Routledge is an imprint of the Taylor & Francis Group, an informa business

© 2020 Taylor & Francis

The right of May Friedman, Carla Rice, and Jen Rinaldi to be identified as the authors of the editorial material, and of the authors for their individual chapters, has been asserted in accordance with sections 77 and 78 of the Copyright, Designs and Patents Act 1988.

Trademark notice: Product or corporate names may be trademarks or registered trademarks, and are used only for identification and explanation without intent to infringe.

Library of Congress Cataloging-in-Publication Data
A catalog record for this title has been requested

ISBN: 978-1-138-58002-2 (hbk)
ISBN: 978-1-138-58003-9 (pbk)
ISBN: 978-0-429-50754-0 (ebk)

Typeset in Bembo
by Integra Software Services Pvt. Ltd.

Contents

Acknowledgments

We are grateful for the community that made this book possible, which came together for critical collaboration, delightful conversation, and delicious cake. Like many such endeavours, the finished volume doesn't convey the many different forms of labour that led to its completion and the many different supports that allowed the book to come to life. May would especially like to thank Carla and Jen for exemplifying what feminist collaboration should look like: support, guidance, challenge, and a lot of love. Carla shares in that gratitude and wants to thank May and Jen for their incredible smarts, Jen for her quirky humour, and May for truly fantastic baking. And Jen owes a great deal to May and Carla for their mentorship and their generosity of spirit. On a final note, Carla needs to thank her body for bearing the burdens of her own and others' punishments, and for teaching her in a small way something of what is required to survive, create, and even celebrate in the face of adversity and injustice.

Before there was a book, there was the splendid Thickening Fat Symposium, a two-day event that enabled authors to present draft chapters. Support for the symposium was generously offered by the Social Sciences and Humanities Research Council of Canada (SSHRC), Ryerson University's Faculty of Community Services and the Office of the Vice President of Research and Innovation; the University of Ontario Institute of Technology; the Re•Vision Centre for Art and Social Justice at the University of Guelph; and the SSHRC-funded Partnership Grant, Bodies in Translation: Activist Art, Technology and Access to Life. We owe thanks to the artists—in particular our Master of Ceremonies Sabrina Friedman—who performed at a fabulous and funky cabaret that reminded us to keep connected to community and to imagine intersectionality on artistic and theatrical registers. The symposium was a success, in part, thanks to the administrative support of the fabulous Farrah Trahan and the management skills of the uber-host, Tracy Tidgwell.

The process of completing this volume was greatly aided by the exceptional organizational prowess of Kelsey Ioannoni. Kelsey supported *Thickening Fat* from its inception as a vague idea and has helped us immeasurably at every stage. She also provided logistic and emotional support for the symposium. We truly would have been lost without her.

We appreciate the guidance we have received from Samantha Barbaro and Erik Zimmerman at Routledge. The tremendously talented Paul Richards created the gorgeous cover artwork, was gracious when we slid into his Tumblr DMs, and gave us permission to use his work. We thank the anonymous reviewers who offered useful commentary and helped to strengthen our conviction about the necessity of the collection.

Finally, our deep gratitude goes to the authors of this volume. The symposium and subsequent chapters allowed us to engage in conversation that truly thickened our understanding of fat in the best possible ways. The wisdom, sensitivity, and thoughtfulness that authors offered to this topic have genuinely pushed our thinking further and, we hope, will thicken Fat Studies as a field.

Introduction

Jen Rinaldi, Carla Rice, and May Friedman

We are in constant dialogue with fat. We consider where our fat lives on our bodies—how to grow it, contain it, remove it, and prevent it. We check fat grams and make choices about what types of fat to put into our bodies. The historical and contemporary absence of fat—whether in flesh or in food—is not benign but is typically governed by a range of disciplinary practices designed to keep fat at bay. The presence and history of fat is deeply embodied and deeply emotional but is also bound up in other structural zones of oppression and privilege. It is impossible to think about fat without thinking about colonialism, for example, and the ways that food, wellness, exercise, lifestyle, and health are profoundly and palpably shaped by a colonized landscape. Likewise, thinking about fat in and on, as well as taken into and expelled from, our bodies is inextricably bound up in thinking through our culture's broader notions of normalcy and madness—how the self-governance and the individual responsibility required to adhere to mainstream views of health are inextricably entwined with the anxieties of neoliberalism.

The academic sister of fat activism, Fat Studies has grown more robust in the last 15 to 20 years, creating a body of literature that interrogates the experiences of fat people and the nuances of fat stigma in a range of times and spaces. Fat Studies looks at the negative impacts of fatphobia but also extrapolates from the embodiment of fat people as a potential rebuttal to normativity, as a form of liberation and revolution that resists conformist discourses and practices. As a field, Fat Studies is in close dialogue with other interdisciplinary fields—Disability Studies, Mad Studies, d/Deaf Studies, Aging Studies, Feminist and Gender Studies, and Queer Studies—while it has yet to integrate other liberation scholarships. *Thickening Fat* is an attempt to take the robust and cheeky canon of Fat Studies, as a growing interdisciplinary field, and to grow it further by considering fat in dynamic and unstable yet indivisible and intricate dialogue with other identity markers and materializations, liberation struggles and academic fields. Without maligning the excellent scholarship which has developed this field, *Thickening Fat* aims to grow and stretch Fat Studies into a complicated and dynamic engagement with non-normative bodies of all shapes, sizes, races, abilities, genders, and sexualities, as well as with impactful socioeconomic and historical forces underpinning these, including colonialism, neoliberalism, geopolitics, and beyond.

We began this quest by literally embodying our scholarship. In February 2018, two dozen Fat Studies scholars from around the world convened in Toronto, Canada, with a lofty goal: to make Fat Studies thicker. Over the course of two days, participants—including the authors of this volume, as well as graduate students, activists, artists, performers, and community members—presented, argued, laughed, ate, danced, sang, and, in short, showcased the best of what fat scholarship and community has to offer. The event explored an altered and extended literature that situates fat liberation in the context of the full, glorious, messy continuum of human identity. It is important to note that the goal of this event—and the goal of this book—is not consensus. Rather than inscribing dogma, *Thickening Fat* seeks to inhabit possibility, to thicken fat by understanding the ways that fat identities and embodiments are neither singular nor static. In line with our liberationist impulse, we also push against normative tendencies in fat scholarship and beliefs about what constitutes acceptable fat activisms and activists, thus thickening our movements in ways that embrace the intersectional concept of fat justice.

Thickening Fat Identities, Thickening Fat Studies, Thickening Fat

Normative expectations have a habit of creeping into critical studies. Even the progressive field of Fat Studies has sometimes failed to treat gender, sexuality, race, ethnicity, class, indigeneity, citizenship, age, geography and ability to full analysis. The normative subject of the field still tends to be a young(ish), white, cisgender woman, and typically one who is from the Global North. Fat activist spaces, too, tend to materialize as white, middle-class spaces. Like other fields and activisms invested in counter-hegemonic culture-building, Fat Studies and politics run the risk of erring on the side of sameness at the expense of difference when, for example, "Fatshion" campaigns hinge on neoliberal values that celebrate fat embodiment through consumption and attempt to secure fat belonging through commodity capitalism (Rinaldi, Rice, LaMarre, McPhail & Harrison, 2017); when Big Bold Women events (BBW) cast out queerness and gender non-normativity (Farrell, 2011); and when body positivity movements disavow experiences of shame tied to bodily difference and disadvantage (Cooper, 2016; Solovay & Rothblum, 2009). All of these examples indicate the urgent need to stretch Fat Studies and activism, and to find and push its intersectional focus, through dialogue.

Thickening Fat responds to the call for thickening fat identities, thickening Fat Studies, and thickening fat itself. While critiques of Fat Studies are not new, intersectionality theories at the heart of such critiques are themselves evolving. Rooted in Black feminist thought, intersectionality was fully developed into a theory by feminist legal scholar Kimberlé Crenshaw (1989, 1991), who employed the metaphor of the traffic intersection to make visible the multiple, interweaving causes of discrimination against Black women and others experiencing overlapping oppressions. Since then, scholars from different disciplines and theoretical perspectives have elaborated on ways to use the concept in their work. Some have deployed it to theorize anti-essentialist approaches to subjectivity and group affiliation and others, to explain micro-level experiences of multiply marginalized people or to study macro-level interactions between lived experiences and social structures (Rice, Harrison & Friedman, 2019). Still others, like Deleuzian queer theorist Jasbir Puar (2007, 2012), have imagined the intersections as an arrangement or event rather than a static nexus of identities and social structures: momentary, contingent, dynamic.

Crenshaw's now classic traffic metaphor has been treated to myriad interpretations and applications, some of which imply that intersectionality is additive, fixed and strictly socially constructed. However, many of these applications have been critiqued for failing to account for the messiness and fleshiness of identities—for the dynamism of human identities and worlds, and the materialization of embodiments at their conjunctions. An embodied approach to intersectionality points to the impossibility of disaggregating differences or identity categories since embodiment "defies compartmentalization by social category" (Changfoot & Rice, forthcoming). An embodied intersectionality further underscores the need to account for the visceral sensations, agencies, sufferings, and pleasures of bodies in the myriad ways they manifest through the convergence of the social and the material (Rice, Pendleton Jiménez, Harrison, Robinson, Rinaldi, LaMarre & Andrew, forthcoming). Taking an "intrasectional embodiment perspective" (Rice, 2018, p. 537), we might reinterpret embodied subjectivities at the intersections as dynamic, affective, emergent becomings, as "dispersed but mutually implicated and messy networks, draw[ing] together enunciation and dissolution, causality and effect, organic and nonorganic forces" (Puar, 2007, pp. 211–212). When considered through the lens of embodiment, intersectionality theory can capture how societies control multiply marked, differently sized and shaped bodies, and how those bodies act back, through the push and pull of identity interpellation and self-creation as well as through the confrontation of social and nonsocial forces, capacities, and tendencies.

Thickening Fat aims to advance a deeply intersectional project. The text brings Fat Studies into dialogue with intersectionality studies in order to cultivate a new body of critical scholarship and activism that recognizes the entanglements of fat with other identity markers and surfaces the flows of power that crystallize temporarily to shape differently embodied lives. Conscious that intersectionality theory has been mobilized in a plurality of ways (Geerts & van der Tuin, 2013; Rice, Harrison & Friedman, 2019), we seek in *Thickening Fat* to pose critical questions of fatness at the intersections. We ask: How do we render analysis of fatness intersectional and thicken up intersectionality? What happens when we operationalize intersectionality in fat scholarship and politics, and position difference and liberation at the center and start of inquiry? Our collection explores the multiple, variable, and embodied experiences of fat oppression, fat possibilities and fat activisms. Moving beyond an analysis of fat oppression as singular, our book aims to unpack the volatility of fat—the mutability of fatness as it entangles and coalesces with other embodied differences. In addition, *Thickening Fat* explores the range of intersectional analyses that push into the complex alchemy of layered yet unstable markers and forces of difference and privilege.

One aim of this collection is to thicken the field of Fat Studies. Fat Studies, as an emergent interdisciplinary field (Cooper, 2016), draws from and contributes to many other interdisciplinary areas, including Women's, Gender and Sexualities Studies, Critical Disability Studies, legal studies, sociology and anthropology, critical geography and many more beyond. In addition, Fat Studies scholarship is beginning to be taken up in professional disciplines such as social work, medicine, nutrition, midwifery and other health science and social service fields (Cameron & Russell, 2016). While *Thickening Fat* begins from the scholarship of Fat Studies, we are equally grounded in theoretical and practical writing from beyond this field. Specifically, we aim to stretch the capacity of Fat Studies to consider the multiple, dynamic, and complex ways that fat may be layered into and muddled with other markers and materialities of identity and difference. This complexity surfaces the entanglements of fat with queer and trans embodiments and issues; with melanin alongside other physical markers of race as these entwine with racism and white supremacy; with colonial histories and their legacies for Indigenous bodies and lives; with critical approaches to disability and madness. *Thickening Fat* seeks to advance inter- and even trans-disciplinary thinking by tying together social scientific and (post)humanities approaches, and by cross-pollinating the fields of fat and intersectionality studies in ways that grow conversations with potential to transform both.

Finally, we aim in our collection to thicken fat itself. Thinking past discourses that imagine fat bodies as strictly socially constructed or as biologically and behaviourally determined, we argue for a distinctly cultural, material, and intersectional approach to fatness—one that affirms fat's agency and vitality, and also acknowledges the pains and perils of embodying fatness at this historical and cultural moment. Such a move opens the field of Fat Studies to expansive readings that acknowledge multiple, contradictory experiences of fatness; that resist discourses of utopic body positivity as much as those of dystopic obesity epidemic panics; that bring eating pleasure and distress into discussion and trace the agencies of fat in food and in flesh; that make the destruction of bodies and minds seen as non-vital ever more possible in a post-humanist moment marked by proliferating biotechnologies; that build alliances to think across other alterities and non-normative embodiments and to open new terrain from which to ground our scholarship and activisms. Recognizing that representations of a group determine the treatment of that group (Chandler & Rice, 2013; Rice & Chandler, forthcoming), we advance that we need theory that accounts for the disparate socio-corporeal realities of fat people, the vigorous cultural drive to expunge fat bodies and fat from bodies (and food), and the power of cultural production to reassert fat lives as livable, and fat futures as desirable. We assert that generating critical theory and cultural possibility about fat as it intersects with other difference has palpable material consequences for social and fat justice, centering the most marginalized bodies of difference. We turn now to consider the sections of this book and the different discursive techniques used to thicken fat in this volume.

Our Heavy Inheritances

The nuanced analysis in this section traces fat oppression through entangled systems of power and deeply rooted histories. Against paradigms that would problematize fat, we need analytic approaches that pull focus toward the treatment of fat, or "stigma and prejudice (and their consequences) that inspire much of the extensive research in the field of fat studies" (Solovay & Rothblum, 2009, p. 5). These stigmas tend to be clustered in ways that connect constructions of fatness—moralizing attributes like "laziness, gluttony, poor personal hygiene, and lack of fortitude" (Murray, 2005, p. 154; see also Ward, 2016), as well as medicalized attributes like risk, biology, and defect—to other marginalized identity markers, including gender, race, poverty, indigeneity, and disability.

In particular, white supremacist and settler colonial ideologies racialize fat, such that the technologies designed to monitor and expunge fat map onto longstanding anti-Indigenous and racist projects and intentions (LeBesco, 2004; Poudrier, 2016). When "higher obesity rates" are identified in marginalized groups, medical paradigms provide justification for discourses of surveillance and expressions of judgment. That fatphobia emerges as an acceptable stand-in for racial discrimination amplifies experiences of exclusion and violence (Wilson, 2009). From the history of the freak show to that of the bell curve, disability scholars have shown how ableist and racist ideologies overlap and intersect with fatphobic ones through constituting certain bodies as species typical while coding others as aberrant (Clare, 1999; Garland-Thomson, 1997). Today, medical and legal regimes continue to disable fatness through the conflation of obesity with disease and the circulation of a "cure imaginary" that ties access to happiness, love, and life itself to realizing the elusive cure (Kafer, 2013, p. 27). Further, anti-fat discrimination operates in and through hetero-patriarchal systems of logic, such that fat is gendered, feminized, and marked as a site of disgust or undesirability. Fat Studies scholarship has borrowed generously from queer and trans theory to account for the social rejection of fat embodiment (Cooper, 2016; Solovay & Rothblum, 2009; Vade & Solovay, 2009), demonstrating new complexities to the gendering of fat.

Fat is read through these lenses, and violence—both discursive and visceral—against fatness flows through these various, interlocking, long-standing systems of oppression. Oppression is passed down, bestowed upon populations across macro generational relations, and intimately between and through persons (Rinaldi, Rice, Kotow & Lind, 2019). Teasing apart the unfolding of fat discrimination, and its various directions and conflations, calls for careful analytic work.

Exploding Our Expectations

Chapters in this section seek to wrest fat from the interpretive frames of the medical encounter. Processes of medicalization produce narrow versions of fatness as a diagnosis, disease, or disorder (Paradis, 2016). Fat is made legible via diagnostic tools of measurement, particularly the Body Mass Index, which determines whether and to what extent a patient has a health problem (Rice, 2007, 2014). Medical practitioners also conduct snapshot diagnoses according to which their patients' existing and potential ailments are entirely attributable to their fat form (Ellison, McPhail & Mitchinson, 2016). Discourses of medicalization position fatness as a problem on several counts. First, fat is framed as a death sentence—an impediment to good health given its myriad attendant risks (Ward, 2016). Second, fat becomes a matter of public health when read as an epidemic spreading across populations (Wykes, 2014). The fat person is presumed to influence poor behaviours in others, and to use more health care services—a finite resource—than they deserve compared to the normatively non-fat population (Ellison, McPhail & Mitchinson, 2016). This knitting together of affective attachments renders the fat person responsible for seeking out and submitting to solutions for their own good, their health and well-being, but also for a greater communal good. These engagements are exacerbated and amplified when fat bodies are multiply non-normative, exploding expectations of gender, race, coloniality, disability, and madness.

Conditions made medical are treated via medical solutions and are thus ushered into the jurisdiction of health care providers. Solutions include diet and exercise at the recommendation and under the supervision of nutritionists and dieticians; physiological and psychiatric medication; psychiatric treatment; and surgery (LeBesco, 2004; Paradis, 2016). These interventions are designed to expunge fat through medically administered and managed means. Interpretations of fatness maintain the authority of the medical provider to make sense of fat and to oversee approaches to fat. They also engender medical trauma and produce barriers to accessing needed health care services.

Complex theorizing of fat carries the potential to recast and respond to the expectations embedded in the medical encounter. An intersectional reading of fatness lays bare how medical expectation contracts and oversimplifies relationships to eating, exercise and distress. Medicalization—and concomitant problematization—of fat assigns stigma to bodies in particular and debilitating ways, and limits or altogether precludes access to health care support (Rinaldi, Rice, LaMarre, McPhail & Harrison, 2017).

Expanding Our Activisms

Critical responses to fat discrimination flourish outside the academy, in a rich history of community organizing efforts. Just as Fat Studies scholarship can be deepened through intersectional analysis, the chapters in this section illustrate that fat activisms cannot effectively enact social justice without intersectional and intra-sectional consideration. Oversimplified fat liberation projects risk re-inscribing the exclusionary logics that fat bodies are challenging. Further, historical accountings of fat activisms are guilty of themselves oversimplifying the work accomplished. They have, as examples, focused on American movements, and left out of their accountings the work of fat activists of colour (cf. Ellison, 2016). Scholarly lacunae and on-the-ground reticence to do coalition- and community-building work can paper over the experiences that diversely positioned persons have of oppression and can undercut the labour and achievements of social movements.

In her analysis of fat activisms, Cooper (2016) cautions against movements that are not radically critical of capitalism. This critique is levelled against, for instance, strategies to improve fashion choices for fat bodies, or to improve representation of fat persons in film. In her own words: "using capitalism as a basis for activism illustrates how, within the gentrification of fat activism it is access rather than social transformation that has become the main motivator" (p. 175). Fat liberation projects that do not acknowledge the force of poverty in people's lives also risk missing compounding oppressive factors like racism and ableism; and indeed, fat activist spaces have struggled with welcoming persons of colour and being accessible to persons who require accommodation support.

Fat liberation's investment in affirmation has implications that need unraveling. Specifically, body positivity work has been central to fat activist projects in the face of unrelenting social shaming and marginalization; but Cooper cautions that there are fat persons who "cannot conform to an activist orthodoxy of self-acceptance when their lived experience is saturated with ambivalence and pain" (Cooper, 2016, p. 15; see also Murray, 2009). For instance, in her analysis of bariatric surgery and diet, particularly in fat trans populations, LeBesco suggests that: "fat activism is currently wrestling with an important question: how does the movement make sense of a fat activist who intentionally loses weight?" (2014, p. 49). In short, is there room in our movements for feelings more complex than positivity or pride?

Our Gainful Failures

Creative and critical analysis of body positivity surfaces in auto-ethnographic work on fatness. A common approach in Fat Studies scholarship, auto-ethnography connects the personal to the political by illustrating how oppression is experienced, navigated, and felt. Cooper (2016) calls intentional living while fat—for example, wearing a bathing suit, or ordering a dessert in the face of open hostility—a kind of micro fat activism. She describes: "micro fat activism takes place in everyday spaces, is generally performed by one person, sometimes two, but rarely more, and happens in small, understated moments" (p. 78).

Living while fat is a kind of activism because it operates as a productive failure. Failure is conceptualized in queer theory (Halberstam, 2011) as a refusal and rejection of normative paradigms and respectability politics. LeBesco (2004) deals with this subversion by characterizing the fat body as revolting—as both a source of disgust and a catalyst for rebellion (see also Cooper, 2016; Nault, 2009). In her words, "if we think of revolting in terms of overthrowing authority, rebelling, protesting, and rejecting, then corpulence carries a whole new weight as a subversive cultural practice that calls into question received notions of health, beauty, and nature" (LeBesco, 2004, pp. 2–3). Fisanick (2009) explores this idea in the case of persons living with a diagnosis of polycystic ovarian syndrome (PCOS), and specifically takes up an interest in intentional living: "The PCOS body—fat, irregular, infertile, and hairy—attempts to accomplish this subversion, but the body alone is not enough to alter the oppressive system of normative femininity...Rather, it takes an actor to effect change by the way the acts are read and repeated" (p. 107). Artistic performance is another way of presencing fatness in normative space, and in so doing engaging in an art of refusal. For this reason, fat activisms make clear connections to artistic practice. Consider burlesque: "Fat burlesque dancers use the performance space to present, define, and defend their sexualities, resisting a backdrop of medical and social discourses that inform their everyday lives" (Asbill, 2009, p. 299).

These chapters engage with pride, but they also afford theories the opportunity to explore the shame felt from being ridiculed, alienated, hurt and harmed. The exploration of shame can itself be productive, for "tracing some of the manifestations, or 'faces' of shame, whether they be personal or collective [enables] people to reassess their actions, themselves and, importantly, their politics" (Longhurst, 2014, p. 19; see also Probyn, 2005).

Conclusion

Bringing Fat Studies and intersectionality literatures together will always be an uneasy truce: both fields are justifiably defensive, eager to establish their credibility in the face of endless commentary to the contrary. At the same time, neither canon can be truly revolutionary without acknowledging the impact of the other. While this book exists as an attempt to explore the overlaps and tensions between Fat Studies and intersectionality, we are mindful that there is enormous work yet to be done. As academics and scholars, we embrace the impact of words, but we are also cognizant of the ways that truly revolutionary work—perhaps especially work on embodiment— may require us to move into more creative realms. We may require a thickening of our fields and scholarships, but also the very nature of scholarship and academic work. To sit in the nuance may require a true engagement of story as scholarship, of dance as research, of creative and uncategorizable work as a new frontier of academia.

Our *Thickening Fat* symposium provides one such example of creative new approaches. While much of the event was taken up with traditional—though exciting—scholarship, one evening was set aside for a different approach to thickening fat. Community members, artists, singers, dancers, poets, drag performers and others sought to thicken fat in creative and thought-provoking ways. Digital stories about identity and weight stigma were screened. Wine was consumed. Snacks were eagerly handed around. The broad community that gathered was inspired and ignited and the possibilities seemed limitless.

Our hopes for this volume are to capture some of the energy of that event. We hope that this book will truly result in a thickened approach to fat, a version that lives in textbooks and lecture halls but also in dance and song, in popular and private culture, in shifting conversations, graffiti, protests, spoken word, and selfies about identity and justice. Rather than replacing existing knowledge with a new version of events, our hope is that *Thickening Fat* will engender dialogue and debate and will inspire traditional and creative scholarship, organizing and activism.

To truly thicken fat we must sit in discomfort. To trouble identities we must be open to confusion and uncertainty. We invite you to join this conversation in all its glorious ambiguity and to commit to a thicker understanding of fat, of justice, and of identity.

References

Asbill, D. L. (2009). "I'm allowed to be a sexual being": The distinctive social conditions of the fat burlesque stage. In E. Rothblum & S. Solovay (Eds.), *The fat studies reader* (pp. 299–304). New York: New York University Press.

Cameron, E., & Russell, C. (Eds.). (2016). *The fat pedagogy reader: Challenging weight-based oppression through critical education*. New York: Peter Lang.

Chandler, E., & Rice, C. (2013). Alterity in/of happiness: Reflecting on the radical possibilities of unruly bodies. *Health, Culture and Society, 5*(1), 230–248.

Changfoot, N., & Rice, C. (forthcoming). Aging with and into disability: Futurities of new materialisms. In K. Aubrecht, C. Kelly & C. Rice. (Eds.). *The aging disability nexus*. Vancouver: University of British Columbia Press.

Clare, E. (1999). *Exile and pride: Disability, queerness and liberation*. Cambridge: South End Press.

Cooper, C. (2016). *Fat activism: A radical social movement*. Bristol: HammerOn Press.

Crenshaw, K. (1989). Demarginalizing the intersection of race and sex: A Black feminist Critique of antidiscrimination doctrine, feminist theory and antiracist politics. *University of Chicago Legal Forum, 1*, 139–167.

Crenshaw, K. (1991). Mapping the margins: Intersectionality, identity politics, and violence against women of color. *Stanford Law Review 43*(6), 1241–1299.

Ellison, J. (2016). From "FU" to "Be Yourself": Fat activisms in Canada. In J. Ellison, D. McPhail & W. Mitchinson (Eds.), *Obesity in Canada: Critical perspectives* (pp. 293–319). Toronto: University of Toronto Press.

Ellison, J. E., McPhail, D., & Mitchinson, W. (2016). Introduction: Obesity in Canada. In J. Ellison, D. McPhail & W. Mitchinson (Eds.), *Obesity in Canada: Critical perspectives* (pp. 3–30). Toronto: University of Toronto Press.

Farrell, A. E. (2011). *Fat shame: Stigma and the fat body in American culture*. New York: New York University Press.

Fisanick, C. (2009). Fatness (in)visible: Polycystic ovarian syndrome and the rhetoric of normative femininity. In E. Rothblum & S. Solovay (Eds.), *The fat studies reader* (pp. 106–112). New York: New York University Press.

Garland-Thomson, R. (1997). *Extraordinary bodies: Figuring physical disability in American culture and literature.* New York: Columbia University Press

Geerts, E., & van der Tuin, I. (2013). From intersectionality to interference: Feminist onto-epistemological reflections on the politics of representation. *Women's Studies International Forum, 41,* 171–178.

Halberstam, J. (2011). *The queer art of failure.* Durham: Duke University Press.

Kafer, A. (2013). *Feminist, queer, crip.* Bloomington: Indiana University Press.

LeBesco, K. (2004). *Revolting bodies? The struggle to redefine fat identity.* Amherst: University of Massachusetts Press.

Longhurst, R. (2014). Queering body size and shape: Performativity, the closet, shame and orientation. In C. Pause, J. Wykes & S. Murray (Eds.), *Queering fat embodiment* (pp. 13–26). Farnham: Ashgate.

Murray, S. (2005). Un/be coming out? Rethinking fat politics. *Social Semiotics, 15*(2), 153–163.

Murray, S. (2009). 'Banded Bodies': The somatechnics of gastric banding. In N. Sullivan & S. Murray (Eds.), *Somatechnics: Queering the technologisation of bodies* (pp. 153–170). Farnham: Ashgate.

Nault, C. (2009). 'Punk will never diet': Beth Ditto and the (queer) reevaluation of fat. *Neoamericanist,* 4(1), 1–14.

Paradis, E. (2016). "Obesity" as process: The medicalization of fatness by Canadian researchers, 1971–2010. In J. Ellison, D. McPhail & W. Mitchinson (Eds.), *Obesity in Canada: Critical perspectives* (pp. 56–88). Toronto: University of Toronto Press.

Poudrier, J. (2016). The geneticization of Aboriginal diabetes and obesity: Adding another scene to the story of the thrifty gene. In J. Ellison, D. McPhail & W. Mitchinson (Eds.), *Obesity in Canada: Critical perspectives* (pp. 89–121). Toronto: University of Toronto Press.

Probyn, E. (2005). *Blush: Faces of shame.* Minneapolis: University of Minnesota Press.

Puar, J. K. (2007). *Terrorist assemblages: Homonationalism in queer times.* Durham, NC: Duke University Press.

Puar, J. K. (2012). "I would rather be a cyborg than a goddess": Becoming-intersectional in assemblage theory. *Philosophia, 2*(1), 49–66.

Rice, C. (2007). Becoming the fat girl: Emergence of an unfit identity. *Women's Studies International Forum, 30*(2), 158–174.

Rice, C. (2014). *Becoming women: The embodied self in image culture.* Toronto: University of Toronto Press.

Rice, C. (2018). The spectacle of the child woman: Troubling girls in/and the science of early puberty. *Feminist Studies, 44*(3), 535–566.

Rice, C., & Chandler, E. (forthcoming). Representing difference: Disability, digital storytelling, and public pedagogy. In K. Ellis, G. Goggin, B. Haller & R. Curtis (Eds.), *Routledge companion to disability and media.* New York: Routledge.

Rice, C., Harrison, E., & Friedman, M. (2019). Doing justice to intersectionality in social science. *Cultural Studies Critical Methodologies.* https://doi.org/10.1177/1532708619829779

Rice, C., Pendleton Jiménez, K., Harrison, E., Robinson, M., Rinaldi, J., LaMarre, A., & Andrew, J. (forthcoming). Bodies at the intersection: Reconfiguring intersectionality through queer women's complex embodiments. *Signs: A Journal of Women in Culture and Society.*

Rinaldi, J., Rice, C., Lind, E., & Kotow, C. (2019). Mapping the circulation of fat hatred. *Fat Studies: An Interdisciplinary Journal of Body Weight and Society*. E-pub ahead of print. doi: 10.1080/21604851.2019.1592949

Rinaldi, J., Rice, C., LaMarre, A., McPhail, D., & Harrison, E. (2017). Fatness & failing citizenship. *Somatechnics*, 7(2), 218–233.

Solovay, S., & E. Rothblum (2009). Introduction. In Rothblum & S. Solovay (Eds.), *The fat studies reader* (pp. 1–10). New York: New York University Press.

Vade, D., & S. Solovay (2009). No apology: shared struggles in fat and transgender law. In E. Rothblum & S. Solovay (Eds.), *The fat studies reader* (pp. 167–175). New York: New York University Press.

Ward, P. (2016). Obesity, risk, and responsibility: The discursive production of the "ultimate at-risk child." In J. Ellison, D. McPhail & W. Mitchinson (Eds.), *Obesity in Canada: Critical perspectives* (pp. 218–244). Toronto: University of Toronto Press.

Wilson, B. D. M. (2009). Widening the dialogue to narrow the gap in health disparities: Approaches to fat Black lesbian and bisexual women's health promotion. In E. Rothblum & S. Solovay (Eds.), *The fat studies reader* (pp. 54–64). New York: New York University Press.

Wykes, J. (2014). Introduction: Why queering fat embodiment? In C. Pause, J. Wykes & S. Murray (Eds.), *Queering fat embodiment* (pp. 1–12). Farnham: Ashgate.

Part I

Our Heavy Inheritance

1 The Big Colonial Bones of Indigenous North America's "Obesity Epidemic"

Margaret Robinson

I have grown fat again. My body size waxes and wanes like phases of the moon. As a fledgling professor, I worry how my fat impacts my ability to obtain a tenure-track position in Mi'kmaki, the traditional territory of my people, the Mi'kmaq, on what is currently Canada's eastern seaboard. Authority and truth, qualities valued by students, colleagues, and tenure or promotion committees, are not often ascribed to fat bodies (Fisanick, 2007). Instead, fatness is uncritically associated with "laziness, greed, and moral slackness" (p. 237), posing challenges for the academic credibility and success of people with larger bodies (Bacon, 2009; Cameron, 2016; Fisanick, 2006; Hunt & Rhodes, 2018). As a queer woman whose Indigeneity already evokes negative stereotypes, I worry my intersecting identities stretch the boundaries of academic collegiality too far, as my chest stretches the blazer that fit me last summer. So I control what I eat, skip meals, and walk to work and back, but feel complicit in shaping my body to meet colonial standards beyond my reach.

In this chapter I examine how Indigenous fatness—particularly that of women —is used to justify ongoing colonial domination and control by settlers and their governments. I explore this connection through a visual discourse analysis of fatness in the historical personification of America, content analysis of contemporary health research funding, and visual discourse analysis of a health promotion poster targeted at Indigenous people. My analyses demonstrate the colonial logic embodied in "the obesity epidemic" as applied by Canadian health research and health promotion campaigns. I focus on Canada, but practices that norm Indigenous bodies and maintain the occupation of Indigenous lands occur across Turtle Island and beyond.

French philosopher Michel Foucault used the term "biopower" to describe practices that shape and control populations (1990, p. 140). Biopower is manifested in biopedagogies, "the loose collection of moralized information, advice, and instruction about bodies, minds, and health that works to control people by using praise and shame alongside 'expert knowledge' to urge conformity to physical and mental norms" (Rice, Chandler, Liddiard, Rinaldi & Harrison, 2016, p. 4–5). Both the historical personifications of America and contemporary research funding practices train Settlers to perceive Indigenous bodies and land as requiring domination. Contemporary health promotion frames Indigenous bodies and populations as excessive and attempts to train them for absorption into the body politic. Such biopedagogy produces political and medical knowledge that is simultaneously moral and sexual, marking Indigenous bodies and populations as conquered, unhealthy and immoral, requiring ongoing intervention (Rice, Chandler, Liddiard, Rinaldi & Harrison, 2016).

America Is a Rich Fat Woman

To understand the colonization of Indigenous bodies we must start with the colonization of Indigenous land. Indigenous scholars Waziyatawin Angela Wilson (Dakota) and Michael Yellow Bird (Mandan, Hidatsa, and Arikara) define colonization as methods to "maintain the subjugation or exploitation of Indigenous Peoples, lands, and resources" (2005, p. 2). Biopower is one such method, especially as it produces knowledge and expertise about Indigenous fatness.

Efforts to control and discipline fat, feminine, Indigenous bodies have a long history. Settler literary theorist Louis Montrose (1991) notes that by the 1570s European artists had begun to personify America as a large-bodied woman with bare breasts and a feathered headdress. *The Discovery of America* (circa 1587–1589), a drawing by Jan van der Straet (best known via an engraving of it done by fellow Dutch artist Theodoor Galle ca. 1600), portrays the territory as a thick nude woman in a hammock encountering a fully dressed European man (Amerigo Vespucci) (see Figure 1.1). Vespucci is armed with a cross, navigational astrolabe, and sword, emphasizing the "mutually reinforcing emblems of belief, empirical knowledge, and violence" (Montrose, 1991, p. 4). The presence and danger of food is in the background, where Indigenous people roast a human leg over an open fire. Montrose notes that the position of the leg on the spit "inverts and miniaturizes" (2007, p. 4) Vespucci's own leg. Professor of American Indian Studies M. Elise Marubbio refers to this personification of unconquered America as "the Native American Queen," noting that her nakedness and repose "invite[s] the colonizer's gaze, his exploration, and his exploitation" (2006, p. 10), even as the cannibalism motif suggests that Indigenous womanhood may consume European masculinity.

In an engraving called *America, a Personification* (c. 1590) by Flemish artist Adriaen Collaert, America is again a naked woman in a feathered headdress, armed with bow and arrows, riding a giant armadillo (see Figure 1.2). She turns her gaze to the right (the symbolic future, since English reads left to right), where naked people with axes battle armoured Europeans armed with guns. In the left background (the symbolic past), naked people hunt deer in a pastoral setting, a naked man butchers a human body with an axe, and a naked woman roasts a human leg on a spit. The message is that if left undominated, Indigenous people (especially women) resort to ungodly overconsumption, treating what

AMERICA.

Americen Americus retexit , &   *Semel vocauit inde femper excitam*.

Figure 1.1 The Discovery of America. Galle, T. (ca. 1600). *Discovery of America*. After a drawing by Jan van der Straet.

Retrieved from https://www.metmuseum.org/art/collection/search/659655

Christians see as the very image of God—the human body—as mere meat. Once the image of the axe is connected with cannibalism, the European invaders on the right are fighting for their very lives (and for Christian values of the body) against an all-consuming enemy.

Spanish and English visitors to the Americas personified the land as a large rich woman and conflated political and sexual conquest. Sir Walter Raleigh, in a passage from his 1597 book, *Discovrie of the Large, Rich, and Beautiful Empire of Guiana*, wrote:

> Guiana is a country that hath yet her maydenhead, never sackt, turned, nor wrought... It hath never bene entred by any armie of strength, and never conquered or possesed by any Christian Prince.
>
> (Raleigh, 2006)

The merging of sexual and colonial possession is a recurring pattern. Early settler colonist Thomas Morton described what is currently New England as:

Figure 1.2 America, a personification. Collaert, A. (c. 1590). *America, A Personification.* From *The Public Domain Review.* https://publicdomainreview.org/collections/america-a-per sonification-ca-1590/

> Like a faire virgin longine to be sped
> and meete her lover in a nuptial bed,
> decked in rich ornaments t'advance her state.

(Morton, 2011, p. 10)

Similarly, in *A Relation of the Second Voyage to Guiana*, English explorer Law-rence Keymis, a contemporary associate of Raleigh, described the New World as "shires of fruitfull rich grounds, lying …waste for want of people," that "prostitute themselves unto us, like a faire and beautiful woman, in the pride and floure of desired yeeres" (Kaymis, 1968, p. 487). The theme that emerges is of a sexualized and fertile fat female body demanding to be conquered.

The representation of America as eager for domination is one of the earliest tropes of Indigenous land as a feminine body. The portrayal of Indigenous territories as the "feminine Other" partakes of a colonial Christian binary in which men are associated with intellect and women with the body. Literary scholar Susanne Scholz (1998) notes that the association of men with intellect is made possible by the over-association of the body with women. In this gendered binary, the mind must dominate the body as men dominate women. The control of the body by a hyper-developed will justifies the leadership of men and masculinized subjects, such as England's Virgin Queen Elizabeth I, over women, populations, and domains framed as feminine (Montrose, 1991). This ideology connects the colonial occupation of Indigenous land with the subjugation of Indigenous people and with Christian practices of body intended to display mastery of the mind or spirit over the flesh. Such practices concretize in movements from early Christian asceticism to the "muscular Christianity" of the nineteenth century (Webb, 2009), influencing European children's literature and producing organizations such as the Scouting movement and the Young Men's Christian Association (later, YMCA). Fatness becomes a metaphor for moral laxity.

America's Puritan Makeover

Settler sociologist Abigail C. Saguy (2013) details how fatness came to be framed as both a moral crisis and a health crisis. Originally associated with success, nineteenth- and early twentieth-century America used categories of fatness and thinness to distinguish itself from Europe, reframing fatness from a sign of God's favour to a marker of sloth, gluttony, and lack of the self-control (Saguy, 2013; Stearns, 2002). This process of reframing body fat into a foundational character flaw is inescapably raced, sexed, and classed:

> [T]hinness (at least in women) has been associated with self-control and whiteness since early in U.S. history. In this national context, fatness has long been associated with lack of control, immorality, barbarity, and blackness.
>
> (Saguy, 2013, p. 41)

Although briefly fashionable due to a wave of wealthy German immigration, once associated with poor Irish Catholic immigrants in the nineteenth century, fatness became indicative of laziness and moral laxity (Saguy 2013; Strings, 2012). More recently, stereotypes portray Black and Latina women as having voracious appetites for food and sex to justify punitive social control (Saguy 2013). In this way, campaigns against "obesity" can be used where more overtly racist, sexist, or classist campaigns might be challenged (Campos, Flegal, Carroll, Kuczmarski & Johnson, 1998; Saguy, 2013; Sobal & Stunkard, 1989).

Marubbio (2006) notes that as Settler norms around body size shifted, the large, fecund body of the militant "Native American Queen" became refigured as the "Squaw," marked by excess fat, excess sexual appetite, and excess reproduction. By 1953, for example, Disney's animated film *Peter Pan* has a fully developed "Squaw"—a fat, bullying woman with a child strapped to her back. The "Squaw" represents Indigenous women as taking too much space, physically, morally, and socially. She exemplifies what Geneviève Rail and Shannon Jette describe as the "bio-Other": "the weak-willed, the lazy, the amoral, the unruly, those who do not live responsibly and engage in "risky" behavior or do not get involved in preventative behavior" (2015, p. 4). The "Squaw" image evokes shame and disgust, key emotions for internalizing the "normalizing and moralizing instructions for life" that constitute biopedagogy (Rice, 2015, p. 387).

Like the "Black Welfare Queen," the "Squaw" reaffirms White body norms and sexual morality, justifying White domination over populations framed as lacking self-control (Roberts, 1999; Saguy, 2013; Witt, 1999). Implications of literal cannibalism shift to sexual, emotional, and economic "maneating." Marubbio (2006) contrasts the sovereign and militant "Native American Queen" with the "Indian Princess" who sides romantically and politically with male Settlers against her own nation. The most familiar "Indian Princess" is Pocahontas, who rescues Captain John Smith from death and befriends colonists at Jamestown, in what is currently Virginia. The Princess is no longer large and rich—only beautiful. By the time we get to Walt Disney Pictures' 1995 animated film *Pochahontas*, the flirtatious "Princess" is as slender as Barbie. Muscogee scholar Dwanna Lynn Robertson notes the racist binary of "sexy maiden" and "dirty squaw" promotes "the idea that Indigenous women are highly sexualized, act wild, like to be held captive, and become sexually active at earlier ages than other racial groups of women" (2013, p. 53). Such representations mark Indigenous women's bodies as targets for sexual aggression, justifying the rape of bodies and lands as a civilizing practice.

"Obesity" Knowledge Production in Federal Research Funding

While controlling the symbolic body of America, colonial practices also strive to shape the literal bodies of Indigenous people through health discourse. Saguy traces the framing of fat as a crisis requiring government intervention, arguing that defining fatness as "obesity" "was crucial in convincing public opinion that fatness represented a medical problem" (2013, p. 42). Medical historian Robert Aronowitz, a Settler, argues that the medicalization of fatness distinguishes between upper and lower classes in America (Aronowitz, 2008). Saguy (2013) likewise notes how race, class, and gender intersect to prevent stigmatized women from uniting in solidarity while the image of elite Americans as thin both marks and justifies their authority over others. Here the "good citizen" is constructed as embodying "masculine" virtues of autonomy, responsibility, and self-control, manifested in physical, mental, economic, and moral strength (Rail & Jette, 2015; Rice, 2015). Within this framework, body sovereignty is reserved for those citizens who best reflect the political and economic sovereignty of the nation-state, while bio-Others require intervention.

Increasingly, public health research funders are framing "obesity" as "epidemic" among the Indigenous peoples of North America. As early as 1992, the National Institutes of Health in the United States initiated funding for school-based interventions to prevent obesity in American Indians and Alaska Natives. Since 2014 the Canadian Institutes for Health Research have funded the Pathways to Health Equity for Aboriginal Peoples initiative, which identifies "obesity" (conflated with diabetes) as one of four priority areas. My analysis of funded health research below sheds light on colonial biopower as it pertains to the promotion of an Indigenous "obesity epidemic" in Canada. Federally funded health research frames "obesity" in ways that erase the impacts of colonialism and neoliberal consumerism on Indigenous bodies, and shifts focus to interventions that discipline the bodies and practices of Indigenous women.

In May of 2018, I conducted a search of The Canadian Research Information System (http://webapps.cihr-irsc.gc.ca/cris/search) using the terms "Aboriginal," "Indigenous," "First Nation," "Métis," or "Inuit" and "weight," "obesity," "adipose," "fat," or "diabetes" (often conflated with fat), obtaining 271 results. I read research abstracts for context and relevance and excluded studies that did not address Indigenous body weight or that focused on populations outside Canada, leaving 117 relevant studies. Between 2001 and 2021, the Canadian Institutes of Health Research and allied funders will have invested $29,936,497 in studying "obesity" among Indigenous people in Canada, comprising 13% of their Indigenous health research funding in the same period. In the United States, funding from the National Institutes of Health for "obesity" research rose from approximately $50 million in 1993 to over $400 million in 2004 (Spiegel & Nabel, 2006).

Examining the abstracts of funded projects, I note that 20 studies frame "obesity" as a general health problem, 16 identify it as a risk factor for health problems, 11 frame it as a negative health outcome, and eight use it as a quality or attribute (e.g., obese women). Thirty-eight abstracts associate "obesity" with diabetes (e.g., obesity and diabetes) or conflate it with diabetes (e.g. obesity/diabetes), 27 frame it as a disease, and eight abstracts incorporate "abdominal weight" into a concept they name "cardiometabolic syndrome," defined to include insulin resistance, impaired glucose tolerance, high lipoprotein cholesterol, high blood pressure, and fat deposits at the waist (Liese, Mayer-Davis & Haffner, 1998). Forty abstracts use "obesity" as a keyword but do not provide enough information to determine how it is being framed. These findings suggest that health researchers and/or the committees that fund them perceive "obesity" as a health issue, but disagree whether it constitutes a disease, a risk factor for disease, or a generally negative health outcome. This lack of specificity makes "obesity" extremely flexible as a tactic for Indigenous population control.

Research funding practices both reflect and generate knowledge about the body, ensuring that Indigenous "obesity" is perceived and treated as a health priority. The demand for knowledge about the "epidemic" reinforces the legitimacy of the "obesity" concept and financially rewards those who demonstrate mastery of the subject. Nine of the 177 funding awards (13%) are in the form of Doctoral, Master's, New Investigators, or emerging team grants. Such training funds promote "obesity" as a legitimate issue among emerging scholars, and "obesity science" as a lucrative field. Like the symbology of America that preceded it, this knowledge production focuses primarily on Indigenous women. Among the 19 research abstracts that address gender, women are almost always the target, with 14 of the abstracts revealing an emphasis on pregnant women (usually in the context of gestational diabetes); only one study focuses exclusively on men. Young indigenous people are broadly targeted, with 26 of the abstracts indicating a focus on youth.

The knowledge being produced through "obesity" studies funded by the Canadian government manifests biopower by norming and controlling the bodies of Indigenous women. Where interventions form part of the funded project, 56 promote changes to diet and exercise at the individual, family, or community level, and six imply a genetic cause for weight gain. Only 12 indicate the project will develop, seek, or promote policy solutions, and only two mention colonialism as a factor shaping Indigenous health. These data indicate that government funding practices of biopower locate the "problem of obesity" in Indigenous women's failure to understand nutrition, to control our eating, to exercise enough, or to resist assimilating to eating practices promoted by colonial food industries. The tendency to focus interventions on individuals or populations labeled "obese" shifts research attention away from policy-driven and government-controlled practices, and from the benefits accrued by colonial corporations profiting from the loss of traditional foods resulting from the destruction of traditional territories, animal habitats, and ways of living.

Saguy argues that the medical framework defines fat bodies as diseased, making it "difficult, if not impossible, to see these bodies as healthy or good" (2013, p. 6). Framing fatness as a health problem obscures the role of sex in biopower. As Saguy states, "women are judged more harshly based on their appearance than men and are more likely to go on weight-loss diets, take weight-loss drugs, and undergo weight-loss surgery" (p. 13). The promotion of "obesity" as a problem requiring intervention is therefore about sex, race, and class, even as the political and social elements of these factors are reduced to mere demographics of research participants. The promotion of weight-control interventions for Indigenous populations supports a framework in which Indigenous people are pressured to assimilate to White Settler middle-class economic, religious, moral, and body norms.

Interlocking Oppressions of the Body

Colonialism interlocks with complementary oppressions, and the interplay of heteronormativity and middle-class White Settler values can be seen in my analysis of an image from Health Canada's Aboriginal Diabetes Initiative, released in 2002, to "promote active living and eating nutritious foods" (Wallace, 2002, p. 8). Established to reduce type 2 diabetes among Aboriginal people, the Aboriginal Diabetes Initiative received $448 million in funding between its inception in 1999 and 2013 (Government of Canada, 2013). The Health Canada (2002) poster I examine is sometimes called "Family in Kitchen," and portrays an Indigenous grandmother, mother, father, and child (see Figure 1.3). The poster presents diabetes within a personal responsibility framework: "Eat right. Be active. Have fun. *You can* prevent diabetes" (Health Canada, 2002, emphasis in original). We can also see communal responsibility: "*Our lifestyle* is important to us as a family," the text reads. "*We know* the best way to avoid diabetes is to eat healthy foods" (Health Canada, 2002, emphases mine). The locus of power is framed at the family level, through bullet points such as "We have: a healthy lifestyle; a spirit; a goal"; and "*the power to prevent diabetes*" (Health Canada, 2002, emphasis in original).

The grandmother, in the centre background, stands at the counter touching green-topped carrots. In the left foreground, the mother chops celery at the kitchen table, smiling at her toddler who eats cut-up fruit from a white bowl. In the back right, the father stirs something at the stove. The eyeline of both parents is on the child, framing Indigenous parents as responsible for the size and health of their children.

The kitchen reflects middle-class values of cleanliness and consumerism: the white gas stove has a digital readout; there is a white dishwasher; a white coffeemaker is nestled behind a bowl of fruit on the counter. All the objects in the room are new, and white dominates in cabinets, windowframe, and blinds. The sparking silver faucet over the sink indicates this is not one of the many First Nations families living without running water (Galway, 2016). In front of the mother are carrots, fennel, squash, a large bowl of seeds or nuts, half a red onion, a portabello mushroom, and three large tomatoes. In the foreground lies two-thirds of a trout and some parsley. The missing section of fish may explain the frying pan on the stove, whose contents are not visible. The image implies financial and nutritional abundance. Using May 2018 Grocery Gateway prices for downtown Toronto, items on the table alone retail for $52.29. Food preparation is idealized; although the father appears to be cooking, no steam or smoke emerges from the pans.

Indigeneity is symbolized in embroidered potholders featuring a person with braids, a medicine-wheel-and-feather suncatcher, the "Indian" corn in a basket hanging on the cupboard, and in the long braided hair of the man at the stove. These images are loosely associated with nations of The Plains, but the fish on the cutting board may reference traditional coastal foods. The models sport new clothes. The child (aproximately three years old) sits in a booster seat, wearing lavender overalls and matching top. The women wear modest long-sleeve shirts and minimal silver jewelry. The mother's maroon top is tucked into her jeans, which are belted at the waist, making them just

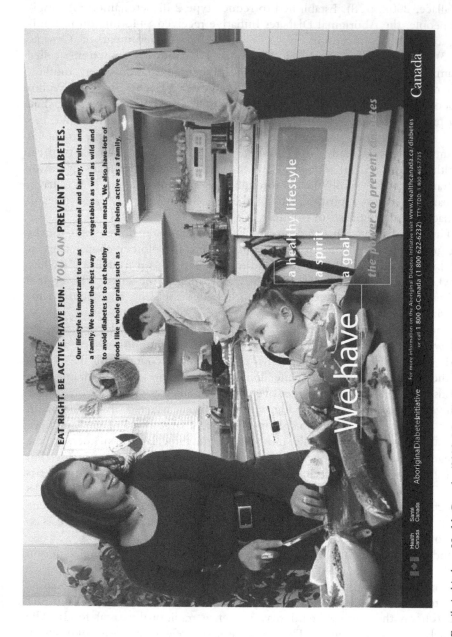

Figure 1.3 Family in kitchen, Health Canada. (2002, May 3). Eat right. You can prevent diabetes. Aboriginal Diabetes Initiative. Copyright 2002 by Health Canada, reprinted with permission. http://web49.radiant.net/~nada1/docs/4/142.pdf

body-conscious enough to demonstrate the appropriate size for the Indigenous female during her reproductive years. The parents wear matching wedding bands, assuring us of their socially respectable heterosexual union.

Just as the control of appetite is demonstrated by the mother's body size, so too is her sexual restraint. While First Nations women average 2.7 children each (Arriagada, 2016), this poster models a fertility rate lower even than that of White women (who average 1.6 children each, the lowest in Canada) (Todd, 2013). Susanne Scholz argues that women's chastity is "the body practice which corresponds to a commodified vision of the sexualized female body," that scrutinizes and disciplines body orifices toward monogamous heterosexuality (Scholz, 1998, p. 297). The representation of the mother as disciplined in eating and reproduction protects her from the category of Squaw and shifts her to that of Princess, whose support for colonial authority (and here, health expertise) brings Indigenous people in line with colonial standards of civilization (Marubbio, 2006). As part of the curricula of biopedagogy, this poster manifests a "health imperative" (Rail & Jette, 2015, p. 2) that overwrites Indigenous body sovereignty with colonial norms and participates in a teleology of cultural extinction (Rice et al., 2016).

Conclusion

Interventions to control and discipline the bodies of Indigenous women and children emerge during a resurgence of political activism led by Indigenous women and youth (e.g., Idle No More, Sisters in Spirit) (Barker, 2015). Campaigns designed to colonize Indigenous body values and eating practices, and to assimilate them into a white Christian middle class, is a form of biopolitics rooted in a long-standing and pernicious colonial symbologies and ideologies. Such interventions partake in a strategy of colonial biopower that has included starvation through the deliberate destruction of traditional food sources (Smits, 1994), residential school nutritional experiments in which Indigenous children were intentionally malnourished (Mosby, 2013), and the coercive sterilization of Indigenous women (Stote, 2012). The message implicit in such practices is that the Indigenous body is too big, out of control, and getting larger. Saguy notes that framing "obesity" as a deadly threat is used to justify "imposing elite white preferences for thinness onto working classes and people of color" (2013, p. 13). She argues that "obesity" discourse is an example of what French sociologist Pierre Bordieu calls "symbolic violence" (Saguy, 1991, p. 23). Framing "obesity" as an "epidemic" justifies ongoing colonial intervention into the practices of Indigenous nations and the daily lives of Indigenous people in ways that undermine our sovereignty.

The colonial health lens of the "Indigenous obesity epidemic" relates to colonial symbols such as Native American Queen, Princess, and Squaw, and to systems of oppression that interlock with or are rooted in colonialism. How might practices of colonial biopower be challenged if we centred

Indigenous body sovereignty in issues of food and body size? That is a conversation worth having among Indigenous women and men, our youth and elders, and Indigenous health researchers. Paula Gunn Allen (Laguna, Sioux, Pueblo) (1986) details the social benefits that would result if Settler society adopted the values and traditions of Indigenous Nations, including a re-valuation of fat bodies. Some research has found that Cree adults, for example, view fatness "as a sign of robustness and strength" (Willows 2009, p. 533), and young Indigenous women have identified their culture(s) as able to buffer negative messages about their bodies (McHugh, Coppola & Sabiston, 2014).

As I look for ways to buffer the impact of colonial discourse on my own body, I find strength in the photographs of woman in the Mi'kmaq Portraits Collection (https://novascotia.ca/museum/mikmaq/), whose traditional dress reveals their round, soft bodies. Like the representations of early America, they are large, culturally rich, and beautiful.

References

Allen, P. G. (1986). *The sacred hoop: Recovering the feminine in American Indian traditions.* Boston: Beacon Press.

Aronowitz, R. (2008). Framing disease: An underappreciated mechanism for the social patterning of health. *Social Science & Medicine, 67*(1), 1–9.

Arriagada, P. (2016). First Nations, Métis and Inuit women. [Report No. 89-503-X]. Women in Canada: A Gender-based Statistical Report. Ottawa: Statistics Canada.

Bacon, L. (2009). Reflections on fat acceptance: Lessons learned from privilege. Speech, National Association to Advance Fat Acceptance. Retrieved from https://lin dabacon.org/wp-content/uploads/Bacon_ReflectionsOnThinPrivilege_NAAFA.pdf

Barker, A. J. (2015). 'A direct act of resurgence, a direct act of sovereignty': Reflections on idle no more, Indigenous activism, and Canadian settler colonialism. *Globalizations, 12*(1), 43–65.

Cameron, E. (2016). Challenging "size matters" messages: An exploration of the experiences of critical obesity scholars in higher education. *The Canadian Journal of Higher Education, 46*(2), 111.

Campos, P. F. (2004). *The obesity myth: Why America's obsession with weight is hazardous to your health.* New York: Penguin.

Collaert, A. (c. 1590). America, a Personification. [engraving] The Public Domain Review. Retrieved from https://publicdomainreview.org/collections/america-a-per sonification-ca-1590/

Fisanick, C. (2006). Evaluating the absent presence: The professor's body at tenure and promotion. *The Review of Education, Pedagogy, and Cultural Studies, 28*(3–4), 325–338.

Fisanick, C. (2007). "They are weighted with authority": Fat female professors in academic and popular cultures. *Feminist Teacher, 17*(3), 237–255.

Flegal, K. M., Carroll, M. D., Kuczmarski, R. J., & Johnson, C. L. (1998). Overweight and obesity in the United States: Prevalence and trends, 1960–1994. *International Journal of Obesity, 22*(1), 39.

Foucault, M. (1990). *The history of sexuality: An introduction, volume I.* Trans. Robert Hurley. New York: Vintage.

Galway, L. P. (2016). Boiling over: A descriptive analysis of drinking water advisories in First Nations communities in Ontario, Canada. *International Journal of Environmental Research and Public Health*, *13*(5), 505.

Government of Canada. (2013). Diabetes. Retrieved from https://www.canada.ca/en/indi genous-services-canada/services/first-nations-inuit-health/diseases-health-conditions/ diabetes.html

Health Canada. (2002, May 3). Eat right. You can prevent diabetes. Aboriginal Diabetes Initiative. http://web49.radiant.net/~nada1/docs/4/142.pdf

Hunt, A. N., & Rhodes, T. (2018). Fat pedagogy and microaggressions: Experiences of professionals working in higher education settings. *Fat Studies*, *7*(1), 21–32.

Keymis, L. (1968). A Relation of the Second Voyage to Guiana: London 1596 (No. 65). Da Capo.

Liese, A. D., Mayer-Davis, E. J., & Haffner, S. M. (1998). Development of the multiple metabolic syndrome: an epidemiologic perspective. *Epidemiologic Reviews*, *20*(2), 157–172.

Marubbio, M. (2006). *Killing the Indian maiden: Images of Native American women in film*. Lexington: University Press of Kentucky.

McHugh, T. L. F., Coppola, A. M., & Sabiston, C. M. (2014). "I'm thankful for being Native and my body is part of that": The body pride experiences of young Aboriginal women in Canada. *Body Image*, *11*(3), 318–327.

Montrose, L. (1991). The work of gender in the discourse of discovery. *Representations*, *33*(1), 1–41.

Morton, T (2011). *New English Canaan*. Carlisle: Applewood Books.

Mosby, I. (2013). Administering colonial science: Nutrition research and human biomedical experimentation in Aboriginal communities and residential schools, 1942–1952. *Histoire Sociale/Social History*, *46*(1), 145–172.

Rail, G., & Jette, S. (2015). Reflections on biopedagogies and/of public health: On bio-others, rescue missions, and social justice. *Cultural Studies <=> Critical Methodologies*, *15*(5), 327–336.

Raleigh (1597). *The Discoverie of the Large, Rich, and Beautifull Empire of Guiana*. Urbana: Project Gutenberg. Retrieved from https://www.gutenberg.org/files/2272/2272-h/ 2272-h.htm

Rice, C. (2015). Rethinking fat: From bio-to body-becoming pedagogies. *Cultural Studies <=> Critical Methodologies*, *15*(5), 387–397.

Rice, C., Chandler, E., Liddiard, K., Rinaldi, J., & Harrison, E. (2016). Pedagogical possibilities for unruly bodies. *Gender & Education*, *28*(8), 1–20.

Roberts, D. E. (1999). *Killing the black body: Race, reproduction, and the meaning of liberty*. New York: Vintage Books.

Robertson, D. L. (2015). Invisibility in the color-blind era: Examining legitimized racism against indigenous peoples. *The American Indian Quarterly*, *39*(2), 113–153.

Saguy, A. C. (2012). *What's wrong with fat?* New York: Oxford University Press.

Scholz, S. (1998). Pleasure island, or when Guyon discovered Guiana: Visions of the female body in English Renaissance literature. *European Journal of English Studies*, *2*(3), 285–305.

Smits, D. D. (1994). The frontier army and the destruction of the buffalo: 1865–1883. *Western Historical Quarterly*, *25*(3), 312–338.

Sobal, J., & Stunkard, A. J. (1989). Socioeconomic status and obesity: A review of the literature. *Psychological Bulletin*, *105*(2), 260.

Spiegel, A. M., & Nabel, E. G. (2006). NIH research on obesity and type 2 diabetes: providing the scientific evidence base for actions to improve health. *Nature Medicine*, *12*(1), 67.

Stearns, P. N. (2002). *Fat history: Bodies and beauty in the modern west*. New York: New York University Press.

Stote, K. (2012). The coercive sterilization of aboriginal women in Canada. *American Indian Culture and Research Journal*, *36*(3), 117–150.

Strings, S. A. (2012). *Thin, white, and saved: fat stigma and the fear of the big black body* (Doctoral dissertation, UC San Diego).

Todd, D. (2013, November 27). High birthrate among immigrant women has implications for Canada. *Vancouver Sun*.

Galle, T. (Engraver). (ca. 1600). Discovery of America. After a drawing by Jan van der Straet. Retrieved from https://www.metmuseum.org/art/collection/search/659655

Wallace, J. (2002, December). Aboriginal Communities Confront Type 2 Diabetes Epidemic. *National Aboriginal Diabetes Association Newsletter*, *8*.

Webb, J. (2009). 'Voracious appetites': The construction of 'fatness' in the boy hero in English children's literature. In K. K. Keeling & S. T. Pollard (Eds.), *Critical approaches to food in children's literature* (pp. 105–121). New York: Routledge.

Willows, N. D., Marshall, D., Raine, K., & Ridley, D. C. (2009). Diabetes awareness and body size perceptions of Cree schoolchildren. *Health Education Research*, *24*(6), 1051–1058.

Wilson, W. A., & Yellow Bird, M. (2005). *For Indigenous eyes only: A decolonization handbook*. Santa Fe: School of American Research Press.

Witt, D. (1999). *Black hunger: food and the politics of US identity*. New York: Oxford University Press.

2 Origin Stories

Thickening Fat and the Problem of Historiography

Amy Erdman Farrell

Origin stories are important. They map the roots, the contours, the beliefs about who a people or a nation is, who the polity includes, who it excludes, who is recognized as a citizen, who is "illegal" or, at best, a refugee or a recent immigrant. The origin stories of social movements and fields of study are equally important. They name the creators and their foundational questions; they identify whose perspectives are important and whose are irrelevant; and they demarcate the central goals, tactics, and methods, and exclude those that are superfluous or even dangerous. Origin stories set the terms. They provide the yardstick by which either to measure lineage and belonging or, conversely, to serve as the foil which initiates the rejection and then serves as the point of comparison for the new, improved, and presumably different approach. Nevertheless, that "different" approach is recognized by the extent to which it diverges from the original. With each articulation of a particular origin story, the roots grow deeper, the vision more certain. It becomes more daunting to challenge or re-imagine meaning, purpose, and trajectory outside of those boundaries initially constructed.

Despite being a nascent field, Fat Studies already has an origin story, repeated frequently and with increasing detail. It serves an important purpose, providing evidence of historical roots, demonstrating the deep thinking, activism, and theorizing that happened prior to the present, giving our contemporary field the status of "real." This origin story makes the field of Fat Studies "feel" solid; however, it actually constrains what we mean by, and what we imagine as, Fat Studies. In particular, it delineates a field that is inherently white, yet it generally does not explore the significance of that whiteness. It excludes the complexities of race and ethnicity, age and (dis) ability. In order to challenge this limiting vision, this paper outlines a different genealogy, one of Black fat activism, in order to challenge the dominant origin story and to offer at least one other origin story of Fat Studies. The chapter concludes with a note of caution, however, urging scholars and activists to be wary of setting up any particular group as the sine qua non of "intersectional" fat activism. Instead, I argue, scholars and activists need to connect fat activism to the broader project of ending body oppression wherever it emerges.

The Origin Story of Fat Studies

This dominant origin story of Fat Studies, as an academic field, is that of US fat feminism, written almost as it happened in the US by some of its own activists, then picked up by scholars as the field of Fat Studies emerged within the academy. The details may differ in the telling, even to the point of being argued over in print, online and verbally, in scholarly texts and colloquially, but that simply gives more proof that it's an important story, one worthy of dispute. It goes something like this: Emerging at the same time as other social movements in the United States, fat activism first showed up in groups organized by white men, such as Steve Post's 1967 Fat-In held in Central Park, and Lew Louderback and William Fabrey's creation of the National Association to Aid Fat Americans in 1969. Lesbian activists in California, feeling limited by the social and heterosexual focus of NAAFA, broke away in the early 1970s, creating the Fat Underground (also known as FU), enacting zap actions resisting diet clubs and dominant psychology and eventually writing the *Fat Liberation Manifesto*. The growing number of women's centers across the United States, but especially on the East Coast, the West Coast, and particularly liberated college towns like Iowa City, generated fat consciousness raising groups, out of which emerged Fat Liberator Publications which later coalesced into the important 1983 publication *Shadow on a Tightrope*. All this activism happened within and in relation to other feminist organizing, such as the Michigan Womyn's Music Festival (during which connections happened that moved the Fat Liberator Publications to Iowa City which resulted in the eventual publication of *Shadow)* to the Boston Women's Health Book Collective (which published fat activist material connected to Boston and New Haven feminist fat activist conferences) to the National Organization for Women (which in 1988 passed a resolution regarding body size discrimination and which led to other legal battles.)

This basic origin story, rooting the academic field of Fat Studies in the early activism of white, US fat feminism, is repeated frequently. It sandwiches Esther Rothblum and Sondra Solovay's *Fat Studies Reader* (2009), which begins with a narrative recounting of the basic story and concludes with the actual *Fat Liberation Manifesto* in the appendix. Charlotte Cooper lovingly traces the details of this origin story in her textured *Fat Activism: A Radical Social Movement* (2016). In *Queering Fat Embodiment* (2014), Jackie Wykes quickly summarizes the origins of fat activism by explaining that it emerged out of fat women's consciousness raising groups and was then collected in the *Shadow on a Tightrope* anthology. Le'a Kent narrates a similar basic history in her pathbreaking essay on fat and personhood, "Fighting Abjection: Representing Fat Women," in Kathleen LeBesco and Jana Evans Braziel's *Bodies Out of Bounds: Fatness and Transgression* (2001). It begins Jenny Ellison's (2016) wonderfully nuanced chapter on the development of Canadian fat activism. This is the history that I, too, recount, in my book *Fat Shame* (Farrell, 2011). I've even double-downed on this history in an article for an *American Periodicals* special issue on feminist publishing, tracing in great detail the precise meanderings through feminist periodicals and presses that eventually produced *Shadow on a Tightrope* (Farrell, 2018).

This story about the roots of the academic field of Fat Studies in US fat feminisms is neither bad nor wrong. Indeed, it's important and it's (increasingly!) well-documented, with archival records, written texts, and oral histories. It's not surprising, considering that those who author the story can generally trace their own activism directly back to these radical feminist roots, either as fat feminist activists themselves or as feminist academics whose fields are direct offshoots of these earlier feminist consciousness raising groups. It's also not surprising because this history is of people who most strongly identified with fat as a source of oppression. As one of the members of the Fat Underground explained, "Fat was the crisis area, the area where our identification ran highest and where we felt most strongly persecuted" (Farrell, 2011, p. 140). There is something startlingly clear and beautiful about such a laser focus.

But this origin story also constitutes a serious problem. Even with the caveat that often precedes its telling ("this is only one of the stories") the frequency with which this origin story is repeated means it is becoming more entrenched, situating fat activism as a largely US, white, lesbian movement. Its repetition flattens fat, erasing complexity and contradiction, ignoring other voices, many of whom do not necessarily see fat as *the* crisis area, but rather as one crisis area out of many.

A Disappeared Fat Genealogy: Black Fat Activism

A very important genealogy of Fat Studies and fat activism that disappears in this dominant story is that of Black writers, activists, and artists who have articulated a "thickened" fat activism from the origins of fat liberation. In the 1972 first full issue of *Ms.* Magazine, for instance, the welfare rights organizer Johnnie Tillmon wrote, "I'm a woman. I'm a black woman. I'm a poor woman. I'm a fat woman. I'm a middle-aged woman. And I'm on welfare. If you're any one of those things, you count less as a person. If you're *all* of those things, you just don't count, except as a statistic" (1972, p. 111). Connecting her identities as a woman, an African American, a poor person and an aging person to being fat, Tillmon put her finger on the ways that these cultural stigmas and oppressions interlock, denying personhood and making one, as she put it, a "statistic," the object of scientific and political inquiry, rather than a person, a complex human being within her own right. Guyanese-British poet Grace Nichols' 1984 *Fat Black Woman's Poems* lovingly evokes the ways that "beauty is a black fat woman" (p. 7), a being of explicit and enticing sexuality, as she writes in "Invitation":

> I'm feeling fine
> feel no need
> to change my lines
> when I move, I'm target light.
> Come up and see me sometime.

(p. 12)

This explicit sexual invitation, however, contrasts sharply with her political jab in "The Black Fat Woman Remembers": "This black fat woman ain't no Jemima" (p. 9). In other words, Nichols claims her fat and its beauty, but only for those with whom she wants to share it. She shakes off the historic layering of oppression, the claims of white people who seek her body for pleasure and sustenance, whether through "flipping pancakes" or sexual domination. She rejects the controlling image, in Patricia Hill Collins's words, of a stereotypical Black fat mammy, an image designed to simultaneously soothe whites and disempower Blacks, all while selling products at a profit (Collins, 2000; Farrell, 2011).

The artist Kerry James Marshall represents a similar tension in his 1993 *Beauty Examined*, in which we see a woman of colour laid out on an examining—presumably autopsy—table, with sections of her body labeled as in historical anatomy lessons. Indeed, many critics have noted the similarity of this painting to Rembrandt's (1632) *The Anatomy Lesson of Dr. Nicolaes Tulp*. While Marshall's *Beauty Examined* gestures to Rembrandt's *Anatomy Lesson*, I would argue it also explicitly evokes the history of scientific racism and its practitioners, such as the nineteenth century French scientist Georges Cuvier. In Marshall's painting, the woman's body is labeled, part by part: "big tits," "big thighs," "big legs," "big butt." Singling out these particular body parts for investigation was typical of Cuvier and other European scientists of the time, whose work categorizing human body types was used to "prove" the evolution of civilization and white supremacy. Most specifically, the painting calls to mind the particular case of the early nineteenth century South African Khoikhoi woman known as Sara Baartman, taken by Dutch traders in her home region and then forced to participate in both public fairs and laboratory studies as an oddity and scientific curiosity in England and then in France. After Baartman died, while still a young woman, Cuvier performed an autopsy in which he recounted what he identified as her barely human, almost animalistic characteristics. His work paved the way for later scientists, scholars, and philosophers, such as Cesare Lombroso and Havelock Ellis, who attributed criminality, lack of beauty, and animalistic traits to people of non-European origin. Along with skin colour and hair texture, body size, particularly fatness, was identified as a key element of primitiveness (Farrell, 2011). What is so powerful about Marshall's work, however, is that even as he conjures this painful, oppressive history of scientific racism and the way that it "painted" Black women as both not-quite-fully-human and as ugly, he twists and re-names it. Most explicitly, the title of the painting, *Beauty Examined*, identifies the woman lying on the table as a specimen of pulchritude, and that word used to punish—"big"—becomes a marker of attractiveness. It's also imperative to place *Beauty Examined* in conversation with all of Marshall's other work, which paint in joyful colour and buoyancy the beauty and liveliness of Black men and women in beauty shops, playgrounds, picnics, and bedroom scenes. If his

1993 *Beauty Examined* explores the confines and degradation of oppressive Euro-American medical and philosophical articulations of health and beauty, his 2012 *School of Beauty, School of Culture* left those confines behind completely in his celebration of a beauty shop, where we see women talking, preening, moving, bending, their round buttocks emphasized, their robust thighs highlighted.

Almost 20 years after Marshall's *Beauty Examined*, Sonya Renee Taylor's spoken word poem, *The Body is Not an Apology*, became the title of her new virtual community (https://thebodyisnotanapology.com). Her organization includes blog posts, editorials, educational sessions, and speaking engagements all focused on the complex routes of body hatred and body love. Taylor explicitly links the challenges faced by people of colour, people with mental health problems, trans and queer people, fat people, and disabled people to a perspective that perceives the body as "illegal" if it doesn't fit some dominant conception of normal. In her spoken word poem, she says, "Do not present the body as communion, confession, raised in contrition, the body is not an apology, do not ask for it to be pardoned as criminal" (Ravengal101). The body, to Taylor, is the source of pleasure, of movement, of life, and of pain, but what it isn't is a litmus test measuring humanity. Humanity, as she explains in her newest book, *The Body Is Not an Apology: The Power of Radical Self-Love* (Taylor, 2018), is already a given.

As co-founder of Body Confidence Canada, activist, and now member of the Ontario Parliament, Jill Andrew speaks to a similarly comprehensive understanding of what constitutes both body oppression and body liberation. She powerfully recounts an experience she had as a young, 15-year-old teenager, traveling to a youth empowerment event. Dressed in a new, figure shaping dress she loved, Andrew found herself seated next to a large man with a menacing dog. When she scootched over to create some space between her and the dog, the man yelled at her, "If you weren't such a f—ing fat, black, b—h, you wouldn't be afraid of my dog." While some other travelers looked at her in pity, most either laughed or looked away. She was devastated. It was a "tri-fecta of hate," she explained, her self-hood reduced to and punished for her size, her colour, and her gender (Vella, 2018).

There is a genealogy unfolding here, from the activism of Tillmon to the poetry of Nichols to the paintings of Marshall, to the contemporary spoken words of Sonya Renee Taylor, to the activism of Jill Andrew, all of whom connect the oppression and vitality of Blackness, fatness, and gender. As Andrea Shaw puts it, fat Black women "embody disobedience" by their very existence, and have through their lives, actions, and theorizing constructed what we regularly now call an intersectional philosophy (Shaw, 2006). Indeed, while the term "intersectionality" itself was coined relatively recently—in 1989—by the legal scholar Kimberlé Crenshaw in her insightful essay "Demarginalizing the Intersection of Race and Sex: A Black Feminist Critique of Antidiscrimination Doctrine, Feminist Theory and Antiracist Politics" (1989), the idea itself goes back much further, at least as far as to the pointed remarks of Sojourner Truth in her "Ain't I a Woman?" Akron, Ohio, speech, in which she challenges white, middle class women to understand not only the multitude of ways that she has been oppressed but also the fact that womanhood does not always look the same (Truth, 1995). For the purpose of thinking through the genealogy of fat activism, Shaw's 2006 commentary that Black women "embody disobedience" by their very existence illuminates the ways that fat oppressions work in tandem with other forms of oppression and the ways that fat knowledges—the pleasure and embodiment of fatness—work with other forms of knowledge "from the margins," in bell hooks' words, to construct a fuller understanding of human life, meaning, and power (hooks, 2000). Yet these lineages—as histories—are traced much less frequently than the origin story I articulated above, regarding the white, lesbian roots of fat activism, much to the detriment of Fat Studies. And in order to map these histories, it's going to be necessary to do more than looking beyond the stories already being traced. It's going to be necessary to look for places where fat is not necessarily considered the singular or primary form of oppression, but rather is articulated in conjunction with other identities. Such an approach would truly begin to thicken fat.

A Note of Caution: No Group Can Serve as the "Intersectional Wedge"

As scholars begin to turn to other archives and articulate these other genealogies, particularly those of women of the African diaspora, scholar Jennifer Nash (2008) voices a note of caution. As Nash argues, intersectionality often relies on "black women as the basis for its claims to complex subjectivity render[ing] black women prototypical intersectional subjects." "To that end," she continues, "black women's experiences are used as a theoretical wedge, designed to demonstrate the shortcomings of conventional feminist and antiracist work" (p. 8). And, indeed, the examples I gave above—of Tillmon, Nichols, Marshall, Taylor, Andrew—are working as that wedge, providing evidence of the limitations of conventional Fat Studies historiography. Nash worries that not only does this make Black women's lives more of an exemplar than a lived reality, but it also ignores the ways that all identities are "always constituted by the intersections of multiple vectors of power" where "privilege and oppression" can co-exist and even produce each other (p. 10). In other words, all lives are intersectional, all histories are intersectional, and it is only our (un)critical lens that sometimes makes certain lives appear "singular."

What I'm working through here is the importance of underscoring that in our work of "thickening fat" we cannot make women of the African diaspora the picture of already and always existing fat activism. As Haitian-American writer Roxane Gay expresses so eloquently in her memoir *Hunger* (2017), fatness is a source of shame and frustration in both her familial community and in her present public life as a writer. Her Blackness never insulated her from the pain of fat stigma; indeed, it has exacerbated it. And for most African

American "achievement feminists," fat was and is a problematic bodily attribute. By "achievement feminism" I gesture to a theoretical perspective and a set of practices that is most similar to what has been identified as liberal feminism. Liberal feminism refers to thinkers and activists who generally articulate an agenda that focuses on the law as the locus for change, emphasize individualistic approaches, and seek incremental reforms rather than radical upheaval. As Zillah Eisenstein explains in her now canonical work *The Radical Future of Liberal Feminism* (1981), however, even liberal feminism potentially creates sufficient change to cause significant and fundamental repercussions for patriarchy and capitalism. "Achievement feminism," in contrast, seeks to gain power and upward mobility explicitly within the systems already in place. Interestingly, one might identify aspects of achievement feminism within many different theoretical and activist approaches to feminism. And, generally, when achievement feminism blossoms, fat stigma and the belief that fat is incommensurate with personhood continues to flourish. That is, within a feminism that seeks achievement within already existing hierarchical arrangements, bodily signification regarding the superiority of thinness and the degeneracy of fatness may exist undetected and even be celebrated.

Historically, feminist thinkers—again, in that most capacious sense of that word—*chipped away* at the idea that the body itself did *signify*, that it did *mean something*, eliminating certain characteristics that were irrelevant: the uterus, upper body strength, the weight of brains. Feminists of colour challenged the significance of dark skin. But few eighteenth, nineteenth and early twentieth century Western feminists fundamentally disavowed the idea that certain aspects of the body *did* signify, that it could be read for signs of status, intelligence, willpower, for signs of being "civilized" or a "throwback" to some earlier, less evolved state, that it could, in other words, tell you *something* about the humanity of that body. One of the major untouched areas of body meanings was *fat*, particularly for those feminists whom I call above "achievement feminists."

We see this particularly well in the activism of nineteenth and early twentieth century US and British suffragists. During the campaigns for suffrage, anti-suffrage propaganda lampooned white suffragists as old, manly, and fat; many of their mocking cartoons drew from the stock portrayals of Irish and Black people, portraying suffragists with oversized lips, bulging eyes, and red or black skin. Significantly, however, prominent white feminists did not challenge the meaning of those attributes; they concurred that Black, fat, old, and manly were all negative characteristics, signifying "ugly," "degenerate," and "uncivilized." The predominant visual defense suffragists used in their propaganda were images of suffragists as white, youthful, and *thin* (Farrell, 2011, p. 82–117).

It's not only white women who traded in fat phobia, however. Fat stigma weaves its way throughout the history of African Americans' campaigns for full equality and rights. In what was likely one of the first public speeches by an African American woman about women's rights, Maria Stewart in 1832 took up the "evidence" that African American women, with their strong, thick bodies, were obviously not made for thinking, for education, for full rights. In a fascinating passage, she makes clear her argument, not that a strong, thick body could think as well as a thin one, but rather, that it was the labour that had hidden, and defaced, the true slender and delicate person within:

> Most of our color have dragged out a miserable existence of servitude from the cradle to the grave.... O, ye fairer sisters, whose hands are never soiled, whose nerves and muscles are never strained, go learn by experience! Had we the opportunity that you have had, to improve our moral and mental faculties, what would have hindered our intellects from being as bright, and our manners from being as dignified as yours? ... And why are not our forms as delicate, and our constitutions as slender, as yours? Is not the workmanship as curious and complete?
>
> (Stewart, 1995, p. 32)

In other words, the real person, inside the body of an African American labouring woman—whether enslaved or free—was a delicate and slender person. Labour and drudgery had simply overlaid a false façade. And this belief—that the real civilized *person* was thin, manifested itself by the early part of the twentieth century in African American professional women's lives as a very robust culture of exercise and dieting to lose weight and maintain a slender figure, as the historian Ava Purkiss has demonstrated in her finely argued article "Beauty Secrets: Fight Fat" (2017). In other words, among African American middle class women, among those who considered themselves professional, concerned about the uplift of their race and their sisters, fat was never "accepted," but rather was a trait that might be understandable (the result of drudgery and overwork) but certainly needed to be controlled and eliminated if a woman were to be seen as "fit" for citizenship. Interestingly, we can see the same focus on weight loss and a slender figure in contemporary versions of the professional Black women who Purkiss describes, namely Oprah Winfrey and Michelle Obama. Both women represent and advocate for women's place in public life, women's economic opportunities, women's reproductive rights and freedoms, and Black equality and achievement in general. And, for both, weight loss and a slim figure are key: First Lady Michelle Obama launched her Let's Move campaign in 2010 to "combat the epidemic of childhood obesity" because the "security of our nation is at stake" (Let's Move! Campaign, 2014). She even appeared—twice! —on the long-running television show *The Biggest Loser*, working out with Bob Harper in the White House, demonstrating how to do jumping push-ups (*Politico*, 2014). Likewise, for media mogul Oprah Winfrey, fat is the betrayer, the curtain of shame and excess that envelopes and smothers the real, fit person who resides inside. As she said in a video piece announcing her 10% ownership of Weight Watchers (which sent the stock price soaring), "Inside every overweight woman is a woman she knows she can be" (Hines,

2016). For Michelle Obama, the fat body connotes an unfit citizen, a danger to the nation; for Winfrey, it's a loss of potentiality, a threat to self-actualization, the result of behaviours—overeating, feigning injury—that are understandable but ultimately defeating (Dowd, 2016).

Thickening the Historiography of Fat Studies

I am rehearsing these stories of white and African American feminists who have and are trafficking in fat condemnation to point out that, in the endeavour to "thicken" the history of fat activism, we must listen to Nash's caution to avoid making any particular group the simple "wedge" in an already existing historiography. Instead, we need to look for the myriad ways that resistance to fat oppression has interlocked with resistance to other forms of oppression in complex and sometimes contradictory ways. And these contradictions run deep! For instance, in my own work, I have demonstrated the powerful and destructive ways that fat stigma is rooted in racialization and the blossoming of white supremacy. That is, in the Western thinking that I studied, particularly within the development of scientific racism, fat was a clear and definite sign of a primitive and degenerate body. Scholar Margaret Robinson traces this idea out in her work on Indigenous peoples in Canada, in her essay in this collection. But complicating this picture is Deborah McPhail, in her book *Contours of the Nation: Making Obesity and Imagining Canada, 1945–1970* (2017), who demonstrates how in post-war Canada, "obesity" was considered a modern malady, afflicting white, middle class Canadians. Indigenous people were considered immune to fatness. When the federal government began noting obesity as an increasing problem among Indigenous people, it was taken as a sign, not of their primitiveness, but of being "almost white," a sign of their modernizing and a way to dismantle claims to sovereignty. As she put it, "This discourse of Northern obesity helped characterize Inuit and Northern First Nations populations as 'almost-modern,'" ordinary citizens whose claims to 'special status' would be null and void" (p. 132). And this example is very important, as we thus see the ways that "fat" can serve as a malleable and tricky tool of oppression.

I end with a thought that as we trace the multiple routes of fat activism, and the multiple starting places for the academic field of Fat Studies, we may be best served by looking to those who are working and who have worked to dismantle the complex and contradictory projects of oppressive body signification, who seek ways to allow people and bodies to thrive in all their "brilliant imperfection," in the words of poet and essayist Eli Clare (2017). As we add stories about the beginnings of fat activism and Fat Studies, we may not see the "pure" and "clear" vision that our initial origin story provided. But, then, if we look to the ways that power, privilege, and oppression intersect, that original story itself is really quite complicated, even if the re-telling of it has tended to smooth out those tangled histories.

Acknowledgements

I would like to thank very much the creators of the Thickening Fat conference in Toronto, May Friedman, Carla Rice, Jen Rinaldi; the organizer extraordinaire Kelsey Ioannoni; and all the participants whose work, energy, and vitality I value so much. I wish to thank Kayleigh Rhatigan, Dickinson College class of 2019, who worked to clean up this manuscript and format it correctly. And, finally, I wish to thank Eli Clare, whose writing and whose visit to Dickinson have profoundly shaped my thinking on bodies.

References

Clare, E. (2017). *Brilliant imperfection: Grappling with cure.* Durham, NC: Duke University Press.

Collins, P. H. (2000). *Black feminist thought: Knowledge, consciousness, and the politics of empowerment.* New York: Routledge.

Cooper, C. (2016). *Fat activism: A radical social movement.* Bristol: HammerOn Press.

Crenshaw, K. (1989). Demarginalizing the intersection of race and sex: A black feminist critique of antidiscrimination doctrine, feminist theory, and antiracist politics. *University of Chicago Legal Forum, 1,* 139–167.

Dowd, K. E. (2016, April 10). Oprah Winfrey says Weight Watcher opportunity 'felt like an intervention from on high.' *People.* Retrieved from http://www.people.com /article/oprah-winfrey-talks-weight-watchers-body-image-super-soul-sessions

Ellison, J. (2016) From 'FU' to 'Be Yourself': Fat activisms in Canada. In W. Mitchinson, D. McPhail & J. Ellison (Eds.), *Obesity in Canada: Critical Perspectives* (pp. 293–319). Toronto: University of Toronto Press.

Eisenstein, Z. R. (1981). *The radical future of liberal feminism.* Lebanon: University Press of New England.

Farrell, A. E. (2011). *Fat shame.* New York: New York University Press.

Farrell, A. E. (2018). "In the position of fat women is shown the true position of woman in our society": *Shadow on a Tightrope* and the centrality of feminist independent publishing. *American Periodicals, 28*(2), 139–152.

Gay, R. (2017). *Hunger.* New York: Harper Collins.

Hines, R. (2016, March 11). Oprah unveils her weight loss transformation, talks 'best body' in O. *Today.* Retrieved from https://www.today.com/health/oprah-unveils-her-weight-loss-transformation-talks-best-body-o-t79376

hooks, b. (2000). *Feminist theory: From margin to center.* London: Pluto Press.

Kent, L. (2001). Fighting abjection: Representing fat women. In K. LeBesco & J. E. Braziel (Eds.), *Bodies out of bounds: Fatness and transgression* (pp. 130–150). Berkeley: University of California Press.

Let's Move! Campaign (2014, October 1). Learn the facts. Retrieved from http://www .letsmove.gov/learn-facts/epidemic-childhood-obesity

Marshall, K. J. (1993). *Beauty examined.* Acrylic and collage on canvas. The Metropolitan Museum of Art.

Marshall, K. J. (2012). *School of beauty, school of culture.* Acrylic and glitter on canvas. The Metropolitan Museum of Art.

McPhail, D. (2017). *Contours of the nation: Making obesity and imagining Canada, 1945–1970.* Toronto: University of Toronto Press.

Nash, J. C. (2008). Re-thinking intersectionality. *Feminist Review, 89*, 1–15.

Nichols, G. (1984). *The fat black woman's poems*. London: Virago.

Politico. (2014, October 2). Michelle Obama works out on the *Biggest Loser*. Retrieved from http://www.politico.com/multimedia/video/2012/04/michelle-obama-works -out-on-the-biggest-loser.html

Purkiss, A. (2017). "Beauty secrets: Fight fat": Black women's aesthetics, exercise, and fat stigma, 1900–1930s. *Journal of Women's History, 29*(2), 14–37.

Ravengal101. "The body is not an apology" by Sonya Renee [Video file]. Retrieved from https://www.youtube.com/watch?v=B7lKPdh_y-8

Rothblum, E., & Solovay, S. (Eds.). (2009). *The fat studies reader*. New York: New York University Press.

Shaw, A. E. (2006). *The embodiment of disobedience: Fat black women's unruly political bodies*. Lanham, MD: Lexington Books.

Stewart, M. (1995). Lecture delivered at the Franklin Hall, Boston, September 21, 1832. In B. Guy-Sheftal (Ed.), *Words of fire: An anthology of African-American feminist thought* (p. 32). New York: The New Press.

Taylor, S. R. (2018). *The body is not an apology: The power of radical self love*. Oakland: Berrett-Koehler Publishers.

Tillmon, J. (1972). Welfare as a woman's issue. *Ms.*, Spring, 111–16.

Truth, S. (1995). Woman's rights. In B. Guy-Sheftal (Ed.), *Words of fire: An anthology of African-American feminist thought* (p. 36). New York: The New Press.

Vella, E. (2018). 'It was a trifecta of hate': Body image activist recalls moment she was accosted by a man over her weight, race. *Global News*. April 17. Retrieved from https://globalnews.ca/news/4106084/jill-andrew-body-confidence-canada/

Wykes, J. (2014). Introduction: Why queering fat embodiment? In C. Pause, J. Wykes & S. Murray (Eds.), *Queering fat embodiment* (pp. 1–12). Farnham, UK: Ashgate.

3   Fat Pedagogy for Queers

Chicana Body Becoming in Four Acts

Karleen Pendleton Jiménez

Prelude: Body Becoming Theorists

Do not see bodies as bounded, stable entities, but as fluid forms that come to be through relations with natural and cultural forces that surround them (Rice, 2014, pp. 431–432).

Act 1: Mothers and Daughters: Snow White's Legacy

1935

My nana (my mother's mother) walks into the studios to audition for the main character of what people are calling "Mr. Disney's Folly" (Barrier, 1999, p. 229), "the first full-length cell animated feature in motion picture history" (Smith, 2006, p. 33). She has a sweet high voice, a little girl's voice, that has landed her parts in cartoons. Her claim to fame is her role as Minnie Mouse en Español.

Walt Disney makes the celebrated film Snow White, *but without my nana's voice. She is a part of the film though. At that audition, they took her image instead of her voice to create the character of Snow White without consent. So says my nana and her husband in an unsuccessful lawsuit against Disney. While the history books say otherwise, looking at a side-by-side comparison of their 1930s photos, I would have ruled in her favour.*

My Mexican grandmother is "the fairest one of all" with "lips as red as the rose. Hair black as ebony. Skin white as snow" (IMDB, Snow White and the Seven Dwarfs*), and she demands to be compensated properly for it. The only child of a single mother who worked the factories, she has survived on her looks. She gets gigs at the studios, gets a husband for a dime a dance, gets certified as a beautician in 1935 Hollywood.*

The body is a pedagogical device, a location of recentering and recontextualizing the self and the stories that emanate from that self.

(Cruz, 2006, p. 72)

What has the survivalist Snow White learned about her body, and how will she teach it to her daughter?

1954

    My mom is sitting in the doctor's waiting room beside my nana. She is a 14-year-old girl with dark brown eyes, and hair almost black. She is a beautiful tall and plump girl. She is the copy, once removed of her mother's image. She loves to wear brightly embroidered skirts and blouses from México. She loves to read books. She pleads to get a gift of a model train from her parents, even though it is meant for her brother. Her adoring father gives in, as he often does, to the irritation of my nana. My grandpa sings "Maria Elena" to my mom, and whispers how she will be the first one in her family to go to college. She will get the education that he craves.

    My nana is in a panic. My mother's chubby girl body has transformed into an even larger adolescent shape. My nana is certain that my mom will be unable to find a man to marry her. She isn't pretty enough to work at a salon. My nana doesn't have the money to pay for her. She will instruct my mom to find some babysitting to cover the costs of her clothes for now. She's gotta cut down on her weight though if she's gonna make it.

    "Elaine," the nurse calls for her, and she and my nana enter the doctor's office. The doctor smiles at her and asks that she stand on a scale in the corner of the white room. My nana looks away, but she hears the sound of the metal slide as he pushes it further and further to the right to accurately identify the number of pounds. The doctor winks at my mom to reassure her. He informs her about the new dieting pills that will solve the problem and writes out the prescription.

    She swallows the pills and whips through her classwork, joins clubs and watches the neighbours' kids after school. The amphetamines cut a few pounds and make her heart race. It doesn't seem to stop her mother's stream of comments though. Her mother doesn't like her body.

Learning is never a done deal, and ongoing critical consciousness is of great relevance when attempting to make a more loving world (Freire, 1999). Carla Rice (2014) reminds us that the ongoing process of learning applies to our bodies as well. Each day our bodies rub up against the world, they learn, transform, and reconstitute themselves. Citing Grosz, Rice wants us to understand that "the unexpected, accidental, and everything that befalls people – from insults and injuries to technologies and pleasures – become new ingredients in their bodies' history and development" (Grosz, 1999, 2008, cited in Rice, 2014, pp. 431–435). My relationship with my body is a culmination of the harmful biopedagogies endured by three generations of women in my family, as well as the healing body becoming pedagogies, those active moves of resistance and transformation, that I, my mother, and my grandmother took to reclaim power over our bodies (Rice, 2015). My biopedagogies follow the history of the hurt of my mother's body under the gaze of my grandmother, and the insidiousness of a homophobic/transphobic culture that renders ugly my butch woman's body. My body becoming pedagogies have been formed by my mom's refusal to carry on the tradition of harming daughters' bodies. My body becoming pedagogies included years of the shape of my mother's arm hanging down onto my shoulder when she wrapped her arm around me.

> *1993*
>
> *I am 21. We are lying in bed together side-by-side. I show my mom a flier from our theatre show, where my girlfriend is featured, while I appear in a group shot on the back. I say something to my mom about how pretty (feminine) my girlfriend is.*
>
> *My mom would frankly rather see more of me. She responds, "You do know that you're pretty, right?"*

She must have been worried about how many times I had been mistaken for a boy. She must have been trying to quiet the laughter that sometimes followed me. I remember feeling insulted by her response, though. I got it in my head that she thought I was trying to be a lesbian because I didn't think I was pretty. I wish I could shake that 20-year-old self. Shake her and tell her that my mom was just giving me a compliment. She wanted to make sure that I knew to value my body, something her mother had never offered her.

I can't see my grandmother's vision of my mother's body. It is not visible to me. I can only see my mother's body as the most beautiful substance on earth.

> *1978*
>
> *I am 6. My mom lets me watch her get dressed in the early mornings before school. She rolls on nylons and pulls up a black skirt with yellow and burgundy flowers. She wrestles with a great big silky bra, covers it with a burgundy blouse, and sprays on some Opium perfume.*

When does the curriculum of our bodies begin? Is it when a baby begins to enjoy the recognition of her mother (Benjamin, 1995, p. 33)? What about when that recognition coincides with a recognition of the mother's body as beautiful?

> *2018*
>
> *At 46, my 8-year-old daughter tells me with a sincerity and passion that my body is "really pretty." We are in a little stall changing after swimming in the pool. I've removed my swimsuit and she stares at me naked and tells me that she loves my tummy. When she says it, it's like she has no idea that big stretch-marked tummies are often frowned upon or that butches look weird. She is convinced that I am a most gorgeous thing, and she convinces me. I tell her about how much I loved carrying my mom's body, full in my arms, around in a swimming pool when I was a kid.*

I hope my adoration of my mother's body had the same healing effect on her as my daughter's has had for me.

How important is the mutual recognition of beauty between mothers and daughters to the body becoming curriculum? My grandmother never offered to my mother a mutual recognition of beauty. My mother's biopedagogies were rooted in the desperate and hateful gaze of her mother. I want to be clear that I don't think my grandmother hated my mother, but I do think she hated her body. My own body pedagogies include an investigation of this hatred.

Act 2: Chicana Bodies: "Real Women"

> We need more fat histories to explore the way in which the category "obesity," and its invisible, unmarked counterpart, "thin," serve to secure certain oppressive power relations. What role do they play in defining what it is to be non-white, poor, and foreign, on the one hand, and white, upper-class, and native, on the other?
>
> (Levy-Navarro, 2009, p. 16)

The United States possesses an abundance of propaganda targeting big women's bodies. My grandmother found hers in the quest for the American dream and the frenzy of early twentieth century Hollywood. She was part of an aspiring show business family, where "good looks" could be cashed in. "Good looks" could trump social stigma against Mexican ancestry and poor education. "Good looks" was fair skin and thin bodies, or the illusion and promotion of fair skin and thin bodies even in their absence. "Good looks" was about survival, money and the middle class.

My mother had a wandering eye and a big round body. She failed to embody studio "good looks," and faced her mother's wrath, an anger born of unconscious fear. How could a Chicana survive without beauty? How could she find a man, make a family, establish an economic safety net without beauty? My grandmother attempted to shame my mother into a better body to no avail. My mother challenged the shame and kept the pounds. She was hurt but not defeated.

Chicanas receive contradictory responses to their bodies from their families. In Elena Levy-Navarro's (2009) essay "Fattening Queer History," she offers examples of positive body language within Latina culture: A "fat" Latina might understand herself to be "bien cuidada" or well-cared for, as opposed to a mainstream perception of her body pathologized as "obese" (p. 16).

In another study, Chicanas are probed for signs that their families are complicit in preventing the women from losing weight (McLaughlin, et al., 2017). They offer numerous examples of Chicanx families pressuring the women to cook unhealthy food, urging them to eat more than they desire, teasing them if the women express concern or interest in their health. However, the researchers never ask whether Chicanx families do anything loving or helpful for the women's bodies. There is no opportunity afforded to consider the benefits of feeling "bien cuidada." In addition, the only weight-loss strategy employed by one participant's family members, which was also a favourite of my grandmother's, is when "they'll tell you you won't find a boyfriend if you get too fat!" (McLaughlin, et al., 2017, p. 1515).

My grandmother always couched her comments about women's bodies in a concern over their capacity to attract men. If I grew hair on my legs, I wouldn't be able to get a boyfriend. If the neighbour wasn't married, it was because the size of her nose was too big. If my mom left her husband, it was because she had probably put on too much weight to keep him.

This obsession with controlling women's bodies in an effort to appeal to men is a central theme in Josefina López's play (and later, movie) *Real Women Have Curves*. The story centres on the protagonist Ana, a young full-figured Chicana coming of age who is coerced into working at her sister's sewing factory, even though her dream is to go to college. As part of her struggle to assert her independence, she is faced with her mother's remarks about her body. "Carmen [Ana's mother] constantly nags Ana to lose weight and she attempts to control what Ana consumes" (Perez, 2009, p. 128). As with my grandmother, family and fertility drive Carmen's behaviour, "This is all part of Carmen's scheme to maintain a traditional family structure and get another baby in the family" (p. 128).

Act 3: Bodies of Resistance: Revolution on Olvera Street

> We need more histories that consider the experiences of the defiantly and happily fat in our culture.
>
> (Levy-Navarro, 2009, p. 16)

Body pedagogies don't finish there. They are not stuck in the controlling words of a fearful mother. Chicanx culture also includes big women who fight for the autonomy of their bodies. As Ana calls out her mother, "'Mama, I do want to lose weight. And part of me doesn't because my weight says to everybody, fuck you!' then she adds, 'How dare anyone tell me what I should look like or what I should be when there's so much more to me than my weight'" (Perez, 2009, p. 136). Ana will claim her body on her own terms. Chicanas fight to be recognized as beautiful and legitimate, no diets taken, no changes to their lifestyle to appease others, no apologies.

> Through resisting her mother's tutelage, and patriarchy in general, Ana is able to legitimate herself and her curvy body as that of a 'real woman'.
>
> (Perez, 2009, p. 139)

1992

My mom, my nana, my aunt, and I are browsing the stalls on Olvera Street, a Mexican shopping district in Los Angeles. There are brightly coloured blankets, tiny red clay pots, beaded jewelry, turquoise rings, dancing marionettes, Aztec calendars, guayaveras. Mariachi music flows over from the restaurant three doors down, along with the smell of carne asada roasting on the grill. My aunt buys me a silky rust coloured guayavera with white flowers. I put it on immediately and feel handsome. I hold my mom's hand and look up at the next stall, which features velvet paintings. We used to have one years ago hanging in our living room, and they make us nostalgic: torreros, tigers, revolutionary soldiers, and Guadalupes. My mom smiles when she gets to the glowing lime green Elvis and points it out to her mother. My nana peers up at Velvet Elvis, but shakes her head, "I used to like him," she sighs, "until he got fat."

My mom drops my hand and begins the battle. Right there in the middle of Olvera Street, with neon Velvet Elvis strumming his guitar above her, my 52-year-old mom unleashes her fury. People gather round to watch the show.

"I don't want you to make any more fat comments around me ever again!!" she yells.

My nana responds with surprise, "What do you mean? I didn't say anything."

"Yes, you did, mom. You made a look of disgust on your face when you described Elvis getting fat."

"I didn't mean anything by it," she responds in her high voice.

"Yes, you do, mom. You make some comment against fat people every single time you see me," she retorts, "I can't stand it. I don't want to hear it anymore," she finishes exasperated, "You got that, not one more time!"

It was a dramatic moment. The colours. The audience. The demand to be rid of toxic words, even and especially those from family. It is such a flamboyant scene in my body becoming pedagogy. It is more exciting than upsetting; it is theatrical and empowering.

My mom's body becoming pedagogy consisted of five decades of knowledge garnered from the perspective of a fat girl and woman. It was a pedagogy of resistance to bullshit, like the underhanded comments from her mother, or the food vendors who would try to give her less taquitos, or the man in the meeting who ignored her because he decided that her weight coincided with less intelligence.

My mom's body becoming pedagogy also involved the pleasure of beautiful clothing. She proudly abstained from walking long distances, so that she could enjoy pretty leather and suede heels. She was a skilled shopper, scouring department store racks in search of deals on fancy 2X skirt suits, even as she complained that the skinny women could look beautiful in a $20 outfit.

My mom's body becoming pedagogy included cases of diet sodas, pork chop stews, enchiladas for celebrations, white rice and Campbell's soup.

My mom's body becoming pedagogy for me was also profound in its silence. My mom never commented on my weight. Not when I was skinnier, not when I was chubbier. Never once. I didn't know that was remarkable until I went off to university and found out how other people lived.

"You need to eat more. You need to eat less. You've put on weight. You look good (when you've lost weight). Here, have some more mashed potatoes."

She never did that. The only comment I ever remember her saying about my eating, probably offered when I was a teenager, was that she felt I would be ok. I would be well nourished because I instinctively enjoyed a range of foods: meats, vegetables, and carbs. That is the comment, the truth that has guided my good feelings about eating for the thirty years since. That I would be ok.

My mom's body becoming pedagogies valued intellect over body. At 21, my mother left the valley of show biz, and fled to the other valley, the hot and boring valley, the post-war tract home valley for young families with little money. It was geographic distance, an attempt at the protection of her body from her mother. She sought survival through intelligence, found elegance in numbers and budgets, found sanctuary in schools. Her soft and awkward body could be maneuvered by a strategic use of intellect. The intellect could not salvage the damage done to body and psyche, but it could provide for economic stability.

I inherited my mother's lessons of survival. I inherited the hurt, the helplessness I felt when her body was the object of ridicule. I learned the confusion of multi-perspective and partial knowledge; why couldn't the rest of the world perceive her as the great beauty that I saw?

My family's body becoming pedagogies were based on Chicana knowledges of survival. Both my nana and mom taught me to survive, but survival has looked differently for each of us. I learned that it would be my smarts that would save me. My body would not be my chance for economic opportunity. My butch body would not be marriage-ready. "You don't have to get married to get the silver," my mom told me, "But you could get a PhD in whatever you like." By the end of the 20th century, (some) big women and queer women get to be intelligent and don't have to depend on men for economic stability.

My mom's fat pedagogies also taught me a sensitivity around bodies, a carefulness, a respect for bodily autonomy. Her lessons spared me the ubiquitous North American obsession with weight and dieting. I was also provided an example for how to accept a nonconforming body, in my case a chubby butch lesbian body. Such are the gifts of fat pedagogies for queers.

Act 4: Queer Fat Solidarity: Big Fat Pussy

The body prompts memory and language, builds community and coalition.

(Cruz, 2006, p. 72)

"Did your mother feel badly about her body?" My sister-in-law asks as I recount my mom's weight war stories.

"I don't know," I had gotten so wrapped up in the stories that I don't know how she actually felt about her body. I know that she often lifted her sweater to hide her face if someone tried to take a photo of her. I know that while she always had boyfriends, she was very private about her sexuality.

She handed me *Our Bodies, Ourselves* and smutty romances to read, but we never had a conversation about bodies and sex. She said once that her mother would buy her lingerie or sexy nightgowns and it made her feel uncomfortable. She didn't want us to feel that discomfort, and we each were afforded a wide zone of privacy.

Her body becoming pedagogies were often chosen as the polar opposite to what her mother had done. They were acts of resistance to her mother's controlling commentary. If my nana pushed conversation of bodies, my mother retreated into silence about bodies. If my nana pushed sexy lingerie, my mom avoided any mention of sexuality. My mom's fat body becoming pedagogies offered me a love and legitimacy of my queer body, they offered me a lifelong desire for round women's bodies, but they did not grant me the knowledge to enjoy sexiness without shame.

1998

July in Toronto means bright colours of flowers bursting from every postage stamp garden. It means that bodies carefully hidden and layered in sweaters and jackets after months of winter are revealed. It means women walking all over the sidewalks in cotton sundresses. It means hot, sticky days.

I have a new girlfriend, the Canadian who brought me here. She has round arms that I love to stroke. Her curvy ass presses against her blue and white sundress as she leads me up to her bedroom. I am dying to jump her, to push open her legs, to start working my hand against her damp, baby-blue underwear. I will stretch her dress above her cream breasts and kiss her tummy still loose from the daughter she had the year before. I know the rhythm of my taking her, and I'm ready to go.

Hilary has another idea though. She is the one pushing me down. I am struggling with this. It's hard for me to pull off being a bottom mid-afternoon. If it's the morning before I've woken into myself, or the night after a couple drinks and I've forgotten myself, I can slip more easily into being a woman with a body. But in full consciousness, how am I to face it. I insist that she fight me for me. Luckily she's the stronger, can block my fists, can pin me down, can force me to accept it, can make me feel so much pleasure.

We must also learn to write fat histories that are more imaginative and playful in nature.

(Levy-Navarro, 2009, pp. 16–20)

1999

"Maybe I should use a pen name," I suggest. I don't feel very comfortable writing about sex. How can a butch top, who feels like a guy, who is also a feminist, really write about how great it feels to devour a woman? How can a butch top, who feels like a guy, who momentarily loses her feminism, shamefully admit to being devoured as a woman? Either scenario scares the hell out of me to put into print, to live up to.

"I don't get that," tatiana (de la tierra – poet friend and lover) responds to me in an irritated voice. "Why wouldn't you use your name?" She's not impressed with sexual cowards.

"I don't know," I mumble, "Could it affect my chances of getting a job?" I don't think that's my actual reason for worrying about it, but I can't confess to my shame.

"Agh!" she grunts in disgust, "What's the point?" She is whirling around her apartment in a long tie-dye dress that highlights her lush Botero body, making chicken, putting on salsa music, pouring a little glass of aguardiente.

She hands me the shot, looks me in the eye, and tells me, "I wouldn't hide my sexuality from anyone."

My body becoming pedagogies have been guided by my fat mother and my fat queer lovers. My mom made the space for my body, the queers have offered me the luxury of enjoying the sexiness of my body. I propose a solidarity of queer and fat. I don't mean allies. I mean two overlapping groups of peoples targeted by the claws of normality. Such shared experiences of body marginalization have led some theorists to include fatness as a kind of queer. As Levy-Navarro (2009) writes, "The queer historiography that I discuss here embraces a more expansive definition of "queer" that is more expressly inclusive of all who challenge normativity, including fat people" (p. 15). However you conceive of their connection, fat and queer are a particularly valuable intersectionality that at times produce loving knowledge, representation and action.

Returning to the film *Real Women Have Curves*, the protagonist Ana does go to work in her sister's sewing factory, but she ultimately leads a rebellion. She is not resisting the work, instead uses it as her opportunity to defy her mother's control over her body. Under hot working conditions, she removes her blouse and skirt and urges the other women to follow suit. Despite her mother's objections, the scene erupts into laughter and dancing as they examine each other's round bodies, talk about them, and show them off to one another. While they do not identify as queer, the movie offers us a "queer" scene of sexy, playful full-figured women admiring each other's bodies that "redefine[s] Chicana/Latina aesthetics by designating their large-sized bodies as erotic and beautiful" (Perez, 2009, p. 139).

Latina poet tatiana de la tierra's work "Big Fat Pussy Girl" is another personal favourite of mine that celebrates queer/fat fusion. Upon finding a stone butch lover who adores her pussy, she learns that,

Papayona. Big fat pussy. She said it. She named it. I didn't just have any pussy. I had a big fat pussy. And this was a good thing. Papayona. Bigger, softer, better. Papayona. Wider, deeper, wetter. Panochota, 3X double-wide extra padded. Chochachona. Big fat pussy. Queen-size cunt. A whaler of a cunt, the cruise ship of cunts, the World Wide Web of cunts, the Cadillac of cunts, the castle of cunts, the eagle of cunts, the Jupiter of Cunts. Papayona. The Library of Congress of cunts. Papayona. The Disney World of Cunts. Papayona. The Sonora Matancera of Cunts.

(de la tierra, n.d.)

de la tierra's delight and humour abounds in this tribute to queer desire and fat pussy. She reinscribes the meaning of fat pussy with the grandest locations and best inventions in the world. This bilingual ode to her papayona also shows the way in which race and ethnicity overlap with queerness and fatness as a path toward pleasure. Women of colour can be simultaneously discriminated against and celebrated because their bodies do not conform to white western ideals of beauty, as in the popularity and contestation of Jennifer Lopez's big "butt" (Burns-Ardolino, 2009, p. 273) de la tierra's Latinidad is central to her adoration of her transgressive big fat pussy. In both life and in writing she celebrated Latina queer fat sexuality and challenged the rest of us to step up.

While I do not have a story to match the exuberance of the two above, I will conclude with a return to the space of the women of my family. It is a recounting of one personal intervention of queer desire and fat pedagogy and a small tribute to my mother's body.

1997

I'm riding in the back of my aunt's Ford. Snow White (my nana) sits in the passenger seat and gossips with my aunt. It is a year after my mother's death, and the three of us are thrown together for a family outing. The outing was probably planned because my mom was gone. Each of us were intimately tied to the woman whose body had failed her. The sister, the mother, and the daughter were missing the woman who had connected us.

I don't know how it started, but it was a familiar refrain. My nana started talking about my mother's body, how fat it was, how she needed to lose weight, how it would be difficult for her to find a man. My mother was dead, and my nana so accustomed to trashing my mother's body, kept right on doing it even after her body was gone. My mouth hung open. I knew that if my mother was with us, she'd be telling her off. Then my nana would appear innocent and confused and note that my mom had always been very sensitive. This would further enrage my mother and the family outing would deteriorate into an argument. This was the routine. But my mother wasn't there to play her part.

My beautiful aunt intervened, "Elaine never had any trouble finding a man," she retorts, "She always had boyfriends."

My nana continues, "A lot of men won't go for a woman with that much weight."

"No, that's not true, mom," my aunt signals on the highway, "Many men prefer bigger women, I've got a friend-"

I interrupt her. Here is my chance. "Yes, she's right, and I prefer bigger women too."

I really hadn't wanted to yell at my nana because she was an old lady relative of mine, and I wasn't raised to do that kind of thing. But she was insulting my mother after all, and I couldn't let that slip by. And then, there it was. The perfect opportunity to challenge fatphobia and homophobia with one clever line. "I prefer bigger women." (FYI, I was out to my aunt but not my nana). Silence. That shut her up.

I felt such naughty glee when I said it. My mom would have burst into laughter. One woman loving and wanting another woman. No men required. No need to seek approval. No need for a man's salary. No need for weight reduction. Just my desire for a big woman's body.

References

Barrier, M. (1999). *Hollywood cartoons: American animation in its golden age.* New York: Oxford University Press.

Benjamin, J. (1995). *Like subjects, love objects: Essays on recognition and sexual difference.* New Haven, CT: Yale University Press.

Boston Women's Health Book Collective. (2011). *Our bodies, ourselves.* New York: Simon & Schuster.

Brown, E. (Producer), & Cardoso, P. (Director). (2002). *Real women have curves* [Motion Picture]. USA: HBO Films.

Burns-Ardolino, W. A. (2009). Jiggle in my walk: The iconic power of the "big butt" in American pop culture. In E. Rothblum & S. Solovay (Eds.), *The fat studies reader* (pp. 271–279). New York: New York University Press.

Cruz, C. (2006). Toward an epistemology of a brown body. In D. Delgado Bernal & C. A. Elenes (Eds.), *Chicana/Latina education in everyday life: Feminista perspectives on pedagogy and epistemology* (pp. 59–75). Albany, NY: State University of New York.

de la tierra, t. (n.d.). Big fat pussy girl. Retrieved from http://delatierra.net/?page_id=1037

Freire, P. (1999). *Pedagogy of the oppressed* (20th anniversary ed.). New York: Continuum.

Grosz, E.A. (1999). Becoming … An introduction. In E.A. Grosz (Ed.), *Becomings: Explorations in time, memory, and futures* (pp. 1–11). Ithaca, NY: Cornell University Press.

Grosz, E.A. (2008). Darwin and feminism: Preliminary investigations for a possible alliance. In S. Alaimo & S. Hekman (Eds.), *Material feminisms* (pp. 23–51). Bloomington: Indiana University Press.

IMDB. (n.d.). *Snow White and the Seven Dwarfs* (1937) Quotes. Retrieved from https://www.imdb.com/title/tt0029583/quotes

Levy-Navarro, E. (2009). Fattening queer history: Where does fat history go from here? In E. Rothblum & S. Solovay (Eds.), *The fat studies reader* (pp. 15–22). New York: New York University Press.

McLaughlin, E. A., Campos-Melady, M., Smith, J. E., Serier, K. N., Belon, K. E., Simmons, J. D., & Kelton, K. (2017). The role of familism in weight loss treatment for Mexican American women. *Journal of Health Psychology, 22*(12), 1510–1523. doi:10.1177/1359105316630134

Perez, D. E. (2009). *Re/thinking Chicana/o and Latina/o Popular Culture.* New York: Palgrave Macmillan.

Rice, C. (2014). *Becoming women: The embodied self in image culture.* Toronto: University of Toronto Press, Scholarly Publishing Division. Kindle Edition.

Rice, C. (2015). Rethinking fat: From bio– to body becoming pedagogies. *Cultural Studies ↔ Critical Methodologies, 15*(5), pp. 387–397.

Smith, D. (2006). *Disney A to Z: The Official Encyclopedia* (3rd ed.). New York: Disney Editions, 2006.

4 "May My Children Always Have Milk and Rice"

Problematizing the Role of Mothers in Childhood Fatness in India

Sucharita Sarkar

This chapter is an attempt to decolonize fat discourses—specifically, childhood fatness—by inserting India into a debate that has been, thus far, overwhelmingly situated in Europe and North America. "Childhood obesity" has become—as part of a global trend—a fraught site of moral panic, body-image anxiety, medical-industrial regulation, neoliberal consumerism, and mother-blaming (Boero, 2009; Friedman, 2015). While this is undoubtedly manifest in globalized, urbanized India, there simultaneously exists an older, traditional, contrary narrative that celebrates fat as good. This is the point of difference (vis-à-vis western fat discourses) wherein I frame my inquiry and consider how, in India, childhood fatness is *also* a site of an ongoing epistemological conflict between cultures and generations, and how *both* these competing narratives (of fat-as-bad and fat-as-good) responsibilize mothers for childhood fat or its absence.

In the first section, I investigate how these dual narratives persist in mainstream fat discourse, focusing on three maternal categories that are intensely scrutinized—the traditional (over)indulgent mother, the working mother, and the fat mother. I unpack a controversial clinical study on Indian urban childhood obesity written by Gulati and others (2013) and related media articles to expose the amplification of mother-blame through these three risky figures. In the second section, I draw on my own primary research to analyze the responses of ten heterosexual Indian mothers implicated in this binarized fat politics. Following their lead, I use the terms "underweight," "normal weight," "overweight," and "obese" to reflect the new fat lexicon in India, although I acknowledge that these terms are discriminatory and disciplinary. I also emphasize that my research focuses on the experiences of relatively privileged urban middle-class mothers, and does not address the responses to childhood non/fat among poor mothers.

For my primary research, I conducted semi-structured interviews, through e-mail and telephone, of a purposive sampling of eight married and two divorced Hindu mothers from Mumbai, Kolkata, New Delhi and Chennai, each with one or two children aged 10–19 years. Six respondents were full-time working mothers, two worked part-time, and two were stay-at-home mothers. Three lived in multigenerational families and the other seven in nuclear families where parents and parents-in-law were frequent visitors. The respondents' educated, urban, middle-class demographics correspond to the mothers surveyed by Gulati et al.'s report and, hence, their responses are crucial to my critique of the report's politics. The respondents were familiar with obesity management terminology like Body Mass Index (BMI) and most of them uncritically used medical body-weight categories—underweight, normal weight, overweight, and obese—to define themselves, with six self-identifying as normal-weight, three as overweight, and one as obese. They also used these categories to describe their children, but as disputed rather than absolute terms. They often expressed a disjuncture among their own categorization of their children's weight, the medical expert's assessment and the opinion of older family relations; and these taxonomic interstices expose the contestations in Indian childhood fat discourses.

The Contrary Discourses of Childhood Fatness in India

The supplication in this chapter's title is an often expressed wish by Bengali parents. It can be traced to Bharatchandra's eighteenth-century ballad, where a poor boatman asks the mother goddess, Annapurna: "Let my children have enough rice and milk for their meals" (Raychaudhuri, n.d., para.6). This metaphor of food as a boon of plenty suggests how fat has been culturally valorized as a marker of health and prosperity in India from precolonial times. Bharatchandra's male supplicant represents the patriarchal desire for fat children to ensure familial prosperity and continuity. Brahminical patriarchy casts Hindu women as "symbolic and literal providers (*Annapurna, Lakshmi*) rather than consumers of food" (Roy, 2005, p. 392). The patriarchal strategy of maternal glorification transfers the role of the benevolent goddess to mothers, who are culturally expected to be nurturers of appropriately fat children, especially sons; although the idealization of maternal self-sacrifice has meant that mothers—indeed, all women—usually under-eat and perform hunger through ritualized fasts and dietary restrictions.

The gendered perception of fat as health/wealth was buttressed by the colonial history and post-colonial socio-economic context of India. As a "developing" nation abetted by conditions of colonialism, a majority of the population of India has historically been poor and hungry. Dr. Anoop Misra, one of the co-authors of the 2013 childhood obesity study mentioned earlier, states that older generations, especially women, who had "known famine" often insist on "fussing over" the food intake of their children (and grandchildren), and even if "the child is overweight they consider them healthy rather than fat" (Nelson, 2013, para. 3–4). Misra's disapproving comment replicates the colonial stigmatization of fat bodies and fat status in non-white, "foreign" (non-western) cultures as primitive and uncivilized (Farrell, 2011, pp. 59–81). It also indicates the responsibilized association of women with food: both in its scarcity (famine) and in its excess (fatness). Indeed, gendered and colonial readings of fatness have become conflated following the devastating Bengal famine in 1943; caused by artificial food scarcity produced, in part, by the wartime policies of the colonial British government, the famine has been documented primarily through "an iconography of female suffering" (Roy, 2002, p. 393). My grandmothers, having witnessed the famine, always insisted that children (and guests) be fed until "the stomach is filled." They valued excess food intake—and the resultant, visible weight gain—as a talisman against deprivation. Misra repositions this historical-cultural response as obesity-causing overindulgence.

A recurrent trope in Indian religious iconography is the fat son being lovingly fed by the mother: for instance, Yashoda pampering the butter-stealing child-god Krishna, or goddess Parvati feeding her pot-bellied son, Ganesha. In these works the child embodies patrilineal prosperity, while the mother performs ideal maternal devotion. However, this direct correspondence of meanings—of the fat child as desirable, and of the overfeeding mother as good—is becoming increasing muddled as the traditional cultural valorization of fat childhood is epistemically challenged by the modern, urban, "western" norm of the "slim and fit" child. Iyer Mohanty writes,

> For a long time in India, fat has meant good. ... Being fat means you are rich enough to afford a lot of food and to avoid physical labor. Being fat means you're well-loved and cared for. ... Now we are in the midst of a historical change in connotation: Being fat no longer means that you are prosperous, but rather that you don't have the time, money or wherewithal to keep yourself in shape.
>
> (2011, paras. 4–6)

As childhood fatness is redefined as liability and poor health, the shift of meaning from "well-fed" to "overfed" effects a strategic shift from glorifying devotedly feeding mothers as ideal, loving, and dutiful to blaming such mothers as overindulgent, outmoded, and harmful.

Traditionally in India, the fat child is protected through prayers and linguistic taboos. Any direct mention of the child's "healthiness" or "fatness" is taboo because it may bring on *"buri nazar"* (evil eye). The persistence of such taboos explains why external interventions diagnosing childhood fatness are often rejected by older family members. Conversely, the new medical-media narrative projects benevolent practitioners of non-rational indigenous customs as superstitious, ignorant, disease-causing villains (meaning in the etymological sense bad and rustic or unsophisticated). A 2013 BBC documentary, *India's Supersize Kids*, narrates the story of Sagar Balani, who "became one of the youngest kids in the world to undergo weight loss surgery" at the age of seven (Wells, 2013, para. 2). At 14 stone (89 kg), the child—by then "almost unable to walk"—was "finally" put on a diet by doctors, but his mother would "still feed him on the sly" (Wells, 2013, paras. 2–3). Sagar's mother desisted only after "doctors explained that he was close to eating himself to death" (Wells, 2013, para. 3). The narrative positions Sagar as the victim, his mother as the backward culprit, and the medical expert as the savior. Echoing gendered and racialized colonial binaries of civilized/savage and discipline/excess that is central to the western worldview of progress, the (male) obesity expert implicitly contrasts his prescriptive knowledge (of western medicine) with the mother's lack of knowledge and control. The medical narrative—of mothers "fussing over" fat children and ignoring their obesity—diminishes indulgent mothers as obstructive and unfit as modern caregivers.

As in the west, in contemporary India, too, the narrative of childhood obesity as an "epidemic" of excess is constructed and circulated by a nexus of medical, media and corporate industries. Dr. Shashank Shah, the bariatric surgeon who operated on Sagar, uses the term "diabesity pandemic" (Wells, 2013, para. 8). The neologism pathologizes fatness by coupling it inextricably with diabetes. Significantly, mother-blaming and mother-shaming seems to increase during "epidemics," whether socially constructed "epidemics" like childhood obesity, or politically suppressed epidemics like the 1943 Bengal famine, which was "never officially designated as a famine" by the colonial government (Roy, 2002, p. 394). Roy references several creative works that depict famine-afflicted mothers prioritizing their own hunger over that of their children, and comments how famine became a "testing ground," with many mothers failing to meet cultural standards of "maternal self-denial" (Roy, 2002, p. 401). In contemporary discourses, mothers are likewise systemically essentialized as natural nurturers, and any inversion of the normative order of nurture evokes panicked projections of maternal failure.

As the perception of what constitutes an over/indulgent and a nurturing mother is altered due to contemporary fatphobia, other maternal categories like the working mother or the fat mother—which potentially destabilize the norm of intensive, sacrificing motherhood—also become targets of indictment. The 2013 report embeds mother-blame in a clinical framework by concluding that maternal obesity, ignorance, and working motherhood are causative factors of the rapid rise of urban childhood obesity. Based on a "cross-sectional observational study of 1800 children aged 9–18 years and their mothers," of whom 64.8% were either overweight or obese, the report "highlights the poor knowledge, faulty attitudes and practices of urban Asian Indian mothers and their children in a highly correlated manner" (Gulati et al., 2013, p. 279).

The report vilifies working mothers because they are "now feeding their babies and children commercial pre-packaged, ready-to-eat meals, rather than taking the time to prepare food from scratch as previous generations had" (Ghosh, 2013, para. 8). Urban, middle-class working mothers in India are often perceived as potentially disrupting the domestic sphere of the patriarchy-assigned wife-and-mother roles. The "figure of the new woman" (including the urban working mother) embodies "paradoxes of globalization" as it is both "iconic" of neoliberal India and also indicates an "unruly modernity that ha[s] to be controlled and tempered" to protect Hindu patriarchy and nation from western contamination (Oza, 2006, p. 35) Indian working mothers are doubly damned: the traditional narrative perceives them as a threat to patriarchal family structures, and the modern medical narrative stereotypes them as uncaring and under-devoted. The maternal derogation of the 2013 report has been reproduced and magnified through multiple media articles (Khan, 2013; Mail Today Reporter, 2013; Nelson, 2013). Only a few media articles interrogate the gendered politics of this report: "[t]here's not a word here about men who are not expected to take on the burden of feeding their children, nor the blame for what they are fed" (Chaudhry, 2013, para. 4). The medical-media matrix demonizes mothers while suppressing the gendered inequity of familial food work, underreporting the profit motive that drives the obesity panic-mongering, and marginalizing other causative factors.

Lakshmi Chaudhry's media piece (2013) points out how, along with working mothers and old-fashioned, overindulgent mothers, the "fat Indian mommy" is also the "perfect scapegoat for child obesity" in the 2013 medical report. Both fat discourses merge in the scapegoating of the fat mother: her visible fatness deviates from the traditional norm of the self-abnegating mother and also from the globalized norm of the disciplined body. As obedient, self-controlling neoliberal subjects, mothers are inundated with media-circulated triumphant stories of fatness controlled, as well as cautionary horror tales of uncontrolled fat: a carrot-and-stick disciplinary strategy that overdetermines their lifestyle "choices." The mediatized discourse counters the bad fat mother with the good neoliberal "yummy mummy" who has disciplined her own and her children's bodies into approved contours of slimness and health. Yummy mummy is a construct embodied by celebrity mothers, popularized in print and online media, and often aspired to by urban mothers; the latter tend to use and embody the term uncritically and approvingly. The shift in desirable dimensions of feminine/maternal beauty (like slimness and, to a lesser extent, fairness) indicates how cultural/aesthetic differences are gradually flattening out in post-globalized India, although this neo-colonization of feminine beauty (and sexuality) by westernized standards often coexists uneasily with traditional beauty norms and the cultural protectionism of Hindu patriarchy. Neoliberal, neo-colonial feminine beauty presented in Indian film, fashion and beauty industries (Runkle, 2004) frequently evokes conflicted, anxious responses in Hindu patriarchy (Oza, 2006, pp. 79–101).

Maternal bodies are policed not only as sites of neoliberal beauty and fitness, but also as indexes of caregiving ability. The *Times of India*, India's largest circulating English daily, published a participatory lifestyle series called "FAT BUSTER," where readers shared their "weight loss story that can inspire others" (TNN, 2017). In one such feature, mother Shuchi Sharma Bhatnagar recounts how she had "always been overweight and had learned to manage it with confidence" *till* her nine-year old son's doctor "warned" her about the pathological consequences of her son's rapid weight gain:

> As a mother, it was my job to ensure he took the steps he needed to. And the first step in motivating him was to set the right example. ... I decided to lose weight so that I can motivate him and become his role model.
>
> (TNN, 2017, paras. 4–5)

The aspirational narrative rewards the deviant fat mother after she "decides" to redeem herself and her child by obeying the expertized (Western) norms. By losing weight for her child, Bhatnagar also performs a maternal sacrifice that maps onto the traditional ideal of good motherhood. Mothers who refuse to follow these norms are stigmatized as failing at their "job" or setting the "wrong example." Unpacking Bhatnagar's story reveals how her initially confident size-acceptance is undermined and substituted by anxiety after the expert's intervention. Although this anxiety seeps through Bhatnagar's fat-to-fit transformation story, such media-manipulated narratives minimize and homogenize the lived struggles of mothers caught between two oppositional fat narratives that either collide or collude to implicate them. In the next section, I attempt to counter this homogenization and pluralize the discourse by documenting and analyzing how Indian mothers in my qualitative study engage with these overlapping narratives and the transitioning perception of childhood fat from aspirational to morbid.

Maternal Responses to Mother-Blame

One of the "normal-weight" working mothers I approached had initially agreed to participate, but eventually did not complete the interview. She writes: "I'm actually scared that [my son] will fall in the over obese category. ... I'm scared to fill the questionnaire as I feel as a mother I didn't inculcate the right eating habits when he was young" (K., reproduced with permission). In spite of giving her son "home-cooked food" and avoiding "junk food" or "eating out," this respondent is "scared" about her son's weight gain. Despite obediently performing good Indian motherhood by feeding her son home-cooked food (prescribed in both old and new discourses), K. internalizes the overt blaming of working mothers. K.'s guilt about not inculcating the "right eating habits when [her son] was young" indicates she has assimilated the assumption that working mothers do not give enough time or effort for the "right" nurture of their children and are, therefore, actively responsible for any lapses in their weight/health. Her panic and confusion are produced by her inability to control her son's obesity in spite of her efforts to become neither the traditional overindulgent mother nor the westernized, packaged-food-feeding working-mother. K. lives in a multigenerational or "joint" family where she often has to defer to the provisioning decisions of her mother-in-law, and such unavoidable negotiations aggravate her helplessness and guilt. K.'s lived experience contradicts the over-generalized claim of the new clinical discourse, exemplified by Gulati et al.'s report, that maternal diligence will ensure childhood fat control, yet her anxiety mimics the perceptions and biases of this discourse.

K.'s anxiety is shared by the other mothers I interviewed. They all agreed that in India, like in other cultures, mothers are held responsible for the child's body weight; most of them felt that this was, in their words, "unfair." However, this feeling of "unfairness" is directed neither at the fatphobia of the new discourse, nor at the gendering of care work endorsed by both old and new discourses. None of the mothers I interviewed challenged the medical-media framing of fat as a disease or a problem; most of them also accepted their assumed central role in domestic food provisioning as normal and natural. Sanghomitra, an "overweight" single working mother of a normal-weight daughter, says that "it is correct" that mothers should be held responsible for a child's weight, because the mother performs "the whole role of the family [in the] upbringing [of] a child." Among respondents, the desire to conform to the traditional norm of devoted motherhood coexisted with their desire to be perceived as modern mothers equipped with the knowledges of the new discourse. Most of them endorsed the fit childhood goal promoted by this new discourse. This twofold desire to be both rooted and advanced is symptomatic of the neoliberal construct of the new Indian woman who "can be modern and assertive while continuing to inhabit traditionally prescribed gender roles as mother, wife, and sister" (Oza, 2006, p. 33). The compulsion to embrace both traditional Indian values and westernized models of progress is embedded in India's hybridized Hindu patriarchal and colonial legacy, and, thus, the new Indian woman/mother figure represents—and is socialized to perform—both neo-colonialism and neo-patriarchy.

The constant negotiation between traditional and modern value systems is a messy and vexing task, especially in the context of the binarized fat discourses jostling in India. The feeling of "unfairness" expressed by the respondents can be unpacked as being generated by their specifically Indian location: of being *caught between* the two colliding-yet-colluding discourses and two contrary sets of expectations. The prevalence of a culture of deference to elders and experts as holders of wisdom/knowledge makes it difficult—and socially unacceptable—for mothers to openly challenge either pediatricians or the older relations in close-knit and often multi-generational families. Deepanjali, an "overweight" working mother with an "overweight" son, narrates this double bind:

> Mother-in-law is indulgent and sees nothing wrong in being overweight. Her response is it is all puppy fat which will get shed if he runs around the block a couple of times. Mother is a doctor and is very strict about obesity. She is more particular than me about her grandson's weight issues.

She articulates the impossibility of pleasing both: whereas her traditionally oriented mother-in-law insists on unchecked indulgence, her medically trained mother wants her to monitor her son's diet and exercise. Jhumpa, a "normal-weight" working mother with a "normal-weight" teenage son, has to navigate a similar, mutually conflicting taxonomic impasse: "Although my child was always normal as per the doctor's parameters yet my in-laws always found him to be below normal and [too] thin." Although none of the mothers endorse the traditional valorization of fat—projecting this older discourse as old-fashioned and unscientific—they still feel pressurized by familial expectations to adhere to it in their nurturing practices.

Significantly, it is usually older women, often within the family, who blame and shame mothers for their children's over/underweight, indicating how patriarchy coopts older women to socialize younger women into their assigned roles as nurturers. To maintain patrilineal prosperity, the nurturing of children is heavily skewed in favour of sons. Sandhya, stay-at-home mother of a "normal-weight" son and an "obese" daughter, recounts:

> If the child is not within the range they consider normal, people feel free to give advice and even check up on whether you are following the advice religiously too. *My MIL [mother-in-law] tells me how I should give more and more nutritious food and in larger quantities to my son so that he gains weight and at the same time forbid my daughter from eating between meals or even eating too much during meals so that she doesn't put on any more weight.* Though I did not express my horror to her face, I never paid attention to such advice (emphasis added).

Sandhya's narrative reveals how Indian mothers struggle to navigate the tangled discourses of fat-as-good and fat-as-bad. The intergenerational negotiation becomes messier because it is often, as here, underpinned by the patriarchal custom of son-preference. Sandhya remembers the trauma and frustration she experienced at the "advice and accusations" of being a failed mother: "I used to feel pressurized by such comments and used to get totally frustrated when kids don't eat properly despite my efforts to present a lot of variety at every meal." Sandhya's experience exposes both the collision and collusion of the two fat narratives. While the figure of the normal-weight son is approved of by the new medical-media narrative but disapproved by the traditional narrative as underweight and underfed (indicating maternal failure), this collision is ironically absent in the reception of the overweight daughter. Both narratives collude to stigmatize the figure of the fat girl: the new discourse pathologizes *all* obesity, while the old discourse heroizes self-abnegation in women, which is embodied through thinness and inculcated through ritualized fasting from girlhood.

The deviancy embodied by the fat girl becomes even more threatening in the figure of the fat mother, especially if she has a thin child. Susmita, an "obese" working mother with a daughter who her neighbors and family "always view as underweight" writes:

> My neighbors and even my church Aunty would say … Your daughter is so slim … Doesn't she eat and drink milk every day, some ask her …

Mummy sab … kha leti hain na? [Does your mummy eat up all your food?] Very awkward situation as I know she is choosy about her food and I munch on everything eatable. I often get pressurized and lost in such situations. Moreover, they will say that *as I go to office she is not taken care properly* (emphases added).

Here, the consuming fat mother of a thin child is imaged as a monster preying on her child's food (figuratively devouring her offspring). By embodying the intersecting, risky categories of fat *and* working motherhood, Susmita becomes doubly deviant: she is criticized as both devouring and negligent. Her concern about her daughter's pickiness about food (constructed in opposition to her self-acknowledged gluttony) indicates her struggle against being cast as the self-indulgent mother who cannot discipline either herself or her daughter. She admits her maternal failure: "I started health drinks which she never liked, neither would she regularly drink milk." The intersecting of all the three risky maternal categories of fat/working/undisciplined motherhood made Susmita's responses the most fraught and angry. Susmita's experience of feeling "pressurized and lost" also stems from the contradictory perceptions of the two discourses: while her pediatrician confirms that her daughter has "perfect weight but no one believes." Although Susmita is equipped with the new medical knowledge about her daughter's "perfect weight," the persistence of the old fat-valorizing discourse shapes her inability to wholly believe or be reassured by the expert: "Sometimes yes, I felt guilty that all children look healthy and maybe I am doing something wrong with her diet, so she is not getting fat. Maybe I am a bad mother."

It is significant that Susmita's guilt about her "bad motherhood" stems from her concern about her daughter's apparent underweight. In western, fatphobic cultures, mothers are incriminated for their own or their children's obesity. In India, the simultaneity of fatphobic and fat-philic discourses implicate mothers for either or both overweight and underweight children. Natalie Boero, writing about the "distinct trend of 'mother blame' in common sense and professional understandings of … [the] 'epidemic of childhood obesity,'" remarks how "the weight of one's children has increasingly become a litmus test of good mothering (2009, p. 113). For Indian mothers, this test is literally double-edged: the weight of their children (and, consequently, their own maternal ability) is perceived as dissatisfactory by either or both old and new discourses. May Friedman, writing about "mothers of fat children" in English-speaking countries, notes how "the requirement for intensive mothering is taken to a different degree as they are assumed to have control over their children's size and are hyper-scrutinized for 'compliance' with healthy choices" (2015, p. 20). In India, this scrutiny is extended to mothers of "normal-weight" children also, as with Sandhya and Jhumpa. It is especially intensified if they deviate from the ideal of the hearth-bound, self-denying mother, as Susmita visibly does.

Although many of the mothers seem to internalize the guilt produced by discriminatory accusations of bad mothering, their maternal practice manifests a deep concern about the fat discrimination experienced by their children. Deepanjali discloses how her "overweight" son "is teased by his friends for being fat, a giant, sometimes called a monster." Sandhya's daughter, too, has been traumatized by fat shaming: "A family member once asked my 12-year-old daughter how many months pregnant she was. This was extremely painful for the little child." Most medical reports and fat-to-fit guidebooks mention low self-esteem as a psychological effect of obesity. However, they overlook the links between self-esteem and body-shaming, pushing through a disciplinary agenda of correctional weight management. Instead, it is the mothers I interviewed who engaged in more mindful and versatile engagement with fat discrimination. Sandhya, for instance, reassures her daughter by emphasizing size acceptance, and in the Indian context, both underweight and overweight are discriminated size categories. Critiquing the BMI equation of weight and health, she says,

> The weight should not be a concern as there are different types of body shapes and the weight will differ accordingly—what is healthy for someone else might not be healthy for me. The form that our body takes is the way it is supposed to be. Our job is to just keep it healthy.

Even Susmita, whose experiences with fat are so conflicted, asserts: "I remember my daughter asking my mom to give me less roti or I will get fat when she was small. Now, of course, she says she likes a fat mom." These instances of mother-daughter bonding over size acceptance may be read as resistant and enabling, especially in the Indian contexts of son-preference and body-shaming.

While contradictory fat discourses compress and vex mothers, their coexistence also offers a range of fat-valuations that Indian mothers use as a defensive or coping strategy. They sometimes play off opposing perceptions of fat-is-bad and fat-is-good against each other to shield themselves and their children from invasive and negative criticism. Some respondents discussed how they often defend their child's underweight, when accused by older relations, by referencing the medical opinion that slim is fit; conversely, they defend their child's overweight, when accused by medical experts, by shifting the onus to grandparental indulgence. Another recurrent maternal coping strategy that emerged from these interviews is flexibility. Some of the mothers accept the social regulation of childhood fatness and pragmatically adapt it to their own care practices. They endorse fat-consciousness in their children hoping that this would encourage self-regulation through diet and exercise. Even Deepanjali, whose "overweight" son encountered body-shaming, approves of his recent weight-consciousness: "He is now conscious of what he eats and enjoys eating salads. He does not ask for aerated beverages. He exercises whenever he feels he has overeaten." For Indian mothers, public scrutiny of childhood fatness often becomes a usable tool in child weight management.

Although such fat-consciousness appears to conform to, rather than resist, the negative fat narrative and although the mothers interviewed are in many ways still colonized by the expectations of both fat discourses, they demonstrate resistance in indirect ways. Most refuse to submit to the medical-media circulated obesity panic. Here, too, mothers deploy the co-existence of the older narrative to defuse the modern obesity panic and to refuse the homogenized prescriptions for managing childhood fatness. Sumana, a "normal-weight" mother of a "sometimes overweight" daughter, for instance, advocates that "balancing is necessary" and counters the contemporary obesity panic with the "earlier days" when "there was no concept of overweight." Selecting advice from both discourses that she considers "good for [her] child's well-being," Sumana is unperturbed by her daughter's weight gain: "I was not worried because she was always a little overweight and with exercise that can be controlled." Mimi, a working mother who categorizes both herself and her daughter as "slightly overweight," summed up her complaint/resistant position with a similar self-assurance:

> I take responsibility to a point since I am taking care of my kids and family and the meals, etc., are also generally decided upon by us (my husband and me). However, it has not yet stressed me out to the point where I feel panicky. I try to work around the busy schedules to give healthy options.

Sharon Dalton discusses three parenting approaches to childhood obesity: "authoritarian (overcontrolling)," "permissive (no limit setting)," and "authoritative parenting, which uses role modeling, negotiation, and reasoning to support healthy food behaviors" (2004, p. 91). In the context of the medical/media vilification of the over/indulgent mother, and considering that, in India, it is fathers who are traditionally expected to be disciplinarians, most of the respondents positioned themselves as "authoritative" mothers: Mimi described this as "work-(ing) jointly with the child to a manageable goal."

To conclude, I would emphasize how Sumana's and Mimi's enabling self-assurance differs from K.'s disabling panic or Susmita's guilt and anger, because the surveyed mothers are situated differently within dualistic fat discourses. They experience different degrees of blaming and shaming, and, thus, respond in unique as well as shared ways. Each of them mobilizes the prescribed definitions and regulations of childhood obesity while negotiating the conflicting maternal expectations in individual ways. Along with individual differences, "perceptions about fat" and "fat stigma" are "relative, dependent on the historical and cultural context" (Farrell, 2011, p. 7). Scholars have noted how "the lack of a multicultural perspective" in Fat Studies "reiterates tired models of western cultural dominance" (Cooper, 2009, p. 330). In order to interrupt this dominance, there is a need to study fat in other cultural contexts and also through individual experiences. While the binarized, mother-blaming fat discourses in India partly replicate western biases, the distinctive persistence of an alternative fat-is-good, mother-implicating narrative and the complicated, heterogenous maternal responses that arise from this juxtaposition open up spaces for more intercultural conversations on, and intersectional understanding of, childhood fat.

References

Boero, N. (2009). Fat kids, working moms, and the 'epidemic of obesity': Race, class and mother blame. In E. Rothblum & S. Solovay (eds.), *The fat studies reader* (pp. 113–119). New York: New York University Press.

Chaudhry, L. (2013, June 3). Fat Indian mommy: Perfect scapegoat for childhood obesity. *Firstpost*. Retrieved from http://www.firstpost.com/living/the-fat-indian-mommy-the-perfect-scapegoat-for-child-obesity-827453.html

Cooper, C. (2009). Maybe it should be called fat American studies. In E. Rothblum & S. Solovay (eds.), *The fat studies reader* (pp. 327–333). New York: New York University Press.

Dalton, S. (2004). *Our overweight children: What parents, schools and communities can do to control the fatness epidemic.* Berkeley: University of California Press.

Farrell, A.E. (2011). *Fat shame: Stigma and the fat body in American culture.* New York: New York University Press.

Friedman, M. (2015). Mother blame, fat shame, and moral panic: 'Obesity' and child welfare. *Fat Studies: An Interdisciplinary Journal of Body Weight and Society, 4*(1), 14–27.

Ghosh, P. (2013, 29 May). Fat of the land: In India, obesity affects the affluent, not the poor. *IBN Times*. Retrieved from www.ibtimes.com/fat-land-india-obesity-affects-affluent-not-poor-1282445

Gulati, S., Misra, A., Colles, S.L., Kondal, D., Gupta, N., Goel, K., Bansal, S., Mishra, M., Madkaikar, V., Bhardwaj, S. (2013, May). Dietary intake and familial correlates of overweight/obesity: A four-cities study in India. *Annals of Nutrition and Metabolism, 62*(4), 279–290. doi: 10.1159/000346554

Iyer Mohanty, R. (2011, September 14). The rise and fall of fat in India. *New York Times*. Retrieved from www.nytimes.com/2011/09/15/opinion/15iht-edmohanty15.html

Khan, A. (2013, June 8). Obese kids, blame it on overweight moms. *DNA*. Retrieved from www.dnaindia.com/pune/report-obese-kids-blame-it-on-overweight-moms-1845515

Mail Today Reporter. (2013, May 26). Parents to blame for obese children. *Daily Mail*. Retrieved from www.dailymail.co.uk/indiahome/indianews/article-2331253/Parents-blame-childhood-obesity-India-study-finds.html

Nelson, D. (2013, May 27). Indian mothers blamed for spreading child obesity. *The Telegraph*. Retrieved from www.telegraph.co.uk/news/worldnews/asia/india/10082494/Indian-mothers-blamed-for-spreading-child-obesity.html

Oza, R. (2006). *The making of neoliberal India: Nationalism, gender and the paradoxes of globalization.* New York: Routledge.

Raychaudhuri, T. (n.d.). Mother of the universe—Motherland-2. *The rite stuff 1.4.* Retrieved from www.littlemag.com/rite/trc2.html

Roy, P. (2005). Women, hunger, and famine: Bengal, 1350/1943. In B. Ray (ed.), *Women of India: Colonial and post-colonial periods* (pp. 392–423). New Delhi: Centre for Studies in Civilizations.

Runkle, S. (2004). Making "Miss India": Constructing gender, power and the nation. *South Asian Popular Culture, 2*(2), 145–159. https://doi.org/10.1080/1474668042000275725

TNN. (2017, May 8). FAT BUSTER: I lost weight to set the right example for my son. *Times of India*. Retrieved from https://timesofindia.indiatimes.com/life-style /health-fitness/weight-loss/fat-buster-i-lost-weight-to-set-the-right-example-for-my -son/articleshow/58572255.cms

Wells, A. (2013). India's supersize kids. *BBC Two: This World*. 2013. Retrieved from www.bbc.co.uk/programmes/articles/2BcMW01VVrf3TZTnT7Jhl2b/indias-supersize-kids

5 Tracing Fatness Through the Eating Disorder Assemblage

Andrea LaMarre, Carla Rice, and Jen Rinaldi

In this paper, we present an analysis of interview data collected for a collaborative research project titled *Through Thick and Thin*. In this project we explored the embodied experiences of folk who make up assemblages of queer sexualities, gender expressions, and other privileged or minoritized identifications (race, Indigeneity, class, and age, to name a few) in confrontation with weight stigma, expectations around eating and exercise, and pathologization. We took an intentionally intersectional approach to data collection as we aimed hear from participants with diverse experiences.

We found that most participants in our study endorsed a history of disordered eating, yet few had been diagnosed with clinical eating disorders. Many identified having fraught histories with eating and exercise, both personally and in relation to public shaming and stigma. Many shared they had complex relationships with their own body shape and size that they held in tension, pride, and shame. Rather than seeing these findings as evidence for "sub-threshold" eating disorders, we consider how systemic discrimination leads to the de-legitimization of pluralist experiences and the perpetuation of the "single story" of eating disorders. Participants contextualized their different and often difficult relationships with food against histories of racism, ableism, sexism, and more. We explore the intersections between oppressions and eating distress, foregrounding participants' descriptions of embodying a thicker narrative around eating disorders than what we have been led to believe eating disorders "are."

> When you're fat, no one will pay attention to disordered eating or they will look the other way or they will look right through you. You get to hide in plain sight ... I didn't think anyone in my life would even care about the truth so long as I was dealing with my body by any means necessary. We have to worry about the emaciated girls being fed through a tube in the nose, not girls like me.
>
> (Gay, 2017, pp. 196–199)

An intersectional analysis of eating distress, one that brings fat into focus, carries the potential to push back against monolithic, static, medicalized framing devices. If we rely on standard diagnostic criteria for phenomena currently known as eating disorders, fat becomes something to be feared, something to resist, and something to prevent. Likewise, if we do not engage with eating practices as we theorize fat, we miss critical connections between fat, eating, and the reading of bodies. Here, we aim to deepen our analysis of fat in relation to eating disorders/distressed eating, by exploring the complex ways that fat moves through the eating disorder assemblage. Specifically, we consider the multiple and often conflicting sets of medical expectations placed on those experiencing distress, and the ways that fat materializes around these expectations to preclude or open the possibility of diagnosis and treatment. We also explore the modes of regulation that operate in cultural contexts to calibrate the kinds of options available to people who are fat and experiencing distress around food—the way that fat emerges in food and flesh as pivotal to the eating disorder assemblage. Providing examples from interviews with participants who were a part of a study on LGBTQ+ women's embodiment, we demonstrate the vitality of fat and the innovative ways that people carve out alternative framings of their distress and "recoveries" when they do not engage with dominant diagnostic and treatment systems (Rice, 2014). We explore how fat materializes through interactions and intersections—how it is relational, dynamic, and assembled or congealed in socio-historical contexts.

Moving beyond characterizations of experiences of "eating disorders" based on pre-defined clinical norms, we assert that exploring a wider range of embodiments and behaviours around food—and the meanings that these hold beyond clinical labels—opens space to redefine relationships with food and body (LaMarre & Rice, 2016; Rinaldi, LaMarre & Rice, 2016a; Rice, 2014). Recognizing the social power of diagnostic labels, and their possible "tyranny" (Rosenberg, 2002), we chose not to focus on experiences of "eating disorders" that have been so labelled. This enabled rich accounts that reconfigure expertise on distress and empowerment at the intersections of food and body. Being fluid in our conceptualizations beyond diagnostic labels also allowed us to move beyond un-reflexive associations often made between body size and eating behaviours, such as the assumption that restrictive eating always yields emaciation, that binge behaviours necessarily lead to corpulence, or that fatness and eating distress are inevitably incommensurate. We draw on interview data analyzed for a collaborative research project titled *Through Thick and Thin*.[1] In this project, we explored embodied experiences of folks who narrated assemblages, or collections of knowledges, affects, meanings, events, practices, bodies, etc. configured in dynamic and transitory ways and crystallizing in moments (Deleuze & Guattari, 1988). These assemblages were comprised of queer sexualities, gender expressions, and other privileged or minoritized identities (race, Indigeneity, class, age, etc.) as they intersect with what is expected in regard to eating, exercise, and assigned labels (Lind et al., 2018; Rinaldi, Rice, LaMarre, McPhail & Harrison, 2017; Rinaldi et al., 2016b).

We took an intentionally intersectional approach to data collection as we aimed hear from participants with diverse experiences (see Rice et al., forthcoming, for elaboration). Here we use the term "intersectionality" in ways that build on the paradigm-shifting work of Kimberlé Crenshaw (1989), Patricia Hill Collins (2002), and Black womanist thinkers (Walker, 1983) more generally. We recognize the concept's wildfire movement and widespread adoption across diverse disciplines, temporalities, and geographies, and the heated debate it has sparked (Rice, Harrison & Friedman, 2019; Rice et al., forthcoming; Changfoot, & Rice, accepted; Hobbs & Rice, 2018). Structuralist scholars tend to use intersectionality to predict and explain the relatively stable ways that social systems reproduce social identities and axes of inequities, an application that anti-essentialist scholars have critiqued for failing to account for the dynamism of human subjects and sociality (Garry, 2011; Lugones, 1994; Puar, 2007, 2012). For critics, identifications may unpredictably intermix and coalesce in subjects' embodied experiences, and new subjectivities emerge in shifting social relations. In response to this constraint, we turned to intersectionality scholars who bring the construct into conversation with other critical frameworks, particularly feminist Deleuzian assemblage theory (Puar 2007, 2012; Rice 2018). We have found that our interviewees' accounts resonate with this pairing insofar as assemblage theory generates theoretic space to analyze participants' contradictory, changeable, and ambiguous experiences of embedded and embodied difference.

We, the authors, each write from a particular relational history with distressed eating that we enunciate as part of our feminist intersectional ethic and efforts to presence our research assemblage—how our positionalities, philosophical commitments, and life experiences inflect our readings of participants' accounts. I (LaMarre) am a thin, white, young, educated, middle-class, heterosexual, cisgender woman of Scottish/British settler ancestry. I struggled with an eating disorder in my late teens; while in many ways my experience and identities fit within the "told" story of eating distress, I faced barriers to treatment including time and physician lack of awareness. Since completing treatment, I have problematized what it means to be in recovery in a world that ascribes significant weight to eating and bodily practices (and body sizes). I (Rice) am a queer, white, middle-class woman with working-class roots who has been involved in fat activist/body positivity movements for over 30 years. Having struggled with eating distress and having worked (and been treated) in and around psychiatry-controlled treatment regimes, I have witnessed and experienced the negative effects of diagnostic categories, and I have yearned for more difference-affirming spaces in which to tell messy, contradictory (yet faithful) stories of problem bodies and eating behaviours that still hold possibilities for resistance. For these reasons, and because I recognize the need for specific language to make sense of experiences of food/fat distress, I align with critical psychology/mental health/mad studies perspectives that reject psychiatric frameworks in favour of generating "experience-near" discourses that consider the ethics of language and knowledge systems for those affected. Finally, I (Rinaldi) am a cis-gender, white woman of French settler and Italian immigrant origins invested in articulating and enacting the responsibilities of allyship. I recognize my positionality informs my apprehension of subjectivity as relational, extending beyond skin and into community; and fluid, running through privilege and disadvantage. I am especially cognizant of how power throbs and thrums contingent on time and politics of passing. In particular, I am of a family that has oscillated between extreme states of wealth and poverty; I am queer, but am also in a longstanding heteronormative partnership; I have thin privilege and no overtly visible disability, but I also have a complex relationship with food and weight, madness and recovery.

Methods

We focus on interviews conducted with 19 participants who identified as having a history of distressed eating, with most reporting that they had never received a diagnosis. Among those who identified as having had an eating disorder, a majority (12) also described themselves in relation to fatness, using various words, including: "fat," "big girl," "thick," "chubby," "superfat," "considered big in Asia," "depending," "unsure, curvy, bigger than typical," and "fat but sometimes pass". The use of these terms starts a process of unravelling the relationship between "external" and "internal" worlds, bodies, and affects. Exploring their stories in relation to the landscape of eating disorder/distressed eating literatures, both mainstream and feminist, offers insight into how the very categories used to construct diagnoses and research studies render some people invisible in clinical and social contexts—or as Gay (2017) puts it, "hidden in plain sight." In our effort to enrich fat and disordered/distressed eating research, we articulate experiences often made unintelligible by an assemblage of factors ranging from diagnostic labelling and the power structures imbued with social dictates about eating, body size, and discipline. We relied on participants' words to determine our usage of "disordered" or "distressed" eating. Readers may agree or disagree with these framings; this openness itself speaks to the dynamic and contextual read of eating and bodies we invite in this chapter.

Without a diagnosis, people's experiences may be de-legitimized in the clinical and public eye; and yet, diagnosis itself carries stigma (Rosenberg, 2002). On the other side, significant barriers exist to receiving a diagnostic label, including racist, heterosexist, ableist, sizeist, and other assumptions that inform clinical perceptions of whose experiences might be so-labelled (Becker, Hadley Arrindell, Perloe, Fay & Striegel-Moore, 2010). Further, attracting a label may invite bodily surveillance and treatment modes that are incongruous with folks' orientations to the world, and to their health. Disease and disorder categories carry with them imperatives of cure, as well as specific "objective" treatment practices that may ignore individual needs and desires; "in providing seemingly value-free frameworks for thinking about the normal and the deviant" (Rosenberg, 2002, p. 246), such categories offer incomplete and often unsatisfying "solutions" to distress. This social life of diagnosis calls into question the un-reflexive adoption of diagnoses as preconditions for inclusion in research or accounting for lived experience. Here, we offer an alternative framing, foregrounding participants' experiences of distress in relation to systemic discrimination alongside histories of racism, ableism, sizeism, heterosexism, and more. We argue that in order to thicken eating disorder/distressed eating research, we must attend to embodied experiences as assemblages across time. We suggest that fat—both the substance itself and the affective experience of eating, feeling, or being fat—emerges as a significant force in the eating disorder assemblage.

Participant interviews were transcribed verbatim and coded for meaningful groupings across the data. We analyzed this data using a thematic analysis (Braun & Clarke, 2006) driven by new materialist, feminist theories. We focus here on themes specifically related to being at odds with bodies, experiences that might elsewhere be coded as "eating disordered." In our analysis, we attend not only to themes on a symbolic level, but also to the "semiotic echoes" of codes, or the ways that they carry "rhythms, forces, and corporeal residues necessary for representation" (Grosz, 1989, p. 43, cited in Chadwick, 2017, p. 59).

Analyses

Medically Prescribed Shaming

Participants described medical mistreatment of and disregard for their bodies. These encounters affected participants' relationships to their bodies, their fat, and their eating and exercise practices. Fat shaming in medical contexts helps to explain how most people in our study could identify as having a history of disordered eating or experiences of eating distress despite not having been diagnosed. Namely, medical professionals may be so focused on weight and oriented to prescribing weight loss strategies that they do not recognize markers of diagnosis or distress in their patients (see also Lebow, Sim & Kransdorf, 2015). They may not recognize that advice flowing from dominant framings of fat (e.g., as problem, as itself pathological, as abject) may push people to adopt practices that feel deeply disordered to those experiencing them—yet that are framed as "healthy" for those whose bodies are read as fat. Harper, a pansexual cis femme woman of colour who identified as "plus size" and as having an undiagnosed eating disorder, noted:

> I think the first time I noticed my body must have been when I was very young and I went to the pediatrician and the pediatrician told me I was obese for my age. Until that moment, I never looked at my body any differently. I never saw my body as anything that was bad. I never had any issues with my body. Until someone told me it was wrong.

Harper's reflection foregrounds the role medical practitioners assume: 1) as gatekeepers of eating disorder diagnosis and inducers of distress about fatness, insofar as her pediatrician catalyzed the shifts in her relationship with her body; and 2) as arbiters of how fat, both in terms of food and flesh, is interpreted and managed. Her pediatrician's words affected her body image by moving her to attach to her body attributes like "bad" and "wrong"—associations that are flagged in the clinical field as pathological and problematic. In the doctor's office, fat presents itself as intermediary between person and physician; here, fat makes actions that privilege the mind-over-matter "management" of fat appear necessary or justified.

Leigh, a racialized fat woman who frequents medical spaces to manage a degenerative physical disability, described a number of traumatic encounters with doctors and nurses who provided counsel on weight loss that was unsolicited, unrelated to her medical needs, and articulated disrespectfully. She used "eating disorder" language (e.g. restricting, unsafe exercising) when describing health provider impact, which was magnified for her given her physical disability:

> I start restricting—especially after [medical appointments] … I don't really know where that comes from per se, because I've never really had particularly disordered eating habits, but there's just something about a medical practitioner telling me that I need to lose weight, and especially being in a position where—I also after last time came home and started angry exercising, tendons be damned! I was doing weight bearing cardio, and I just get totally destructive! I stop eating, and if I am physically able to, I will start unsafe exercising, and I don't—I've gotten it more under control. Like, the last time it happened, I didn't really do that, but it's really hard for me not to do that.

Here, again, doctors' responses to fat set in motion practices that urge embodied reactions "against" fat, actions that encourage disconnection from the body's needs and requests. The response to fat works its way in and through corporeality, driving embodied practices that enact violence on fat. Fat is rendered an entity separate from the body—something to be managed or worked on, rather than an integral aspect of the embodied self.

Similarly, Vaska, a white femme woman who identifies as "fat" in size-affirming contexts and "plus sized" in conventional spaces, wondered whether she had a binge-related eating disorder after a medical practitioner made presumptuous statements about her eating:

> She pushed back her clipboard and started launching into this speech about how I shouldn't be eating burgers and fries and fettuccini alfredo, and I said, "I don't," and she said, "You must, look at you." And I was kind of frozen. I didn't know what to do, what to say. And I went home and I remember reeling from that. And I remember thinking how

does one get to be this size without binging on burgers and fries and fet-tuccini alfredo. Maybe I do it and I don't know that I do it. So maybe I've got some subconscious eating disorder that I don't know about. And maybe—all of my intuition around what to eat is wrong? So for weeks, I was terrified of eating ... And I realized just how far this alienation from your own body can escalate when we've got these doctors as intermediaries between us and our bodies?

Here we encounter the doctor's presumptions about the links between corporeal outcomes (e.g. fatness) and consumption of fat. The doctor's words come to supplant Vaska's self-knowledge as a legitimate form of expertise, through the privileging of "expert advice." The doctor becomes intermediary between person and body, prescribing minded advice for embodied experience.

The Omnipresence of Eating Discord

Participants' accounts challenged how eating habits are normalized and pathologized. Specifically, they push us to reexamine how body, eating choices, and relationships to "health" may not be easily sorted into "normal" or "disordered." Bodies tend to be a starting point for guidelines on health—and how to be healthy—such that dictates directed toward fat bodies, around food management with the object of weight loss, resemble the very behaviours that are diagnosed as eating disorders in thin people (Burgard, 2017). Participants articulated their experiences with food in rela-tionship to or against clinical conceptualizations of eating disorders/distress, which tend to attach only to those who are culturally intelligible as having eating disorders—thin, young, white, middle class, able-bodied, cis-gender women, with uniform narratives of distress as pathological disruption (LaMarre & Rice, 2016; Rabinow & Rose, 2006; Rinaldi et al., 2016a; Rinaldi et al., 2016b; Rice, 2014).

Although most participants expressed feeling concern that their eating was disordered, many did not bring this to the attention of loved ones or medical professionals. Their cognizance of what an eating disorder "is" informed their reactions to and interpretations of their own behaviours. Ella, a Chinese-Canadian participant, described her body size as being interpreted differently according to context; in white Western contexts, her body was considered "normative," whereas in Asian cultural contexts, she was thought to be "big." This contextual reading of fat makes clear its relational and dynamic quality. These fluctuating interpretations informed Ella's bodily understand-ings and experiences. As she described:

[I]n my mind, I have a certain image of what an eating disorder looks like, and I think having depression—my understanding of an eating dis-order is that it adversely impacts the quality of your life, and for me, I've never been hospitalized for eating or not eating. It has caused me anxiety, but a lot of things caused me anxiety. So it's—it's kind of part of the landscape of anxiety that my life kind of exists in.

Ella's understanding of what an eating disorder "is" calls out a framing where eating disorders exemplify distress around food that consumes day-to-day tasks of living and identity formation and calls for hospitalization or intensive attention and treatment.

Other participants described awareness of the ways that their eating deviated from the norm, but again hesitated to label their experiences. Cas demonstrated a commitment to ambivalence in their identification as gender-queer, gender fluid, and both butch and femme. They also expressed ambivalence when asked whether they considered themselves fat, stating instead they were "unsure," "bigger than typical," and "muscular." Cas moved through liminal representation especially when explaining their relationship to diagnosis:

I knew what I was doing wasn't normal, but I—it's a tricky question, because at some points, it was almost like a goal. Like … there was some points where mental health and being a fuck up was kind of my identity, so it was kind of an achievement, like, if I can't be perfect or be viewed as worthwhile, then fuck it, my identity is going to be the opposite. So in some way, I knew that I had an eating disorder, or disordered eating or whatever, but I didn't realize how deep it went. But I think that moment clarity was an interaction with my friend—we were eating, and I had the takeout container, and my friend was like, "What is going on with you?" and I was like, "I don't even know". So yeah, yes and no, I knew, but yeah.

For Cas, knowing that their eating "wasn't normal" did not immediately compel them to define what it was. Instead, they developed clarity around having "an eating disorder" in interaction (with a friend, with the interviewer), which they qualify as "disordered eating or whatever," thus alternately focusing and softening the clinical lens on their behaviour. While some participants avoided labelling their relationships with food as "disordered" or approaching medical professionals because they did not feel that their experiences "qualified," others feared that their eating would be called out as disordered despite not feeling this was so.

Cultural Abjection

Participants' explorations of food in relationship with their cultural and socio-economic contexts provides us with another site of entry into a critique of the normal-pathological divide (see also LaMarre, Rice & Bear, 2015; LaMarre & Rice, 2016). This entry-point opens envisionings of eating disordered/distressed experiences as continuous assemblages with other aspects of people's lives and allows for a deeper understanding of experiences of bodies in society, some of which induce stress. Melissa described her experiences of growing up white, working poor, and with immigrant parents. While her self-identification of her body size ranged from average to voluptuous, Melissa interpreted her size and eating practices against the backdrop of food being framed in relation to lack and wanting. These experiences affected access to organic foods and coloured her relationship with food and its purposes. For her family, food was about survival:

> [C]lass has definitely impacted. I think that growing up working poor—that also impacts the relationship you'll have with food and the access you'll also be able to have, um. I think that when both of your parents are immigrants and they're both working minimum jobs, it's really hard to get organic things on the table. The survival is to pay rent and make sure you feed everybody in the family. And us being 4 kids—I think that was a lot to—for them to survive, so you eat a lot of the carbs or the potatoes or whatever can stretch a meal. So I think that definitely has an impact on how we relate to food.

Relationships with food were also informed by culture and spirituality, as Raine, a Black participant who did not identify as fat and understood herself to have an "undiagnosed eating disorder," described. In her family, eating animal flesh carries that animal's soul into the human's body. In a mass-producing society, the fear is that the torture of the animal will be retained upon its consumption. In her own words:

> I eat less animal products because I worry spiritually about what that means—having the flesh of another living being in my body. I believe that animals have souls, and I also worry about the way they're being murdered. Because in Jamaica, you have a goat, and the goat lives with you, the goat hangs out with you, you name the goat, and then at some point, the goat is slaughtered. And probably there's a lot of traditions from your ancestors, too—the animals are respected. They're food and stuff, but they're nice, and you talk to them. That's not the meat we're getting. We're getting tortured meat. And I worry about the emotion of an animal when its adrenaline is being pushed through its body as its being murdered, and I'm consuming that meat. I worry about that. And maybe there's nothing on physical level. I worry about that on an energy level, and so by virtue of taking care of my soul, I now eat less meat products, which I guess is going to mean I lose weight. I drink more water because I really want to cultivate what's happening with my soul.

The choice to eat less meat, then, is informed not by a fear of animal flesh per se, but rather by the emotions and energies that the food carries. Given that eating disorder treatment—and food cultures in general—are imbued with white Western rationality, such an explanation might be treated as a post hoc "excuse" for restrictive behaviours. Yet, delving into the compassion with which Raine describes sources of food, we might open to a new kind of food-body relationship that has nothing to do with the corporeal outcome of eating that food, but rather the energetic outcome of such.

Conclusion

Fat—in food and as flesh—floats along the borders of interactions about and around eating disorders; often unnamed, it carries material implications for the relationships people have with food and in their bodies and with health-care providers. Implicating fat within the eating disorder/distressed eating research assemblage and in relation to people's other spaces of belonging brings into relief the need to more meaningfully engage with fat embodiment in relation to practices around food. Fat, in relation to other contextual factors, including the spaces of belonging of healthcare providers and those seeking care, often tacitly impacts the way that lines are drawn between "normal" and "pathological" behaviours—or, at least, what kind of pathology might be inscribed on bodies (LaMarre & Rice, 2016; Rinaldi et al., 2016a). Participants' intentionality around food, and their interpretations of their behaviours as more or less disordered, also invites insight into collective awareness of the multi-layered food and bodily contexts in which people live. They were often acutely aware of discourses around eating disorders/disordered eating—and who is "legitimately" disordered—which belies the logic in some texts that presumes clinical expertise over disordered eating with limited insight from those experiencing eating distresses. This "legitimacy" is informed not only by others' interpretation of body size, but also of their racial, classed, and other identifications in a white Western context.

Thickening research around food and body beyond "eating disorder" research entails moving beyond, for instance, a simplistic perspective on anosognosia—the idea that people with eating distress lack insight into their "condition" and require external intervention for change (Kaye, Frank, Bailer & Henry, 2005). This framing risks ignoring the perspectives and experiential knowledge of those with lived experience as invalid. Moreover, while people diagnosed with "eating disorders" are routinely described as experiencing anosognosia, even studies using positivist analysis have found that only a fraction of these individuals suffer lack of insight (Konstantakopoulos, Tchanturia, Surguladze & David, 2008). We might then consider how this frame's deployment is imbued with power; diagnostic labels and behaviours associated with them are taken as guidelines for treatment not only in the clinical sense but also in a social one. Eating disorders have a "social life," that is, they are inscribed with levels of public understanding—and often a public understanding that views them as choice-borne disorders of the vain, young, and female (in the case of anorexia nervosa; O'Hara & Clegg Smith, 2007), uncontrolled and reckless women (in the case of bulimia nervosa; Burns, 2004; Rice, 2014), and as tantamount to gluttony and the purview of those in fat bodies (in the case of binge eating disorder; Brown-Bowers, Ward & Cormier, 2017). So too does fat carry its own social legacy, informing as it does calls for comment and intervention, self-management, and responsibilization (McPhail, 2013; Rice, 2007; Rinaldi et al., 2016b; Rinaldi et al., 2019).

Participants' narratives significantly complicate the normal-pathological divide long problematized by feminist scholars (e.g., Bordo, 1993). They reveal the negotiation of food and eating in mainstream food cultures that urge a restrained approach to eating alongside other cultural practices of food in their specific contexts. Had we recruited only individuals whose behaviours had been labelled eating disordered, and/or who had experienced treatment, we likely would not have developed such rich insights into the ways in which these cultures interact with each other and with the localized, embodied, and relational experiences participants had in their bodies. We do not wish to inscribe pathology where it does not exist. On the contrary, we use these experiences around and about disordered/distressed eating to call for a thickening of the way we think about bodies and eating, and an undoing of "eating disorder" research itself. Participants were often neither wholly comfortable nor wholly uncomfortable with their bodies and around food. They variously adopted and resisted practices of dietary restraint, negotiating these relationships in context. Here, we thicken research around "eating disorders" by naming and exploring fat. At the same time, we thicken fat by acknowledging that eating distress can play a significant role in how people experience fat and their fatness—and could perhaps make it hard to embrace fat as vital, or something to be celebrated (Rice, 2015; Rice, 2017). Putting these literatures and activisms into conversation reveals the importance of acknowledging both the struggle and vitality of fat.

Note

1 This project was funded by Women's College Hospital's Women's XChange program with additional cash and in-kind support provided by Re•Vision: The Centre for Art and Social Justice. We thank our research team and participants for working with us on this project.

References

Becker, A.E., Hadley Arrindell, A., Perloe, A., Fay, K. & Striegel-Moore, R.H. (2010). A qualitative study of perceived social barriers to care for eating disorders: Perspectives from ethnically diverse health care consumers. *International Journal of Eating Disorders, 43*(7), 633–647.

Bordo, S. (1993). *Unbearable weight: Feminism, western culture and the body*. London: University of California Press.

Braun, V. & Clarke, V. (2006). Using thematic analysis in psychology. *Qualitative Research in Psychology, 3*(1), 77–101.

Brown-Bowers, A., Ward, A. & Cormier, N. (2017). Treating the binge or the (fat) body? Representations of fatness in a gold standard psychological treatment manual for binge eating disorder. *Health, 21*(1), 21–27.

Burgard, D. (2017) Podcast episode: Food Psych #117: How to practice health at every size with Deb Burgard. Food Psych Podcast, Christy Harrison. August 14th, 2017. https://christyharrison.com/foodpsych/4/how-to-fight-sizeism-embrace-health-at-every -size-with-deb-burgard

Burns, M. (2004). Eating like an ox: Femininity and dualistic constructions of bulimia and anorexia. *Feminism & Psychology, 14*(2), 269–295.

Chadwick, R. (2017). Embodied methodologies: Challenges, reflections and strategies. *Qualitative Research, 17*(1), 54–74.

Changfoot, N., & Rice, C. (accepted). Aging with and into disability: Futurities of new materialisms. In Aubrecht, K. Kelly, C. & Rice, C. (Eds.) (accepted). *The Aging/Disability Nexus*. British Columbia: UBC Press.

Crenshaw, K. (1989). Demarginalizing the intersection of race and sex: A Black feminist critique of antidiscrimination doctrine, feminist theory and antiracist politics. *University of Chicago Legal Forum, 140*, 139–167.

Deleuze, G. & Guattari, F. (1988). *A thousand plateaus*. Massumi, B. (trans.). Minneapolis: University of Minnesota Press.

Garry, A. (2011). Intersectionality, metaphors, and the multiplicity of gender. *Hypatia, 26*(4), 826–850.

Gay, R. (2017). *Hunger*. New York: Harper Collins.

Grosz, E.A. (1989). *Sexual subversions: Three French feminists*. London and Boston: Unwin and Hyman.

Hill Collins, P. (2002). *Black feminist thought: Knowledge, consciousness, and the politics of empowerment*. London, UK: Routledge.

Hobbs, M. & Rice, C. (Eds.) (2018). *Gender and women's studies: Critical terrain*. 2nd Edition. Toronto: Canadian Scholars'/Women's Press.

Kaye, W.H., Frank, G.K., Bailer, U.F. & Henry, S.E. (2005). Neurobiology of anorexia nervosa: Clinical implications of alterations of the function of serotonin and other neuronal systems. *International Journal of Eating Disorders, 37*, Suppl S15-159, discussion S20-1.

Konstantakopoulos, G., Tchanturia, K., Surguladze, S.A. & David, A.S. (2008). Insight in eating disorders: Clinical and cognitive correlates. *Psychological Medicine, 41*(9), 1951–1961.

LaMarre, A. & Rice, C. (2016). Normal eating is counter-cultural: Embodied experiences of eating disorder recovery. *Journal of Community and Applied Social Psychology, 26*, 136–149.

LaMarre, A., Rice, C., & Bear, M. (2015). Unrecoverable? Prescriptions and possibilities for eating disorder recovery. In Khanlou, N. & Pilkington, B. (Eds.), *Women's mental health: International perspectives on resistance and resilience in community and society* (pp. 145–160). Toronto: Springer Press.

Lebow, J., Sim, L.A. & Kransdorf, L.N. (2015). Prevalence of a history of overweight and obesity in adolescents with restrictive eating disorders. *Journal of Adolescent Health, 56*(1) 19–24.

Lind, E.R.M., Kotow, C., Rice, C., Rinaldi, J., LaMarre, A., Friedman, M. & Tidgwell, T. (2018). Reconceptualizing temporality in and through multi-media storytelling: Making time with through thick and thin. *Fat Studies, 7*(2), 181–192.

Lugones, M. (1994). Purity, impurity, and separation. *Signs: Journal of Women in Culture and Society, 19*(2), 458–479.

McPhail, D. (2013). Resisting biopedagogies of obesity in a problem population: Understandings of healthy eating and healthy weight in a Newfoundland and Labrador community. *Critical Public Health*, *23*(3), 289–303.

O'Hara, S.K. & Clegg Smith, K. (2007). Presentation of eating disorders in the news media: What are the implications for patient diagnosis and treatment? *Patient Education and Counseling*, *68*(1), 43–51.

Puar, J. K. (2007). *Terrorist assemblages: Homonationalism in queer times.* Durham, NC: Duke University Press.

Puar, J. K. (2012). "I would rather be a cyborg than a goddess": Becoming-intersectional in assemblage theory. *PhiloSOPHIA*, *2*(1), 49–66.

Rabinow, P. & Rose, N. (2006). Biopower today. *BioSocieties*, *1*(2), 195–217.

Rice, C., Harrison, E., & Friedman, M. (2019). Doing justice to intersectionality in research. *Cultural Studies ↔ Critical Methodologies.* doi.org/10.1177/1532708619829779

Rice, C., Pendleton Jiménez, K., Harrison, E., Robinson, M., Rinaldi, J., LaMarre, A., & Andrew, J. (forthcoming). Bodies at the intersection: Reconfiguring intersectionality through queer women's creative accounts of their complex embodiments. *Signs: A Journal of Women in Culture and Society.*

Rice, C. (2018). The spectacle of the child woman: Troubling girls in/and the science of early puberty. *Feminist Studies*, *44* (3), 535–566.

Rice, C., (2017, May) *The Vitality of Fat.* Women's and Gender Studies et Recherches Féminstes Conference, Congress of the Humanities and Social Sciences, Ryerson University, Toronto, Ontario.

Rice, C. (2015). Re-thinking fat: From bio- to body becoming pedagogies. *Cultural Studies ↔ Critical Methodologies*, *15*(6), 387–397.

Rice, C., (2014). *Becoming women: The embodied self in image culture.* Toronto: UT Press.

Rice, C. (2007). Becoming the fat girl: Emergence of an unfit identity. *Women's Studies International Forum*, *30*(2), 158–174.

Rinaldi, J., LaMarre, A. & Rice, C. (2016a). Recovering bodies: The production of the recoverable subject in eating disorder treatment regimes. In Coffey, J., Budgeon, S. & Cahill, H. (Eds.), *Learning bodies: The body in youth and childhood studies* (pp. 157–170). Singapore: Springer Press.

Rinaldi, J., Rice, C., LaMarre, A., Pendleton Jiménez, K., Harrison, E., Friedman, M., McPhail, D. & Tidgwell, T. (2016b). Through thick and thin: Storying queer women's experiences of idealized body images and expected body management practices. *Psychology of Sexualities Review*, *7*(2), 63–77.

Rinaldi, J., Rice, C., LaMarre, A., McPhail, D. & Harrison, E. (2017). Fatness and failing citizenship. *Somatechnics*, *7*(2), 218–233.

Rinaldi, J., Rice, C., Lind, E, & Kotow, C. (2019). Mapping the circulation of fat hatred. *Fat Studies: An Interdisciplinary Journal of Body Weight and Society.* E-pub ahead of print. https://doi.org/10.1080/21604851.2019.1592949

Rosenberg, C.E. (2002). The tyranny of diagnosis: Specific entities and individual experience. *The Milbank Quarterly*, *80*(2), 237–260.

Walker, A. (1983). *In search of our mothers' gardens: Womanist prose.* San Diego, CA: Harcourt.

Part II

Exploding Our Expectations

6   Critiquing the *DSM-V* Narrative of "Obesity" as "Mental Illness"

Sarah Blanchette

In this chapter, relying on multiple theoretical frameworks—Fat Studies, Mad Studies, and feminist bioethics—I critique the *DSM-V* biomedical narrative of "obesity" as "mental illness" to argue that the complexity or thickness of fat Mad subjectivity is obfuscated by reductionist and risk management biomedical models. I introduce the terms obesity and mental illness in quotation marks to signal critique of these terms in Fat Studies and Mad Studies respectively. However, to engage in biomedical discourse, I recognise that it is still necessary to use medicalized terms such as these to illustrate their limitations. I also capitalize Madness to distinguish it as a critical term reclaimed by Mad Studies for neurodiversity, to challenge its pejorative sanist usage, and to assert alternatives to the pathologizing labels of mental illness and mental disorder. I problematize the recent inclusion of obesity in the American Psychiatric Associations' (APA) fifth edition of the *Diagnostic and Statistical Manual of Mental Disorders* (*DSM-V*) as a reason to be recommended to a psychiatrist, which suggests that the fat body is necessarily a product or kind of mental disorder (APA, 2013, p. 22). Inclusion of obesity in the *DSM-V* marks an attempt to solidify a biomedical relationship between obesity and mental illness, such that fat embodiment is surveilled and punished as physical and mental deviance. I argue that there are similarities between hysteria and obesity as discriminatory diagnostic labels that function to pathologize some bodies and/or minds as out of control and dangerous in order to justify violent "treatment" plans rooted in a desire to discipline non-normative gender performance and/or embodiments. The recommendation of the chapter is that the seemingly "objective" *DSM-V* is engaged in groundless discrimination to justify and allow for epistemic, psychiatric, and/or medical violence against marginalized and/or subversive identities.

It is worth considering why it is productive to engage with psychiatric research to argue for the limitations of the *DSM-V*. As Morrow and Weisser (2012) articulate, "[b]iomedicalism ... operates discursively within society to ensure that the dominant way of understanding distress is through the lens of neurobiology, eclipsing all other possible frameworks and approaches" (p. 30). Am I re-inscribing the presumed importance of biomedical narratives by engaging with these texts? LeBesco (2004) offers a response that I find generative:

The master's tools of medical fact seem unable to dismantle the house of fat oppression built on a foundation of scientific rhetoric. Rather than presenting scientific counterfacts to propel fat acceptance, activists might do well to embrace the contradictions of the lived experience of fatness … Pro-fat protesters can challenge received knowledge using these contradictions as a start but will ultimately prove more effective at redefining fat identity if they create new paradigms for thought instead.

(p. 116)

Alongside LeBesco, I am hesitant to believe that the concerns raised by this chapter will be readily accepted in conservative psychiatric discourse. I hope in this chapter to disrupt those who might be receptive to a shift in perspective by disavowing them of the assumed empirical justification of the *DSM-V* inclusion of obesity. As LeBesco articulates, new narratives of fat identity, and fat Mad identity, will come from outside psychiatric discourse. My approach to critiquing psychiatric discourse is grounded by my experiences as a mental health user and as someone with thin privilege. I deploy the terms mental health user/refuser to reframe the passive "patient" as an active consumer of mental health services and/or the resistant person who has "treatment" forced on them through psychiatric paternalism. I have struggled, and sometimes continue to struggle, with disordered eating and my relationship with my body, but my thin privilege means that my body is never read as a sign of physical or mental pathology.

Obesity as Mental Illness in the *DSM-V*

Caplan (1995) describes the *DSM* as the "bible of mental health professionals", elucidating its significance within psychiatric discourse and its presumed infallibility (p. xviii). It is written and published by the American Psychiatric Association, with complete autonomy and for significant profit, as Caplan notes that the *DSM-III* revised edition "yielded more than a million dollars in revenue" (p. xix). The *DSM* currently has five editions, published in 1954, 1968, 1980, 1994, and 2013 respectively. The form of the *DSM* is intended to invoke an "aura of scientific precision," with a numbering system for diagnostic categories, a list of defining symptoms, as well as a threshold limit to determine how many of the criteria must be met to justify a diagnosis (Caplan, 1995, p. xix). I suggest that the *DSM* has a long history of including discriminatory diagnoses not supported by research findings, which has most recently resulted in the limited, but problematic, inclusion of obesity.

In 2007, the APA committee requested editorials for consideration in the formulation of the then upcoming fifth edition of the *DSM*. In response, Volkow and O'Brien released an editorial arguing that "some forms of obesity are driven by an excessive motivational drive for food and [obesity] should be included as a mental disorder in DSM-V" (2007, p. 708). While the *DSM-V* (2013) does not technically classify obesity as a mental disorder, it references obesity in numerous contexts because of the alleged "robust associations between obesity and a number of mental disorders" (APA, 2013, p. 329). In particular, the *DSM-V* associates obesity with "binge-eating disorder, depressive and bipolar disorders, [and] schizophrenia" (p. 329). It also states that "obesity may be a *risk factor* for the development of some mental disorders (e.g., depressive disorders)" (p. 329, emphasis added). Thus, the *DSM-V* frames obesity as being naturally affiliated with certain mental illnesses.

While obesity is not included as a mental disorder, the *DSM-V* states that certain "conditions may be listed as a reason for a clinical visit in addition to, or in place of, the mental disorders listed" which includes "relational problems, problems related to abuse and neglect, problems with adherence to treatment regimens, *obesity*, antisocial behavior, and malingering" (APA, 2013, p. 22, emphasis added). Significantly, obesity is the only condition listed that does not pertain to behaviour or trauma, but to physicality and appearance, suggesting it is the only embodiment that can be directly linked with mental illness. The APA is recommending that obesity is a justification for seeing a psychiatrist in lieu of the individual having any other mental disorder included in the *DSM-V*. As a result, a mentally well and fat individual can be recommended to a psychiatrist based on their embodiment alone.

Mental health users/refusers also can be diagnosed with "Other Specified Feeding or Eating Disorder" (OSFED), which gives psychiatrists discretion to assign a label of an eating disorder to someone who does not meet the standard criteria protocols (APA, 2013, pp. 353–354). As Caplan (2012) notes about the previous term "eating disorder not otherwise specified" (EDNOS), this diagnostic category gives anyone with the power to diagnose the "freedom to declare that the person has an eating disorder (defined as mental illness)" (p. 94). As a result, OSFED potentially allows psychiatric and medical professionals to perpetuate the association between obesity and mental illness with the insinuation that a fat body is necessarily a product of "disordered emotion(s)" that cause disordering eating habits (Caplan, 2012, p. 93).

In particular, "binge-eating disorder (of low frequency and/or limited duration)" is included under the umbrella of OSFED, which is significant because obesity is listed under "differential diagnosis" for binge-eating disorder, suggesting a natural affiliation between an embodiment and a relationship with food (APA, 2013, pp. 352–353). The *DSM-V* states that "binge-eating disorder occurs in normal-weight/overweight and obese individuals", but then claims it is "reliably associated with overweight and obesity in treatment-seeking individuals" (p. 351). Thus, the *DSM-V* uses statistics of fat embodied individuals seeking mental health services to pathologize their embodiment as being naturally affiliated with a mental disorder. There could be statistically more "normal-weight" persons diagnosed with binge-eating disorder, but their embodiment does not make them a target of body and/or food shaming, prompting them to seek "treatment". Thus, the *DSM-V* allows psychiatrists to diagnose individuals with obesity as being mentally ill, in virtue of their embodiment alone, by embedding fatphobic ideology within other diagnostic categories, particularly OSFED and binge-eating disorder.

Insufficient Evidence for Claims of a Biomedical Affiliation

The *DSM-V* states that there is a biomedical affiliation between obesity and mental disorders (2013, p. 329), which suggests that there is clear evidence that points to a biomedical link between a type of embodiment and forms of neurodiversity. However, while many psychiatric studies take this presumed association for granted, the current data is at best inconclusive. Significantly, the articles that propose to have found a link between mental illness and obesity only demonstrate a higher than average statistical overlap of these two labels, particularly in women, and they take for granted that this intersection occurs for biomedical reasons. For instance, Jonikas et al. concluded that women with a "serious mental illness" (SMI), such as bipolar disorder and schizophrenia, are more likely than men with a SMI or the general population to also be classified as obese (2016, pp. 441–442). Similarly, Dickerson et al. (2006) found in their study of 169 "out-patients receiving community-based psychiatric care" (p. 306) that obesity was more likely for women mental health users/refusers: "Our results underscore that obesity is an even more prevalent problem among persons with serious mental illness than in the population at large; a total of 50% of our female psychiatric sample and 41% of the men were obese compared with 27% and 20% in the matched comparison group" (pp. 310–311). I would suggest that these results pose a complex question about why marginalized identities of fat embodiment and Mad experience often overlap, rather than providing straightforward answers. Significantly, Dickerson et al. acknowledge that while their "data support[s] that there is excess obesity among persons with serious mental illness ... the etiology of this obesity is not understood with certainty" (2006, p. 311). However, despite this recognition, the recommendation of the article remains that attempts continue to be made to discover a biomedical link, rather than exploring socio-political influences.

It is even less clear how depression intersects with fat embodiment, even though it is also mentioned in the *DSM-V*. For instance, a study tested the hypothesis that the rise of obesity corresponds to its possible relation to depression, but ultimately their data found no significant relationship between weight and depression in Canada's population (Johnston, et al., 2004, p. 180). Similarly, a study by Mukamal et al. (2010) was premised on the assumption that "overweight and obese individuals would have a higher risk of suicide" because of obesity's presumed association with depression, but they concluded that "higher BMI was strongly associated with a lower risk of suicide mortality among US adults" (p. 82–85). Thus, the proposed biomedical link between fatness and depression has not been confirmed in studies that already presume its existence, which puts into question the objectivity of the *DSM-V* when it includes obesity because of its supposed connection to depression.

Moreover, studies that do show a relationship between fat embodiment and depression do not consider socio-political factors in mediating this relationship and assume that weight must correlate directly to mental health. For instance, a United States medical study found that "[i]ncreased BMI was associated with major depression in women while lower BMI was associated with major depression in men" (Johnston, et al., 2004, p. 179). Significantly, this result has not led to the pathologization of thinness as a cause of depression in men. The US study also stated that "obesity, when defined as a BMI ≥30, was predictive of the development of depression five years later, but the reverse was not true: depression did not predict obesity over the same time frame, suggesting that obesity is a causal antecedent for depression" (p. 179). While Johnston et al. frame the US study's results as being indicative of obesity causing depression, the study results could also be explained by fat discrimination, especially when depression is "characterized by feelings of loneliness, despair, low self-esteem and self-reproach", all of which are the *intended* results of fat shaming (2004, p. 179). Lee et al. (2016) suggests "that obesity could increase the risk of developing MDD [major depressive disorder], and *vice versa*," based on their finding that "MDD/stress and obesity … share common pathophysiological pathways", in that they both activate the HPA axis (p. 9). However, what Lee et al. do not consider is how fat discrimination and medical surveillance of weight contribute to stress, and potentially feelings associated with depression, which cannot be neatly divorced from other feelings of mental distress. In contrast, Jones and Griffiths (2015) found a causal relationship between increased levels of self-objectification, measured by feelings of body shame, appearance anxiety, and/or body awareness, and depression in women (p. 29). Thus, the proposed biomedical link between obesity and mental illness is not adequately supported by current data, which remains at best inconclusive and limited by its lack of consideration of socio-political context.

Psychotropic Drugs and Healthism Risk Narratives

Significantly, neither Jonikas et al. or Dickerson et al. considered the influence of psychotropic drugs on embodiment, especially antipsychotics and antidepressants. Holt and Peveler (2009) found psychotropic drug use to be the "most important predictor of weight gain in people with SMI" (p. 669). They note that "[w]eight gain is the commonest side effect [of psychotropic drugs] and affects between 15% and 72% of patients", but there is a drastic range of possible weight change for some drugs, with consumers potentially losing 50 pounds to adding 66 pounds (p. 669). Jonikas et al. (2016) claim that drug levels can accumulate in fatty tissue and cause weight gain, and if there is a loss of body fat, the medication stored in the fat is released into the bloodstream, increasing drug side effects (p. 412–413). It is relevant to consider how fat embodiment can interact with psychotropic drugs, especially since it potentially increases the side effects of those drugs including weight gain, thus creating a false association between fat embodiment and mental illness that is more accurately described as an interaction between fatty tissue and psychotropic drugs.

Significantly, psychiatric studies seem to be largely concerned with the effect of psychotropic drugs because "weight gain contributes to non-compliance" of drug regimes, suggesting that mental health users/refusers would rather abstain from a treatment plan than potentially gain weight (Holt & Peveler, 2009, p. 669). While there are legitimate reasons to stop consuming psychotropic drugs against medical advice, including intolerable side effects, I remain critical of how anxieties about gaining weight from psychotropic drug use and rejection of drugs for that reason suggests complicity in fatphobic discourse. In that, if the sole reason for drug refusal is weight gain, this reasoning reinforces the social undesirability and healthism risk-narrative of fat embodiment, which is often used to justify fat shaming discourse as being in the best health interest of the individual, even if that now requires refusing potentially alleviating psychotropic drugs.

It is relevant to clarify that I am not attempting to provide what LeBesco (2004) terms a "will to innocence" argument to justify the higher statistical probability of mental health users/refusers with a SMI label also being fat (p. 116). As LeBesco points out, such an argument "perpetuate[s] the search for a cause or an explanation for fatness, whereas no parallel search exists for bodily 'normalcy'" and it "disavow[s] one's own corporeal agency" (2004, p. 116). Fat mental health users/consumers do not need to explain away their fatness as a side effect from psychotropic drugs that they cannot control, because that would suggest that there must be *a reason* for fatness to be socially or medically acceptable. However, since the *DSM-V* uses these statistics to claim that obese individuals should be referred to a psychiatrist, it is relevant to question the numerous factors that those statistics cannot reflect and that remain missing in the *DSM-V* reductionist risk narrative. The suggestion from the statistical data is that individuals, especially women, who are already mental health users/refusers, are more likely to be categorized as obese—not that obesity has in any manner caused these individuals to experience symptoms associated with bipolar disorder, schizophrenia, and/or depression.

Psychiatric articles that presume there is a biomedical link between mental illness and obesity frame obesity in terms of risk for mental health users/refusers, and usually recommend increasing surveillance around embodiment as a result. For instance, Karasu (2011) "recommend[s] that psychiatrists not only discuss, but also monitor, their patients' weight as part of every psychiatric evaluation and treatment" (p. 22). If this recommendation was followed, mental health users/refusers would be perpetually framed as at risk of obesity, and in turn obesity would be constructed as putting them at risk of numerous other health conditions. Along the same lines, McIntyre et al. advocate for the "need to screen and prevent obesity in psychiatric populations" (2013, p. 583). Karasu and McIntyre et al. invoke a risk narrative to justify the weight surveillance and medical intervention around weight in mental health users/refusers. However, the articles do not acknowledge that the persistent harassment of medical and/or mental health practitioners for fat mental health users/refusers to monitor their weight and/or lose weight might provoke mental distress, make medical spaces feel unsafe, or catalyze them to discontinue any ongoing "treatment" plans to end their body surveillance.

Hysteria and Obesity: Continuing a Legacy of Medical-Psychiatric Discrimination

The previous psychiatric diagnosis of hysteria was used to justify disciplinary violence against women whose behaviour or body—specifically the uterus—was deemed to be out of control. (Unaccounted for here is how gendered expectations of social and bodily conformity and gendered forms of medical control, including removal of reproductive organs, might impact trans persons). This mirrors the contemporary fascination with out of control fat bodies, which have been constructed as "domestic bioterrorists" in the "war against obesity" or the ominous *"obesity epidemic"* (Morgan, 2011, p. 205–206). Hysteria was primarily constructed as a unique "female malady" since it was coined by Hippocrates—around 400 BC—based on the Greek word *hustéra* for "uterus", because of his theory that symptoms of Madness in women are a product of deviancy in the uterus or its displacement in the body, also known as "wandering womb" syndrome (Showalter, 1985, p. 3; King, 1993, p. 3–4; Ussher, 2011, p. 217). Common biomedical "treatments" of hysteria ranged from hydrotherapy, electrotherapy, and massage of the vaginal area to stimulate orgasm, to more invasive and violent methods, including bloodletting of the uterus with leeches, cauterization of the womb, ovarian compressors, clitoridectomy, and the surgical removal of the ovaries and/or uterus (Latham, 2015, p. 126; Ussher, 2011, p. 20). Phyllis Chesler (1972/1997), among other feminists, argues that hysteria and other psychiatric diagnoses pathologize women's resistance to androcentrism to justify the suppression of female discontent through psychiatric violence (p. 56).

Similar to the construction of hysteria as a female malady, fat embodiment has been taken up as a feminist issue because aesthetic ideals for female-coded bodies allow less deviation than male-coded bodies (Fikkan and Rothblum, 2012, p. 575), causing girls and women to engage in self-regulatory and surgical practices under the threat or duress of being diagnosed as obese. In the twenty-first century, these surveillance and punitive practices range from self-deprivation to increasingly violent and invasive surgeries that cut through flesh and vital organs, shed blood, and place foreign objects under the flesh and skin to cybernetically regulate the body's access to nourishment (Morgan, 2011, pp. 201–2). Morgan (2011) considers how bariatric surgeries, considered to be the "'gold standard' of weight-loss surgery", involve removing a large portion of the healthy stomach, which can cause "massive kidney stones, liver failure" and death (pp. 204–205). I argue that there is an analogous disciplinary motive between diagnosing a woman as hysterical in order to remove her healthy clitoris, ovaries, and/or uterus to cure her of Madness, and diagnosing a woman as obese, to justify cutting out most of her healthy stomach to cure her of fatness. As a result, the diagnosis of obesity functions similarly to the previous female malady of hysteria in order to discipline women's behaviour and bodies through violent biomedical and psychiatric interventions.

Moreover, both hysteria and obesity transitioned from being conceptualized as a biomedical condition caused by a body out of control, to a psychological mental illness created by a disordered mind. Uterine hysteria theories were a standard medical diagnosis for women exhibiting symptoms of Madness until the end of the nineteenth century, when Freud's talk therapy and cathartic method signaled a theoretical transition from a biological to a psychological cause and "treatment" of hysteria (Porter, 1993, p. 253; Latham, 2015, p. 127). Similarly, obesity is being increasingly constructed as both a symptom and type of mental illness. Thus, both hysteria and obesity as categories of illness were absorbed by psychiatry on the basis that a disordered body was a determinant of mental illness—i.e. the wandering womb or the fat body. Significantly, Mad studies scholar Liegghio (2013) argues that a function of psychiatric diagnoses is to justify epistemic violence against marginalized figures who, once diagnosed, are "disqualified as legitimate knowers at a structural level" and are constructed as fundamentally dangerous to the public order, justifying violent disciplinary interventions, including forced hospitalization, restraints, and involuntary "treatments" (pp. 123–124, 127). As a result, I suggest that the transition of both hysteria and obesity from biomedical condition to mental illness is a form of epistemic violence intended to propagate fear around women whose bodies and minds are deemed to be out of control and a public danger, which is highlighted in obesity epidemic narratives.

Significantly, both the categories of hysteria and obesity are produced by hegemonic social discourses that define which bodies and behaviours are seen as deviant, and are reinforced by psychiatric practices intended to discipline non-normative gender performance. Hysteria is grounded in the traditional Greek medical conceptualization of women's bodies and reproductive organs as being naturally inferior to men's, reinforced in the late nineteenth century with Freud's theory of "penis envy" (Porter, 1993, pp. 250–251). Likewise, fat stigma discourse, and its associated cult of thinness, has historically been aimed at female-coded persons, who are taught from birth that their bodies are "both disgusting in their natural state and inferior to men's" (Jeffreys, 2005, p. 20). Like mental health refusers, dissenting fat women are shamed and pathologized. Both hysteria and obesity are diagnostic categories significantly influenced by discriminatory hegemonic discourses and social prejudice, which remains unacknowledged in the seemingly objective *DSM-V*.

Numerous scholars have critiqued the presumed objectivity of the *DSM*. For instance, Caplan (1995) argues that the contents of the *DSM* are determined by gatekeeping practices that are legitimized through a "veneer of scientific sheen rather than genuine, carefully supported research" (p. 186). The diagnoses included in the *DSM* are often grounded in social discourse of immorality that pathologizes difference from white heteronormative cis-gendered colonial ideals. For example, homosexuality was included as a mental disorder in the *DSM* until 1973 (Drescher, 2015, p. 565). As Drescher notes, the conceptualization of homosexuality as a kind of biomedical illness is rooted in religious morality: "As 19th century Western culture shifted power from religious to secular authority ... eventually, religious categories like *demonic possession, drunkenness,* and *sodomy* were transformed into the scientific categories of *insanity, alcoholism,* and *homosexuality*" (2015, p. 568). While Drescher highlights how 19th and 20th century psychiatric discourse incorporated social constructions of "immorality", a common misconception is that this methodology of creating diagnoses based on social mores, rather than psychiatric evidence, is only true of *past* editions, and not the current *DSM-V*. For instance, Metzl (2009) argues that during the civil rights movement (1960s) in the U.S., the *DSM,* media, pharmaceutical advertisements, and popular discourse suggested there was a natural affiliation between black male hostility and schizophrenia to pathologize black resistance of racism (p. 112). Furthermore, King (2016) asserts that post-colonial racism continues in mental health systems through the diagnosis of schizophrenia and the continued invisibility of white subjectivity and values in diagnostic practices that define "normal" behaviour as white (pp. 69–73). These examples are important to frame the groundless discrimination implicit in the inclusion of obesity in the *DSM-V* within a broader context of biased *DSM* methodology that is nevertheless regarded as scientifically trustworthy.

Conclusion

In this chapter, I suggest that a thickened narrative of fat Mad subjectivity would consider the contributing role of fat discrimination and psychotrophic drugs, among other socio-economic-political influences, at the intersections of fat embodiment and neurodiversity. I argue that the reductionist biomedical risk narrative articulated by the *DSM-V* of obesity as mental illness is both limited and problematic, because the proposed biomedical link is not justified by current data and psychiatric studies ignore the potential role of socio-political forces, including fat discrimination and medical surveillance of bodies. I suggest that the *DSM-V* is engaged in evidence-free discrimination to surveil and discipline "deviant" or "out of control" minds and bodies, a practice that extends back to hysteria. Diamond and Kirby (2013) argue with respect to gender dysphoria disorder, which pathologizes trans-identity as mental illness, that "it's not enough to get our identities out of the DSM, because somebody else's identity is in there ... it's not enough to have this psychiatric model that we tweak. It's a model that we need to get rid of" (p.

170). Alongside scholars like Diamond and Kirby, I urge Fat Studies and Mad Studies scholars and/or activists to work together towards the abolition of the *DSM-V* as a diagnostic tool to deter further epistemic, psychiatric, and medical violence against oppressed identities. It is also important to recognize that it is not just psychiatrists who are invested in the continuation of the *DSM-V*, because some mental health users/refusers find psychiatric labels personally and/or socially validating and/or necessary to receive access to vital services. As a result, the dissolvement of the *DSM* would also require broader changes to psychiatric and social discourse to shift away from diagnosis culture that only legitimizes mental distress when it is categorized and labeled. While the change may be gradual, I am optimistic that there is a future for mental health care that is not dependent on the *DSM* and that does not pathologize human experience, such as fat embodiment, as mental illness.

References

American Psychiatric Association. (2013). *Diagnostic and statistical manual of mental disorders* (5th ed.). Arlington, VA: American Psychiatric Association Press.

Caplan, P. (1995). *They say you're crazy: How the world's most powerful psychiatrists decide who's normal.* Reading, MA: Addison-Wesley.

Caplan, P. (2012). Elephant in the living room: "Obesity epidemic," psychiatric drugs, and psychiatric diagnosis. *Fat Studies, 1*(1), 91–96.

Chesler, P. (1972/1997). *Women and madness.* New York, NY: Four Walls Eight Windows.

Drescher, J. (2015). Out of DSM: Depathologizing homosexuality. *Behavioural Science, 5,* 565–575.

Diamond, S. & Kirby, A. (2013). Trans jeopardy/trans resistance: Shaindl Diamond interviews Ambrose Kirby. In B. Burstow, B. LeFrançois, & S. Diamond (Eds.), *Psychiatry disrupted: Theorizing resistance and crafting the (r)evolution* (pp. 298–308). Toronto: Canadian Scholars.

Dickerson, F. B., Brown, C. H., Kreyenbuhl, J. A., Fang, L., Goldberg, R. W., Wohlheiter, K., & Dixon, L. B. (2006). Obesity among individuals with serious mental illness. *Acta Psychiatrica Scandinavica, 113*(4), 306–313.

Fikkan, J., & Rothblum, E.. (2012). Is fat a feminist issue? Exploring the gendered nature of weight bias. *Sex Roles, 66,* 575–592.

Holt, R. I. G., & Peveler, R. C. (2009). Obesity, serious mental illness and antipsychotic drugs. *Diabetes, Obesity and Metabolism, 11*(7), 665–679.

Jeffreys, S. (2005). *Beauty and misogyny: Harmful cultural practices in the west.* Toronto: Routledge.

Johnston, E., Johnson, S., McLeod, P., & Johnston, M. (2004). The relation of body mass index to depressive symptoms. *Canadian Journal of Public Health, 95*(3), 179–183.

Jones, B. & Griffiths, K. (2015). Self-objectification and depression: An integrative systematic review. *Journal of Affective Disorders, 171,* 22–32.

Jonikas, J., Cook, J., Razzano, L., Steigman, P., Hamilton, M., Swarbrick, M., & Santos, A. (2016). Associations between gender and obesity among adults with mental illnesses in a community health screening study. *Community Mental Health Journal, 52*(4), 406–415.

Karasu, S. (2011). Double stigma of obesity, mental illness. *American Psychiatric Association, 46,* 22.

King, C. (2016). Whiteness in psychiatry: The madness of European misdiagnosis. In J. Russo & A. Sweeney (Eds.), *Searching for a rose garden: Challenging psychiatry, fostering mad studies* (pp. 69–85). London: PCCS Books.

King, H. (1993). Once upon a text: Hysteria from Hippocrates. In S.Gilman, H. King, R. Porter, G. S. Rousseau, & E. Showalter (Eds.), *Hysteria beyond Freud* (pp. 3–90). Berkeley: U of California Press.

Latham, C. (2015). Rethinking the intimacy of voice and ear: Psychoanalysis and genital massage as treatments for hysteria. *Women & Music, 19*, 125–212.

LeBesco, K. (2004). *Revolting bodies?: The struggle to redefine fat identity.* Amherst: U of Massachusetts Press.

Lee, S.H., Paz-Filho, G., Mastronardi, C., Licinio, J., & Wong, M.-L. (2016). Is increased antidepressant exposure a contributory factor to the obesity pandemic? *Translation Psychiatry, 6*, 1–12.

Liegghio, M. (2013). A denial of being: Psychiatrization as epistemic violence. In B. LeFrançois, R. Menzies, & G. Reaume (Eds.), *Mad matters: A critical reader in Canadian mad studies* (pp. 122–129). Toronto: Canadian Scholars,.

Metzl, J. (2009). *The protest psychosis: How schizophrenia became a black disease.* Boston: Beacon Press.

McIntyre, R. S., Cha, D. S., Jerrell, J. M., Soczynska, J. K., Woldeyohannes, H. O., Taylor, V., & Ahmed, A. T. (2013). Obesity and mental illness: Implications for cognitive functioning. *Advances in Therapy, 30*(6), 577–588.

Morgan, K. (2011). Foucault, ugly ducklings, and technoswans: Analyzing fat hared, weight-loss surgery, and compulsory biomedicalized aesthetics in America. *International Journal of Feminist Approaches to Bioethics, 4*(1),188–220.

Morrow, M. & Weisser, J. (2012). Toward a social justice framework of mental health recovery. *Studies in Social Justice, 6*(1), 27–42.

Mukamal, K., Rimm, E., Kawachi, I., O'Reilly, E., Calle, E., & Miller, M. (2010). Brief report: body mass index and risk of suicide among one million US adults. *Epidemiology, 21*(1), 82–86.

Porter, R. (1993). The body and the mind, the doctor and the patient. In S.Gilman, H. King, R. Porter, G. S. Rousseau, & E. Showalter (Eds.), *Hysteria Beyond Freud* (pp. 225–285). Berkley: University of California Press,.

Showalter, E. (1985). *The female malady.* New York, NY: Random House.

Ussher, J. (2011). *The madness of women.* Toronto: Routledge.

Volkow, N. & O'Brien, C. (2007). Issues for DSM-V: Should obesity be included as a brain disorder? *American Journal of Psychiatry, 164*(5), 708–710.

7 Taking Up Space in the Doctor's Office

How My Racialized Fat Body Confronts Medical Discourse

Sonia Meerai

This chapter illustrates an entangling and untangling of fatness at the intersection of weight and race through the auspices of Western medical discourse. Medical discourses permeate our understandings of our bodies' functions and of how we live. These discourses quantify health, and link directly to the socio-cultural values given to different bodies. Racism produces similar discourses about the worthiness of bodies. Particular bodies are subjected to intensified judgments and misunderstandings. For example, Black bodies are subjected to anti-Black racism in many different contexts, including medical settings (Abdillahi, Meerai & Poole, 2017; Benjamin, 2003; Walcott, 2003).

This chapter focuses on the intersections of race/racism, fat, and medical discourse. Specifically, I will explore the intersection of racism and fatphobia through my racialized fat body's experience in the health care system. I use an autoethnographic method to describe and analyze my experiences of racialized fatness through the following themes: how flesh becomes "problematic" (hooks, 2000, p. 35) and/or the instigation and reinforcement of racist fat shaming through fashion; and how I re-signify my flesh, or the reimagining of my embodied realities through counter-discourses of race and fat pride. I use autoethnography to illustrate the processes by which medical discourses manifest at the intersections of fat and race, and of fatphobia and racism, highlighting spaces where my racialized fat body is perceived as evidence of an epidemic. Broadly, autoethnography brings the evocative to the analytic in accounting for my experiences (Le Roux, 2016). I offer a site of resistance by shifting from oppressive perceptions to a new imagining of how we engage with medical discourse in order to reject and destabilize the quantification of health.

Fleshy Problems

Too tall, too big, too wide, too brown, too fat. I am reminded of my size daily. The reminders increase when I decide to engage in the wedding industrial complex, a complicated, capitalist driven entity that dictates how my wedding should look and feel for my partner and me. Reinforced by heteronormative values instilled in every word and action by both of our parents, this process is not as enjoyable as it seemed in all the reality TV shows and magazines. One of the worst parts is finding the outfits. For me, wedding fashion means that my already racialized fat body will be decorated with delicate, yet heavy, and shiny fabrics to illuminate every curve. My body has always been constructed as problematic, and wedding preparations make this clear. Upon reflection, the sites read as most problematic are intricately tied to racism, sexism, ableism, and sizeism among other intersecting isms. At my wedding, my body becomes a site for interrogation; it becomes vulnerable.

I enter the fourth wedding clothing store, specializing in South Asian wear. Born in Toronto, part of the Indo-Caribbean diaspora, I find myself in contradictory spaces such as these shops. The shiny, extravagant fabrics and store owners speaking Hindi feel familiar, but so much has been lost through the migration via indentured servitude of my great, great grandparents from India to Guyana, South America. As I wiggle my way through thick fabric, embellished seams, and shiny buttons, I hear a dreadful ripping, causing the skirt to fall, and my brown skinned body is left exposed, as the sales associate says, "You're too fat."

It doesn't end there. When I enter my doctor's office my body is further criticized, except the criticism comes with a much more powerful force than the shop owner's words. It comes with numbers which convey fear—fear that being in a racialized fat body is dangerous for me. The doctor says, "Your blood pressure is too high." I say, "I'm planning a wedding, dealing with a multitude of family dynamics, and working full-time. I'm pretty sure the reason for the rise in my blood pressure is due to environmental factors." The doctor pauses, "Oh ... you're getting married? Do you plan on having children?" I reply, "Yes, I do." "Your blood pressure is too high; you need to lose weight. Plus, don't you want to lose some weight for your wedding? You will look beautiful in your dress." I'm in disbelief. Is the doctor telling me that my blood pressure is too high and that I need to lose weight for the purpose of lowering my blood pressure, or is the doctor interweaving the rationale for losing weight with the aesthetic of my body for the wedding? The end result is that I feel fat. Fashion makes me feel fat. Health "care" makes me feel fat. The materialized reality that was constructed for me by the shop owner and doctor is one in which fat signifies danger, risk, ill health, ugliness, and despair.

Medical discourses construct and mark racialized fat bodies as the deviant Other (Ahmed, 2012; Saeed, 2007). The intersections between my body's outer stylings and inner workings—the dress shop and the doctor's office—reveal the elaborate interactions between aesthetics, health, representation, size, and risk. Medical discourses are embedded in our daily living, seeping into our habitual enactments. They play on the power dynamics of physical, material, and aesthetic associations with fat, declaring causes for fatness and how fatness can lead to supposedly detrimental physical outcomes: disease, disorder, condition. This framing, which is internalized and embodied, manifests in how we present our bodies in the everyday: do I wear loose clothing, should I hide my arms? My racialized fat body internalizes this rhetoric along with racist micro and macro aggressions.

bell hooks considers the possibilities of "flesh as problematic" (hooks, 2000, p. 35). At the intersection of fatness/sizeism and race/ism, the flesh becomes a site of the problematic within medical discourse as it is read through a racist lens in connection to other intersecting identities, as Crenshaw (1989) outlines. My experience with medical discourses continues to be entangled with the social construction of how and when fat is *too fat* and what is *healthy*. These discourses cannot be understood in isolation of the racist messages that are laid upon my brown body; as with discourse, knowledge is never objective, but rather subjective and ever changing through time (Kirby & McKenna, 2006). In the interactions I experienced with the shop owner and doctor, my flesh is constructed as a problem, one which is absolute in the absence of the "solution" of drastic weight loss. There is no acknowledgement that my body's emotional and physical responses might shift drastically depending on other spatial and intersectional forces. For example, Carolyn Pedwell argues: "the nature of particular embodied 'differences' cannot be known in advance, but rather is continuously (re)formed through located articulations of power" (2010, p. 53). Under the auspices of medical discourse, my racialized fat body is taken up in particular ways. I am told that I am too broken to live and marked as a danger if I do not conform to what is deemed healthy. The distortion within medical discourse of what is healthy becomes complex at the intersections of disability, race, gender, and class, among many other identity markers. I attribute many of the ways in which fat racialized bodies are read and taken up in medical discourses as attempts to perform an embodied whiteness under the guise of health.

Deconstructing the Dichotomy

I barely manage to get through our wedding week. Our wedding lasts days—not hours, not minutes, but days. I completely manifest the emotional stressors accompanied by performing the feminine, by having others judge, observe, and document my body in its fashionable wedding wear, and by not giving myself space to reflect on the emotional impact of such a life changing event. The stress of the wedding and family dynamics following the event shifts my heart health for the worse. My blood pressure readings increase. Between October 2017 and April 2018, I am in the emergency department four times for my heart. The construction of fatness and how it is taken up in medicine hide the realities of what is occurring with my heart—it has undergone life stressors, through the co-construction of fatness/fatphobia and race/racism entangled in my everyday experiences. This entanglement translates into an embodied experience, both physical and emotional.

At 2:00 a.m. on a weekday in February 2018, I find myself holding my chest as it throbs. I go back to sleep, hoping it will stop. By 7:00 a.m. I go to the emergency room. The nurse quickly attaches me to the electrocardiogram, a diagnostic tool that is used to assess the electrical and muscular functions of the heart (Wedro, Kulick & Davis, 2018). As part of my follow up appointment on a later date, I have an echocardiogram that uses sound waves (ultrasound) to create a picture of the heart (Heart and Stroke Foundation, 2018a). These tests, along with other diagnostic testing, are ordered and completed. The outcome is a prescription for 60mg of nifedipine, which is a calcium channel blocker that relaxes and widens the walls of blood vessels (Ogbru, 2018). The nifedipine is to help regulate my blood pressure. Side effects include water retention. Water retention is the swelling of the body, in particular the ankles, feet, stomach, and hands. This swelling makes it difficult for my clothing and footwear to fit. In addition to the prescription, the doctor and the cardiologist repeatedly tell me to lose weight.

Here lies the contradiction: if I were to lose weight, would that automatically mitigate my cardiovascular issues, and importantly, the social disruptions of living in a racialized fat body? The answer is no. Would weight-loss eliminate my high blood pressure altogether, which would void the need for nifedipine? While a definitive answer may be impossible to establish, the idea that obesity is the rationale for, and losing weight the solution to, ending all heart health issues is a long-standing polarized argument made through medical discourses. Deconstructing and challenging the dichotomous thinking of fat and thin is crucial in moving towards a more meaningful and critical engagement with fatness within medical discourses (Campos, Saguy, Ernsberger, Oliver & Gaesser, 2006; Monaghan, 2005). Beyond this, thinking of fatness in medical discourses at the intersections of racism, gender, classism can shift how we understand and alter the view of fatness (Campos et al., 2006). Although there have been numerous evidence-based studies of the effects of weight-loss for health issues that are socially constructed as the effects of fatness (such as diabetes and heart disease), there is no direct evidence clearly indicating that weight-loss diminishes such conditions, let alone alleviates an individual from the negative effects of dealing with society's perceptions of fatness at the intersection of race.

As an example, blood pressure is described by the Heart and Stroke Foundation (2018b) in the following way:

> a measure of the pressure or force of blood against the walls of your blood vessels (known as arteries). Your blood pressure reading is based on two measures called systolic and diastolic. The systolic (top) number is the measure of the pressure force when your heart contracts and pushes out the blood. The diastolic (bottom) number is the measure of when your heart relaxes between beats.

Hypertension (high blood pressure) is common among racialized communities. In thinking about medical discourses at the intersection of fat and race, my narrative demonstrates the contradictions at this juncture. As stated, a main side effect of the anti-hypertensive medication nifedipine is water retention. Water retention swells body parts, which is often perceived as the body gaining fat. Even if weight-loss reduced the systolic and diastolic numbers in the blood pressure reading, it would not address the side effects of medication. These side effects, which may lead to a body that is aesthetically fat, contribute to the stigma attached to racialized, fat bodies.

Reimagining Embodied Realities at the Intersection of Race and Fat

As I continue to grapple with racism and fat shaming in the everyday, I am reminded through this analytic reflection that there are sites of resistance and hope. Specifically, uncovering the operation of medical discourse through this autoethnography reveals that the specific negative perceptions of the intersection of racism and fat are not only pervasive, but also embody a particular kind of everyday problematic made "valid" through the quantification and evidence that medical discourses provide to further marginalize the raced, fat, gendered body into a place of vulnerability and uncertainty.

It is late March, almost the end of the winter term. As I stand in front of the class at noon, about to begin a lecture, the chest pain begins, throbbing and not stopping. I ask the class to begin group work as I sit on a chair. Privately, I am worried, and begin to have an internal dialogue: "I took my medication, I'm doing everything the doctor is telling me to do, so why does it still hurt?" I end class early and get the next bus back home. My partner picks me up from the station. I begin to cry. I'm not sure whether I'm crying out of frustration or pain, but either way, the crying has now exacerbated the pain. It is now 7:00 p.m. and I lay quietly as the pain slowly dissolves. I check my blood pressure and heart rate. It is a "good" reading.

The intersection of race and fat is not simplistic and is far more nuanced than this chapter can fully address in its portrayal of a racialized, fat body that embodies these intersecting experiences in varying ways dependent on the social context. As Narda Razack argues: "Racism insists on critiques of liberalism, political and economic ideology, imperialism, colonization and transnationalism … racism therefore needs to be centralized within the discourse of oppression to avoid disruption through comparison and hierarchical behaviours" (2002, p. 10). To take up Razack's challenge in the context of fatphobia and fat activism would entail a fundamental paradigm shift. My own story illustrates the specific implications of racism and fatphobia in medical discourses, but this is but one site of many that requires a fundamental awareness of race and racism to be fully integrated.

How racism operates needs to be central in how we take up and consume the construction of the racialized fat body. Medical discourses require a fundamental shift away from the Western view that privileges these ideas as dominant and uses them to control the body. How do we shift medical discourses to redress the marginalization of the racialized fat body? With the rise of quick diets and big pharma making exasperating claims based on evidence-based clinical trials, there has been an absence of critical reflection, of any moment to exhale and consider what has occurred, and what is occurring onto and into the human body. We require a fundamental shift in the structural manifestations of medical discourses, and a move towards an acknowledgment of the effects of our emotional responses to marginalization. This shift would involve sustained attention to the ways that racism and fatphobia, and their complex intersections, are internalized and embodied. A call to action in moving towards a critical consumption of medical discourses would require individuals to be aware of the limitations and biases embedded in mainstream evidence-based clinical trials which valorize and normalize thinness, placing a dichotomous and unrealistic view of the body. Recognizing that the internal mechanisms of the body and mind require care suggests a holistic approach in how we think of what health means, and a consideration of the ways that health is intricately tied to our environmental and social factors. Without this recognition, the racialized, fat body will continue to be at a marginalized intersection which will continue to become more complex as we continue to place value on the quantification of health, rather than the realities of lived experiences.

Bibliography

Abdillahi, I., Meerai, S., & Poole, J. (2017). When the suffering is compounded: Towards anti Black sanism. In S. Wehbi & H. Parada (Eds.), *Re-imagining anti-oppression social work practice*. Toronto: Canadian Scholars Press.

Ahmed, S. (2012). *On being included: Racism and diversity in institutional life*. Durham, NC and London: Duke University Press.

Benjamin, A. (2003). The Black/Jamaican criminal: The making of ideology (Unpublished doctoral dissertation). Toronto: University of Toronto Press.

Campos, P., Saguy, A., Ernsberger, P., Oliver, E., & Gaesser, G. (2006). The epidemiology of overweight and obesity: Public health crisis or moral panic? *International Journal of Epidemiology, 35*(2), 55–60.

Crenshaw, K. (1989). Demarginalizing the intersection of race and sex: A Black feminist critique of antidiscrimination doctrine, feminist theory and antiracist politics. *University of Chicago Legal Forum, 1989*(1), 139–167.

Fraser, S., Maher, J., & Wright, J. (2010). Between bodies and collectivities: Articulating the action of emotion in obesity epidemic discourse. *Social Theory & Health, 8*(2), 192–209.

Heart and Stroke Foundation (2018a). Echocardiogram. Retrieved from: http://www.heartandstroke.ca/heart/tests/echocardiogram

Heart and Stroke Foundation (2018b). High blood pressure. Retrieved from: http://www.heartandstroke.ca/heart/risk-and-prevention/condition-risk-factors/high-blood-pressure

hooks, b. (2000). *Feminism is for everybody: Passionate politics*. Cambridge: South End Press.

Kirby, S., & McKenna, K. (2004). Methods from the margins. In W. K. Carroll (Ed.), *Critical strategies for social research* (pp. 67–74). Toronto: Canadian Scholars Press.

Le Roux, C. S. (2016). Exploring rigour in autoethnographic research. *International Journal of Social Research Methodology, 20*(2), 195–207.

Monaghan, L. (2005) Discussion piece: A critical take on the obesity debate. *Social Theory & Health*, *3*, 302–314.

Ogbru, O. (2018). Nifedipine. *MedicineNet*. Retrieved from: https://www.medicinenet.com/nifedipine/article.htm#what_is_nifedipine?

Pedwell, C. (2010). *Feminism, culture and embodied practice: The rhetorics of comparison.* New York: Routledge.

Razack, N. (2002). *Transforming the field: Anti-racist and anti-oppressive perspectives for the human service practicum.* Winnipeg: Fernwood Publishing.

Saeed, A. (2007). Media, racism and islamophobia: The representation of Islam and Muslims in the media. *Sociology Compass, 1/2,* 443–462.

van Amsterdam, N. (2013). Big fat inequalities, thin privilege: An intersectional perspective on "body size." *European Journal of Women's Studies, 20*(2), 155–169.

Wedro, B., Kulick, D. L., & Davis, C. P. (2018). Electrocardiogram (ECG, EKG). *eMedicine Health.* Retrieved from: https://www.emedicinehealth.com/electrocardiogram_ecg/article_em.htm#what_is_an_electrocardiogram_ecg_ekg

Walcott, R. (2003). *Black like who?: Writing Black in Canada.* 2nd Edition. Toronto: Insomniac Press.

8 "You're Just Another Friggin' Number to Add to the Problem"

Constructing the Racialized (M)other in Contemporary Discourses of Pregnancy Fatness

George Parker, Cat Pausé, and Jade Le Grice

> [C]ontemporary proposals to solve social problems by curbing black reproduction ... are similar to past eugenic policies in that they make racial inequality appear to be the product of nature rather than power.
>
> (Roberts, 2009, p. 796)

Introduction

The visiting obstetrician clicks on the first slide of his presentation. A photo of two horses appears on the screen: one, a small white Shetland pony, the other, a large brown draught horse. The obstetrician, representing the hospital that services the southern part of greater metropolitan Auckland[1], which is home to the largest Māori and Pasifika[2] communities in the city, was addressing a study day at Auckland's central city hospital (Counties Manukau Health, 2017). Drawing on long-standing racialized and gendered tropes that have likened women and people of colour to animals (e.g., Dunayer, 1995), the audience was informed that the photo was a visual representation of the embodied difference (in terms of both body size and ethnicity) between the women[3] giving birth in South Auckland – draught horses – versus those women who birth at the central city hospital – Shetland ponies. The audience tittered. The presentation went on to describe the burden of high (and increasing) maternal body weight in South Auckland, an area that has been described as "one of the worlds capitals of obesity" (sic) (Johnston, 2015). The main thesis of the presentation was that the embodied difference between the two hospitals' birthing populations could account for the poorer maternal and child health outcomes in South Auckland, as well as the growing costs of health care delivery to this population. The obstetrician framed this situation as a crisis for his hospital and emphasized the need to improve his populations' health choices. What he did not reference was the overwhelming impact of colonization and systemic racism on the social determinants of health that continue to impact Māori and Pasifika communities in South Auckland and elsewhere in Aotearoa New Zealand (e.g., Reid & Robson, 2006).

The presentation described above referenced a wave of medical science that has centered pregnancy fatness as both the latest manifestation of, and perhaps more significantly, the *cause* of the so-called "epidemic of obesity" (e.g., Gard & Wright, 2005). Fatness has come to represent a causal factor in almost all complications of pregnancy and birth and thus the growing costs associated with the delivery of highly medicalized maternity care intended to manage them (e.g., Poston et al., 2016). Furthermore, through the scientific advancements of epigenetics, fat pregnant (and "pre-pregnant") bodies are described as wiring offspring for future obesity (e.g., Low, Gluckman, & Hanson, 2015). Fat pregnant people have therefore been placed at the very epicenter of contemporary anxieties about the chronic population health problems (and costs) facing Western societies leading to unprecedented opportunities for their discipline and control (Parker, 2014; Parker & Pausé, 2018). However, as the visiting obstetrician so aptly demonstrated, contemporary constructions of the problematized fat pregnant body, and the disciplinary technologies enacted to regulate them, do not target all fat pregnant bodies equally, but in fact are highly racialized. This paper traces a line from the colonial eugenicist and racist reproductive control policies of the past century (e.g., Smith, 2004) through to this contemporary neoliberal moment. We argue that contemporary discourses of fat pregnancy perpetuate and amplify existing raced and classed biases about who is (and isn't) fit to reproduce and to mother. Drawing on the theoretical frameworks of intersectionality and reproductive justice (e.g., Collins, 1986; Ross & Solinger, 2017) we demonstrate how contemporary discourses of pregnancy fatness work to perpetuate the harmful relations of colonization and reproduce legacies of reproductive injustice. Reproductive justice, as articulated by women of colour and Indigenous women, is a framework that highlights the use of reproductive oppression as a powerful instrument of social control and insists that movements for social justice must include demands for reproductive self-determination (Ross & Solinger, 2017). Reproductive justice draws our attention to the use of obesity knowledge as an instrument of reproductive oppression in the lives of women of colour and Indigenous women. We demonstrate how this is achieved through the derogation of socio-economically disadvantaged women of colour and Indigenous women (e.g. Smith, 2004). These mothers-to-be are constructed as unsuitable for pregnancy and are responsibilized with the task of securing their child's future from their risky bodies. This is shown to compromise their health and wellbeing and to perpetuate cultural violence through erasure and silencing.

Race and the Fat Reproductive Body: Critical Approaches

An analysis of the dominant discourses implicated in the construction of pregnancy fatness reveals deeply entrenched gendered, raced, and classed biases and stereotypes that are typical of the popular representation of health challenges facing Indigenous people in Aotearoa New Zealand (e.g., Nairn et al., 2011). Both scientific and popular media discourses have consistently highlighted the higher incidence of pregnancy fatness amongst socio-economically disadvantaged and ethnic minority women, while representing the cause of fatness as almost singularly the result of poor individual lifestyle choices (e.g. Farquhar & Gillet, 2006; Grunwell, 2011). These biases have been reflected in the delivery of health care with socio-economically disadvantaged Māori and Pasifika women targeted with lifestyle-based health interventions and other disciplinary projects designed to tackle pregnancy fatness (e.g., Johnston, 2015). Critical obesity scholars argue that such treatments of fatness contribute to the perpetuation of socially unjust arrangements of power and resources (e.g., Boero, 2009; McNaughton, 2011; Sanders, 2017; Strings, 2015). Scholars have called into question the objectivity of medical knowledges about obesity, pointing to their role in the construction of racialized, gendered, and socio-economically marginalized bodies as diseased, deviant, and inferior (Strings, 2015, p. 111). Scholars have also pointed to the influence of neoliberal politics in contemporary medical knowledges about obesity, with individual responsibility and self-management of health emphasised over social and structural determinants (LeBesco, 2011; Wright & Harwood, 2012). These intersecting dynamics are starkly demonstrated within contemporary discourses about pregnancy fatness, whereby women (mothers) of colour have come to be represented as the leading cause and greatest burden of the "obesity epidemic", and the purported health effects, and associated costs of obesity are linked to poor personal (maternal) choices. Sanders (2017) has argued this leads to the construction of a "highly vilified" public persona of the obesity epidemic: the "obese black/brown woman". This persona is argued to evoke longer-standing colonial and racist stereotypes of women of colour and Indigenous women as irresponsible and unfit reproducers, bad mothers, and an unnecessary and unfair drain on the public purse (Sanders, 2017; Ware, Breheny & Forster, 2017). Scholars have observed that positioning poorer women of colour and Indigenous women in this way is highly convenient in that it leaves uninterrogated the histories of colonization and institutional racism that constrain the choices of such women (e.g., Le Grice, 2014; Pihama, Te Nana, Cameron, Smith, Reid & Southey, 2016; Smith, 2004). This perpetuates a racial and colonial project intent on securing white supremacy and privilege through the derogation of women of colour and Indigenous women, whilst positing that the poor conditions of their lives can be resolved through their own individual effort (Reid, Taylor-Moore & Varona, 2014).

The construction of the obese black/brown woman can be understood as perpetuating and amplifying a much longer legacy of racial and gender injustice directed at socio-economically disadvantaged women of colour and Indigenous women, enacted through the control and marginalization of their sexuality and reproduction (Le Grice & Braun, 2016). Scholars have documented histories of reproductive abuse of black and brown women in which their freedom to procreate has been forcefully controlled, devalued, and discouraged (Roberts, 1992). This has included the legitimization of ideologies such as eugenics that posited arguments for limiting black and brown women's reproduction through: scientific claims about their biological and culturally inferiority; deliberate campaigns to limit fertility through compulsory or coerced contraception and sterilization; the removal of infants and young children under the guise of child welfare; and the outlawing and invalidation of Indigenous and traditional knowledges and practices relating to fertility control, pregnancy, childbirth and infant care practices (Glover & Cunningham, 2011; Higgins, 2014; Le Grice & Braun, 2016; Roberts, 1992, 1995, 2000, 2009; Wepa & Te Huia, 2006). The popular eugenicist movements of the early twentieth century aimed to take steps to prevent those deemed unfit from passing on their characteristics to future generations through state-controlled reproduction (Richardson, 2004; Smith, 2004). By linking social inequities and poor social conditions to biological degeneracy passed on through childbearing, eugenicists advocated for selective breeding (Roberts, 1992). Roberts (1992, p.1963) argues that eugenic policies reinforced the prevailing social order in two ways: it punished social difference and depoliticised social problems. By imposing society's (Europeanized) norms of reproduction, eugenic-based thinking masked racist and class-based judgements about who deserves to procreate and punished those deemed to be outside of those norms (Roberts, 1992, p. 1964). Eugenics also depoliticised social inequities and conflict by providing a biological explanation for poverty and crime. The philosophy of eugenics was widely accepted in the early 1900s in Aotearoa New Zealand, underpinned by a belief in the superiority of British colonisers and enacted through a suite of laws and policies focused on the expansion of a healthy British population and the erosion of Māori birthing and infant care practices (Glover & Cunningham, 2011; Wepa & Te Huia, 2006).

The Study

In this chapter, we draw on the findings of qualitative research interviews conducted with 11 self-identified fat, cis-gender, Māori and Pasifika (Niuean, Samoan, Tokelauan, Cook Islands Māori) women in (predominantly, South) Auckland, Aotearoa New Zealand. Interviews were recorded, pseudonyms were given, and prepared transcripts were analysed using a form of poststructural discourse analysis that incorporates the methodological principles of intersectionality (Staunæs, 2003). Intersectionality was first articulated by women of colour and Indigenous women who were wary of the claims made about women and their experiences by predominantly white feminists (e.g., Crenshaw, 2018; Collins, 1986). Intersectionality aims to avoid hegemonic generalizations that universalise the experiences and problems of privileged women who are (most often) white, Western, middle-class, and heterosexual. It does this by drawing attention to the "interlocking effects of identities, oppressions and privileges" that shape and determine the range and complexity of women's identities and experiences, including those produced by colonization, racism, heterosexism and ciscentrism, economic marginalization, ableism, sizeism and ageism (Price, 2011, p. 55). Analytically, a commitment to intersectionality in poststructural analysis requires a refusal to analyse discourses of gender in isolation, or women as a homogenous group, attending instead to the ways in which the effects of discourse and the processes of subjectification are differentiated and stratified by participants' location within various axes of social power (Signal et al., 2008). In other words, poststructural analyses incorporating intersectionality examine how social categories, including but not exclusive to ethnicity, gender and class, are constitutive of subjectivity, and are, "produced, sustained and subverted in relation to one another" (Staunæs, 2003, p. 105).

Reproducing Obesity

Māori and Pasifika participants described the ways they made sense of, took up, and resisted dominant discourses about pregnancy fatness in their pregnancy health care, highlighting the specific raced and classed effects of these discourses. Participants described the perception that their brownness, intersecting with their fatness, compounded their construction as problematic maternal subjects who are burdensome to care for and costly to the public health system. In turn, this led participants to question the extent to which the problematizing of their fatness actually masked a racist and economically motivated interest in discouraging them from having babies. For example, Kahu (Māori; pregnant with her third child) questioned:

> Honestly, I think the weight is all they see when they look at me – just a fatty and I reckon if they were to say it, "fatties shouldn't have kids" and it's like well what the hell are we meant to do, I mean firstly aren't us brownies meant to be bigger than white people? I know it sounds really wrong, but, but um, I just don't think the health system is made for brownies, and if it is for brownies, it is only for certain ones who aren't going to cost too much to fix.

Leilani (Samoan) also questioned whether the focus on her weight was actually underpinned by a belief, perpetuated in welfare discourses, that brown women having babies were a financial burden society could do without:

> I know Māori and Pacific Islanders have all those heart problems and all these types of things but are we a drain on the health system or something? When we get pregnant, because we're already so large, are we going to be more of a hindrance on it?

Mere (Māori), enduring a long struggle to get pregnant with her second baby but denied access to fertility assessment and treatment because of her Body Mass Index (BMI), suspected that the construction of poorer brown women and their children as an economic burden was at play in the denial of treatment: "Maybe they're just finding ways to save money ... and telling people like me to lose weight so that we don't use their resources."

In contrast to the problematizing of their bodies, as brown and fat, participants described the "ideal" and "normal" reproductive body as white, slender, and middle-class, a construction they felt was affirmed by weight classification systems such as the BMI, which fails to take account of ethnic variations in body composition. Participants expressed strong criticism about the use of non-ethnically specific BMI classifications in fertility and maternity care, describing the BMI as invisibilizing ethnic diversity in body size and promoting an unhealthy, even dangerous, body weight norm. As Kahu described: "Well if I be like that my bones are going to stick out of my fricken skin, I'm going to look weird. The BMI, it's really not for us, they should just chuck it out the window." Participants emphasised the impossibility of trying to get their pregnant or preconceptual bodies to conform to (Europeanized) ideal pregnancy weight guidelines and were critical of the resulting privileging of white embodiment. For example, as Mere described:

> They told me my ideal weight should be 56, 57 kg or something and I was like you're joking me ... that's like so skinny. I'd look hungry. The first thing people would say to me is "are you alright? What's happening?" That's what people would say. They won't say, "oh, you're looking good." It will be, "are you alright?" Meaning "what's wrong with you?" Yeah but that's coming from a Pacific Island perspective.

As Mere demonstrates, the (white) slender reproductive body was not just considered unattainable but was also seen by participants as being in conflict with their own cultural meanings and embodied knowingness based on whakapapa[4] – contexts of past familial patterns of fertility and reproduction and the conditions that support it across the generations.

The discursive construction of their reproductive bodies as unfit to bear children and burdensome to care for was seen by our participants as sanctioning negative attitudes and discriminatory treatment from their health care providers. Participants who were pregnant or who had recently had babies described an absence of warmth, positivity, and support for their pregnancies from their providers. Talia (Samoan) described her experience of approaching maternal health services for care for the first time: "It was like, 'you're just a Pacific Island girl who's overweight, typical! And you're going to have a baby, and you're young, get out.' That's just how it felt." This sense of derogation and dehumanization was echoed by a number of our participants who described feeling treated as more like a number adding to the problem of obesity than a person embarking on the life-affirming journey of pregnancy and childbirth. This is consistent with longer-standing treatments of Indigenous people's reproduction as neither remarkable nor cause for celebration (Le Grice & Braun, 2016). Talia, for example, went on to describe:

> You feel like you're just another number having a baby, another brown fat woman having a child, there's no excitement for you. You know with all three children that I have conceived there's never been a nurse or doctor go "congratulations." It's just been, "ok, so do you want it or not?"

Some participants described overtly discriminatory and abusive treatment from their maternity carers including name-calling and rough handling. For example, Nadine (Cook Islands Māori), recalled her dread at seeing her midwife, who she described as having a "Nazi-like" attitude toward her, and calling her derogatory names such as "piggy". Participants also observed a higher standard of care offered to Pākehā[5] women with similarly large bodies which led them to conclude that at the end of the day the health system's issue with pregnancy fatness was, as Talia remarked: "slowly and quietly based on race". For example, Talia contrasted her own treatment with a fat Pākehā friend when they both became pregnant at the same time. She observed that her friend got special care and attention while she herself was treated as just another number.

Impacts

Participants took up these problematizing discourses of pregnancy fatness in ways that were highly detrimental to the emergence of their maternal identities, and that obscured, invisibilized, and ignored their actual health *needs*. As we have demonstrated, through the compounded effects of racism, classism, and fatphobia, Māori and Pasifika participants were constructed as particularly problematic and undesirable maternal subjects whose pregnancies were unwelcome and burdensome, leading to multiple forms of discrimination and mistreatment. While our participants were highly cognisant and critical of these intersecting discriminations and the inequities in their care, appeals to their maternal care and concern for their babies-to-be induced silence and submission. As Kahu described:

> I don't like being dicked around, um, although there are times when I will keep quiet depending on who's going to benefit from it, and if it's understandable for me to be quiet. And because they told me I'm a danger to my son, I'll keep quiet and I'll do what I'm told.

In turn, participants described the harmful effects of being situated in Western medical gaze and ensuing subject position of the "obese brown woman" who is problematized as unfit to reproduce and mother, and responsibilized with salvaging her child's future from her "problem" body. As Leilani described: "So yeah you feel scared, you feel anxious, you feel depressed, and you feel guilty that, you know, you feel responsible that you're the reason your baby is going to be at risk." In response, participants took up a range of self-managing practices in order to try to control their bodies despite many having limited access to the resources (time and money) required for this task. For some participants, this involved dangerous attempts at weight loss while pregnant by, for example, "trying to starve and limit what I eat" (Leilani), and hyper vigilance and worry that signalled a loss of enjoyment in their pregnancies and a declining self-esteem. For others, the impact of the assault by oppressive meanings attached to the medical gaze which universalized western body norms and disrupted their own knowledges afforded by whakapapa, led to debilitating feelings of shame and guilt. For example, Nadine described being constantly teary thinking she, "had started her son off on the wrong pathway." Ironically, the worse participants came to feel about themselves, the more their own health and that of their babies-to-be was compromised. Participants described a decline in their physical, mental, and spiritual wellbeing, expressed in social isolation, a loss of trust in and care for their bodies, and the desire to withdraw from health care.

The result was ultimately a highly compromised transition to parenthood, and a decline in the health and wellbeing of Māori and Pasifika mothers and their babies, which served to compound existing health inequities. This finding of deleterious health effects is supported by research that identified how racial and ethnic discrimination affects the cortisol activity of pregnant women and their babies (Thayer & Kuzawa, 2015). Undermining the health and wellbeing of Māori and Pasifika mothers and their babies through exposure to stress events stemming from derogation and discrimination is an unjustifiable outcome of maternal health policy and practice developed to address obesity.

Further to this, we found that participants' negative evaluation of themselves as fat maternal subjects had an additional sinister effect on their reproductive decision-making. Questioning whether they should ever have become pregnant in the first place, their suitability as mothers, and whether they could justify, or had the right to have further children, participants reproduced legacies of racist and colonial constructions of black and brown women as less suitable to be mothers. We found this had a negative impact on participants' reproductive self-determination. Nadine, for example, described the toxic effects of her subjectification as the "obese brown woman" on her future reproductive decision making: "I was just feeling so bad about myself and then that's why I don't want to have another baby. Even though I do want another baby I don't want to put that on another baby, basically." Talia also described the curtailment of her reproductive desires as a result of her subjectification under the colonizing medical gaze:

"I've decided that I don't want any more children because of this. I cannot be bothered going through that negativity and that stress, and because of what it's made me as a person." This undermining of Māori and Pasifika women's reproductive self-determination, coupled with the silencing and erasure of their own knowingness about reproduction (see Le Grice & Braun, 2016), constitutes a reproductive abuse that positions the racist and colonizing intentions of past eugenic and reproductive control policies right at the center of this contemporary moment in reproductive politics.

Conclusion

So how might we, as Fat Studies scholars and activists, respond? Given the extent to which contemporary obesity knowledges and practices are entangled in legacies of racist and colonizing reproductive abuses, and impact the lives of women of colour and Indigenous women so disproportionately, we argue that the intersectional framework of reproductive justice must necessarily inform contemporary movements for fat justice (Pausé, 2014; Price, 2010; Ross & Solinger, 2017). In producing our own counter knowledge of fatness and health, reproductive justice demands that we disrupt the universalization of western bodies and knowledges and create space for, and place at the center, Indigenous and further non-western epistemologies of reproduction, that intrinsically value the human existence of Indigenous women and women of colour, and contextualize maternal belonging in a wider network of relationships. As Indigenous scholars have already identified (e.g., Le Grice, 2014; Penehira, Green, Smith, & Aspin, 2014), our participants were not simply the passive recipients of oppressive discourses about pregnancy fatness. Participants challenged the construction of white slender reproductive bodies as normative and ideal, and the racist, colonial, and economic motivations underlying the problematizing of their bodies and pregnancies. Participants also engaged in efforts to negotiate with – and resist – dominant discourses about pregnancy fatness by articulating their own cultural knowing about their bodies and healthfulness (LaFrance & McKenzie-Mohr, 2014). Participants described a very different set of assumptions about embodiment and health than those contained in dominant discourses of pregnancy fatness. Weight was not, in and of itself, explicitly tied to health and wellbeing but rather participants' set of health norms were tied to a normalization of larger embodiment, whereby different considerations were foregrounded as health areas of concern. Nadine (Cook Islands Māori), for example, described how being large and pregnant was normal and accepted in her family, describing their healthful and easeful birthing histories:

> My family is a big family, so my mum was a big lady and she had four of us, and she had four of us all the way through her bigness. And my eldest sisters they all … they have five kids each and they both were healthy mums in their bigness as well. So, I wonder, if it's really a big deal?

As Nadine demonstrates, participants' families were described as a particularly important source of support and affirmation in resisting the problematizing of their bodies and accessing more liveable counter meanings. Participants drew on knowledges afforded by whakapapa, which offered a vital counterpoint to medical knowledge that is predicated on western norms, a devaluing of subjective knowledge, *and* the embodied subjectivities of people who are larger bodied and Indigenous.

Taking seriously the challenge of reproductive justice in movements for fat justice means creating space for whakapapa, familial knowledges, and whānau histories, that clearly indicate cultural differences in patterns of fertility and reproductive norms across cultures (see Le Grice & Braun, 2016 for further discussion about mātauranga Māori[6] pertaining to reproduction). Centering such Indigenous and other cultural epistemologies will help ensure the production of a much more complex and socially just counter knowledge about the relationship between fatness, reproductive health, and mothering. Such counter knowledge will: highlight the structural and social determinants of maternal and child health, including legacies of colonization and racism; insist that health be considered a collective, rather than an individual responsibility; and restore and support the dignity of women of colour and Indigenous women in their transition to parenthood as a critical health intervention.

Notes

1 Auckland is Aotearoa New Zealand's largest city of approximately 1.6 million inhabitants
2 Māori are Indigenous (tangata whenua) to Aotearoa New Zealand. Pasifika people are Indigenous to further islands of Te Moana Nui a Kiwa (The Great Ocean of Kiwa – The Pacific Ocean).
3 We acknowledge that not all gestational parents will identify as women or mothers, and not all parents who identify as women or mothers gestated their children. Our use of language to describe gestational parent experience is imperfect and we are continuing to challenge ourselves to expand our lexicon in order to encompass the diversity of gendered experience in relation to reproduction and family formation.
4 Whakapapa is a fundamental principle in Māori culture that describes human connection and belonging through ancestry, incorporating past influences and future potential
5 New Zealand European ancestry
6 Indigenous knowledges in Aotearoa New Zealand, that are metaphysically, epistemologically and ontologically distinctive.

References

Boero, N. (2009). Fat kids, working moms, and the "epidemic of obesity": Race, class, and mother blame. In E. D. Rothblum & S. Solovay (Eds.), *The fat studies reader*, pp. 113–119. New York: NYU Press.
Collins, P. H. (1986). Learning from the outsider within: The sociological significance of black feminist thought. *Social Problems*, S14–S32.

Crenshaw, K. (2018). Demarginalizing the intersection of race and sex: A Black feminist critique of antidiscrimination doctrine, feminist theory, and antiracist politics [1989]. In K. Bartlett & R. Kennedy (Eds.), *Feminist legal theory*, (pp. 57–80). New York: Routledge.

Counties Manukau Health (2017). *Population profile.* Retrieved from: http://www.countiesmanukau.health.nz/about-us/our-region/population-profile/, (19th October, 2018).

Dunayer, J. (1995). Sexist words, speciesist roots. In C. Adams & J. Donovan (Eds.), *Animals and women: Feminist theoretical explorations*, (pp. 11–21). Durham NC: Duke University Press.

Farquhar, C. M., & Gillett, W. R. (2006). Prioritising for fertility treatments—should a high BMI exclude treatment? *BJOG: An International Journal of Obstetrics & Gynaecology, 113*(10), 1107–1109. https://doi-org.ezproxy.auckland.ac.nz/10.1111/j.1471-0528.2006.00994.x

Gard, M., & Wright, J. (2005). *The obesity epidemic: Science, morality and ideology.* London: Routledge.

Glover, M., & Cunningham, C. (2011). Hoki ki te ukaipo: Reinstating Māori infant care practices to increase breastfeeding rates. In P. Liamputtong (Ed.), *Infant Feeding Practices* (pp. 247–263). New York: Springer.

Grunwell, R. (2011). Big mums risk babies' health. *The New Zealand Herald.* Retrieved from http://www.nzherald.co.nz (8th April, 2018).

Higgins, J. A. (2014). Celebration meets caution: LARC's boons, potential busts, and the benefits of a reproductive justice approach. *Contraception, 89*(4), 237–241. https://doi.org/10.1016/j.contraception.2014.01.027

Johnston, M. (2015). Mums the word in obesity trial. *The New Zealand Herald.* Retrieved from http://www.nzherald.co.nz/nz/news/article.cfm?c_id=1&objectid=11535044

LaFrance, M., & McKenzie-Mohr, S. (2014). Women counter-storying their lives. In S. McKenzie-Mohr & M. Lafrance (Eds.), *Women voicing resistance* (pp. 1–16). London: Routledge.

LeBesco, K. (2011). Neoliberalism, public health, and the moral perils of fatness. *Critical Public Health, 21*(2), 153–164. https://doi-org.ezproxy.auckland.ac.nz/10.1080/09581596.2010.529422

Le Grice, J. (2014). *Māori and reproduction, sexuality education, maternity, and abortion* (doctoral thesis). University of Auckland, Auckland, New Zealand.

Le Grice, J. S., & Braun, V. (2016). Mātauranga Māori and reproduction: Inscribing connections between the natural environment, kin and the body. *AlterNative: An International Journal of Indigenous Peoples, 12*(2), 151–164.

Low, F. M., Gluckman, P. D., & Hanson, M. A. (2015). Evolutionary and Developmental Origins of Chronic Disease. In M. P. Muehlenbein (Ed.), *Basics in Human Evolution* (pp. 369–381). London: Academic Press.

McNaughton, D. (2011). From the womb to the tomb: Obesity and maternal responsibility. *Critical Public Health, 21*(2), 179–190. https://doi-org.ezproxy.auckland.ac.nz/10.1080/09581596.2010.523680

Nairn, R., Barnes, A. M., Rankine, J., Borell, B., Abel, S., & McCreanor, T. (2011). Mass Media in Aotearoa: An Obstacle to Cultural Competence. *New Zealand Journal of Psychology, 40*(3), 168–175.

Parker, G. (2014). Mothers at large: Responsibilizing the pregnant self for the "obesity epidemic". *Fat Studies, 3*(2), 101–118. https://doi-org.ezproxy.auckland.ac.nz/10.1080/21604851.2014.889491

Parker, G., & Pausé, C. (2018). Pregnant with possibility: Negotiating fat maternal subjectivity in the "war on obesity". *Fat Studies, 7*(2), 124–134. https://doi-org.ezproxy.auckland.ac.nz/10.1080/21604851.2017.1372990

Pausé, C. J. (2014). X-static process: Intersectionality within the field of fat studies. *Fat Studies, 3*(2), 80–85. https://doi-org.ezproxy.auckland.ac.nz/10.1080/21604851.2014.889487

Penehira, M., Green, A., Smith, L. T., & Aspin, C. (2014). Māori and indigenous views on R and R: Resistance and Resilience. *MAI Journal, 3*(2), 96–110.

Pihama, L., Te Nana, R., Cameron, N., Smith, C., Reid, J., & Southey, K. (2016). Maori cultural definitions of sexual violence. *Sexual Abuse in Australia and New Zealand, 7*(1), 43–50.

Poston, L., Caleyachetty, R., Cnattingius, S., Corvalán, C., Uauy, R., Herring, S., & Gillman, M. W. (2016). Preconceptional and maternal obesity: Epidemiology and health consequences. *The Lancet Diabetes & Endocrinology, 4*(12), 1025–1036 https://doi.org/10.1016/S2213–8587(16)30217–0

Price, K. (2010). What is reproductive justice?: How women of color activists are redefining the pro-choice paradigm. *Meridians: Feminism, race, transnationalism, 10*(2), 42–65.

Richardson, S. (2004). Aoteaoroa/New Zealand nursing: from eugenics to cultural safety. *Nursing Inquiry, 11*(1), 35–42. https://doi-rg.ezproxy.auckland.ac.nz/10.1111/j.1440-1800.2004.00195.x

Reid, J., Taylor-Moore, K., & Varona, G. (2014). Towards a social-structural model for understanding current disparities in Maori health and well-being. *Journal of Loss and Trauma, 19*(6), 514–536. https://doi-org.ezproxy.auckland.ac.nz/10.1080/15325024.2013.809295

Reid, P., & Robson, B. (2006). The state of Maori health. In M. Mulholland (Ed.), *State of the Maori nation: Twenty-first-century issues in Aotearoa.* Auckland: Reed.

Roberts, D. (2000). Black women and the pill. *Perspectives on Sexual and Reproductive Health, 32*(2), 92–93.

Roberts, D. E. (1992). Crime, race, and reproduction. *Tulane Law Review, 67*, 1945–1977.

Roberts, D. E. (1995). Race and the new reproduction. *Hastings Law Journal, 47*, 935–949.

Roberts, D. E. (2009). Race, gender, and genetic technologies: A new reproductive dystopia? *Signs: Journal of Women in Culture and Society, 34*(4), 783–804. https://www-jstor-org.ezproxy.auckland.ac.nz/stable/10.1086/597132

Ross, L., & Solinger, R. (2017). *Reproductive justice: An introduction* (Vol. 1). Oakland: University of California Press.

Sanders, R. (2017). The color of fat: racializing obesity, recuperating whiteness, and reproducing injustice. *Politics, Groups, and Identities*, 1–18. https://doi.org/10.1080/21565503.2017.1354039

Signal, L., Martin, J., Cram, F., & Robson, B. (2008). The health equity assessment tool: a user's guide. Wellington: Ministry of Health.

Smith, C. (2004). Eugenics and biotechnologies. Auckland: International Research Institute for Maori and Indigenous Education, University of Auckland.

Staunæs, D. (2003). Where have all the subjects gone? Bringing together the concepts of intersectionality and subjectification. *NORA: Nordic Journal of Women's Studies, 11*(2), 101–110. https://doiorg.ezproxy.auckland.ac.nz/10.1080/08038740310002950

Strings, S. (2015). Obese black women as "social dead weight": Reinventing the "diseased black woman". *Signs: Journal of Women in Culture and Society, 41*(1), 107–130. https://doi-org.ezproxy.auckland.ac.nz/10.1086/681773

Thayer, Z. M., & Kuzawa, C. W. (2015). Ethnic discrimination predicts poor self-rated health and cortisol in pregnancy: Insights from New Zealand. *Social Science & Medicine, 128*, 36–42. https://doi.org/10.1016/j.socscimed.2015.01.003

Ware, F., Breheny, M., & Forster, M. (2017). The politics of government 'support' in Aotearoa/New Zealand: Reinforcing and reproducing the poor citizenship of young Māori parents. *Critical Social Policy, 37*(4), 499–519. https://doi-org.ezproxy.auckland.ac.nz/10.1177/0261018316672111

Wepa, D., & Huia, J. T. (2006). Cultural safety and the birth culture of Maori. *Social Work Review, 18*(2), 26.

Wright, J., & Harwood, V. (Eds.). (2012). *Biopolitics and the "obesity epidemic": Governing bodies* (Vol. 3). New York: Routledge.

9 Embodying the Fat/Trans Intersection

Francis Ray White

The literature in Fat Studies devoted to unpacking the complex intersections of fat and gender is theoretically diverse, politically transformative, and ... almost entirely cis-centric. That is to say, not only is there barely a trans person in sight, but even as the shifting experiences, oppressions, and discursive constructions of fatness are painstakingly analyzed, the binary categories of "woman" and "man" are taken for granted (e.g., Gailey, 2014; Hartley, 2001; Monaghan & Malson, 2013; Whitesel, 2014). The aim of this chapter is to avoid the assumption that these categories are stable or self-evident and to highlight some assumptions underpinning existing Fat Studies approaches to gender through an exploration of fat/trans embodiment.

To say there is no mention of trans people in Fat Studies is erroneous. A small but growing literature attending to the intersection of fat and trans does exist and takes two main forms. The first is not, strictly speaking, intersectional work: it compares aspects of trans experience with fat experience but does not consider the formation of subjects or identities at the intersection of the two (see Vade & Solovay, 2009). Lee (2014), for example, couches her analysis in the context of an intimate relationship, and LeBesco (2014) compares "size fluidity" and "gender fluidity." A variant of this type of work includes writing by fat trans people that compares how their fatness is treated and ascribed meaning depending on whether they are perceived as male or female (see Barker, 2009; Bergman, 2009). This work draws on fat/trans experience but does not address the question of how fatness and gender work together in the production of bodies that are then legible as male, female, or both/neither. Rather, this is what distinguishes a second strand of fat/trans academic writing and is the approach this chapter seeks to build on. Such work (e.g., Burford & Orchard, 2014; White, 2014) not only considers heretofore neglected specificities of fat/trans experience, but critiques the emergence and coherence of categories used to name them. These analyses could also be described in McCall's (2005) terms as approaching intersectionality as "intracategorical" and "anticategorical" complexity. In this chapter, I will discuss both deployments of intersectionality through an analysis of qualitative interview data from a small ongoing research project investigating trans embodiment.

Research Sample

This chapter draws on data from 19 semi-structured interviews with trans people in the UK. Participants did not have to satisfy any kind of weight criteria to be included in the study, but rather volunteered to be interviewed about the role weight played in their gender identities, expressions, and transitions. The participants identified as a range of genders: six as male or female; ten as non-binary, genderqueer, or agender; and three as something in between binary and non-binary (for example as a "genderqueer man" or "non-binary female"). Thirteen participants were assigned female at birth, and six were assigned male. They ranged in age from 18 to 59, with a mean age of 34, and had identified as trans for one to 54 years. Eleven out of the 19 participants had undertaken aspects of a medicalized physical "transition"—nine were taking/had taken hormones and five had undergone surgical procedures.

The small sample size means that the findings presented here are not representative or generalizable to the trans population as a whole, but participants' experiences of weight loss and gain, of "fat" and "thin" embodiment, and of diverse gender identity and expression were rich and varied and provide some novel insights into fat/trans embodiment. Although the focus here is on the intersection of fat and trans, the participants' experiences are also shaped by other intersecting aspects of identity, for example sexuality, class, ability, and race. In these terms, the sample was diverse in some ways, and homogenous in others. Only one participant identified as heterosexual, the other 18 largely identifying as queer (10), bisexual, pansexual, or lesbian (7). Twelve participants had completed university level education (4 were currently students); however, only five of those working were on incomes above the UK average wage. Six participants identified as disabled in some way and an overwhelming majority (17) were white and only two were from mixed (Black/white) or minority ethnic (Latinx) backgrounds. Given this, the data has little to contribute to further understanding the embodied experiences of racialized fat/trans people, but the analysis can highlight points at which the unmarked presence of whiteness is revealed in talk about gender and embodiment.

For the purposes of this chapter, two key themes were identified which will structure the main discussion. The first concerns the invisibility of fat/trans in both fat and trans spheres, and the second, main discussion explores the narratives deployed by participants when talking about fat in relation to their lived and desired gendered embodiments.

Trans=Thin, Fat=Cis: Fat/Trans Invisibility

The absence of fat/trans visibility—in community and activist spaces and in online/social media forums—was frequently raised by the participants, echoing similar concerns in the literature (Burford & Orchard, 2014; Ingraham, 2015, p. 126). Some expressed this in terms of not seeing people "like them" especially when first coming out as trans. Eleanor (non-binary) said, "in the early years of questioning my gender there was never anything really to say that I didn't have to be thin to be who I am," while Cato (genderqueer trans man) noted, "there's only so many narratives I had access to and every single trans man I've heard of has looked really skinny … it was always like very cis passing, very skinny athletic type bodies." For Alfie (male) this extended to a lack of practical information for trans men of his size. He said, "I don't feel there's as much advice on passing for larger people as for thinner people."

Participants who had engaged in fat or "body positive" politics also bemoaned the lack of trans inclusion there. This was particularly the case for trans masculine and non-binary participants such as Genesis (agender) who stated, "finding fat acceptance community was amazing, but the looks and everything are very gendered, like the pinup look, the twee look, wearing cute dresses, wearing accessories." Their sense of exclusion was shared by several others who felt that online groups and events such as clothing swaps too easily assume their audience to be femme-presenting and cis-female.

The types of invisibility participants recognized and felt frustrated by were caged almost entirely in terms of fatness and transness. Admittedly, this was the intersection the interviews focused on, but it was notable that only four of the white participants ever explicitly mentioned their whiteness as a source of privilege or inclusion in fat or trans/queer spaces. This failure to mark whiteness also emerged via the implicit whiteness of the "cis passing," "skinny athletic," "pinup," or "twee" bodily aesthetics participants described and experienced as exclusionary. Raising issues around invisibility can sometimes imply that there are potential benefits attached to making visible and recognizing specific experiences and subjects at a particular intersection. However, demanding to make the fat/trans body "visible," present, or legitimate risks replicating the limitations of this deployment of intersectionality. McCall (2005) warns that moves to identify and locate new subject positions at hitherto ignored intersections, which she names as "intracategorical" intersectionality, "inevitably leads to demarcation, and demarcation to exclusion, and exclusion to inequality" (p. 1777). A question raised by the consideration of unmarked whiteness might be around which fat/trans bodies became visible at this intersection and which became further erased? Would white, or for that matter ablebodied or young (to name a few norms), bodies prevail?

A second shortcoming of this type of intersectionality is highlighted by Puar (2014), who argues: "The study of intersectional identities often involves taking imbricated identities apart one by one to see how they influence each other, a process that betrays the founding impulse of intersectionality, that identities cannot be so easily cleaved" (p. 337). Taking this into account, the analysis that follows owes more to McCall's (2005) "anticategorical" variant of intersectionality and will attempt to do more than assert that a fat body can be trans, or a trans body can be fat. Instead it will consider this "intersection" not as one where two previously existing identities "fat" and "transgender" cross, but as the points at which those identities emerge, alongside race, class, ability, and sexuality, simultaneously in/as particular types of embodiment.

Bulges in All the Wrong Places: The Gender(s) of Fat

The role of fat in gendering bodies has been a central concern in Fat Studies, often highlighting the way fat is both masculinizing and feminizing. Gailey (2014) epitomizes this when she says:

> Fat women's bodies tend to demonstrate characteristics associated with both masculinity and femininity. Their bodies are masculine because they take up a large amount of space, and their bodies are ultrafeminine because they are soft, curvy, and fleshy (p. 112).

In relation to men's bodies, Whitesel notes that "fat feminizes male features, threatening masculinity and departing from the archetype of the disciplined hard body" (2014, p. 44); while in their research with fat men, Monaghan and Malson observe that "occasionally, the cultural equation of masculinity with physical bulk mobilized a construction of men's weight or size precisely as an index of masculinity" (2013, p. 307). Fat's seemingly magical ability to simultaneously secure, enhance, and undermine gender also has consequences for non-fat bodies. Writing about (implicitly white, middle class, and heterosexual) women's bodies in US culture, Hartley asserts that, "the thin female body becomes, ironically, hypersexualized, culturally 'feminine' and admired" (2001, p. 68). Conversely, Wooley (1994) suggests, "the rejection of the soft fatty contours in favour of hard and bony bodies is a move towards reshaping women's bodies in the image of men's" (as cited in Sellberg, 2014, p. 98).

Whether it is present or absent it seems fat is doing something to gender. If this is approached from the perspective of trans embodiment, the issue may be less that "'fat' threatens to *spoil* gendered identities" (Monaghan & Malson, 2013, p. 316, emphasis added), and more that it works to prevent an identity from being recognized in the first place. Given Hartley's argument, "that which distinguishes women outwardly from men—the curves of breast and hip—are primarily accumulations of adipose tissue" (2001, p. 68), it becomes clear why, for the research participants, fat was intimately linked with successful "passing," that is, the ability to be consistently read by others as the gender with which they identify. Passing was a priority for some participants, for example Alfie:

My primary concern is being read as male and I will do whatever it takes to make sure that I am read as male … I've lost weight, and I'm losing weight at the moment but I'm still on the larger side, but it's, I do that I guess to help me pass.

Although, like Alfie, many of the participants had engaged in weight-loss projects, the link between fat and passing was more often expressed in terms of having a particular distribution of fat rather than a general concern with being "fat" or "thin." As Norman (non-binary) put it, "I have bulges in all the wrong places"—the implication being that "bulges" would be acceptable in the "right" places, ones congruent with their gender identity. Weight loss/gain was one practice participants discussed for achieving a desired (re)distribution of fat. Others included padding, chest binding, surgery, and the effects of hormones. Fat redistribution is a frequently noted effect of hormone treatment, and Teich's (2012) account typically describes how "estrogen helps to redistribute body fat from a male pattern into a more female pattern (curvier shape; fat shifts from the abdomen to the thighs, hips, and buttocks)" (p. 49), while on testosterone, "body fat will redistribute from a female pattern to a male pattern (fat shifts from the thighs, hips, and buttocks to the abdomen)" (p. 51).

Participants who desired changes to their fat distribution often imbued hormones with the ability to produce gendered arrangements of fat that weight loss or gain alone would not achieve. For example, Norman started taking hormones because of body shape: "I've got big hips and they're never going to go anywhere and so testosterone helps with that a bit." Clarissa (genderqueer) had similar hopes for estrogen: "I'm hoping when I start hormones that weight distribution will change … No diet will change the fact that testosterone gives you a belly and no butt." Horse (female) affected her redistribution in part by having breast implants and liposuction to literally move fat around her body:

It was about transferring the fat into the right place … I wanted the pear shape and I could create that pear shape before by putting silicon hips on and a waist shrinker and I could look really good and I wanted to achieve that in my body [with liposuction]. It's not the absolute amount of weight that I care about. It's … whether I have a feminine shape.

The importance attached to moving fat around the body is rarely reflected in existing literature on transgender embodiment, which tends to reduce embodiment to questions of "genital morphology" (e.g., Davy, 2018; Elliot & Roen, 1998). When other bodily changes are described, they operate with the assumption of slenderness. For example, when Johnson describes the effects of testosterone—"muscles thicken, and even facial structure becomes squarer" (2007, p. 65)—one could argue that a certain absence of fat is required for these changes to be visible enough to be read as male/masculine. An additional assumption is that prior to hormone treatment the body has a gender-typical fat distribution, something many of the fat(ter) participants challenged. Sarah (female) spoke about already having a "female" fat distribution before starting hormones: "I had breast tissue anyway ... I had curves yeah, and I had fleshiness there and the fat distribution anyway and I was secretly quite pleased."

The kinds of bodily proportions desired or prized by these participants not only produce binary-gendered bodies, but ones that reflect raced and classed ideals. As de Vries argues, "only a distinct minority qualifies as 'truly' feminine or masculine, and in the West, this is defined as white, middle class, heterosexual, and in contrast to all 'others'" (2012, p. 58). Shaw further reflects on the racialization of fatness, noting that in the context of African diaspora cultures in the US there has been a "resistance to the idealization of slenderness" (2006, p. 6) at the same time that Black women have been constructed as non-feminine partly on account of their supposed strength and physical bulk. Similar physical attributes are identified by Skeggs (1997) in relation to the de-feminization of working class female embodiment in the UK. What this indicates is the extent to which having "bulges in the right places" also (re)produces the participants' embodiment as white and/or middle class, as well as re-inscribing specifically white and middle class gendered ideals as universal.

Fat as an Obstacle, Fat as a Resource

The link between fat distribution and passing was a persistent feature of the participants' narratives. In these accounts, fat was constituted as an obstacle to passing or successful gendered (and raced and classed) embodiment, and as something in need of reshaping or removal. Sarah, who previously attested to enjoying the feminizing effects of her fatness, also said, "losing weight definitely helped me to get into clothes that would fit and help me to feel good and feminine," thus positioning that same fat as an obstacle to femininity. Alfie drew on a similar narrative speculating:

> It seems a lot more difficult for me [to pass], because of the weight on my thighs and my hips ... I do feel that the added weight makes me seem a bit more effeminate, so getting rid of that I think would help me feel a bit more masculine.

To view fat as an obstacle, or as Alfie put it, "added," imbues it with what Kyrölä and Harjunen call "the expectation of removability" (2017, p. 113). This reflects dominant constructions of fat as malleable and controllable in ways that other aspects of embodiment, including gender, are not thought to be (White, 2014). Casting fat as an obstacle positions it as something masking a less malleable core gender identity—lose the fat and the underlying gender will be revealed. This coincides with Harjunen's notion of fat as "a liminal state that cannot be considered a permanent, valuable and identifiable part of or a base for subjectivity" (2017, p. 100). However, while Kyrölä and

Harjunen argue weight's perceived mutability sets it apart from gender, the participants' experiences of gender mutability (at least in an embodied sense) appeared to contradict this distinction.

Indeed, rather than constitute fat as something outside gender, the participants actively drew on it as a resource to facilitate the emergence of embodied gender identities. The use of fat as a resource was the other clear narrative in the participants' stories, and operated as the flipside to viewing it as an obstacle. Where fat in the "wrong places" did indeed come with the expectation of removability, there was an equally prominent desire *for* fat in the "right places." For example, Ciarán (male) described:

> I had this real image of how I would dress when I had top surgery. It involved wearing a tank top with a shirt and the aesthetic of having the belly in a tank top contained like that, I thought that would be really hot and I really liked that, and that's how I wanted to look so I was, I wanted that redistribution.

Here, the effects of surgery, hormones, and fat in the "right" places produce Ciarán's desired gendered embodiment. Eliott (non-binary female) reflected on how the redistribution of fat changed how it felt:

> I feel less fat at 100 kilos now than I did two years ago ... I didn't really notice that the numbers went up because it didn't feel like it and I used to think gaining weight is horrible, but yeah, it was actually very nice to see because it started like feminizing the shape.

Sarah drew on fat as a resource in a further way. She described how, when transitioning, she used her size to protect her from transphobic violence:

> I got attacked a lot physically and verbally on the street, it was quite difficult for me. Being overweight I think was almost a subconscious act on my part of being intimidating and feeling safer with that. Being fat was a beneficial thing to me rather than being thin and being vulnerable.

This is perhaps an instance where not only fat but whiteness is drawn on as a resource, given it may be more viable for white people to be "big" without becoming "threatening" (for a transmasculine example of bigness as protective, see Bergman, 2009; cf. Mollow, 2017).

There's No Such Thing as a Blank Canvas: Non-Binary Fat

The notion of "right" and "wrong" places for fat, in terms of producing masculine or feminine embodiment, clearly indexes binary gender. What then is the relationship between fat and non-binary embodiment? Many of the genderqueer, agender, and non-binary participants' desires for fat redistribution were similar to the more binary-gendered participants, hence I have not separated them out from the general analysis above. However, some significant differences arose around the participants' experiences of the difficulty, or indeed impossibility, of "passing" as non-binary given that bodies are almost always ascribed binary characteristics. As Freddie (genderqueer) attested, "I feel like, well I can't, I can't present in a way that I'll actually be legible, I can't."

There was, however, a widely recognized model of "androgyny" which participants cited as the body most likely to be read or recognized as non-binary. This model of androgyny was invariably characterized as being very thin, white, and able-bodied (see Yeadon-Lee, 2016), or as Eleanor described it, a kind of "blank canvas," devoid of the fat that produces bellies, breasts, hips, bottoms, or thighs. Participants regarded this form of embodiment as "ideal" to different extents, and generally more strongly viewed it as unattainable—leading to Eleanor's statement that, "there's no such thing as a blank canvas." For the non-binary participants fat also operated as both obstacle and resource, albeit in some different ways.

In constituting fat as an obstacle, Alex (non-binary) clearly had the ideal of fat-less androgyny in mind when they said:

> I do have larger breasts, being fatter. I guess that's the only thing that, yeah, that's not the only thing, but it's the main thing that I think makes it less easy to be gender ambiguous in terms of fatness.

For Chorizo (genderqueer) and Genesis, being fat severely undermined their legitimacy as not-binary. Genesis said:

> The mainstream perception of trans-ness doesn't help either because everyone you see, most of the people you see, are like tiny. Particularly when they're non-binary—it's like androgynous! Androgyny! Flat chest, flat this. Look like Ruby Rose ... so you look for people who are non-binary and they're skinny, and you think, like, they're not gonna believe me if I'm not like that.

Chorizo echoed this fear of not being "believed" saying: "I feel like skinnier people tend to get believed a bit easier as well, because you have a bit more of a gendered body shape if you're not like, kind of flapper-bodied." Though the sample is too small to make any generalizations, it is notable that neither of the participants who made this point about not being "believed" identified as white. This perhaps highlights how the "blank canvas" model of androgyny is marked by race as well as an absence of fat, and how this will impact on how fat non-binary people of colour are read (or not) as androgynous or genderqueer.

Kite (genderqueer) not only reproduced the idea that fat is an obstacle to ambiguous/androgynous embodiment, but also positioned it as making one less flexible in terms of presentation. They said: "I really admire the way that they [thin people] can mix stuff up, and do different things. Whereas I'm just like, oh, I can't buy clothes that would do that for me." However, elsewhere Kite stated: "I don't know how to be a woman because you can't, because being fat isn't a thing that women do, right? ... Being a large person in feminine clothing does feel like a rebellious thing to do sometimes." Here, the fat body was "mixing stuff up" in terms of subverting gender norms, but evidently did not, for Kite, constitute a "resource" for producing a genderqueer or androgynous embodiment. Crucially, their fatness was positioned simultaneously as excluding them from the category of woman and preventing them from successfully embodying anything else.

Kite was not the only participant to suggest that their fatness troubled their inclusion in the category of "woman." Freddie stated:

> I experienced my fatness as something that the concept of womanhood needed to be exploded to make space for, and then realized that I am more comfortable when not doing that work, but instead saying actually, my fatness does not fit, right, my identity doesn't fit within your whole concept of gender.

Freddie was the only participant to further suggest that an ambiguous body might be achieved not by removing gendered features (breasts, hips) but by embracing "maximal gender signifiers":

> There's no way for me to do pop culture's idea of androgyny because I'm not David Bowie/Tilda Swinton thin ... the other option I've got is I could go full Divine basically ... I'm not able to take all gender signifiers off my body but I want to put them all on.

Here, Freddie suggested a way that fatness could function as a resource in the production of an ambiguous or ungendered body.

Conclusions

The body is not simply fleshy matter to be overcome, it is the central vehicle through which identity is lived.

(Sanader, 2011, p. 19)

Though not talking about trans folks directly, Sanader's words sum up the inextricability of fat and gender in the embodied experiences of my research participants. While accounts of frustration with fat as a fleshy obstacle may more easily rise to the surface, the analysis has shown that fat is also desired, cultivated and put to use precisely as a "vehicle" through which to embody gender. It is this "fat positivity"—fat as an active producer, enabler, or even destroyer of gender—demonstrated in the fat/trans intersection that could contribute to rethinking weight loss/change within Fat Studies in ways that do not dismiss it as the invalidation of fat subjecthood, but explore the possibilities it might create. This does not imply that fat can somehow be spontaneously re-signified in the service of any gendered embodiment. The participants clearly illustrate the narrowness of the parameters within which legible gender is produced, and the physical difficulty of shifting fat. To return to Sanader, the aim would rather be to "politicize fat bodies while remaining aware of their corporeal, transient realities" (2011, p. 20).

The analysis of fat/trans embodiment also has implications for future analyses of gender more broadly within Fat Studies. This could perhaps entail a greater attention to how fat enables any body, trans, cis or elsewise, to "pass" as gendered. The experiences of the participants show the gendering (as well as racializing and classing) effects of adding, removing, or repositioning fat in/on the body. In some cases it seems as though fat *is* gender, in that its removal can signify the androgynous or ungendered body. Existing analyses certainly highlight the many powers of fat to masculinize and feminize bodies, sometimes at the same time. They also showcase how fat bodies are perceived as "failed" in relation to the proper embodiment of (binary) gender, how, as Hartley notes, the fat body, "is a reminder of all that a woman cannot and should not be" (2001, p. 66). And yet, such analyses never suggest that a fat woman be perceived as anything other than female, or that fat might relocate those bodies outside the category of, in this case, "woman."

I want to facetiously ask, why not? If gender is produced at the intersection with fat, then what is the status of the fat gender failure? What happens to bodies that don't "pass"? How might fat be deployed in the destabilization of both male/female and cis/trans binaries? Alternatively, if, as participant Freddie contends, womanhood (and manhood) needs to be exploded to accommodate fatness, then is there any point hanging on to the tattered remains of binary gender that are left?

Acknowledgements

I would like to thank the editors and all the organizers and attendees of the Thickening Fat symposium for their joyful encouragement and support. I would also like to thank all my participants for generously and candidly sharing their stories.

References

Barker, J. E. (2009). Transfatty. In C. Tomrley & A. Kaloski (Eds.), *Fat studies in the UK* (pp. 32–34). York: Raw Nerve Books.

Bergman, S. B. (2009). Part-time fatso. In E. Rothblum & S. Solovay (Eds.), *The fat studies reader* (pp. 139–142). New York: New York University Press.

Burford, J., & Orchard, S. (2014). Chubby boys with strap-ons: Queering fat transmasculine embodiment. In C. Pausé, J. Wykes & S. Murray (Eds.), *Queering fat embodiment* (pp. 61–74). Farnham: Ashgate.

Davy, Z. (2018). Genderqueer(ing): "On this side of the world against which it protests". *Sexualities*, 1–17. https://doi.org/10.1177/1363460717740255

de Vries, K. M. (2012). Intersectional identities and conceptions of the self: The experience of transgender people. *Symbolic Interaction*, *35*(1), 49–67.

Elliot, P., & Roen, K. (1998). Transgenderism and the question of embodiment. *GLQ*, *4*(2), 231–261.

Gailey, J. (2014). *The hyper(in)visible fat woman*. New York: Palgrave.

Johnson, K. (2007). Changing sex, changing self: Theorizing transitions in embodied subjectivity. *Men and Masculinities*, *10*(1), 54–70.

Hartley, C. (2001). Letting ourselves go: Making room for the fat body in feminist scholarship. In J. E. Braziel & K. LeBesco (Eds.), *Bodies out of bounds: Fatness and transgression* (pp. 60–73). Berkeley: University of California Press.

Ingraham, N. (2015). Queering porn: Gender and size diversity within SF bay area queer pornography. In H. Hester & C. Walters (Eds.), *Fat sex: New directions in theory and activism* (pp. 115–132). Farnham: Ashgate.

Kyrölä, K., & Harjunen, H. (2017). Phantom/liminal fat and feminist theories of the body. *Feminist Theory*, *18*(2), 99–117.

LeBesco, K. (2014). On fatness and fluidity: A meditation. In C. Pausé, J. Wykes & S. Murray (Eds.), *Queering fat embodiment* (pp. 49–60). Farnham: Ashgate.

Lee, J. (2014). Flaunting fat: Sex with the lights on. In C. Pausé, J. Wykes & S. Murray (Eds.), *Queering fat embodiment* (pp. 89–96). Farnham: Ashgate.

McCall, L. (2005). The complexity of intersectionality. *Signs*, *30*(3), 1771–1800.

Mollow, A. (2017). Unvictimizable: Toward a fat black disability studies. *African American Review*, *50*(2), 105–121.

Monaghan, L., & Malson, H. (2013). "It's worse for women and girls": Negotiating embodied masculinities through weight-related talk. *Critical Public Health*, *23*(3), 304–319.

Puar, J. (2014). From intersections to assemblages. In P. Grzanka (Ed.), *Intersectionality: A foundations and frontiers reader* (pp. 331–339). Boulder: Westview Press.

Sanader, D. (2011). Exceeding the limits: Redefining fat activism and female embodied subjectivity. *Footnotes*, *4*, 15–21.

Sellberg, K. (2014). The philosophy of "the gap": Feminist fat and corporeal (dis)connection. *Somatechnics*, *4*(1), 95–107.

Shaw, A. E. (2006). *The embodiment of disobedience: Fat black women's unruly political bodies*. Oxford: Lexington Books.

Skeggs, B. (1997). *Formations of class and gender*. London: SAGE.

Teich, N. (2012). *Transgender 101: A simple guide to a complex issue*. New York: Columbia University Press.

Vade, D., & Solovay, S. (2009). No apology: Shared struggles in fat and transgender law. In E. Rothblum & S. Solovay (Eds.), *The fat studies reader* (pp. 167–175). New York: New York University Press.

White, F. R. (2014). Fat/trans: Queering the activist body. *Fat Studies*, *3*(2), 86–100.

Whitesel, J. (2014). *Fat gay men: Girth, mirth and the politics of stigma.* New York: New York University Press.

Yeadon-Lee, T. (2016). What's the story? Exploring online narratives of non-binary gender identities. *The International Journal of Interdisciplinary Social and Community Studies, 11*(2), 19–34.

10 Medicalization, Maternity, and the Materiality of Resistance

"Maternal Obesity" and Experiences of Reproductive Care

Deborah McPhail and Lindsey Mazur

A few years ago, one of us—Deborah—who identifies as a fat, white, cis woman attended a fertility clinic because her partner at the time, also a cis woman, was attempting to become pregnant. During the first consultation appointment, the fertility doctor, who was a thin, white-presenting woman, took the opportunity to communicate to Deborah that before she could begin treatment (even though her partner was the patient), she would have to lose 80 pounds. Deborah reflects upon this in her book, *Contours of a Nation* (McPhail, 2017, p. 135):

> After I left the clinic with my partner, I sat and cried. Not because a doctor had told me I was too fat, but because I didn't know what to say to the doctor. I was so taken aback and unprepared that my years of reading and writing in Fat Studies seemed to have completely drained from my brain. I would have said: "but I'm not getting pregnant," or "do you know that the CDC says overweight people live longer?" or even better, "who are you to decide that my body is not fit enough to reproduce?" But I didn't say any of those things. I sat opposite the Medical Gaze and I crumbled.

We open with these words because they exemplify two important phenomena we explore in this chapter. First, Deborah's interaction with the doctor captures the concept of medicalization, whereby a bodily difference, in her case fatness, is deemed diseased, pathological, abnormal, and risky via medical objectification. Second, Deborah's encounter with the fertility doctor reflects a larger experience of fat people in reproductive and fertility care, in which those deemed "obese" face various types of discrimination from healthcare practitioners. This discrimination can run the gamut from continuous warnings about fetal risk to the outright denial of care.

In this chapter, we draw on qualitative research exploring the experiences of fat cisgender women and trans people in reproductive care. Overwhelmingly, participants described a variety of ways discursive practices rendered their bodies objects of the medical gaze. In particular, participants experienced a heightened emphasis on their bodies as calculable, risky objects knowable in their true, horrifying essence to medicine—regardless of how participants themselves lived their bodies and reproductive experiences. Focusing on data gleaned from interviews with a total of 29 participants in Winnipeg, Manitoba, Canada, we explore the ways in which healthcare professionals medicalized fat bodies in reproductive care. We argue that the characterization of fat bodies as risky objects of the medical gaze certainly had negative and sometimes devastating effects on the healthcare experiences of participants, but also, and importantly, created moments of resistance in which participants pushed back against specious attempts to medicalize their bodies. As such, participant accounts demonstrate how medicalization is an ongoing, incomplete process that is at least partially fallible to the lived materialities of fat embodiments.

Literature Review: Pregnancy, Fatness, and Medicalization

Critical health scholars have argued that in Western neoliberal societies such as Canada, where minimal government intervention—and spending—is considered ideal, individual health practices are crucial "techniques of the self" through which subjects can supposedly prevent disease and decrease the strain on government healthcare coffers (Ayo, 2012; Bell et al., 2011). At the same time "risk populations" are produced and singled out as those less willing or able to take up "good" health behaviours, to be "good citizens," and which are therefore in greater need of targeted disease surveillance and health education campaigns (Lupton, 1999a). Pregnant and potentially pregnant women (Longhurst, 2007; Lupton, 1999b; Ruhl, 1999; Salmon, 2011; Weir, 2006) and fat people (Bell et al., 2011; Fullager, 2009; Kirkland, 2008) are two such populations. Indeed, there are overlapping histories of articulation between these two embodiments, particularly in relation to medicalization.

According to Peter Conrad (2007), the key to medicalization is definition. That is, a problem is defined in medical terms, described using medical language, and understood through the adoption of a medical framework, or "treated" with a medical intervention (p. 5). Medicalization, as described by Conrad, is a type of social control—a process of naming that is the result of doctors and other medical professionals pathologizing a phenomenon, but these are not the only agents of medicalization. Pharmaceutical companies have become increasingly important in the process whereby bodies are both defined and treated as pathological. Patient advocacy groups and "consumers" (p. 153) of drugs and other medical services also help to define who and what are diseased. For example, the advocacy group Obesity Canada is at the forefront of the discourse of obesity as "disease" in Canada, as any cursory glimpse at their website makes evident (https://obesitycanada.ca/understanding-obesity/).

Both fat and pregnant people are rendered "objects of medical interest" (Conrad, 2007, p. 151) and subject to processes of medicalization through clinical definition. Both body types are subject to risk discourses that help to define them as ontologically diseased and carry with them long histories in which bodies deemed "out of the control" and hyper-feminine (Murray, 2008) are placed under the purview of the patriarchal medical gaze. And both types of embodiments have, if we conceptualize them as politicized groups, pushed back against medicalization with varying degrees of success through, for example, the rise of midwifery and homebirth in the case of pregnancy, and the emphasis on vitality and health at every size in some fat politics and scholarship (Ellison, 2019). In this vein, fat scholars have also rejected the highly pathological term obesity in favour of fatness (Rothblum & Solovay, 2009).

Thus, pregnancy and fatness, as medicalized embodiments, come together in the pregnant fat woman, and scholars are beginning to explore the result-ing risk discourse (Jette 2006, 2013; Lupton, 2013; McNaughton, 2011; Nash, 2012; Warin et al., 2012; Weir, 2006). They note, in particular, how the obesity of the (potential) mother is automatically transferred to the fetus, which is itself considered "at risk" for all sorts of ailments, from diabetes to death, for which the pregnant woman is held responsible. Research has also demonstrated that such risk discourse is stigmatizing for fat women, who experience discrimination from (perhaps) "well-meaning" healthcare profes-sionals who communicate that healthy pregnancies are impossible for fat women. Nyman et al. (2010), for example, describe "humiliating treatment" in reproductive healthcare settings, where fat women felt disrespected, judged, and objectified. Similarly, Smith and Lavender (2011) found high levels of emotional and psychological distress in fat pregnant women follow-ing their interactions with healthcare professionals. Such discrimination has elicited responses from the American College of Obstetrics and Gynecologists who, in 2014, released an "opinion" urging practitioners to "avoid stigmatiz-ing their obese patients" (ACOG, 2014, p. 6). At the same time, the ACOG did certainly not shy away from continuing medicalization, warning phys-icians to be "cautious that avoidance of stigmatization does not lead to ennui in counseling patients regarding the medical risks of obesity" (ACOG, 2014, p. 4).

Research Methods

Despite literature demonstrating the existence of fat phobia within the repro-ductive healthcare clinic, and the important impact such research is clearly making in the area of medical policy such as in the case of the ACOG, there remains a paucity of work exploring the experiences of fat oppression. As such, we undertook a qualitative study in Winnipeg, Canada, with 25 fat women who experienced reproductive care, and also with reproductive healthcare professionals. These interviews were part of a larger cross-national study which included 59 participants in total.

We recruited participants through a combination of methods, including postering at key venues, social media ads and posts over social media, word-of-mouth, and snowball sampling. Researchers also attended pertinent groups such as government-sponsored mom and baby groups and fertility support groups to recruit participants. Additionally, we developed a project website, and advertised on websites such as Kijiji and Craig's List. Further, we placed ads in community newspapers and city publications. Given our team's commitment to intersectional research, we deployed purposive sampling in order to recruit a diverse group of people accessing care with regards in particular to race and class. As Rice et al. (2019) argue, intersectional inquiry is not only a theoretical lens, but also, and inherently, a methodology. Along these lines, it is important to note the gathered demographics of participants. While participants in the larger Canadian study included trans people, all participants in Winnipeg identified as cisgender women. Within the sample of fat women (that is, excluding healthcare providers interviewed), 13 identified as white, four as Indigenous, two as Metis, two as Jewish, and four as people of colour. Within the second sample of four healthcare professionals, we interviewed one nurse, one physician, one dietitian, and one midwife.

Interviews were semi-structured in nature and lasted approximately one hour. The Principle Investigator conducted all interviews. We then coded the data, paying careful attention to intersectional themes, incorporating this lens in the coding to explore ways in which the fat body was lived differently given vectors of identity such as race, class, Indigeneity, sexuality, and geography.

After coding the data thematically, we returned to the data through the lens of social theory with a particular focus on new materialism, which helps to provide an analytical framework for this chapter. New materialism, drawn in part from the field of science studies (Rice, 2014), is an emerging theoretical stream in Fat Studies (Rice, 2014; Warin et al., 2012) developing in part as a reaction to the social constructionist influence in critical obesity and Fat Studies positing obesity and fatness as entirely social productions. Using new materialism, scholars are beginning to insist that we re-member the at least partial integrity and fleshiness of the body (McPhail et. al, 2016), and explore the ways in which bodies have agentic properties that we may not entirely comprehend or understand. As Rice (2014) argues: "the new materialism conceptualizes the physical body as a source of knowledge in itself and understands matter to have agency independent of people's perceptions or manipulations of it … the becoming of bodies is a relatively open process that cannot be predicted or determined in advance" (p. 22). In more recent work, Rice et al. (forthcoming) draws on Puar's work to argue for an "*intersectional becoming*" theory, in which "embodiments/differences" are imagined as "fluid" or "provisional" rather than as the intersections of self-contained identities. Thus, in thinking about the fat body, new materialism pushes us to think about how adiposity, as a bodily state, can act upon the world in ways that cannot necessarily be anticipated. Within such an understanding, this chapter highlights the ways in which our research participants' very flesh, and in particular the resiliency of their fatty bodies, opened up possibilities for resistance to medical discourse and intense processes of medicalization as a form of social control.

Participant Stories: Experiences of Medicalization and "Maternal Obesity"

Pregnancy and Birth

Participants overwhelmingly described processes of medicalization whereby their bodies were defined by healthcare professionals as medically abnormal, and then subjected to a variety of "curatives" and acts of containment. Most often, participants were subject to a diagnostic process whereby they were regularly weighed. While frequent weighing in pregnancy is typical for all bodies, and part of the general medicalization of pregnancy (Jette & Rail, 2013), participants relayed intensified experiences of weight monitoring during which healthcare professionals would relate a litany of risks for both fetus and participant. Freddi (white, middle class, queer) exemplified this when discussing her experiences with her family doctor:

> He mentioned at one point that I might have difficulty because of how heavy I was to start with. Talked about gestational diabetes and the risks of that, being overweight to start and overweight through my whole pregnancy. Lots of cautionary things. He never actually said, "You know, you are too overweight to do this." But, he always tells me how much I should exercise, and you know, that how, where my weight should be, and if I've gained weight, between visits, he makes comments about that, so.

Samantha (Jewish, middle class, straight) echoed this in relating her first consult with her OB/GYN:

> He looked at me and just saw fat. Like, that's what he saw. Like, I walked into his office. He was like, "Okay, we're putting you on insulin." "You have to have a c-section." "You're getting induced early, because the baby's going to die." He scared the crap out of me.

Such discourse unsurprisingly created a high level of stress for participants during pregnancy:

> I was anxious through the whole pregnancy. Like, would I get diabetes? You know, or would that affect, you know, the baby? It's still something that I think about, ever since I saw Obese Class 1, on my file.[1]
>
> (Freddi)

Thus, high-anxiety pregnancies resulting from risk narratives were common for many participants, who were encouraged to imagine a variety of terrifying consequences from gestational diabetes to miscarriage and stillbirth. It is important to note at this juncture, however, that the health risks associated with "maternal obesity," are not established. Some studies question the link between "maternal obesity" and "childhood obesity" (Beyerlein et al., 2012; Hinkle et al., 2012; Ode et al., 2012), while others indicate little risk to the fetus associated with obesity (Adams et al., 2011; Burstein et al., 2008; Khalil, Saleh, & Subhani, 2008). In addition, some research argues that weight status and gestational diabetes are not well linked in all populations (Winhofer et al., 2015).

And yet, risks between obesity and pregnancy are so common sense that participants in our study faced the reality of spatial segregation into "high risk" birthing wards if they reached a certain BMI during pregnancy. One nurse we interviewed described the ways in which people are shunted to the high risk ward:

> If you've had a previous C-section before, you're high risk. If you're having twins or triplets, then you're high risk. If you are a diabetic on insulin, then you're high risk. If you have high blood pressure on medications, you're high risk. Um, yeah, lots of other major, kind of health concerns, anything kind of unusual ... blood disorders. Anyone who needs to be induced comes to us. ... There's lots more, but yeah, and then also, if your BMI is over 40, then you have to go to high risk.

Thus, a BMI over 40—and that is a BMI taken upon entry to the hospital, ostensibly at the height of pregnancy weight—is equated with such high risk pregnancies as those involving blood disorders, induction, and previous c-section. As such, those in the high risk ward were subjected to a higher level of medical monitoring and intervention during birth.

The possibility of giving birth on a high risk ward was of great concern for some participants. For Janice, a working class, straight and Indigenous woman, concerns about the specialization of high risk were even more pressing given continued underfunding of healthcare in rural Indigenous communities, whereby high risk pregnancies are flown to a larger urban centre, thus isolating those giving birth from friends, family, and community:

> I know for bigger women, the ones with the high risk pregnancies, they send them to Brandon to deliver, because they have the special tools there for them. Because they put a belt on them and it monitors everything inside. Cause I have a cousin that, when she got pregnant, she was three hundred pounds. And then, it was so much weight on the baby they flew her to Brandon and that's where she gave birth. And she was in there for a whole week. The baby was sick; something didn't come out right. Like, something didn't happen right. And then she had infections from being cut open too. Cause she couldn't push it out. And so, so she had really bad infections, so she had to be in there.

While the prospect of giving birth in a high risk ward was stressful for participants living in the city, for rural Indigenous women the geography of high risk delivery was caught up in colonial mechanisms, whereby the consequences of a hyper-medicalized birth went beyond moving wards within the same hospital to medical evacuation, sometimes hundreds of miles away from home.

Conception Care

Similar risk discourses were also experienced by participants seeking conception support either from fertility specialists or from family doctors, many of whom refused care. This refusal of care demonstrates that within processes of medicalization, a *denial* of curative procedures can also help to objectify an "abnormal" body within the medical gaze while, at the same time and ironically, disallowing access to the medical system. An example of this can be found in Breanne's story.

Breanne (Indigenous, middle class, straight) had attempted to conceive for a number of years, bouncing from family doctor to family doctor trying to find one who would help her:

> I had a lot over the years. It wasn't going anywhere. And then I had another doctor who, when I brought up trying to get pregnant, and that, you know, we weren't getting pregnant, he gave me a list of the reasons, he gave me a list of the things that being overweight, like, high blood pressure and not being able to carry the baby. I kind of feel like he talked me out of trying to get pregnant, or like, "Maybe you should be using protection" kind of. "Fat people shouldn't get pregnant." *I really don't feel like anybody particularly wanted me to get pregnant.*

Finally, desperate to receive conception care, Breanne underwent a costly out-of-province gastric bypass surgery. She states: "I wanted to lose the weight so I could get pregnant." And she indeed lost over 200 pounds. Following the surgery, however, Breanne continued to experience barriers to care, as no doctor she encountered had any familiarity with prenatal care following a gastric bypass procedure:

> I was afraid to get pregnant, because nobody would work with me on that part. I didn't feel like there was anybody around that even knew how to keep a baby from a gastric bypass person healthy, because, nobody seemed to know how to keep me healthy. If nobody understands my body, then how are they going to understand a baby inside of my body? All my doctor kept telling me was "Your baby's going to have different nutritional requirements. You're going to have different nutritional requirements, and we just don't have the resources in Manitoba." So, (laugh) either way [fat or newly thinner], I was going to be, like, damaging a baby if I had one.

The litany of risks that doctors rattled off to Breanne whilst denying her conception support—eventually pushing her towards gastric bypass surgery—were common in almost all participants seeking conception care. Indeed, health concerns such as birth defects, miscarriage, heart issues, and gestational diabetes weighed so heavily on the mind of one participant, that: "Every time, right before I got my period, I would always think, 'If I'm pregnant, what have I done to my baby?'" The spectre of gestational diabetes was particularly poignant for Indigenous participants. For example, Janice, who for financial reasons consulted her family doctor and not a fertility specialist about conception issues, was told that if she got pregnant her weight would "squish" the fetus and precipitate birth defects, heart issues, and cause the umbilical cord to strangle the baby to death. She was also told that she would "pass" diabetes to her potential fetus:

> [The doctor] said I could get a severe case of diabetes. I can pass it on to my baby. … That's what he told me, like, just the weight and because I'm Aboriginal, I might get diabetes 'cause our system is a little different, our bloodline and so that could be a big problem too. And ah, that's what he told me about it.

As critical anti-colonial scholars of fatness have argued, Indigenous bodies are not only hyper-associated with obesity, but also, and relatedly, with diabetes (Fee, 2006; Robinson, this volume). While it is important to recognize the myriad ways in which colonization has created and continues to exacerbate health issues in Indigenous communities, such as through the violent denial of Indigenous people's access to traditional lands and thus food sources (McPhail, 2016), the conflation of Indigeneity with obesity and diabetes ideologically helps to further marginalize and contain bodies in that it stereotypes Indigenous people as "too uneducated" and "too lazy" to practice so-called "good" health behaviours related to exercise and diet (Poudrier, 2016). In the case of gestational diabetes, whereby Indigenous people are being told, as Janice was, that they can "pass on" diabetes due to the double risks of fatness and their "bloodlines," such a discourse also constructs Indigenous women as inherently "bad (potential) mothers" due to the very blood and flesh of their bodies. It is no surprise, then, that Janice was extraordinarily concerned about gestational diabetes, and felt like the right thing to do for her potential baby was to lose weight before becoming pregnant and "understood" where her doctor was coming from on the issue: "some people might take [doctors telling patients to lose weight to conceive] as an insult, but some people like me, I kind of don't. Because it's a reality."

Self-Medicalization

It is important to note that a small handful of participants felt under-medicalized by healthcare practitioners, and, out of concern for their fetus, wished that more attention had been paid to the potential risks of which they believed their bodies were capable. Such self-medicalization aligns with Conrad's (2007) contention that pathologized groups often name themselves as "objects of concern." For example, Natalie (Indigenous, middle class, straight), who is herself a healthcare professional, felt at various points that her midwife did not take her weight seriously enough to engage with her in a meaningful way about it, or to help guide her through a "healthy" pregnancy:

> Just like, with being heavier … [that] seemed, like, important to talk about. So I told her a little bit about the weight gain. … And I don't remember exactly what she said. But it was something like, 'Well, you're [in healthcare], so you already know these things,' which wasn't really helpful.

Similar to Janice, much of Natalie's concern with weight gain and its effects on her pregnancy was due to her Indigeneity, and correlations between Indigenous bodies and diabetes. Given that Natalie was herself a healthcare practitioner, she not only knew about but also accepted the views of the medical establishment with regard to maternal obesity. As a result, Natalie eventually convinced her midwife to sign off on an early induction, which was in turn resisted by the staff at the birthing ward:

> I convinced them to do it earlier, at four days. … I said "Just put on it that I'm [in healthcare] and I'm requesting it." And so they agreed, and so I went in four days early. And the obstetrician on call agreed. He was going to give me the medicine to be induced. And I was concerned, and I said "You know, mainly I'm concerned about the baby. And I know, I've obviously gained too much weight. I do not have gestational diabetes, but I am concerned about the effects on the baby." … So they agreed to induce me, and then basically, the nurse in the triage unit, who would have to administer the stuff, said no and argued with my midwife. And it was one of those rotating midwives, who was fairly new, and she basically caved and agreed with the nurse. … So I had to go home and wait for another six days.

Thus, the pathologization of fat pregnant bodies was not just a top-down phenomenon, but was also embraced and sometimes even championed by participants themselves.

While self-medicalization certainly occurred, the pathologization of fat bodies was overwhelmingly experienced by participants at the hands of the healthcare practitioners encountered throughout their reproductive healthcare journeys. Though embraced by some, the medicalization process was certainly not welcomed by many participants, who often developed strategies of resistance against both the definition of their bodies as diseased, and the curatives that resulted from that definition.

"I Said No": Resistance to Medicalization

In the main, participant resistance to medicalization was a highly embodied experience in which participants drew on their own knowledge and intuitions about their bodies to counter pathologization. For example, Wendy's (white, working class, straight) attunement with her body allowed her to decline medication:

> My first visit with her she took my blood pressure and immediately wanted to start me on blood pressure medication. And I said no. (laugh) "Absolutely not." I, I mean, I was fairly active going into this. She was on the fifth floor or something, and I took the stairs up to her office. And I was excited, and anxious and all this other stuff. And I, I, so she took my blood pressure, and resting heart rate, and it was high, but it wasn't really a true reflection of, like, there was so much going on inside me, it wasn't a good reflection of what my normal resting rate was... . For the most part, I am pretty aware of my body, right?

Patricia (white, middle class, straight) also pushed back against the medical gaze. After being refused fertility care based on weight, Patricia decided to take matters into her own hands, and to work with her body to become pregnant without medical intervention:

> I have nothing else wrong with me, other than I'm overweight. I don't have high blood pressure. I don't have high cholesterol. I don't have high blood sugar. Yeah, like, you know, all of those problems that are associated with being overweight. I don't have any of those. ... I found [the fertility specialist] just jumped to the conclusion that, you know, this is all because I'm overweight. Where, you know, I basically, in, it was a year and a half later, proved that, "Hey, I could do it, on my own." And I had the perfect pregnancy until I developed pregnancy induced hypertension, which wasn't because of my weight. Because, anybody can develop it.

Similar to Patricia, Chantelle (white, middle class, straight) simply "knew" her body to be healthy, thus creating for her an articulation of resistance against a fertility specialist's demand that she lose 10 percent of her body weight before conception treatment could begin:

> I know people who are a hundred, two hundred pounds bigger than me, and they've had kids. So I wonder why that's such an issue. I'm healthy. I'm just fat. Like, otherwise, there's nothing wrong with me.
> I: Okay. So when she suggested that you lose 10 percent of your body weight, did she give you any suggestions as to how you might do that?
> P: No. I don't think that's possible for any human in three months. Like, that's asking someone, what are you going to do, stop eating? Well,

how good is that for fertility, when you're supposed to be nourishing your body? Like, I'm not a huge eater. I don't eat junk. I don't eat processed food. I don't eat fast food, nothing.

Chantelle, then, is both exerting her own claims to knowledge about bodies and fertility in order to resist the medicalization process – "well how good is that for fertility?" – as well as claiming what Fellows and Razack (1998) have called a "toehold on respectability" whereby members of a marginalized group claim dominance by claiming white, middle class behaviours and norms in relation to more "deviant Others" within the same marginalized group. In this case, Chantelle is distancing herself from "super fat" people who weigh "two hundred pounds more" than she does who presumably also eat "junk," "processed food," and "fast food." As both "excessive" largeness and "unhealthy eating" have been associated with marginalized groups such as working class, racialized, and Indigenous people in Canada (Ellison, McPhail & Mitchinson, 2016; McPhail, Chapman & Beagan, 2011), the toehold Chantelle, who is white and middle class, is making, is a race- and class-based claim to "good" motherhood.

For the most part, participants did not articulate their counter-knowledges to their healthcare providers, doctors in particular, due to the profound power imbalance between doctors and patients and especially between patients and specialists such as OB/GYNs and fertility doctors. This is captured eloquently by Wendy:

> It's scary to say "No, I reject your diagnosis." or "Prove it to me." Like, those are scary things to say to doctors. And things you shouldn't have to say to doctors.

Thus, even though Wendy at one point in her reproductive healthcare journey was able to resist blood pressure medication from one doctor, as related above, she found her resistance to her fertility specialist's fat phobia to be difficult to state out loud. She then avoided care to communicate her dissatisfaction.

One exception to the inability to discuss alternative knowledges with healthcare professionals is provided by Natalie. In Manitoba, midwives are required to transfer obstetric care to obstetricians/gynaecologists in the case of "high risk" pregnancies, which include those of people with a BMI of 40 with "related complications" like gestational diabetes (College of Midwives of Manitoba, 2011). Natalie pushed back against this professional guideline, thus demonstrating her complicated relationship to medical knowledge about pregnancy; on the one hand, she accepted and welcomed medical discourse pathologizing her body, yet on the other hand critiqued it:

> [The midwife] basically said "We're not supposed to care for women over a certain BMI, and you're already there." And this was pretty early on in my pregnancy. And I said "Well, two things about that." Two

things, maybe more. First of all, BMI's not a valid measurement in a pregnant person, so, I have a bit of an issue with obstetrical care that's based on a BMI, when it's not a measure that's supposed to be used during pregnancy. Secondly, if I develop any of the associated risks or concerns, then I'd be happy to have my care transferred, but in the absence of any other risk, you know, I don't see a reason for that. And so, we agreed not to have a referral. … I felt like when she said that, it was kind of a scare tactic, like, "If you don't stop gaining weight, at this rate, then we're going to have transfer your care." So.

Even though racism and colonial power could have created a situation whereby the resistance of Natalie, an Indigenous woman, would go unheard, or indeed be punished in some fashion, in this case the power dynamics within medicine worked in Natalie's favour, or at least mitigated such racism. Natalie practiced within a healthcare field typically imagined as superior to midwifery and was thus able to articulate a resistance to BMI measurements—one of the primary tools of the medicalization of the fat body.

Conclusion: Medicalization and the Materiality of Resistance

Almost all participants in our study related experiences of medicalization, whereby their bodies were objectified through measurements such as BMI classification, defined as obese and "high risk," and therefore subject to a number of curatives and controls which differed according to race and position within colonialism. Ironically, one such mechanism of control included a denial of care by healthcare practitioners who characterized participants as "unfit" to reproduce thus demonstrating the flexibility and seemingly all-encompassing nature of medicalization; one can indeed be medicalized even whilst labeled "abnormal" enough to exist beyond the scope of healthcare procedures.

And yet, participant stories demonstrate that medicalization is not in fact all-encompassing. While a small handful of participants welcomed pathologization, sometimes engaging in self-medicalization, the majority of the participants questioned and even pushed back against medical discourse characterizing their (potential) pregnancies as risky and unhealthy. Often, participants relied on their embodied experiences and knowledge about health and reproduction to build for themselves a lexicon of resistance. While this resistance was not always expressed directly to healthcare practitioners, it provided for participants an important counter-narrative to the continuous, high frequency risk discourse that permeated almost all facets of participants' reproductive journeys.

As such, participants' stories point to the new materialist contention that bodies—the material—can serve as a conduit for resistance in that they demonstrate the ways in which practices of dominance are never complete. Articulations of medicalization define fat pregnant bodies as "risky," and this risk discourse has impact. But this discourse does not over-determine the reality of reproductive care in that the material can demand a re-articulation of medical meanings of fatness that include recognition of fat bodies as healthy and capable of carrying a child to term with no major obstetrical concerns. Such a re-articulation was undertaken by one participant, Saavni (South Asian, working class, straight), and as such we close the chapter with her words, reminding us that if we look to the material, to the body, we can see how processes of subjection produced through and undertaken by medicine are never neat, never total, and never complete. Embodiment provides space to resist seemingly totalizing processes of the medicalization of fatness:

> We want a baby. We really want a baby, right? And then, on top of it, you're saying, "Oh by the way, good you want a baby, but it's your fault that you don't have it." That's what it sounds like. ... But, bottom line is this – everybody's different. Like, you know, your body is so different. Bodies react in a different manner. ... I understand if everything could be according to people's desire, then the best would be the skinny. But we aren't. So just work with us, instead of making our lives so difficult.

Note

1 "Obese Class 1" refers to the classification system for obesity as purported by the World Health Organization (WHO, 2018), which relies on Body Mass Index (BMI) to establish an individual as Obese Class 1, 2 or 3 (http://apps.who.int /bmi/index.jsp?introPage=intro_3.html).

References

Adams, S. V., Hastert, T. A., Huang, Y., & Starr, J. R. (2011). No association between maternal pre-pregnancy obesity and risk of hypospadias or cryptorchidism in male newborns. *Birth defects research. Part A, Clinical and molecular teratology, 91*(4), 241. doi:10.1002/bdra.20805

American College of Obstetrics and Gynecologists. (2014). Challenges for Overweight and Obese Women. *Committee Opinion Number 591*.

Ayo, N. (2012). Understanding health promotion in a neoliberal climate and the making of health conscious citizens. *Crit. Public Heath, 22*(1), 99–105. doi:10.1080/ 09581596.2010.520692

Bell, K., Salmon, A., & McNaughton, D. (2011). Alcohol, tobacco, obesity and the new public health. *Crit. Public Heath, 21*(1), 1–8. doi:10.1080/09581596.2010.530642

Beyerlein, A., Nehring, I., Rzehak, P., Heinrich, J., Müller, M. J., Plachta-Danielzik, S., Wabitsch, M., Weck, M., Brenner, H., Rothenbacher, D., von Kries, R. (2012). Gestational weight gain and body mass index in children: Results from three German cohort studies (pregnancy weight gain & childhood body mass index). *PloS one, 7*(3), e33205. doi:10.1371/journal.pone.0033205

Burstein, E., Levy, A., Mazor, M., Wiznitzer, A., & Sheiner, E. (2008). Pregnancy outcome among obese women: A prospective study. *American Journal of Perinatology, 25* (09), 561–566. doi:10.1055/s-0028-1085623

College of Midwives of Manitoba. (2011). Guidelines for providing care for women with high body mass index. Retrived from http://www.midwives.mb.ca/policie s_and_standards/guideline-providing-care-women-w-high-body-mass-index.pdf

Conrad, P. (2007). *The medicalization of society: On the transformation of human conditions into treatable disorders.* Baltimore: Baltimore: Johns Hopkins University Press.

Ellison, J. 2019. *Being fat: Women, weight, and feminist activism in Canada.* Toronto: University of Toronto Press.

Ellison, J., McPhail, D., & Mitchinson, W. (eds.) (2016). *Obesity in Canada: Critical perspectives.* Toronto, Ontario; Buffalo, New York; London, England: University of Toronto Press.

Fee, M. (2006). Racializing narratives: Obesity, diabetes and the "Aboriginal" thrifty genotype. *Social Science & Medicine, 62*(12), 2988–2997. doi:10.1016/j.socscimed.2005.11.062

Fellows, M.L., and Razack, S. (1998). The race to innocence: Confronting hierarchal relations among women. *Gender, Race & Justice, 335,* 335–352.

Fullager, S. (2009). Governing healthy family lifestyles through discourses of risk and responsibility. In J. H. Wright, V. (Ed.), *Biopolitics and the obesity epidemic: Governing bodies* (pp. 108–126). New York: Routledge.

Hinkle, S. N., Sharma, A. J., Swan, D. W., Schieve, L. A., Ramakrishnan, U., & Stein, A. D. (2012). Excess gestational weight gain is associated with child adiposity among mothers with normal and overweight prepregnancy weight status. *The Journal of Nutrition, 142*(10), 1851. doi:10.3945/jn.112.161158

Jette, S. (2006). Fit for two? A critical discourse analysis of Oxygen fitness magazine. *Sociology of Sport Journal, 23*(4), 331. doi:10.1123/ssj.23.4.331

Jette, S., & Rail, G. (2013). Ills from the womb? A critical examination of clinical guidelines for obesity in pregnancy. *Health, 17*(4), 407–421. doi:10.1177/1363459312460702

Khalil, H. S., Saleh, A. M., & Subhani, S. N. (2008). Maternal obesity and neonatal congenital cardiovascular defects. *International Journal of Gynecology & Obstetrics, 102* (3), 232–236. doi:10.1016/j.ijgo.2008.05.005

Kirkland, A. R. (2008). *Fat rights: Dilemmas of difference and personhood.* New York: New York: New York University Press.

Longhurst, R. (2007). *Maternities: Gender, bodies and space.* New York: Routledge.

Lupton, D. (1999a). Introduction: Risk and sociocultural theory. In D. Lupton (Ed.), *Risk and sociocultural theory: New directions and perspectives* (pp. 1–11). Cambridge: Cambridge University Press.

Lupton, D. (1999b). Risk and the ontology of pregnant embodiment. In D. Lupton (Ed.), *Risk and sociocultural theory: New directions and perspectives* (pp. 59–85). Cambridge: Cambridge University Press.

Lupton, D. (2013). *Fat.* New York: Routledge.

McNaughton, D. (2011). From the womb to the tomb: obesity and maternal responsibility. *Critical Public Health, 21*(2), 179–190. doi:10.1080/09581596.2010.523680

McPhail, D. (2016). Indigenous people's encounters with obesity: A conversation with Barry Lavallee. In Ellison, J., McPhail, D. and Mitchinson, W. (eds.), *Obesity in Canada: Critical perspectives,* (pp. 175–186). Toronto, Ontario; Buffalo, New York; London, England: University of Toronto Press.

McPhail, D. (2017). *Contours of the Nation: Making Obesity and Imagining Canada, 1945–1970.* Toronto: University of Toronto Press.

McPhail, D., Bombak, A., Ward, P., & Allison, J. (2016). Wombs at risk, wombs as risk: Fat women's experiences of reproductive care. *Fat Studies, 5*(2), 98–115. doi:10.1080/21604851.2016.1143754

McPhail, D., Chapman, G. E., & Beagan, B. L. (2011). "Too much of that stuff can't be good": Canadian teens, morality, and fast food consumption. *Social Science & Medicine, 73*(2), 301–307. doi:10.1016/j.socscimed.2011.05.022

Murray, S. 2008. *The "fat" female body*. Houndmills, UK: Palgrave Macmillan.

Nash, M. (2012). Weighty matters: Negotiating "fatness" and "in-betweenness" in early pregnancy. *Feminism & Psychology, 22*(3), 307–323. doi:10.1177/0959353512445361

Nyman, V. M. K., Prebensen, Å. K., & Flensner, G. E. M. (2010). Obese women's experiences of encounters with midwives and physicians during pregnancy and childbirth. *Midwifery, 26*(4), 424–429. doi:10.1016/j.midw.2008.10.008

Poudrier, J. (2016). The geneticization of Aboriginal diabetes and obesity: Adding another scene to the story of the thrifty gene. In Ellison, J., McPhail, D. and Mitchinson, W (eds.), *Obesity in Canada: Critical perspectives*, (pp. 89–121). Toronto, Ontario; Buffalo, New York; London, England: University of Toronto Press.

Ode, K. L., Gray, H. L., Ramel, S. E., Georgieff, M. K., & Demerath, E. W. (2012). Decelerated Early Growth in Infants of Overweight and Obese Mothers. *The Journal of Pediatrics, 161*(6), 1028–1034. doi:10.1016/j.jpeds.2012.06.001

Rice, C. (2014). *Becoming Women: The Embodied Self in Image Culture*: Toronto; Buffalo; London: University of Toronto Press.

Rice, C., Harrison, E., & Friedman, M. (2019). Doing justice to intersectionality in research. *Cultural Studies ↔ Critical Methodologies*. https://doi.org/10.1177/1532708619829779.

Rice, C., Pendleton Jiménez, K., Harrison, E., Robinson, M., Rinaldi, J., LaMarre, A., & Andrew, J. (forthcoming). Bodies at the intersection: Reconfiguring intersectionality through queer women's complex embodiments. *Signs: A Journal of Women in Culture and Society*.

Rothblum, E. D., & Solovay, S. (2009). *The Fat Studies Reader*. New York: New York University Press.

Ruhl, L. (1999). Liberal governance and prenatal care: Risk and regulation in pregnancy. *Economy and Society, 28*(1), 95–117. doi:10.1080/03085149900000026

Salmon, A. (2011). Aboriginal mothering, FASD prevention and the contestations of neoliberal citizenship. *Critical Public Health, 21*(2), 165–178. doi:10.1080/09581596.2010.530643

Smith, D., & Lavender, T. (2011). The maternity experience for women with a body mass index > or = 30kg/m2: A meta-synthesis. *BJOG, 118*(7), 779–789. doi:10.1111/j.1471-0528.2011.02924.x

Warin, M., Zivkovic, T., Moore, V., & Davies, M. (2012). Mothers as smoking guns: Fetal overnutrition and the reproduction of obesity. *Feminism & Psychology, 22*(3), 360–375. doi:10.1177/0959353512445359

Weir, L. (2006). *Pregnancy, risk and biopolitics*. London: Routledge.

WHO (Producer). (2018, July 11). Global database on body mass index: An interactive surveillance tool for monitoring nutrition transition. Retrieved from http://apps.who.int/bmi/index.jsp

Winhofer, Y., Tura, A., Thomas, A., Prikoszovich, T., Winzer, C., Pacini, G., Kautzky-Willer, A. (2015). Hidden metabolic disturbances in women with normal glucose tolerance five years after gestational diabetes. *International Journal of Endocrinology, 2015*(2015). doi:10.1155/2015/342938

Part III
Expanding Our Activisms

11 No Bad Fatties Allowed?

Negotiating the Meaning and Power of the Mutable Body

Heather Brown and April M. Herndon

Introduction

People exist within complex constellations of identities and power, and so, too, do our discussions of who can speak with authority within a movement. Like many movements and fields before it, Fat Activism and Fat Studies began as a means of centering the lived experiences of fat people, specifically centering those narratives against the monolithic socio-medical narrative of fatness as inherently unhealthy, flawed, and damaging. Yet, tensions remain about which narratives best counter stigmatizing discourses of fatness and what to do with narratives that may sometimes echo the storylines of suffering or pain that activists and scholars have worked so very hard to counter.

This article aims to work through the important questions of how we assign, vet, and perhaps even control, narratives within the movement for fat justice as it manifests within activist communities and within Fat Studies as a field. We don't seek to establish a strict set of guidelines for determining the legitimacy of any individual's narrative or determine who is and isn't allowed to speak on behalf of fat people, but we do hope to outline the key issues to be raised in such discussions about narrative authority. We argue that if we hope to truly "thicken" our description of fatness/Fat Activism/Fat Studies, we must not disavow or silence voices that are also influenced by experiences of race, sexual assault, trauma, and weight loss surgeries. We must engage with these voices in a way that positions such narratives as learning moments that challenge the movement in the best possible ways.

In the interest of full disclosure, we arrive at the writing of this article from similar yet different places that have both spurred our interest in this subject and given us a particular lens through which to view these questions. As researcher Beatrice Beebe once said, "most research is me-search" (as cited in van der Kolk, 2014, p. 111). Thus, we have taken up this issue, at least in part, because we have lived experiences of fluid bodies and the questions those fluid bodies evoke within our lives, others' lives, and within Fat Studies and Fat Activist communities. We also come to this writing from a point of privilege as two women who identify as white and who haven't had to negotiate the politics of being marginalized via race while we've negotiated the politics of being fat.

Good Fatty or Bad Fatty?

Language is powerful. Fat Studies and Fat Activism acknowledge this when interrogating dominant "obesity" discourse and the use of language within it. For example, Aphramor (2018) calls out the phenomenon of "obgobbing," in which words like "overweight" are used to describe the fat body, reinforcing power hierarchies and harmful stereotypes about fatness through language. Certainly, word choice is one of the core foundations of Fat Studies and Fat Activism (Brown, 2016, 2017; Cooper, 1998; LeBesco, 2004; Wann, 2009). Both Wann (2009) and Cooper (1998) argue that the word "fat" is *the* word to be used when talking about fat people. Not only is using the word "fat" value neutral and descriptive, but it also is a collective and individual reclaiming of the fat body from stigma, shame, and self-hatred (Saguy & Ward, 2011).

Fat Studies scholars and activists enjoy reclaiming language in other ways, such as the reclamation and flipping of the "good fatty" and "bad fatty" labels. Within mainstream discourse, the "good fatty" is one that seeks to conform to neoliberal standards of health and physical appearance (McMichael, 2013; Pausé, 2015). The "good fatty" does not "glorify obesity"; instead, she polices her food choices and works at changing the shape and size of the body. The "bad fatty," by contrast, buys all the cupcakes and eats them, too.

In an effort to reclaim corporeal autonomy and to subvert the idea that bodies ought to "fit" and be policed in particular ways, Fat Activism and Fat Studies suggest we ought to aspire to be the "bad fatty" (although how bad we actually can get is complicated, especially for those with bodies marginalized by race, sexuality, or disability) (Chalkin, 2016; Mollow, 2015). This task also calls into being a certain spurning of the "good fatty" as a troubling figure whose values fall outside the shared community values of Fat Studies and activism. Maor (2013) argues that setting boundaries in social justice movements is important, and, indeed, the "good fatty vs. bad fatty" dichotomy described above is a critical one that challenges how we exist in and relate to our own bodies. However, permanent, inflexible boundaries can create an environment that leads towards an "imperative for singular political identities" (Cooper & Murray, 2012, p. 132). Maor (2013) suggests that fat acceptance groups in a western context actually have started to divide themselves based on a singular political identity that has a "stable, unitary 'resisting' consciousness" (p. 280). One might, therefore, argue that within Fat Activist and Fat Studies arenas the "good fatty" and "bad fatty" types get flipped. "Bad fatties" are, in this context, "not able to fully accept their fat bodies, either by wanting to lose weight or by actually losing weight, [and] are regarded as a threat to the integrity of the movement's political messages of self-acceptance" (Maor, 2013).

An example of how labeling someone as a "bad fatty" within fat communities might play out can be seen in a recent online reaction to Roxane Gay's (2017) *Hunger: A Memoir of (My) Body*. An individual in a Fat Studies Facebook group indicated:

> I haven't read it, but I understand it's problematic in the sense that she attributes her weight to disordered eating, stemming from abuse. This may be true (*or at least, she believes it to be true*) in her case, but of course that stereotype is wrong for most fat people. This book's mainstream acceptance seems to stem at least in part from its conformity to the 'fatness is caused by dietary choices' and 'fat people eat their feelings' myths (emphasis added).

Thus, within the movement, Gay may be considered by some to be a "bad fatty." Yet, Gay herself has no desire to be seen as a "good fatty" within the fat community, at least not in her memoir. Gay (2017) pointedly writes, "This is a book about my body, about my hunger, and ultimately, this is a book about disappearing and being lost and wanting so very much, wanting to be seen and understood" (p. 5). Gay is not identifying herself as a member of the fat acceptance community. She is interrogating the messiness of her own body and her own experiences—a position not entirely surprising from the woman who embraces "the label of bad feminist because I am human. I am messy. I'm not trying to be an example. I am not trying to be perfect. I am not trying to say I have all the answers" (Gay, 2014, p. xi).

This sentiment is echoed in Gay's writing about her recent weight loss surgery: "I worried that people would think I betrayed fat positivity, something I do very much believe in even if I can't always believe in it for myself. I worried that everyone who responded generously to my memoir, *Hunger*, would feel betrayed. I worried I'd be seen as betraying myself" (Gay, 2018). Gay writes honestly about why she had the surgery, noting that "I step outside the safety of my home, I hate how visible I am" and that she knows she lives in a world where despite any achievements she "will always be fat first" (Gay, 2018). In fact, it's that visibility and people responding to it that Gay says finally pushed her to make the decision to undergo the procedure. She writes: "After 15 years of refusing it, I made the decision to get weight-loss surgery on an ordinary day. At home in Lafayette, Indiana, a young man yelled at me to move my fat black ass while I was crossing a grocery store parking lot to my car. It was the last straw" (Gay, 2018).

Gay (2017) screamed out on the page all the pain and messiness and frustrations of her fat, female, black body in a culture that abuses and hates the fat, female, racialized body. There's so much Fat Activists and Fat Studies scholars can learn from her experiences, yet her narrative and her understanding of her own life risk being rejected because they reflect the messiness of human existence rather than an approved political positionality. The notion of accepting one's body as it is doesn't take into account complex factors like race that might also be at play. To ignore Gay's experience of having made a life altering decision, at least in part, because a young man pointed to two of her visible characteristics—fatness and blackness—ignores the constellation of factors around decisions to lose weight.

Who's Allowed in Fat Community?

In many ways, the singular political identity of the resisting "good fatty" serves to establish the boundaries of who belongs in Fat Community, and who is rejected or not allowed to enter. Cooper and Murray (2012) note that while community ought to be about shared identity, it often revolves around a "tacit social contract that depends on insiders, codes of behaviour, non-shifting identities, and Others" (p. 129). This social contract is "frequently problematic and yet I hear from fat activists all the time that community is sacrosanct, the ultimate expression of fat activism" (Cooper & Murray, 2012, p. 129). In other words, there's community and Community. Good, resisting fatties belong to the Community, while bad fatties, who struggle with the shifting realities of body and fat and self-acceptance, might not.

The mutable, fluid, human body proves problematic to a sacrosanct Fat Community delineated by fatness—and a certain way of being a good fatty. The body changes, and the definitions associated with individual and cultural understandings of that body change based on personal context, culture, place, and time (for examples, see Farrell, 2011; Gilman, 2008; Stearns, 2002). Add in race, disability, gender presentation, and other bodily markers, and "belonging" becomes even more complicated. An example of this can be found in a 2016 critique of LeBesco's work on fat activists who are also trans, gender-queer, or fluid. The critique, based on a reporter's short summary of a speech LeBesco gave at a conference, resulted in a calling out of LeBesco's work by dozens of netizens. There was anger that LeBesco equated weight loss with gender confirming surgeries. There was distress that she may have suggested that it is possible to lose weight. There was rejection of individuals pursuing intentional weight loss. There was reaffirmation of the individual's right to do what they pleased with their own body, while still affirming the rights of other individuals not to associate with those who do what they please with their own bodies. Toward the end of the comment thread, one individual wrote: "Katie LeBesco you sound uninformed and inexperienced. I think you should wait until you think clearly before coming to these con-clusions. You've really missed the boat. Your ideas divide unnecessarily and are hurtful" (Karnik, 2016).

LeBesco (arguably one of the founders of Fat Studies as an academic discip-line) is also being positioned as a "bad fatty." Yet, LeBesco was doing noth-ing more than exploring the messy realities of the fat body, the queer body, the trans body from the viewpoint of the people in those bodies—something we say we want in Fat Activism and Fat Studies. The backlash against LeBesco suggests that bad fatties may sometimes be rejected from Community by a "them vs. us" definition that "fails in the face of the messy realities of lived experience" (Throsby & Evans, 2013, p. 335).

If My Body Changes, Am I Allowed to Speak?

For many people, body weight is mutable, and weight loss is possible (whether desired or not)—sometimes for long periods, if not forever. This may partly explain why those who lose weight are sometimes seen as suspect or somehow less than ideal Fat Community members; these people represent the ultimate "bad fatty" since their weight loss and very bodies seem to support mainstream socio-medical narratives about fatness and the ability to lose weight, which is then constructed as a demand to do so.

However, when a person who is fat loses weight, their past experiences as a fat person in the world are not erased. Nor are their current political commitments necessarily rejigged. To suggest this is to value embodiment above all else, which replicates a troubling trend that's often used to question fat people or to relegate the critique of essentialism to the waste bin. Although many fat people report eating what would be considered statistically normal diets, they often aren't believed; their bodies are read as the ultimate evidence of their diets. In the same way, not believing those who have lost weight when they say they are still committed to the cause of Fat Justice or to Fat Studies as a field implies that their bodies are the ultimate evidence of commitment to the cause or lack thereof. In both cases, the body becomes testimony in ways that erase the agency of the person in question, and the interpretation of that body by an outside observer gains precedence over the understandings and agency of the person who is embodied.

The question of who is allowed to speak within the movement becomes further heightened when the weight loss has occurred due to weight loss surgery. Weight loss surgery, which has long been thought of as a kind of mutilation or "stomach amputation" (Longhurst, 2012; Murray 2010; Throsby, 2008; Wann, 1998) within many Fat Activist communities, is often thought of as the ultimate betrayal because it engages with the medicalized narrative that fatness is a disease for which surgery is the cure. However, we are left to wonder if this is a place where Fat Studies and Fat Activism might consider allowing the voice of the weight loss surgery survivor primacy—since it is their understanding of their own experience that we claim to value—rather than the external interpretation of activist, advocate, or researcher. As LeBesco asserts, "Those who intentionally ... change their body size, erasing the line between thin and fat get read as ambitious dieters and sad regainers, dupes of the system. In both cases, observers busy themselves with the ascription of meaning, unconcerned with the self-determination of those whose embodiment they're reading." (2016, p. 52). In short, the personal narratives of those losing weight are overshadowed by witness narratives in order to help support the "good fatty" and "bad fatty" dichotomy.

We would like to be clear here that we are neither advocating for nor promoting dieting or weight loss surgeries. We are, however, suggesting that to co-opt the narratives of people who lose weight, and to possibly oust people from the Fat Community based on weight loss, is something about which we should think carefully. In terms of LeBesco's scholarship and a comparison of weight loss to members of the trans community and body modification that affirms gender, Fat Activists and Fat Studies scholars might do well to adopt what Whitesel and Shuman (2016) note as a "soft opposition" to weight loss surgeries (p. 32). In their study of Girth and Mirthers, a club for "big gay men who are ostracized from the larger gay community because of their size," Whitesel and Shuman found the men they interviewed most often "positioned themselves as personally against bariatric surgery, but tolerant of others who might choose to have it" (pp. 32–33). When interviewing one subject who expresses his own lack of desire for weight loss surgery—even though he might consider rhinoplasty—Whitesel and Schuman note that "his laissez-faire attitude creates a momentary, situated discursive entanglement between tolerance for personal choice and rejection of any practices that stigmatize size" (p. 42). And while this might seem like a tenuous position to hold, this is a position occupied by feminists such as Kathy Davis, who has argued that "feminism and cosmetic surgery are not entirely incompatible. [It] can either be a resource for personal empowerment or an industry that is dominated by an oppressive medical establishment that profits from people's insecurities about their appearance when held up to rigid beauty ideas" (as cited in Whitesel & Shuman, 2016, p. 42).

Davis (1997; 2013) found that while people assumed women who underwent plastic surgery were doing so because they were cultural dupes who had bought into the beauty ideal, many of the women knew that even after surgery they would not be ideal; most of them wanted to take control of their lives after having been through divorces or some other disempowering experience. Modifying their bodies was a way to enact control and feel like they were agents in their lives rather than simply being acted upon. As Whitesel and Shuman (2016) note, choosing weight loss surgery may be a moment when, at least for the Girth and Mirther, "personal authority... can oppose medical authority" (p. 44). In short, the choice of weight loss surgery presents us with a knotty problem when it comes to drawing a line between personal choice and the problematic medicalization of fatness. The "good fatty" and "bad fatty" dichotomy isn't as clear as it appears.

After all, the voices of those who have undergone surgeries, especially people who remain physically fat or even identified as Fat are important sources of information about a host of issues: the different ways they're treated when they're fat versus thin, how the medical establishment talks to people who have had the surgeries, etc. Further, what if engaging in weight loss through dieting—or even surgery—isn't just about the medicalized account of fatness? Continuing to engage with those who intentionally lose weight and allowing them a voice in the community may be especially important if Fat Studies and Fat Activism wish to be truly inclusive and develop a deeper understanding of how different groups of people are affected by fatphobia, fat prejudice, and just the aesthetics of how gendered and racialized bodies are expected to look or how individuals wish to style their own bodies. Allowing these voices into the conversation—and maybe sometimes even centering them—may help to promote an understanding of how, for example, race and class differences do and don't affect people's experiences of being large in a world that privileges thinness. To deny them a voice ignores the very real and oppressive nature of fatphobia that leads to individuals undergoing surgery in the first place. What if, like the Girth and Mirth community, it's about a kind of aesthetics? What if this is the case for folks who identify as trans? What if losing weight is about one's ability to get a job? Buy certain clothes? The ability to be read as one would choose to be read and engaged in the world in keeping with other parts of one's identity? These are all questions to take up alongside criticisms of people who deliberately lose weight if we hope to understand identity as intersectional.

Furthermore, if we harken back to the scholarship of Becky W. Thompson (1994), we know that how women engage with their bodies and eating is deeply influenced by race, class, sexual trauma, and sexual preference. Her work offered a new lens on disordered eating, a field that up to that point had been dominated by explanations that privileged troubled mother-daughter relationships as the primary reasons young women had eating disorders. She did so by conducting interviews with young women of color, poor women, young women who identified as lesbian or queer, and survivors of incest and sexual assault. She listened to their reasons for engaging in disordered eating and found that for many of them it felt like a taking back of control they had lost through dominant power structures that had subjected them to racism, homophobia, and trauma. In short, they took control of their bodies because they were living under oppressive systems that seemed out of reach and controlling food and weight was a means of having some kind of agency in a world that offered them very little agency otherwise. Again, we're not suggesting here that all fatness or thinness is born out of eating patterns. Weight is much more complicated than that. But so are people's reactions to weight and people's decisions about weight and bodies. And so, too, our frameworks should be much more complicated and able to deal with both the power and the nuance of decisions around bodies.

What If I Reject Your Cunning Use of Flags?

In *Dressed to Kill*, comic Eddie Izzard (1998) skewers the first step in the Colonial Playbook, which is to declare ownership of Indigenous lands by planting a colonial flag. Here, we suggest that Fat Studies and Fat Activism engage in a "cunning use of flags" by creating and defending a narrow definition of acceptable fatness that may reject the lived experiences of many fat individuals.

Pushing against narrow notions of acceptable fatness, we may need to find space for those who don't necessarily identify as "fat" or don't like the word and who also have complicated relationships with their bodies and weight. Fat Activists seek to reclaim power over their fat bodies by controlling the use of language. For those individuals who have come out as fat, this empowerment is healing. But we must be conscious of the power differential between our theoretical framework and the individuals with whom they engage with through research. What happens when fat people's interpretations of their own experiences challenge the foundational tenets of fat liberation? What happens when fat individuals participating in research reject the language of "fatness" as harmful or hurtful?

The young women who participated in a research project exploring the experiences of fat women learners in college settings were smart, creative, caring, and also very, very angry (Brown, 2012). The research was designed using a Fat Studies theoretical framework and, therefore, used the word "fat" in advertising, discussion, and interviews. However, the young women in the student actively rejected the word "fat," a word they felt was harmful. "I think it's a really harsh word. I'm not really a fan of that word. Fat is really strong. It's almost like using a racial slur. It's to classify someone as being different from other people in a negative way," said Ann.

These young women knew they were fat. They did not reject their bodies. Some were ashamed of their size but others were not. But they all demanded that they have the right to define their own understanding of their bodies and to use the language they wanted to use. Participants in the study rejected the Fat Studies argument that fat is a positive (or, at worst, neutral word). "I realize in 'fat studies' or whatever, maybe that's what you would call me, but, understand, I feel like that shouldn't be my defining fact, that shouldn't be what everyone thinks of me. I'm a learner! I'm a student! I am NOT my weight. I feel like that is a part of who I am but it's not who I am!" yelled Kari. They exhibited resistance and agency by insisting that their own judgments about their own bodies be taken seriously and respected on their own terms. They demanded that others not impose "meaning onto people's experiences of food and body without considering people's own meanings" (LeBesco, 2004, p. 15).

They demand that we rethink the power dynamic. Who was in control of interpreting their experiences—them or others? Whose interpretation of their experiences should hold power? Should they be allowed to truly speak for themselves, or should we give lip service to their own understandings of their lives and then speak for them with a veneer of fat liberation language that shifts the power from them?

Final Thoughts

The oppression faced by large people is real—regardless of how they personally identify or describe themselves. Some might argue that those who have participated in "bad fatty" behaviors, such as dieting and, especially, weight loss surgeries, have forfeited their ability to speak within the community or for the community. But we would ask for an approach much more like that voiced by Samantha Murray (Cooper & Murray, 2012):

> Fat activism and/or fat scholarship does not (and should not) require one to maintain absolutes. Fat activism and Fat Studies scholarship needs to provide a critical space where debate about the problems attendant on weight loss practices can be included and can productively contribute to counter-discursive strategies – in short, fat activist community space is limiting its own political and ethical potential by silencing those whose experiences are not 'model' examples of what some perceive 'proper' fat activism should look like. ... My concern, then, is not to institute a counter-discourse in fat activism that encourages a slippage into recuperating prescriptive ways of bodily being. I think we can do this by not silencing others, not maintaining a psychic (or concrete) checklist of what 'real' fat activism looks like, not universalising fat experience(s).
>
> (p. 131)

While we don't necessarily have definitive perspectives on these issues or answers to what are tangled questions about agency, medicalization, personal empowerment, and oppressive systems, we do know that these are discussions that need to be had and that in order to "thicken fat" we might need to engage in what philosopher Lisa Heldke (2007) has called "radical listening," listening even when we might not like what we hear.

Perhaps, then, what we're asking for is an accounting of fatness and the experiences of fat people and people within the movement that "thickens" our ability to understand and listen to why people might lose weight or opt to engage in weight loss—even willingly—in a world where fatphobia is admittedly rampant. There is no doubt, of course, that to participate in weight loss efforts and in the medicalization of fatness is thorny and means engaging with a system that has sought to discipline and even eradicate fat people's bodies and fat people. And, yet, people losing weight are not just "fat" and their bodies and identities and social lives exist at complex intersections of power to which we necessarily need to attend.

References

Aphramor, L. (2018). Terms of belonging: Words, weight and ethical autonomy. *Network Health Digest*, 131, 41–45.

Brown, H. (2012). *Fashioning a self from which to thrive: Negotiating size privilege as a fat woman learner at a small liberal arts college in the Midwest* (Doctoral dissertation). Northern Illinois University, DeKalb, IL.

Brown, H. (2016). Fat studies in the field of higher education: Developing a theoretical framework and its implications for research and practice. In E. Carter

& C. Russell (Eds.), *The fat pedagogy reader: Challenging weight-based oppression in education* (pp. 201–209). New York, NY: Peter Lang.

Brown, H. (2017). "There's always stomach on the table and then I gotta write!": Physical space and learning in fat college women. *Fat Studies: An Interdisciplinary Journal of Body Weight and Society, 7*(1), 11–20. doi: 10.1080/21604851.2017.1360665

Chalkin, V. (2016). Obstinate fatties: Fat activism, queer negativity, and the celebration of "obesity". *Subjectivity, 9*(2), 107–125. doi.org/10.1057/sub.2016.3

Cooper, C. (1998) *Fat and proud: The politics of size.* London, UK: Cox & Wyman.

Cooper, C., & Murray, S. (2012). Fat activist community: A conversation piece. *Somatechnics, 2*(1), 127–138. doi: 10.3366/soma.2012.0045

Davis, K. (1997). Cosmetic surgery as feminist utopia? *European Journal of Women's Studies, 4*(1), 23–37.

Davis, K. (2013). *Reshaping the female body: The dilemma of cosmetic surgery.* New York, NY: Routledge.

Farrell, A. E. (2011). *Fat shame: Stigma and the fat body in American culture.* New York, NY: New York University Press.

Gay, R, (2014). *Bad feminist.* New York, NY: HarperPerennial.

Gay, R. (2017). *Hunger: A memoir of (my) body.* New York, NY: HarperCollins.

Gay, R. (2018, April 24). *What fullness is: On getting weight reduction surgery.* Retrieved from https://medium.com/s/unrulybodies/the-body-that-understands-what-fullness -is-f2e40c40cd75

Gilman, S. L. (2008). *Fat: A cultural history of obesity.* Cambridge, UK: Polity Press.

Heldke, L. (2007). The radical potential of listening: A preliminary exploration. *Radical Philosophy Today, 5,* 25–46.

Izzard, E. (1998). Dress to Kill [DVD].

Karnik, L. A. (2016, June 30). Katie LeBesco you sound uninformed … [Facebook comment]. Retrieved from https://www.facebook.com/marilynwann?hc_ref=ARRQJ G A 5 j c T 1 S I u Y L h 9 w W s A s j a - a S s f Y n x W E g F 7Cv136Ebm93H18qQopjxocWA8aiic&fref=nf

LeBesco, K. (2004). *Revolting bodies?: The struggle to redefine fat identity.* Amherst, MA: University of Massachusetts Press.

LeBesco, K. (2016). On fatness and fluidity: A meditation. In C. Pausé, J. Wykes, & S. Murray (Eds.), *Queering fat embodiment* (pp. 49–60). New York, NY: Routledge.

Longhurst, R. (2012). Becoming smaller: Autobiographical spaces of weight loss. *Antipode, 44*(3), 871–888. doi: 10.1111/j.1467-8330.2011.00895.x.

Maor, M. (2013). "Do I still belong here?" The body's boundary work in the Israeli Fat Acceptance Movement. *Social Movement Studies, 12*(3), 280–297. doi: 10.1080/ 14742837.2012.716251

McMichael, L. (2013). *Acceptable prejudice? Fat, rhetoric and social justice.* Nashville, TN: Pearlsong Press.

Mollow, A. (2015). Disability studies gets fat. *Hypatia: A Journal of Feminist Philosophy, 30*(1), 199–216. doi:10.1111/hypa.12126

Murray, S. (2010). Women under/in control? Embodying eating after gastric banding. In S. Vandamme, S. van der Vathorst, & I. Beaufort (Eds.), *Whose weight is it anyway? Essays on ethics and eating* (pp. 43–54). Leuven, Belgium: ACCO.

Pausé, C. (2015). Rebel heart: Performing fatness wrong online. *M/C Journal: A Journal of Media and Culture, 18*(3). Retrieved from http://www.journal.media-culture.org.au /index.php/mcjournal/article/viewArticle/977.

Saguy, A., & Ward, A. (2011). Coming out as fat: Rethinking stigma. *Social Psychology Quarterly*, *74*(1), 53–75. doi: 10.1177/090272511398190

Stearns, P. N. (2002). *Fat history: Bodies and beauty in the modern west.* New York, NY: New York University Press.

Thompson, B. W. (1994). *A hunger so wide and so deep: American women speak out on eating problems.* Minneapolis, MN: University of Minnesota Press.

Throsby, K. (2008). Happy re-birthday: Weight loss surgery and the "new me". *Body & Society*, *14*(1), 117–133. doi: 10.1177/1357034X07087534

Throsby, K., & Evans, B. (2013). "Must I seize every opportunity?" Complicity, confrontation and the problem of researching (anti-) fatness. *Critical Public Health*, *23*(3), 331–344. doi: 10.1080/09581596.2013.802290

van der Kolk, B. (2014). *The body keeps the score: Brain mind and body in the healing of trauma.* New York, NY: Viking.

Wann, M. (1998). *Fat! So?: Because you don't have to apologize for your size!* Berkeley, CA: Ten Speed Press.

Wann, M. (2009). Foreword: Fat studies: An invitation to revolution. In E. Rothblum & S. Solovay (Eds.), *The fat studies reader* (pp. ix–xxv). New York, NY: New York University Press.

Whitesel, J., & Shuman, A. (2016). Discursive entanglements, diffractive readings: Weight-loss-surgery narratives of Girth & Mirthers. *Fat Studies: An Interdisciplinary Journal of Body Weight and Society*, *5*(1), 32–56. doi: 10.1080/21604851.2016.1112146

12 Oppressive Liberation

BBW Bashes and the Affective Rollercoaster

Crystal L. M. Kotow

It's noon on Sunday as I make my way back to Toronto after a weekend spent partying with friends. Fifteen minutes into the ride I begin crying quietly to myself. This outburst of emotion is a consequence of a combination of extreme fatigue and intense hangover. It's likely I haven't eaten enough the last four days, and I certainly haven't slept enough. I find myself longing for the company of my most recent ex one minute and in the next minute, I'm wondering if I'll hear from the person I slept with last night.

This scene is familiar. It's something I experience after every BBW (big beautiful woman) bash weekend. People in the BBW community refer to this phenomenon as "bash blues" – a dramatic low that follows the adrenaline-fueled high of a weekend of uninhibited fun with hundreds of fat people and their admirers. While lack of sleep and the residue of alcohol and drugs in my system contribute to this low, there is always something else happening that can only be described as the utter melancholy associated with returning to the "real world" where my body feels inhibited by size once again.

The BBW community is a network of fat people, admirers, and allies from around the world, and BBW social events serve as spaces of relative body size freedom and fat community building. It is primarily a social scene, and several times each year various BBW groups host "bashes" that last anywhere from three to five days. Some of the more popular bashes, like those held in Las Vegas, host approximately 500 attendees and offer themed parties at night and workshops during the day (e.g. yoga for fat bodies, fat sex education, fat fashion, fatness and mental health). Fat-specific social spaces like bashes offer options for social engagement to those interested in addressing their experiences of social ostracism, shame, and isolation—experiences that often shape the lives of fat people in a society that puts pressure on all of us to either remain thin or to continuously work to achieve thinness (Farrell, 2011). In general, bashes try to be spaces where fat people may be able to relax into their bodies in ways they cannot do in their daily lives. Bashes are promoted as spaces of acceptance for all bodies—where boundless bodies are celebrated.

In February 2017, I undertook autoethnographic research at a BBW bash. I was interested in the affective environment of this bash and its influence on my embodiment. I kept a journal of my experiences, paying attention to how and what I learned about my body by focusing on feelings and emotions and the events that seemingly triggered these affects. My approach to autoethno-graphy reflects my feminist and reflective positioning as a white, queer, and femme fat woman. Theoretical underpinnings of this chapter integrate "freak-ishness," affect, and fat embodiment as central themes through which I analyze my experiences. This chapter begins with an overview of the histor-ical connections of the intersections of fatness and race to freakishness. In the second section, I analyze sexual attraction and sexual objectification within bash spaces, exploring the complexities associated with the construc-tion of fatness as both asexual and over-sexualized and the ways by which bashes intensify these phenomena. Additionally, I consider the potential for bashes to provide attendees with opportunities to have "normal" social experiences that are otherwise tainted by fatphobia in their day-to-day lives. The chapter ends with a section exploring intensified body hierarchies in bash spaces that significantly impact how I feel in and about my body.

Fat-specific social spaces are necessary for escaping the anxiety that accom-panies being fat in public. Overall, this chapter aims to explore what happens when the promise of body freedom is troubled by the reality of power that circulates throughout a space.

Fat as Freakish: The Intersections of Size, Gender, and Race

Stigma associated with fatness feeds social ostracism and shame. Fat bodies are constructed as "freakish," a construction connected to the history of the freak show. Eli Clare (2015) explains that freak shows became big business between the mid-1800s and mid-1900s, writing that many of the "freaks" had agency over their work and shared in profits, unless they were cognitively disabled or brought to the United States from among non-white populations of other nations. This illustrates how freak shows and their financial success relied on racism and ableism.

In his exploration of the place of the freak show in the social construction of fat, specifically, as freakish, Robert Bogdan (1996) confirms that "freakery" was often based on physical attributes, and that "fat people" exhibits used humour by way of exaggeration to attract audiences. Fat people were so common in freak shows that eventually carnivals featured sideshows called "Congresses of Obesity," made up exclusively of fat people. These sideshows "exhibited women dressed in dainty, frilly lace dresses and other trappings of stereotyped petite femininity," (Bogdan, 1996, p. 32). Perhaps one of the most well-known examples of the exploitative display of Black female fat bodies in freak shows is that of Sara Baartman. Baartman was a South African Khoikhoi woman who, due to European colonizers' fascination with her physical make-up—in particular her large buttocks—was exhibited as a freak show attraction in 19th-century Europe. In Baartman's case, commodifica-tion, exploitation, and objectification turned the embodied subject into an objectified body—into a body seen as inherently deserving of violence. As Rosemarie Garland-Thomson (1996) notes, bodies that are visually different, that "stray from what is typical or predictable," by their very presence, "compel explanation, inspire representation, and incite regulation," (p. 1). This fascination and tendency toward regulation especially is taken up by Patricia Hill Collins (2009) who writes of Western science's historical pre-occupation with Black women's genitalia, for instance. As a result of this pre-occupation, violence enacted on Baartman's Black body continued after her death in 1815, when she was dissected and her genitalia and buttocks were placed on display in a museum.

Clare (2015) explains that there was nothing natural about the "freakish-ness" of performers, but that instead, it was the freak show itself that "care-fully construct[ed] an exaggerated divide between 'normal' and Other" (p. 87). Popular culture is rife with modern examples of the way fat bodies con-tinue to be constructed as "freakish," including their representation on reality television programs like *My 600-lb Life, Supersize vs. Superskinny,* and *The Big-gest Loser.* Like the freak show, these types of weight-focused media are like the proverbial train wreck—you can't not look. But in looking, messages about fatness as grotesque, unhealthy, painful, and dirty are reinforced. More significantly, however, weight transformation shows often position fatness as the fault of the individual and therefore as avoidable, promoting the idea that if the subjects featured could muster up some self-control, they could become "normal." Perhaps, instead of fatness being constructed as freakish for the purpose of humour in freak shows, these modern examples of "freaky" fatness are meant to evoke feelings of pity, anger, and disgust, serving neoliberal ends that frame societal problems as individual problems, and self-improvement as something citizens must consistently practice.

In addition to its construction as "freakish," Jeannine Gailey (2014) writes that in terms of visibility, fat is both hypervisible and invisible. She introduces the concept of "hyper(in)visibility," which is defined as a state of being in which "a person is sometimes paid exceptional attention and is sometimes exceptionally overlooked" (Gailey, 2014, p. 7). She contends that this can happen simultaneously, and so often does for fat women whose bodies are hypervisible because of the amount of physical space they take up, while the complexity of their lives is entirely disregarded.

Discussing the historical construction of fatness as "freakish" is meant to further illuminate the necessity of bashes as safer social spaces for a marginalized population. But it is also possible to see bashes as a liberating form of the modern day freak show where exceptional bodies congregate to challenge fatphobic constructions of fatness that serve to dehumanize and degrade fat people. Challenging fatphobia in a cultural climate that thrives on hatred of fatness is indeed "freaky." At bashes, I have experienced my own hyper(in)visibility fading, allowing me to be viewed not only as physically and sexually attractive, but often also as a complex human. To an outsider, however, 500 fat people and their admirers coming together for a week to socialize and build community is, no doubt, "freaky" in a less empowering way. Recently, a YouTuber named Chris Maverick published a video chronicling his experience at a Las Vegas bash he attended in summer 2018. The first 13 minutes of the video are mostly non-offensive, but seem to be invasive of the safer space bashes try to maintain as he films attendees from a distance. In the last four minutes, however, Maverick, in seemingly disgusted wonder, describes one woman's breasts as "a rectangular type thing ... it was just nasty," and her "huge ass muffin top" that made her look like her body had been "sucked right in like a fricken blueberry muffin," (Maverick, 2018). He also comments on one of the men, saying he looks like the type of guy who drives "one of those big ass, white, rape vans," (Maverick, 2018). At the time of this writing, Maverick's video has almost 19,000 views.

Infiltration of bashes by people like Maverick is one way the safety of the spaces is compromised for everyone. But in my time attending bashes, especially those in America, it occurred to me that a subsection of the fat population seemed underrepresented—fat Black women. I wondered about this low turnout. First, between flights, hotel costs, bash passes and food and alcohol, bashes are often expensive to attend. One reason for lower turnout of fat Black women may be due to economic barriers, especially given that Black women in general make less money than white women and other women of colour (Brown, 2012). Research also shows that fat women face economic barriers because of how fatphobia operates in the workplace (Fikkan & Rothblum, 2012). The intersection of fatphobia and racism ensures Black and other racialized fat women face multiple economic barriers to attending bashes. Additionally, I suggest that another significant reason so few racialized women attend bashes in comparison to white women is because of a body hierarchy maintained in the BBW community that marks fat women's bodies that adhere closest to Eurocentric beauty ideals (i.e. white, cis, thin, able-bodied) as most valuable and desirable. While Black women have historically been perceived as hypersexual, fat Black women have specifically been stereotyped via the asexual controlling image of the Mammy and, as was the case with Sara Baartman, fat Black women's bodies are routinely objectified and stripped of autonomy and their ability to make meaning of and for themselves (Collins, 2009; Adia Story, 2010; Shaw, 2005). As a result of Eurocentric beauty ideals, the safer space extended by bashes to fat white women may not extend to fat Black women, playing a role in their conspicuous absence. I explore these ideas further later in the chapter.

Sexual Attraction and Self-Objectification: Sexualizing the Oversexualized Body

Alone in my hotel room, I'm excited and nervous about tonight's event – a roaming room lingerie party where I'll drink wine and meet many people. I give myself two hours to get ready, ensuring I have time to decompress after spending today swimming and socializing. Makeup application is never as precise nor as anxiety-inducing as it is for me during bash weekends. There's a palpable feeling of pressure to perfect winged eyeliner, flawlessly blend face foundation, highlight cheekbones, and sculpt eyebrows that walk the line between intimidating and approachable (I think it's all in the angle of the arch). I finish the look with hot pink lipstick, carefully accentuating my Cupid's bow and note that I'm exhausted before the night has begun. Performing femininity to this degree for an entire weekend differs from my day-to-day beauty regimen: first, I am currently wearing quadruple the number of beauty products on my face; and second, if I weren't, I would feel invisible in this space. I am troubled by the idea that I do this work to ensure I receive a significant level of appearance-based attention from men. I'm even more troubled by how I would feel if I didn't try this hard and received no attention. In fact, I would blame myself for failing to construct a sexy, sensual, and alluring look (a look I rarely care to achieve outside of these events). My self-esteem would suffer. Everything feels different in BBW spaces. My politics are seemingly pliable, and sometimes I feel like I barely recognize myself. The trouble, however, is that I deeply recognize myself in these practices and it shows me that no matter how invested I am in my feminist politics, I still easily succumb to heteropatriarchal ideals of beauty, attraction, self-esteem, and sexuality.

Reflecting on this vignette, the inner conflict is clear. On one hand, I am concerned with re-sexualizing a body that is already read as sexually insatiable. On the other hand, I recognize that BBW social event spaces offer opportunity to play with sexiness and recover my fatness from its other construction as asexual. Feeling sexy and confident and engaging with other bodies in ways that feel good are things that fat people are told they can't be or do by the broader fatphobic society.

Exploring this conflict further, I am interested in my compulsion to perform heightened femininity in bash spaces. Gailey (2012) writes that "[t]he fat female body is frequently not considered to align with the feminine ideal because it symbolizes domination or resistance to idealized femininity and overconsumption," (p. 116). In later work, she explains that fat women's bodies contain both masculine and feminine associations. By taking up space, fat women's bodies exhibit masculine characteristics, while the fleshy, curvy, and soft characteristics of fat women's bodies construct them as ultrafeminine (Gailey, 2014). Significant to note, for Black and other racialized fat women who attend bashes, the work required to perform femininity is amplified by the racism inherent in Eurocentric feminine beauty ideals, which simultaneously requires them to "make up" for fatness *and* race.

Outside of bashes, I am usually the largest person in the room, and whether I'm viewed with disgust or wonder, I am guaranteed to garner significant attention. But at bashes, as one of many fat and superfat women in the room, if I want attention—sexual or otherwise—I work harder to get it. The body/beauty work I feel pressured to do in bash spaces is connected to what Raewyn Connell (1987) calls "emphasized femininity," a concept that refers to the expectation that women must meet normative beauty standards. In general, hyper-feminizing my appearance is fueled by insecurity around my inability to adhere to one of the most valued feminine beauty standards—thinness. This insecurity is intensified in bash spaces, so wearing makeup and dressing "sexy" is work performed to create the most acceptable form of femininity my particular body can achieve—not only to make up for my fatness, but also to set myself apart from the crowd of other fat, feminine bodies. Ultimately, the question I return to when I think about this body work is: as a queer woman who is acutely aware of the insidious nature of heteronormativity and its tendency to shape attraction, why does attention from men still matter so much to me in these spaces?

In addition to Gailey's (2014) discussion of fat bodies exhibiting characteristics that mark them as both masculine and feminine, Carla Rice's (2014) examination of the impact of image society on the embodied experiences of women reveals that, for women, being designated as fat "impose[s] an unfit identity by highlighting their supposed incapacities and unfemininity" (p. 127). This perception of fat as masculine, or "unfeminine" informs the second way I view my participation in the body work it takes to create "sexiness" within BBW spaces—one in which I consider bashes as opportunities to feel attractive in ways unavailable to me in everyday life.

In her work on the cultural politics of emotion, Sara Ahmed (2014) explores emotion not as something that exists within or outside of an individual, but instead suggests that "objects of emotion" circulate in spaces, shaping the surfaces of bodies in different ways. She explains that an object of emotion may evoke a feeling in one person that is different from that evoked in another, describing these objects as "sticky, or saturated with affect, as sites of personal and social tension," (Ahmed, 2014, p. 10). The notion of objects of emotion as sticky, as saturated with affect, and as capable of shaping what bodies can do is useful for my analysis. For instance, each interaction I have at this bash can be taken as an object of emotion. Whether it's a look, compliment, hug, or other such flirtatious gesture, my body is affected—impressed upon, shaped—and emerges as something different from what it was the moment before. In performing femininity to a particular degree, I affect the emotional environment and in turn the emotional environment affects my embodiment in the ways it validates (or doesn't) my fat body. These objects of emotion are saturated with a history of women's investment in patriarchal approval. bell hooks (2002) writes about this phenomenon, explaining that the devaluation of women under patriarchy ensures that women of all sexualities are unable to determine their self-worth and therefore seek to find it in the approval of men. hooks' analysis provides insight into why my desire for men's attraction and approval feels significantly heightened in these relatively heteronormative bash spaces.

Being able to express my sexuality in this way, however, allows me to participate in what I will call "normal" expressions of sexuality. As a white, queer and femme superfat woman, I have access to certain forms of privilege —whiteness and class privilege specifically. My queerness and fatness, however, intersect to ensure that interactions with my world are often coloured by my body being perceived as "too much," as evidence of pathology and gluttony and the various emotionally debilitating associations connected to fatness, especially when it intersects with queerness. When I'm at a BBW event and I have various interactions coded as "normal" by our culture, I gain access to what it feels like to just "be" in my body, much like I expect many (white, able) non-fat people experience daily. I'm not concerned about the space I take up. I'm not worried about whether people view my body as indication of disease or moral deficiency. I don't try to correct my gait, exacerbating pain in order to mask a waddle, nor do I monitor my breathing, allowing myself to breathe heavily if I need to. At these events, I can feel emotionally uninhibited by my body size, and still receive positive, attraction-based attention when I want it.

Body Hierarchies and Self-Perception

There aren't as many people at the hotel tonight, but there's a pool party planned at the private pool. When my friend and I arrive, I immediately notice three men sitting at one end of the room taking in all of the bodies around them. They're attractive and this matters to me. I can tell, because I'm suddenly nervous. About 15 minutes later, a woman walks into the pool room, and all eyes are on her. She's a smaller fat woman and is perfectly proportioned with an hourglass body shape. She's wearing a brown dress that fits tightly against her body and appears to be oblivious to the attention she's getting in this moment. One of the three men I noticed earlier approaches her. I'm overtaken by feeling: I'm envious; I'm questioning why I'm even in this space; and I'm wishing I had a more acceptably fat body that attracted this type of attention. These feelings are unwelcome, negative. I view this woman as a competitor in a competition neither of us signed up for.

Bashes are a microcosm where patriarchal ideals that organize broader society operate even more intensely. A hallmark of the way patriarchy operates as an organizing principle within women's relationships is by putting women into competition with one another, especially for men's attention. This helps to explain some of the envy I was feeling in the vignette above. But there are other factors at play within bash spaces that seem to intensify competition and significantly impact my self-perception and experiences in and of my body. Why do I question my beauty, sexuality, and worth in bash spaces when it rarely, if ever, happens in my regular life? And what does this teach me about my fat body?

My search for meaning made in these moments is illuminated by an understanding of affect offered by Sara Ahmed (2014) and Beverley Skeggs (2010), which posit that affect (the forces that culture codes as emotion) generates meaning. Drawing from Ahmed's (2004) assertion that emotions align individuals with communities, I suggest that the affective experiences shared by fat people are what attract many of us to the BBW community. Making meaning of the complex emotions and affective moments I experience at and after bashes alters how I might navigate future events. Affect theorist Brian Massumi (2015) contends that meaning is produced in every encounter, and that affect is bound up with the lived past of any particular body. How an individual experiences an encounter or an event is intricately tied to their lived experience. In the affective moment—or emotional object—described above, where envy led to shame, these feelings hook into, drum up, and build upon my history of body-based rejection.

Many of the women who attend bashes know fat embodiment well, and this shared experience is made more complex by intersections of race, sexuality, class, and ability. Literature tells us that dating while fat comes with its own unique set of challenges, such as navigating fetishization, dehumanization, being viewed as an "easy target," and being kept a secret (Gailey, 2012). It is therefore likely that at least some of the women who attend bashes have experienced higher levels of rejection and mistreatment by romantic and/or sexual partners than their non-fat counterparts.

Bashes seem to offer a more "normal" social experience in terms of flirting, hooking up, and even going on dates. As it turns out, it's not that normal. Experiences of rejection are heightened *because* bashes are spaces designated *for* fat people and people who are attracted to fat bodies. Experiencing rejection at an event designed specifically to facilitate socializing between fat people and people who admire and find beautiful that very element of fat embodiment that is so often rejected by broader society is often more debilitating than being rejected outside of BBW spaces. If I am rejected in my regular world, fat hatred has conditioned me to blame it on my body size. But if I'm rejected at a bash, it's all too easy to blame it on not having the *proper* proportions, or not being *as* pretty or *as* feminine as other women (and it could also be none of these things).

Importantly—and infuriatingly—within BBW spaces, women's bodies are taken apart, categorized, and slotted into an existing hierarchy that maps to Eurocentric feminine beauty ideals. Alluded to earlier, this body hierarchy positions bottom-heavy and hourglass body shapes as most attractive. While it's true that differently shaped fat bodies are also desired, they are not *as* popular as bodies that simply mimic larger versions of Eurocentric feminine beauty ideals. In fact, I suggest that the body hierarchy in the BBW community is shaped by the sticky residue of racism and fatphobia, inseparable entities rooted in upholding Eurocentric beauty ideals. In his work exploring the interconnectedness of racism and fatphobia, Christopher Forth (2012; 2015) describes the disgust with which European colonizers viewed African, Turkish, Inuit, and Australian Indigenous people's appreciation for fatness. This admiration, especially for fat women, became inseparable from colonizers' views of racialized people as savage and uncivilized. Forth (2012) writes that as far as colonizers were concerned, "any self-respecting European would dismiss [fatness and fat bodies] as unhealthy, unattractive and frankly disgusting," (p. 214). If the ideal fat body in bash spaces is that which fits standards of beauty created and upheld by whiteness, then it stands to reason that the farther a fat body strays from this ideal, the more it is read through the racist lens of fatness as ugly and morally deficient.

Taking the analysis one step further, I suggest that fat body hierarchies persist in the BBW community *because* of stigma associated with liking fat women. The deviancy of the fat admirer is not quite as strong nor easily condemned if the bodies of the fat women he admires closely adhere to Eurocentric feminine beauty ideals, thinness excluded. In other words, for men who are attracted to fat women, there is safety in preferring fat bodies at the top of the body hierarchy.

What all of this means is that in spaces where I should reasonably be able to meet someone who is attracted to my body, I am still at risk of being rejected because my body does not fit what is constructed as most desirable. As a result, I perceive myself as less likely to be found attractive. The consequences of this bring my chapter full circle: the body hierarchy informed by racist and fatphobic beauty ideals strengthens my desire to perform femininity more intensely in order to compete with women positioned at the top of the hierarchy.

Conclusion

A community that organizes around a specific interest or experience cannot avoid attracting members from across the political spectrum. During my time in the BBW scene, I have witnessed attempts to keep BBW online spaces politically neutral. The groups value body positivity—and it is questionable the extent to which body positivity is political or useful at this point (Kessel, 2018)—but anything else of significance is kept at bay to ensure the spaces remain fun and welcoming to as many people as possible. Sometimes I wonder whether I might benefit from investing in this political neutrality, focusing on the ways that I enjoy myself. For instance, future research should analyze fat women's subjectivity and sexual agency at bashes. For me, experiences of sexual agency in bash spaces have involved reveling in attention paid to my body by people who appreciate fatness and know how to work with my fat body sexually. Liberating sexual experiences at bashes certainly impact fat women's embodiment and also provide an entry point for speaking back to the construction of fat women as objects.

A thickened understanding of BBW culture recognizes the culture to be profoundly political because it exists within and in spite of societal structures that firmly and consistently treat fatness as disease, as grotesque, as the worst thing a body can be or become. It is incumbent upon those of us who enjoy BBW social events to question and analyze our affective experiences to determine how to improve them, not only for ourselves, but for anyone else who enters the community with expectations that end up being dashed by the various ways that power operates within it.

References

Adia Story, K. (2010). Racing sex—sexing race: The invention of the black feminine body. In C. Henderson (Ed.) *Imagining the black female body: Reconciling image in print and visual culture.* New York: Palgrave, 23–43.

Ahmed, S. (2004). Affective economies. *Social Text, 22*(2), 117–139.

Ahmed, S. (2014). *The cultural politics of emotion* (Second edition.). Edinburgh University Press.

Bogdan, R. (1996). The social construction of freaks. In R. G. Thomson (Ed.), *Freakery: Cultural spectacles of the extraordinary body*. New York: New York University Press.

Brown, T. (2012). The intersection and accumulation of racial and gender inequality: Black women's wealth trajectories. *Review of Black Political Economy*, *39*(2), 239–258.

Clare, E. (2015). *Exile and pride: Disability, queerness, and liberation*. Duke University Press.

Collins, P.H. (2009). *Black feminist thought: Knowledge, consciousness, and the politics of empowerment*. New York: Routledge.

Connell, R. W. (1987). *Gender and power*. Sydney, Australia: Allen and Unwin.

Farrell, A. E. (2011). *Fat shame: Stigma and the fat body in American culture*. NYU Press.

Fikkan, J. & Rothblum, E. (2012). Is fat a feminist issue? Exploring the gendered nature of weight bias. *Sex Roles*, *66*(9–10), 575–592.

Forth, C. (2012). Fat, desire and disgust in the colonial imagination. *History Workshop Journal*, *73*, 211–239. doi: 10.1093/hwj/dbr016

Forth, C. (2015). On fat and fattening: Agency, materiality and animality in the history of corpulence. *Body Politics*, 51–74.

Gailey, J. A. (2012). Fat shame to fat pride: Fat women's sexual and dating experiences. *Fat Studies*, *1*(1), 114–127. doi:10.1080/21604851.2012.631113

Gailey, J. A. (2014). *The hyper(in)visible fat woman: Weight and gender discourse in contemporary society* (First edition). Palgrave Macmillan.

Garland-Thomson, R. (1996). Introduction: From wonder to error—A genealogy of freak discourse in modernity. In R. G. Thomson (Ed.), *Freakery: Cultural spectacles of the extraordinary body*. New York: New York University Pres.

hooks, b. (2002). *Communion: The female search for love*. New York: HarperCollins Publishers.

Kessel, A. (2018, July 23). The rise of the body neutrality movement: If you're fat, you don't have to hate yourself. *The Guardian*. Retrieved from https://www.theguardian.com/lifeandstyle/2018/jul/23/the-rise-of-the-body-neutrality-movement-if-youre-fat-you-dont-have-to-hate-yourself?fbclid=IwAR0bcNXgqLR9lHY_i1LK0ow9zvfFDDrMxaoLDs8afTsc8oS3VBdJO4S3DEE

Massumi, B. (2015). *Politics of affect*. Polity Press.

Maverick, C. [Chris Maverick]. (2018, August 1). *BBW Bash 2018 Las Vegas Vlog* [Video File]. Retrieved from https://www.youtube.com/watch?v=QX3PgXwaZIo

Rice, C. (2014). *Becoming women: The embodied self in image culture*. University of Toronto Press.

Shaw, A. (2005). The other side of the looking glass: The marginalization of fatness and blackness in the construction of gender identity. *Social Semiotics*, *15*(2), 143–152.

Skeggs, B. (2010). The value of relationships: Affective scenes and emotional performances. *Feminist Legal Studies*, *18*, 29–51.

13 Thick Sistahs and Heavy Disprivilege

Black Women, Intersectionality, and Weight Stigma

E-K. Daufin

Black girls (and women) don't get some kind of "Get-Out-of-Weight-Stigma-Free" card. Contrary to popular belief, especially among many White people, weight stigma exists in the Black community and harms fat Black women wherever we may be (Daufin, 2015, 2016). As a visibly identifiable, higher weight African American woman who is a Health At Every Size (HAES) expert, Fat Studies scholar, and fat liberation activist, I spend much of my time negotiating weight stigma in the White community *and* communities of colour, including African American spaces.

I also spend a lot of time, and experience considerable heartache, convincing White people, "even" many White Fat Studies scholars, that weight stigma exists in Black communities. Popular media representations of fat Black women may provide some justification for these misunderstandings. The increasingly powerful and pervasive media representation of the happy, fat, bossy, Black woman may convince even many fat Black women that they themselves are just lazy overeaters who deserve weight stigma. They sometimes simultaneously join the chorus that weight stigma does not exist for Black women, *contrary to their own experiences*. This chapter uses media representation and intersectional critical theory with an applied autoethnographic focus to explore the disprivilege of women at the intersection of fat, Black, and female.

Intersectional Hurdles for Fat Female Sisters Seeking Social Justice

In *Intersectionality*, Patricia Hill Collins and Sirma Bilge (2016) identify interconnected domains of power: interpersonal, disciplinary, structural, and cultural. Black women and girls are affected by weight stigma and experience painful exclusions from those who have thin privilege in all these domains.

Interpersonal

Black girls experience interpersonal fat stigma from strangers, friends, potential mates, doctors, teachers, community members, and their families, even if those others are fat themselves. I grew up in New York City, where no one can ever be "too thin or too rich." My working class Black family had Southern roots. Though Black women of the South tend to be fatter than their Northern sisters (Gillum, 1987), that doesn't mean I experienced less fat stigma from my family. My mother was an undiagnosed bulimic who prized the thinness of her youth and put me on a weight loss diet when I was five years old. She did not acknowledge that some bodies are just designed to be bigger and that diets make us fatter, as neuroscientist Sandra Aamodt confirms (Fain, 2016).

The younger you start dieting, the fatter you are likely to get. My family considered my fat body an embarrassment to them and proof that I was a worthless, unattractive excuse for a girl. Black girls experiencing fat stigma in their families is common. After speaking on the first Fat Acceptance panel in the history of the University of Alabama, Birmingham's medicalized campus, in February 2018, a thin, young, Black male audience member asked if Black girls and their families had more important challenges to be concerned about than their daughters' fatness. The other Black panelist, Doula Melodi Stone, immediately and adamantly responded that Black families deal with all those other oppressions *and* hate their daughters' fat bodies.

Disciplinary

In the United States, Black girls are 50% more likely to be fat than their non-Hispanic White counterparts (Office of Minority Health, 2017). Black girls are also 500% more likely to be disciplined more frequently and harshly. They are more likely to be considered as less innocent and less worthy, or in need, of protection than non-Hispanic White girls (Crenshaw, 2015). In 2002, 82% of Black women were so-called overweight and higher, as were 60% of White women (CDC, 2002). More recent race/gender data only includes the highest weights (obese), showing Black women at 55% and White women at 38% (National Center for Health Statistics, 2018). Fat Black women suffer from a toxic intersectional combination of hypervisibility (when one needs someone to blame for a bad outcome) and invisibility (when it comes to inclusion in sharing the good) (Mowatt, French & Malebranche, 2013).

Structural

Prevalent use of the non-intersectional term "women and minorities" in research and popular parlance often leads scholars and the public to (largely unconsciously) perpetuate and exacerbate White supremacist and patriarchal assumptions (Daufin, 2017). Ironically, most knowledge about the inequities of "women and racial minorities" doesn't clearly include people who are *both* women *and* racial minorities. Research report statements such as: "*x* improved for women but not for minorities," reinforces the malignant stereotype that only White women are "true" women. It simultaneously allows people to assume that racial minority women are more privileged than minority men, and/or White women, which is rarely, if ever, the case.

African American women have long faced the problem of how their needs simply fall through the cracks of anti-racist social movements and feminism (Hill Collins & Bilge, 2016). Anti-racist movements focus on *men* of color and feminism on *White* women. Anthems of self-acceptance and body positivity of largely White fat activists disavow experiences of shame tied to bodily race and disadvantage (Cooper, 2016).

If research on women doesn't include enough, or any, Black women or other women of color in gender questions, then the authors and media reporters should state that study findings focus only on *White* women. If populations in race studies do not include enough or any Black women or other women of colour, then the authors of those studies should report that their work is only about *men* of colour. Imprecise and often inaccurate language ("women and minorities") leads many people of all races to believe the White supremacist and patriarchal fallacies that Black women have all the unearned privileges of White women but don't suffer the sexism that White women do, and/or don't suffer racial disprivilege as Black men do (Daufin, 2017).

Too few studies and social justice movements deal with the race and gender intersectionality of Black women. Virtually no studies or movements look at the intersections of race, gender, *and* fatness. Instead, studies and media reporting of them often compare weight stigma to racial stigma, as if there were no people of colour living in the crossroads of the two (e.g., Puhl, Andreyeva & Brownell, 2008).

Researchers who *do* look at weight stigma and African American girls and women often assume that Black women and girls will experience weight stigma in the exact same ways as White ones do. They often don't consider intersectional, internalized oppression and social context. Also, the few studies on fat Black women that have been conducted don't include the intersectionality of Black Hispanic fat women and girls who represent a large and growing demographic.

Of relatively few studies that look at Black women, most neglect to account for the fact that 82% of us are at higher weights (so-called overweight or obese) whereas fewer than 64% of non-Hispanic White women are at higher weights (CDC, 2017). Black women seeking to lose weight usually aspire to a fatter goal than do White women. This goal weight difference is erroneously and often used as a measure of Black women's and girls' so-called greater body positivity and lack of experiences of weight stigma (Averett & Korenman, 1999; Hendley & Zhao, 2011). In fact, this difference is merely a reflection of Black women's overall higher weight status. Also, though long-term weight loss is unsustainable for all but the smallest percentage of people, many Black women lose less weight, and more slowly, even initially, while following the same weight loss diet and exercise regimes as White women (Delaney, Jakicic, Lowery, Hames, Kelley & Goodpaster, 2014). For African American women, the genetic propensity for higher weight and lower metabolism may be, in part or in whole, a result of our ancestors' bodies' adaptation to performing arduous physical and emotional labour, with little food and under extreme stress and emotional and physical distress, during the centuries-long American slave and breeding industry heyday (Daufin, 2015).

Health At Every Size proponents champion the fact that health is not equal to thinness and health itself is a relative goal that most human beings cannot reach or sustain as they age (Burgard, 2009). A fat Black woman's imagined goal weight of a size 8 is no more safely, sustainably, or even possibly obtainable than a fat, White woman's goal weight of a size 2 (Daufin, 2015). That difference in the sizes to which different groups of women might aspire should not be mistaken for greater body esteem or less weight stigma. This is a problematic limitation for White scholars and activists, both fat and thin, as well as for virtually all thin, Black scholars/race activists and even some of the fat Black ones, too. In my experience and research, there is no shortage of weight stigma in Black communities, especially among thin Black people.

For example, a thin Black woman who had sought my help to gain an adjunct position in my department had no problem sending me condescending, ridiculing, fat stigmatizing emails when I suggested to her that fatness is not necessarily a result of overeating and under exercising. This came up after she made the unsolicited suggestion that I join her running club to end my fatness, rather than write more articles about weight stigma and Black women.

Fat stigma is perpetrated in higher education in other ways. For over two decades, over 85% of my students at an Historically Black University were African American, usually more than half of them female and upperclassmen. All African American students readily accepted being Black as a powerful, disprivileged, immutable identity, especially for men. Yet many predictably regurgitated the sexism and fatphobia that they had learned from Black communities when discussing the disprivilege of female gender and race, much less higher weight. The number of higher weight students in my classes ranged roughly from 0% to 20%.

Virtually all my fat Black female students privately expressed their gratefulness that someone was talking about fatness as an oppressed identity rather than a personal, mutable character flaw. Their very presence made teaching about the interpersonal and intrapersonal media impacts on fat Black women easier because other students generally did not want to hurt their classmates' feelings. When the fat students were absent, the task was harder as the Black students were especially reticent about recognizing their thin privilege. Some thinner Black students felt free to publicly and in class use my size to disparage me, up to and including one thin man who repeatedly screamed at me from just inside his dorm window, "Dr. D(aufin)—*fatass!*"

Cultural

The three classical media stereotypes of Black women are Mammy, Sapphire, and Jezebel (West, 2017). Sapphire is the castrating (of Black men in general and her husband in particular) spitfire, and Jezebel is the amoral, seductress nymphomaniac. Both Sapphire and Jezebel stereotypes are damaging but they typically present as thinner (with perhaps disproportionately large sexual characteristics of breasts/buttocks/thighs). The Mammy stereotype began first as a justification for slavery, later for segregationist policies, and now for the oppression of fat Black women. The Mammy is a higher weight Black woman, usually dark skinned and supposedly asexual, who happily serves all the domestic needs (emotional and physical) of a White family with apparently no family bonds or responsibilities of her own. Though she is a work horse, ironically it is assumed that the Mammy got and stays fat by eating too much soul food and not getting enough exercise. Fat Black women are less likely to have a support system, more likely to be the single head of household, and more likely than any other race/gender category, perhaps by virtue of the Mammy stereotype, to be expected to happily care for others (Harris-Perry, 2011). Though many of these stereotypes find fertile ground in the United States or North America, discrimination against fat Black women is not confined to nations of North America and Europe (Hill Collins & Bilge, 2016). International export of US popular culture spreads fatphobic, mysogynoir stereotypes globally.

The Mammy stereotype can be a hurdle in academic publishing. For example, of the three Black female editors of a book on Black culture to which I was contributing, two were thin and one was fat. At every stage of manuscript development, the two thin Black women wanted to reject my chapter on HAES. Even the fat Black woman who championed the inclusion of my work defended to me the notion that fat Black women don't face weight stigma, *not* based on her own research *or* personal experience (both rife with weight stigma) but based on a sassy Black woman in the reality show, *Atlanta Housewives*, who made no apologies for being fat. Reality shows are only real in that they don't pay actors guild scale, or real writers to script the forced scenes they set up but rather foist that job upon underpaid producers (Nededog, 2016). This brilliant, beautiful, hardworking, fat Black woman book editor, professor, and professional leader knows that. Additional fat stigma came from the two thin Black book series editors, one male and one female, who kept changing my affirmative fat sentences to negative ones, repeatedly "thinking (I'd) made (the same) typos."

Internalized oppression occurs when members of an oppressed group believe and act out stereotypes created about their own group (Community Tool Box, 2018). Intersectional identities allow for intersectional internalized oppression too. Therefore, it should not surprise anyone that even fat Black women sometimes believe and reinforce negative stereotypes about themselves *and other* fat Black women (as do fat White women who internalize fat stigma).

My own fat body esteem is hard won and requires daily reinforcement as I did not grow up with it and I am exposed to daily disparagement that is mediated interpersonally and structurally. Many White women who have seen me defend myself against race stigma from other White Fat Studies scholars and HAES proponents assume it does not bother me because I do not break down crying in front of them but save that for a safer, private space (Lawrence, 2018). That seems to make them feel they do not have to publicly defend me against their White colleagues or spend any time comforting me, even if they normally would be so inclined. Then again, Harvard-trained anthropologist Jason Silverstein notes that White supremacy allows people of all races to believe that Black people feel less pain than White people, which affects the poor treatment of people of colour socially and even in the prescription of insufficient pain medicine from healthcare providers (NPR, 2013).

Media

James W. Potter effectively argues in *Media Effects* (2012) that pervasive, overwhelming, repetitive multimedia exposure teaches us more about how to behave, and what to think and feel, than any other force. This influence is rarely direct but is incredibly powerful (hooks, 1992; Potter, 2012). It takes place whether media practitioners intend to teach, or merely entertain, and whether we intend to be "taught." All but the most isolated populations are exposed to some form of media. Over half of the world's population has Internet access. In North America 70% and in the US 81% of the population has at least one social media account (Statista, 2018).

Some media effect scholars argue that other people, whether in person or through social media, are the greater influence over public opinion, interpersonal, political, and social behaviour and identity, than the media themselves (Chowdhary, 2018). However, these human influencers are also profoundly affected by the media, which colours their influence on others. So either way, whether consciously or unintentionally, media representation in content and advertising grossly informs how we behave, what we think about, and how we treat ourselves and others. Thus media justice is an integral part of social justice because of the huge intersectional media influence. Like the rising temperature of the water in the slowly warming pot in which we "frogs" sit, media influence goes unnoticed until it is too late to leap out. Unlike the frog in the pot metaphor, there is virtually nowhere to leap.

Some White female Fat Studies scholars (yet another one during the editing of this chapter) have argued with me that they believe fat Black women face no weight stigma based solely on the existence of the rapper, TV show host and actress Queen Latifah (Dana Owens), popularized in the sitcom *Living Single*. This US TV program aired for five seasons on the Fox network from 1993 through 1997 (IMDB, 2018). To begin with, we need to remind ourselves that media stories, even documentaries (which *Living Single* was not) are consciously constructed narratives, based on often unconscious White supremacy, patriarchy, classism, and consumerism (hooks, 1992).

Concerning race, it was indeed delightful to see six Black people as principal characters in *Living Single*, rather than as the lone Black sidekick character, temporary sub-character, or inconsequential extra, as is the case in most television series produced outside of the sub-Saharan African continent. Indeed the more commercially popular sitcom *Friends* appropriated and "Whitened up" the *Living Single* storyline one year later and ran twice as long (Mock, 2017). The all-Black *Living Single* cast also allowed White viewers to mistakenly believe the fantasy that the show allowed them a realistic view of Black life that was foreign to them; thus the White Fat Studies scholars' vehemence that they knew more about the fat Black female experience from watching the show than did I who lives the life and researches the rigmarole.

Concerning gender in *Living Single*, the two thin Black men lived upstairs "above" the women and were thus conceptualized, some media scholars would argue, as superior to the women living below. The women of the show were relatively light skinned except for the actress who played the character Maxine. All had their natural kinky hair usually straightened or covered with wigs (though sometimes braided), except for Maxine, whose hair was always in a natural style. As a fat, Black, kinky haired, female, Fat Studies, media scholar, I found the most liberating representation to be about appetite. Most media tropes have Black fat women as bossy, voracious, weight loss losers (see the main characters in the films *Narberth, Precious*, and even *Fat Girlz*, to name only a few). However, the darkest skinned, most naturally kinky haired, *thinnest* Maxine was portrayed as the one obsessed with food, not Queen Latifah's fatter character, Kadijah. Though this representation further stigmatized the darkest and most kinky haired Black woman character, I was glad that for once it was at least *not* related to a woman of higher weight, as is constantly represented in the media and enacted upon me in my life.

The lack of the fat-girl-always-eating trope and the fat-girl-self-loathing trope (Lawrence, 2018) may have also misled White audiences unaware of their reliance on media representation as reality, to believe there is no weight stigma in Black America. Also, especially for Black women, Latifah was and is only moderately fat. Even by the standards of the predominately White NAAFA (National Association to Advance Size Acceptance), Latifa is a "mid-size" rather than a "supersize" fat. Still, to see Queen Latifah as an exemplar of, or argument for, the idea that real Black women enjoy weight stigma-free lives requires some White-privileged selective perception. As a Cover Girl spokesmodel, Latifah is constantly made to appear thinner through multiple media techniques including make-up, camera angles, digital manipulation, clothing, staging, lighting, etc. And as a Jenny Craig spokeswoman, she has endorsed intentional weight loss, not fat esteem. White-privileged selective perception also ignores the two episodes (at least) of *Living Single* that explore how weight stigma negatively affects Kadijah's ability to find straight, Black males who want to date her.

Kadijah often fit the comfortable (for White consumption) classical Black female media stereotype of Mammy (Prater, 2004)—the fat, jovial servant who is also very strong and assertive (Bogle, 2001). A selfless woman who is happy to be the servant of others is less intimidating to White viewers. Granted, Kadijah was what the Black community calls a "good race woman," more preoccupied with uplifting the race than with personal fulfillment. She was also an entrepreneur rather than a maid, serving mostly other Black characters rather than White employers. However, the emotional labor is still the same (Hochschild, 2012).

Fat Studies as a White Space

Sometimes White people tell me they believe Black women face no weight stigma because some sassy Mammy type of reality TV, or real-life Black woman said so, as in the reality TV character of the fat, Black female book editor example. They also don't see many Black women in fat acceptance advocacy circles. In addition to internalized oppression, despite the weight stigma we may face, many Black women experience other impediments to adopting a size acceptance stance, much less joining the size acceptance movement (Daufin, 2016). I outline five myths that create these impediments in *The Politics of Size* (2016). Included are the non-intersectional notions that racism is the primary or only oppression Black women have to confront in mainstream society; that Black women don't face weight discrimination in the Black community; and that issues of fat acceptance and sizeism are narrow, apolitical concerns that diminish the "more important" concern of racism.

In a study of collegiate journalism faculty (Daufin, 2001), women of colour were often the only female faculty at all, and their only colleagues of colour were *men*. Compared to men of colour, women experienced such disprivilege that they often volunteered that they identified sexism as a greater factor than racism in their job dissatisfaction (Daufin, 2001). However, those women didn't really know if *White* women would experience the same type of disprivilege as they did in the department.

White fat women in fat activist movements notice fat discrimination because they see clearly that thin White women in similar situations enjoy privileges that fat White women do not. White people and Black men have posed to me and other Black women the *non*-intersectional question of whether we are more oppressed by our gender or our race. The problem with this question is that when one is at the intersections of oppressed identities, absent the context of the treatment of others with the exact same intersection of gender, weight, race, and all its signifiers (skin colour, kinkiness of hair, etc.), rarely can one pinpoint which of the oppressed identities is being targeted. One thing is clear: the fat Black woman is more likely to be on the disprivileged end of the stick than those more privileged at *each* intersection.

Conclusion

Using media representation as well as intersectional critical theory, with an applied autoethnographic focus, this chapter explored the disprivilege of women at the intersection of fat, Black, and female. I examined how Black women and girls face fat stigma and social injustice on interpersonal (familial), disciplinary (in the educational and criminal justice systems), structural (language and research), and cultural (media representations and effects, and publishing) levels. Using intersectional media literacy examples, particularly those using the actress Dana Elaine Owens/Queen Latifah in the television series *Living Single*, and analyzing their effects on audiences, I have illuminated some of the reasons why Fat Studies is still predominantly a White space. Internalized oppression plays a part in why some fat, Black women may deny experiencing weight stigma. These examples display the need for more truly intersectional research, clarifying whether subject groups and results are based on White women, or racial minority men or women of colour, and a greater consideration that weight stigma may present differently in some ways, but no less importantly for Black fat women and girls.

References

Adams, T., & Fuller, D. (2006). The words have changed but the ideology remains the same: Misogynistic lyrics in rap music. *Journal of Black Studies*, *6*, 938–957.

Averett, S., & Korenman, S. (1999). Black-White differences in social and economic consequences of obesity. *International Journal of Obesity Related Metabolism Disorders*, *23*(2), 166–173.

Bogle, D. (2001). *Toms, coons, mulattoes, mammies, and bucks: An interpretive history of Blacks in American films.* New York: Continuum.

Burgard, D. (2009). What is "Health At Every Size"? In E. Rothblum & S. Solovay (Eds.), *The fat studies reader* (pp. 42–49). New York: New York University Press.

Centers for Disease Control and Prevention (CDC). (2002). National Center for Health Statistics: National health and nutrition examination survey. Health, United States, 2002. Retrieved from http://www.umich.edu/~ac213/student_projects05/la/obesity.html

Centers for Disease Control and Prevention (CDC). (2017). Health United States, 2016. Table 58. Retrieved from http://www.cdc.gov/nchs/data/hus/hus16.pdf

Chowdhary, M. (2018). Three ways to determine if an influencer's impact is real or fake. *Adweek.* Retrieved from https://www.adweek.com/brand-marketing/3-ways-to-determine-if-an-influencers-impact-is-real-or-fake/

Community Tool Box. (2018). Healing from the effects of internalized oppression. Lawrence: University of Kansas Center for Community, Health and Development. Retrieved from https://ctb.ku.edu/en

Cooper, C. (2016). *Fat activism: A radical social movement.* Bristol: HammerOn Press.

Crenshaw, K. (2015). *BlackGirlsMatter: Pushed out, overpoliced and underprotected.* New York: African America Policy Forum Center for Intersectionality and Social Policy Studies.

Daufin, E. (2001). Minority faculty job experience, expectations and satisfaction. *Journalism & Mass Communication Educator*, *56*(1), 18–30.

Daufin, E. (2015). Big, Black, beautiful and healthy at every size. In V. Berry, A. Fleming-Rife & A. Dayo (Eds.), *Black culture and experience: Contemporary issues* (pp. 115–130). New York: Peter Lang Publishing.

Daufin, E. (2016). Black women in fat activism. In R. Chastain (Ed.), *The Politics of size: Perspectives from the fat acceptance movement* (pp. 163–186). Santa Barbara: Praeger Publishers.

Daufin, E. (2017). The problem with the phrase "women and minorities": Racism and sexism intersectionality for Black women faculty. In K. Cole & H. Hassel (Eds.), *Surviving sexism in academia: Strategies for feminist leadership* (pp. 52–68). New York: Routledge.

Delaney, J. P., Jakicic, J. M., Lowery, J. B., Hames, K. C., Kelley, D. E., & Goodpaster, B. H. (2014). African American women exhibit similar adherence to intervention but lose less weight due to lower energy requirements. *International Journal of Obesity, 38*(9), 1147–1152.

Fain, J. (2016, June 7). A neuroscientist tackles, "why diets make us fat." *The Week's Best Stories NPR Books*. Retrieved from https://www.npr.org/sections/thesalt/2016/06/07/481094825/a-neuroscientist-tackles-why-diets-make-us-fat

Gillum, R. F. (1987). Overweight and obesity in Black women: A review of published data from the National Center for Health Statistics. *Journal of the National Medical Association, 79*(8), 865–871.

Harris-Perry, M. (2011) *Sister citizen: Shame, stereotypes, and Black women in America.* New Haven: Yale University Press.

Hendley, Y., & Zhao, L. (2011). Differences in weight perception among Blacks and Whites. *Journal of Women's Health, 20*(12), 1805–1811.

Hill Collins, P., & Bilge S. (2016). *Intersectionality*. Cambridge: Polity Press.

Hochschild, A. R. (2012). *The managed heart*. Berkeley: University of California Press.

hooks, b. (1992). *Black looks: Race and representation*. Boston: Southend Press.

Imdb.com, Inc. (2018). Living Single (TV Series 1993–1998). Retrieved from https://www.imdb.com/title/tt0106056/?ref_=ttfc_ql

Lawrence, B. (2018, August 22). In the age of body positivity, why is it so hard to imagine fat girls as more than sad & alone? *Black Youth Project*. Retrieved from http://blackyouthproject.com/in-the-age-of-body-positivity-why-is-it-so-hard-to-imagine-fat-girls-as-more-than-sad-alone/

Mock, B. (2017, January 18). The gentrification of city-based sitcoms. *City Lab*. Retrieved from https://www.citylab.com/life/2017/01/the-gentrification-of-city-based-sitcoms/513302/

Mowatt, R., French, B., & Malebranche, D. (2013). Black/Female/Body hypervisibility and invisibility. *Journal of Leisure Research, 45*(5), 644–660.

National Center for Health Statistics (2018). Age-adjusted prevalence of obesity among U.S. adults ages 20 and over, by sex and race and Hispanic origin. *National Health and Nutrition Examination Survey, 2015–2016*. Retrieved from https://stateofobesity.org/obesity-rates-trends-overview/

Nededog, J. (2016, June 7). Here's how reality TV shows get away with paying people nothing. *Business Insider*. Retrieved from: https://www.businessinsider.com/reality-tv-shows-pay-nothing-2016-6

National Public Radio (NPR). (2013, July 11). Study: Whites think Black people feel less pain. *Tell Me More*. Retrieved from https://www.npr.org/templates/story/story.php?storyId=201128359

Office of Minority Health: U.S. Department of Health & Human Services. (2017). Obesity and African Americans. Retrieved from https://minorityhealth.hhs.gov/omh/browse.aspx?lvl=4&lvlid=25

Potter, W. J. (2012). *Media effects*. Los Angeles: SAGE Publications.

Prater, A.D. (2004). An African American cultural critique of weight, race, gender and class using semiotic analysis of Queen Latifah's film roles. *Master's Theses 647.* Retrieved from http://scholarworks.wmich.edu/masters_theses/647

Puhl, R., Andreyeva T., & Brownell, K. (2008). Perceptions of weight discrimination: Prevalence and comparison to race and gender discrimination in America. *International Journal of Obesity (London)*, *32*(6), 992–1000.

Statista (2018). *Social media usage worldwide.* New York: Statista. Retrieved from https://www.statista.com/statistics/273476/percentage-of-us-population-with-a-social-network-profile/

West, C. (2017, October). Mammy, Sapphire, Jezebel, the bad girls of reality television: Media representations of Black women. Retrieved from https://www.researchgate.net/publication/320726561_Mammy_Sapphire_Jezebel_and_the_Bad_Girls_of_Reality_Television_Media_Representations_of_Black_Women/

14 Photographing Fatness

Resisting Assimilation Through Fat Activist Calendars

Rachel Alpha Johnston Hurst

Introduction

Photography is a site of ongoing objectification and dehumanization of fat people, and many fat artists and activists contest and reclaim the medium in their work to redefine fatness. Fat Studies scholars aptly critique the "headless fatty" photograph – depicting a portion of a fat person's body, typically as an embellishment for a news article related to "obesity" – as positioning fat people as abject failures, incapable of overcoming the burden of embodiment (Cooper, 2007).[1] The "before" photograph is the other common photographic representation of fatness, redeemed through its "after" counterpart, which triumphs over unruly embodiment through weight loss. A wide range of photographic counter-practices emerge to challenge these visual narratives of dehumanization and create new representations.

This chapter asks critical questions about the effects of photographic representation for fat activism, which is not always liberating from an intersectional perspective. Beginning with an overview of visual culture analysis in Fat Studies, I provide an in-depth inquiry into two fat activist calendars, separated by almost 35 years – the Seattle Fat Avengers' *Images of Our Flesh: 1983 Calendar for Lesbians Only* and Substantia Jones' *The Adipositivity Project 2017* calendar. A comparative analysis of these calendars is valuable for intersectional Fat Studies because it can reveal the pitfalls and the possibilities of deploying photography as a medium to combat fat oppression. Through an examination of the calendars, I argue that radical possibilities exist in fat activist photographic work that endeavours to dislodge the viewer's identifications based on cultural ideals and their own image of their body by facilitating a look that originates from a position other than the viewer.

A comparative analysis is useful for examining how intersectionality is mobilized within fat activist photography in two significant historical moments: the 1980s, when intersectionality crystallises into a conceptual resource, and the present, when intersectionality enters into popular discourse. I maintain that there is a radical kernel of intersectional possibility to disrupt normativity in photographing fatness, precisely because this practice fixes fat in time and does not aspire to a thin future (for other ways of re-thinking fat temporality, see Lind et al., 2017).

By resisting the normative command for fat people to envision themselves as temporarily fat – a central way that fat bodies are disciplined – the photographic practices in these calendars open up possibilities to resist other ways that bodies are repudiated through modalities of domination. As ordinary, quotidian objects that are displayed in the private space of the home and potentially public spaces like queer and feminist organizations, fat activist calendars hold potential for interventions at the level of "micro fat activism," defined by Cooper as small acts of resistance to oppression that engage others at the individual level and that are often conversational in nature (2016, pp. 78–85).

Fat Studies scholars have analysed visual representations of fat in popular culture, education, and public health, yet Snider comments that the realms of fine art and visual culture are comparatively ignored and "unexplored areas in fat studies" (2012, p. 13). Women, especially queer, lesbian, and bisexual women, have made substantial contributions to the field of fat activist art, including photography (see Cooper, 2016; Snider, 2009; Snider, 2010a; Snider, 2010b). Kargbo argues that contemporary fat activists are drawn toward the photograph as a place for fat to be "reimagined," particularly online, which marks a shift from earlier text-based representations (2013, pp. 163–4). The promise of photographic images for fat artists and activists creates a space to challenge fat prejudice, rehumanize fatness, and celebrate fat bodies (Gurrieri, 2013); disrupt stereotypes (Gurrieri, 2013; Kargbo, 2013; Snider, 2010a); and interact with viewers in online environments (Lupton, 2017).

However, as Cooper (2016), LeBesco (2004), and Sastre (2014) caution, image work carries the risk of validating fatness through assimilation and acceptance of other dominant ideals. Sastre singles out the online body positivity movement as "readily becom[ing] mimetic of the very norms they seek to counter" (2014, p. 931). Here Sastre is critical of those interventions that represent fatness as worthy by aligning fat bodies with prevailing ideals of beauty, ability, whiteness, class, heteronormativity, and femininity. Interventions that reinforce dominant ideals are inadequate because they fail to consider how devaluing fatness is a process interlocked with other forms of oppression. Such strategies aim to increase access to relations of power and oppression for fat people, which results in new ways of disciplining fatness and reinforcing normativity. For these reasons, Fat Studies scholars have looked to transgressive artistic practices that subvert the pathologization of fat by presenting fat people as relational subjects (Kargbo, 2013); picturing fat people as an alluring signifier of danger and immorality (Snider, 2010a), as sexual and desiring (Ratliff, 2013; Snider, 2009) or as disturbing the social realm (Hladki, 2016); demanding the viewer's engagement with bodily difference (Hladki, 2016); and depicting ordinary fat people in everyday contexts, a practice that in itself is "extraordinary" (Snider, 2012, p. 22). Photographing fatness is a critical activist and artistic intervention with many possibilities, not only due to the openness of images for interpretation (Cooper, 2016; Hladki, 2016), but also because photographs of fat people can disrupt the temporal logic of "before" photographs (Kargbo, 2013; Levy-Navarro, 2009), as well as the socio-cultural demands of the forever-malleable body in the west (Hurst, 2015; Kargbo, 2013; Kyrölä and Harjunen, 2017; White, 2014).

A tension that reappears in Fat Studies and fat activism concerns what representation *does* for fat people. A predominant theme is increasing representation of fatness in visual media, and more specifically, the assumption that *positive and celebratory* representations of fatness reduce fat oppression through offering relatable images of fat people.[2] However, such representations often aim to make the fat photographic subject desirable primarily through an appropriation of dominant cultural ideals, which is the lens through which viewers are encouraged to identify with the fat subject. Representational strategies in fat activism have often centred white, able-bodied, heteronormative, cis, feminine, and middle-class fatness, and consequently reify relations of power by "claiming" these for fat people (Cooper, 2016; LeBesco, 2004). Centring intersectionality in the creation and interpretation of photographs of fatness is a way out of the limitations of identification, and toward questioning idealization based on dominance as a strategy for fat activism.

Seattle Fat Avengers, *Images of Our Flesh: 1983 Calendar for Lesbians Only*

The Fat Avengers was a Seattle-based lesbian feminist fat activist group that formed in November 1981 with two major objectives which the calendar works toward: first, to establish nationwide connections between fat lesbian activists, and second, to "fully realize our own beauty and power as fat dykes" (Seattle Fat Avengers, 1983, n. p.). Cooper notes that fat activism in the 1970s and 1980s used publishing as a means to greater legitimacy (2016).[3] *Images of Our Flesh* is remarkable within the historical context of fat activism of the time, marked by ephemerality due to infrequent communication between groups and the scarce documentation that survives from this period (Cooper, 2016). Little is known about its circulation, though the calendar possibly circulated amongst those who placed advertisements in its final pages, including announcements for the books *Feminismo Primero/Feminism First* and *Coming Out Coloured/Saur A La Luz* by Tsunami Press, the photographic services of Deborah Hillwomon, the Women's Bookcenter, and "Out and About," a lesbian feminist newsletter (all based in Seattle), as well as Umoja, a national network for lesbian moms (based in Columbia, South Carolina). The Fat Avengers situated the calendar within a broader network of fat lesbian feminist activists, citing the Fat Underground, Fat Liberator Press, the Fat Activists Together newsletter, and The Gorgons as "inspiration" for their project (1983, n. p.). In the introduction to the calendar, the Seattle Fat Avengers described the calendar as a "labor of love," yet they also directly solicited feedback on the calendar, saying it was "still too white, too young, and ablebodied," didn't "do justice to our full and glorious diversity," and should be received as "the opening note in an expanding chorus" (1983, n. p.).

Images of Our Flesh contains 39 black and white photographs, including head-and-shoulders or full-body portraits of women, images of women working (farming, fixing a VW Beetle), playing (ping-pong, softball, flying kites), enjoying hobbies (writing, radio, reading, playing a flute), and a photograph of fat dykes on bikes at San Francisco's Lesbian/Gay Freedom Day parade in 1982. Eleven of the photographs are nude portraits, which tend to focus more on the facticity of the fat body rather than eroticism or sexuality. The overall feeling of the calendar is that it is a snapshot of a community that resists fat oppression through showing fat women joyfully engaged in a range of activities. These interventions can guide viewers to form identifications based not on cultural norms and the assimilation of difference, but on learning to look productively (Silverman, 1996). Identification is a psychical process whereby a characteristic of an other is recognized by the subject, and integrated into the subject's self-concept; identifications are complex, and can involve assimilating the difference between the subject and an other (idiopathic identification) or maintaining that difference (heteropathic identification) (Laplanche & Pontalis, 1998 [1973]). The calendar facilitates productive looking, I argue, because the photographs often place their subjects in relation to someone other than the viewer, encouraging the viewer to additionally look at the subject from a distanced perspective that is other to their own. This facilitates an openness to becoming displaced and to "identify at a distance" with subjects who are culturally repudiated and devalued (Silverman, 1996, p. 26). Through such productive looking, the viewer acknowledges unexamined and seemingly automatic "acts of incorporation and repudiation" that reify dominant relations of power (Silverman, 1996, p. 184).

Although Kargbo's focus is on contemporary online fat photo blogs, her argument – that radical and subversive potential comes not from presenting fat people "positively" (in contrast to "negatively") in photographs, but rather through establishing an "intimate relationality" between viewers and fat subjects – is fully relevant for my analysis of the photographs in *Images of Our Flesh* (2013, p. 170). Kargbo argues that fat photo blogs introduce an "ethical dimension" to looking because they present fat people fixed in the present, not waiting for a thin future (2013, p. 169), and refusing to be erased as relational subjects (2013). And to Kargbo's argument—that fat activist photography can resist the erasure of fatness epitomized by the "headless fatty" photograph through depicting fat people in *relation*—I would add that visualizing fat people in relation is also fundamentally an intersectional intervention. Rather than picturing fat people as isolated ("headless fatty") or in individualistic ways ("body positive"), picturing fat people in relation is disruptive work that can form coalitions across multiple oppressions and decentre normative viewing practices.[4] This intervention invites the viewer to imagine the women not only in relation to the Seattle Fat Avengers, but also as subjects in relation to a range of communities and activist struggles.

Pandoura

© Cathy Cade 1982

Figure 14.1 "Pandoura," woman playing Ping Pong

A Black woman stands at the end of a ping-pong table, holding a paddle and waiting for the ball (see Figure 14.1). In the photograph on the left, she bites her bottom lip in concentration, focused on the ball that is approaching; on the right, she stands in a more relaxed pose, smiling with open-mouthed joy but still with her eyes on the ball. She is wearing a velour top, dark pants, a ring, a necklace, and glasses; her hair is coiffed but natural. Intriguingly, the viewer is situated not in the position of her unseen opponent, but instead in a slightly elevated position and on her side of the net. As photographs of play, the images resist negative representations of fat people as sedentary and isolated, and indeed it is through the pleasure of play that the viewer is interpellated into these images. She is having fun with someone that the viewer cannot see, and the viewer is drawn into an identification with her through the action and her enjoyment.

In her discussion of Cindy Sherman's series *Untitled Film Stills* (1977–1980), where Sherman poses as many different tropes of female film characters, Silverman argues that the series is productive because the viewer identifies not with the ideals the characters are trying to approximate, but rather with the women themselves (1996). The identification in *Untitled Film Stills* happens because the women *fail* to achieve the ideal image they seek, exposing achievement of the cultural ideal as not just impossible, but undesirable. The overarching strategy of the photographs in *Images of Our Flesh* is one that does not engage with cultural ideals, and instead presents fat lesbians in relation to one another. However, there are significant exceptions where the photographic subjects engage with – and subvert – American cultural ideals of femininity and masculinity. Silverman characterizes such work as "disruptive and transformative labour at the site of ideality," where the photograph displaces the cultural ideal and facilitates an identification at a distance through an idealization that does not reify cultural norms, but instead exposes them (1996, p. 206).

The triptych of photographs of Cat Gonzales by A. D. Gee (see Figure 14.2) is amongst the best examples of this disruptive and transformative photographic work in *Images of Our Flesh*. On the left, Gonzales stands with her hands behind her head in a pose reminiscent of cheesecake pinup; it is unclear whether her eyes are lowered or closed, but the effect is a desirous expression on her face. The photograph is undeniably sexy, but it is here that the parallels to conventional erotic photography end. Because the photographer is situated beneath Gonzales, the viewer looks up at her, and her torso is the focal point of the image. Gonzales' head thus appears smaller, and her

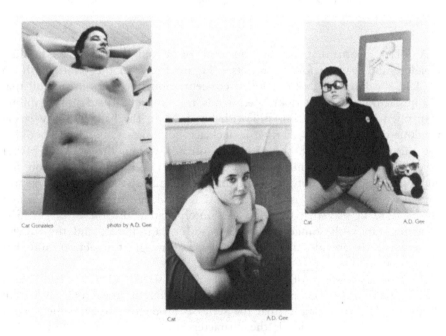

Figure 14.2 "Cat Gonzales," triptych image

belly and broad chest larger, due to the angle. The light shines on her body from above, and slightly to her left, and her belly casts a shadow that obscures visual access to her genitals. In the second photograph, Gonzales sits nude on a bed with her legs crossed, and hands pressed together. Her body is not the focus of this photograph, and instead she looks up at the viewer/photographer with eyebrows slightly raised. The expression on Gonzales' face is ambiguous, as she could be looking up in anticipation or with vulnerability. In the final photograph, she is confidently seated, and this time her eyebrows – which are raised above her mirrored sunglasses – convey toughness, echoed by the scorpion-like insect in the framed art to her left. When considered together, these three photographs not only present a complex representation of queer fat Chicana sexuality, they undermine dominant fictions of masculinity and femininity. The camera angle of the first nude photograph emphasizes Gonzales' sexual power and corporeal presence, and in the second nude photograph – which is more vulnerable – she holds her body in a self-protective position and her questioning look destabilizes a gaze that would situate her as passive. The final photograph is a humorous queering of masculine codes of hardness, because the stuffed bear beside her also sports a pair of sunglasses and the viewer sees that Gonzales' pose imitates the toy. Rather than interpreting Gonzales as a tough macho dyke, the bear suggests she is sweet and fun to cuddle; the triptych disrupts normative ideals of gender and exposes them as performative and playful. This is a very different engagement with ideality than seen in the 2017 calendar.

Substantia Jones, *The Adipositivity Project 2017* Calendar

The Adipositivity Project 2017 calendar emerges out of an online fat activist photography project that Substantia Jones started in 2007, described on the website as "part fat, part feminism, part 'fuck you'" (2017). Jones is an award-winning photographer, radio show host, media personality, lecturer, and fat activist. The project endeavours to present body size as "benign," not through providing detailed arguments for why fat people are excellent, meritorious, and beautiful, but rather "through a visual display of fat physicality… that's normally unseen" (Jones, n.d.). The website houses hundreds of photographs of fat people – primarily nudes – created through professional photoshoots with Jones. The *Adipositivity Project* is funded by Jones' voluntary labour, a Patreon account, as well as the sale of art prints and the calendar. The calendar is printed on demand through the self-publishing platform Lulu. com, and Jones promotes its sale through her Facebook (~25,000 followers), Instagram (~10,100 followers), Twitter (~5,400 followers), and Tumblr pages. Eleven photographs feature one woman, and one photograph depicts a man and a woman in a romantic embrace (for February). Unlike *Images of Our Flesh*, none of the subjects are named, and none of the photographs have a title. The subjects of the photographs are aptly called "Adiposers" by Jones, carefully posed within an artful setting (luxurious pool, dressing room, library, dance studio, on opulent vintage furniture) or background (stone wall, ocean, wall of Adipositivity photographs, old fence, green trees). Three women are clothed (in a sari, a burlesque outfit, and a beach towel or cover-up), and nine women are nude. All the photographs emphasize fat beauty, sensuality, or power, which is conveyed primarily through pose.

The Adipositivity Project 2017 calendar's primary focus is representing fat women as sexy and powerful. The selected photographs present in the calendar are not representative of the Adipositivity Project and present a narrower vision of fat embodiment that is more closely aligned with dominant norms of femininity shaped by standards of whiteness, ablebodiedness, and heteronormativity. This engagement is shaped by idealization, the psychical process through which the characteristics of an object are exalted to the level of perfection (Laplanche & Pontalis, 1998[1973]). Feminist and psychoanalytic theorists have rightfully observed, in their distinct ways, that idealization is frequently based upon culturally sanctioned norms and values that strengthen existing relations of power. Although I think it would be an overexaggeration to characterise the calendar as a fat assimilationist endeavour using LeBesco's framework (2004), it falls short as a fat liberationist endeavour because the celebrations of fatness in the calendar frequently validate fatness through reference to other dominant relations of power. And remarkably, none of the photographs' subjects directly address the viewer, photographer, or others – ten of the subjects have their eyes closed, one is looking at herself in a mirror, and one is looking off to her right. In this section, then, I begin with a photograph that helps better understand these shortcomings, then I discuss a photograph that offers something different than the majority of the calendar's images.

Against the backdrop of an empty studio space, a nude Black woman leans back on her hands, squatting with her knees together, balanced between her hands and the balls of her feet as she brings her body into a backbend.[5] Her back is gently arched and her breasts are jutting toward the ceiling. Her chin is lifted and her head falls backward. Positioned against a backdrop of three large windows opening out to a cityscape and a white wall, she appears luminous. This photograph is representative of the majority of the images in the calendar: the Adiposer is nude, she does not have a visible disability, she does not address the camera, and the overall intent of the photograph is to present her as beautiful and sexy. It is also unrepresentative, as the majority of the calendar's subjects are white and not engaged in activity. There are tensions in this photograph, between making fat Blackness visible and assimilating her into the whiteness of the calendar, between fat liberation and fat assimilation, and the photograph does not fit neatly into any of these poles. Shaw argues that the visual presence of a fat Black woman's body is primarily a "resistive and transgressive" act due to the historical and ongoing effects of white supremacy, which erase and "diminish black womanhood" through absence and racist iconography (2006, p. 128).

Representing fat Black women as powerful sexual subjects mobilizes the fat Black woman's embodiment as a "polyvalent retaliatory agent [responding] to the impact of colonization," resisting ideals of whiteness and thinness and demanding acknowledgement (Shaw, 2006, p. 9). However, in her astute analysis of Black women's participation in American beauty pageants – which could be construed as an expansion of beauty ideals – Shaw notes that Black women's participation is contingent upon their assimilation into whiteness and an erasure of their Blackness (2006). This is a warning in line with LeBesco's observation that fat assimilationist work aims to "secure tolerance for fat rights and experience" within the current societal structure, rather than challenge and overthrow that structure (2004, p. 42). Shaw's insight about the distance between the "resistive and transgressive" fat Black woman and the Black beauty pageant contestant gives pause for the viewer of this photograph, as it suggests that this image does not have a fixed meaning and should be read within its context (in this case, the calendar). This photograph risks being interpreted through an assimilatory idealizing gaze, a risk that arises due to the context of the calendar overall, which overwhelmingly emphasizes whiteness. However, it is important to recognize that this image could be read very differently within another context (for example, the Adipositivity website).

As noted, there are spaces in the calendar that rupture the idealizing gaze and point to intersectional possibility. A white woman leans to her right, with her left hip jutting outward and her left foot firmly on the ground.[6] She gently holds on to the doorframe with both hands, and her body fills the space. Her face looks slightly to the right; her eyes are closed and she appears to be smiling slightly as she stands at the threshold between a kitchen and another room. She is nude, and her long dark hair falls over her left shoulder but does not cover her breast. The room that she enters is sunlit and the wall is covered with photographs of fat women, giving the impression that she too is framed (by the door), but also that she exists within a community of fat women. The framed photographs are more varied than the calendar itself, showing fat women posing and moving through the world with their eyes open.

In this photograph, however, fatness is situated not in relation to these dominant visual tropes but rather, in relation to other photographic representations of fat women. This is a remarkable move away from idealizations based on cultural norms, and toward establishing a foundation for identifications within a fat frame of reference. Looking at this woman contextualized within a range of photographs dismantles the myth of a homogeneous experience of fatness, opening up a space to visually "behold" this body in relation, an act of generosity and intimacy (Garland-Thomson, 2009, p. 294). Further, by situating the woman in relation to new representations of fatness, Jones' intervention here refuses to leave existing regimes of cultural ideals untouched and intact, thus avoiding what Silverman calls a "strategic mistake" to reject idealization completely (1996, p. 2). As idealization is also "the psychic process at the heart of love," the work of artists who create singular representations of fatness is central to the project of social change (Silverman, 1996, p. 2). Jones' work in this final image destabilizes and reimagines the connections between idealization and identification by facilitating a heterogeneous form of identification evidenced in the wall of photographs.

Conclusion: Photographing Fatness

The photographs in the calendars are possible sites of productive looking and seeing differently and intersectionally, beyond dominant modes of idealization. A deeper investigation of the photographs reveals, however, that there are complex and sometimes contradictory relations of looking solicited by the calendars. Specifically, I am challenged by my analysis of the 1983 calendar as a more radical and complex intervention into photographing fatness from an intersectional perspective than the 2017 calendar. Given the abundant discussion of the importance of intersectionality in contemporary scholarly and activist communities as well as popular media, I hoped that its importance would be more fully realized in the 2017 calendar. It is for this reason that I maintain throughout this chapter that analysing photographs of fatness through the psychoanalytic insight that the bodies that can be loved and desired are limited by the ego's image of the body as well as culturally normative images offers a valuable perspective through which an intersectional analysis of fatness can be realized. This perspective illuminates the need for what Silverman terms an "externalizing logic" of identification, one which is excorporative rather than incorporative and "respects the otherness" of bodies, identifying and idealizing not according to cultural ideals or one's own bodily parameters, but through the other's full embodiment (1996, p. 2). Photography is a powerful medium for creating the kind of social change that Rice describes as happening not through trying to change attitudes, but rather visualizing an embodied and material change that can speak back to "social scripts" about fatness (2016, p. 431).

Throughout this chapter, I presented the argument that centering intersectionality in photographic analysis and practice is a way to undertake the disruptive and transformative work of exposing cultural ideals and facilitating new idealizations and identifications that do not rely on normativity in fat activist art. Crenshaw argues that single axis organizing and theorizing not only marginalizes and distorts one's analysis, but in fact provides a "descriptive and normative view of society that reinforces the status quo" (1989, pp. 139, 166–167). A concrete example of this is apparent in fat activist photography that redeems fatness through an appeal to cultural ideals that are structured not only by fat-phobia, but misogyny, racism, classism, homophobia, transphobia, and ableism, which undermines only the fat-phobic axis of the ideal while leaving the other axes untouched – this is not liberatory. Instead, in this chapter I focused on moments where coalitions of fatness are realized through photography by depicting fatness in relation and exposing dominant cultural ideals. Within an intersectional fat activist photographic practice, a politics of fat visibility might emerge that is premised not on the notion of a common fat identity but rather a political subjectivity that is intrinsically interlinked with, and shaped by, other multivalent relations of power.

Acknowledgments

I am grateful to the editors for the opportunity to attend the "Thickening Fat" symposium and for the gracious feedback and encouragement I received there from participants. Thanks to Cathy Cade, Charlotte Cooper, the GLBT Historical Society, and the Bancroft Library for their support and assistance in locating and reproducing the images from *Images of Our Flesh*, and to the Associate Vice-President—Research at St. Francis Xavier University for permissions and duplication funding.

Photographs provided courtesy of the Gay, Lesbian, Bisexual, and Transgender Historical Society: "Pandoura" diptych of woman playing Ping Pong by C. Cade, and "Cat Gonzales" triptych by A.D. Gee, in Seattle Fat Avengers, *Images of Our Flesh: 1983 Calendar for Lesbians Only*, Judy Freespirit Papers (2008-48, Series 5, Box 4).

"Pandoura" © The Regents of the University of California, The Bancroft Library, University of California, Berkeley [Cathy Cade photograph archive], BANC PIC 2012.054–NEG, TEMP Ctn. 6, Roll 828 frames 36A and and 39A.

Notes

1 Cooper's concept of the "headless fatty" is so resonant that it is cited in almost all the sources related to visual culture and fatness cited in this chapter.
2 This is closely aligned with what Charlotte Cooper calls the proxy of body positivity, made to stand in for all fat activism, through self-acceptance and self-love (2016).
3 *Images of Our Flesh* has two pages of advertising and community notices. Amongst these is a call for submissions to a "Fat Issues Book" by Iowa City Women's Press Collective, which became the foundational *Shadow on a Tightrope: Writings By Women on Fat Oppression* (edited by Lisa Schoenfielder and Barb Wieser) by Aunt Lute Books in 1983.
4 Such transformational work – which does not easily fit into aligning oneself "with" or "against" majority cultures – could also be described as "disidentification" (Muñoz, 1999).
5 The image can be retrieved from: https://theadipositivityproject.zenfolio.com /prints/h1BAA6201#h1baa6201. I am grateful to Dr. Jennifer Musial for assisting me in describing this woman's body pose.
6 The image can be retrieved from: https://theadipositivityproject.zenfolio.com /prints/h40DBA289#h40dba289.

References

Cooper, C. (2007, January). Headless fatties [blog]. Retrieved from http://charlottecoo per.net/fat/fat-writing/headless-fatties-01-07/.
Cooper, C. (2016). *Fat activism: A radical social movement*. Bristol: HammerOn Press.
Crenshaw, K. (1989). Demarginalizing the intersection of race and sex: A Black feminist critique of antidiscrimination doctrine, feminist theory, and antiracist practice. *University of Chicago Legal Forum*, 1(9),139–167.
Garland-Thomson, R. (2009). *Staring: How we look*. New York: Oxford.
Gurrieri, L. (2013). Stocky bodies: Fat visual activism. *Fat Studies* 2(2),197–209.

Hladki, J. (2016). Fat politics photography: The stareable body and "openings" for social justice. *InTensions*, 8, 1–30.

Hurst, R. A. J. (2015). *Surface imaginations: cosmetic surgery, photography, and skin.* Montreal: McGill-Queen's University Press.

Jones, S. (2017). *The Adipositivity Project 2017* [calendar]. New York: Substantia Jones.

Jones, S. (n.d.) About [webpage]. Retrieved from: http:///theadipositivityproject .zenfolio.com/about.html.

Kargbo, M. (2013). Toward a new relationality: Photography, shame, and the fat subject. *Fat Studies*, 2(2),160–172.

Kyrölä, K., & Harjunen, H. (2017). Phantom/liminal fat and feminist theories of the body. *Feminist Theory*, 18(2),99–117.

Laplanche, J., & Pontalis, J.-B. (1988 [1973]). *The language of psycho-analysis* (D. Lagache, Trans.). London: Karnac.

LeBesco, K. (2004). *Revolting bodies: The struggle to redefine fat identity.* Amherst: University of Massachusetts Press.

Levy-Navarro, E. (2009). Fattening queer history: Where does fat history go from here? In E. Rothblum and S. Solovay (Eds.), *The Fat Studies Reader* (pp. 15–22). New York: NYU Press.

Lind, E., Kotow, C., Rice, C., Rinaldi, J., LaMarre, A., Friedman, M., & Tidgwell, T. (2017). Re-conceptualizing temporality in and through multi-media storytelling: Making time with Through Thick and Thin. *Fat Studies*, 7(2),181–192.

Lupton, D. (2017). Digital media and body weight, shape, and size: An introductory review. *Fat Studies*, 6(2),119–134.

Muñoz, J. (1999). *Disidentifications: Queers of Color and the Performance of Politics.* Minneapolis: University of Minnesota Press.

Ratliff, J. (2013). Drawing on burlesque: Excessive display and fat desire in the work of Cristina Vela. *Fat Studies*, 2(2),118–131.

Rice, C. (2016). Revisioning fat: From enforcing norms to creating possibilities unique to different bodies. In J. Ellison, D. McPhail, & W. Mitchinson (Eds.), *Obesity in Canada: Critical Perspectives* (pp. 419–439). Toronto: University of Toronto Press, 2016.

Sastre, A. (2014). Towards a radical body positive: Reading the online body positive movement. *Feminist Media Studies*, 14(6),929–943.

Seattle Fat Avengers. (1983). *Images of our flesh: 1983 calendar for lesbians only* [calendar]. Seattle: Seattle Fat Avengers.

Shaw, A. E. (2006). *The embodiment of disobedience: Fat Black women's unruly political bodies.* Lanham: Lexington.

Silverman, K. (1996). *The threshold of the visible world.* New York: Routledge.

Snider, S. (2009). Fat girls and size queens: Alternative publications and the visualizing of fat and queer eroto-politics in contemporary American culture. In E. Rothblum & S. Solovay (Eds.), *The Fat Studies Reader* (pp. 223–230). New York: NYU Press.

Snider, S. (2010a). Revisioning fat lesbian subjects in contemporary lesbian periodicals. *Journal of Lesbian Studies*, 14(2),174–184.

Snider, S. (2010b). *Envisioning bodily difference: Refiguring fat and lesbian subjects in contemporary art and visual culture, 1968–2009* [PhD dissertation]. Retrieved from http://digitallibrary.usc.edu/cdm/ref/collection/p15799coll127/id/362633.

Snider, S. (2012). Fatness and visual culture: A brief look at some contemporary projects. *Fat Studies*, 1(2),13–31.

White, F. R. (2014). Fat/trans: Queering the activist body. *Fat Studies*, 3(2),86–100.

15 Queering Fat Activism

A Study in Whiteness

Emily R.M. Lind

Scene: Toronto Pride Week, June 2012. The Gladstone Hotel ballroom was filled to capacity for an event co-sponsored by Rainbow Health Ontario and various faculties at Ryerson University. Charlotte Cooper, famed activist, scholar, artist, and blogger, was the keynote speaker for an evening exploring "The Queerness of Fat Activism." Small children ran up and down the aisles while rounded bodies, filling out the best of plus-sized fashion, strutted in and out of conversation, blowing kisses to each other across the crowd. A local artist was selling out of T-shirts and posters that featured erotic sketches of fat nudes used in the event's publicity. And if I may, dear reader, the sexual energy of the room could have scorched the walls.

Charlotte Cooper took to the podium with a tiara and fairy wings, disclaiming that she wasn't planning to speak long—there was an activist panel discussion to follow her talk, after all—but she wanted to provide an overview of her argument that fat activism was both informed by, and contributed to, queer cultural projects. She reminded us that queers trouble gender, and that fatness does the same. Cooper reminded us of how queer bodies disrupt gender binaries and taxonomies of desire through their presence, their legibility or illegibility, and how they seek new vocabularies for embodied experiences and identities. She then made the link between queer cultural activism and fat cultural activism by highlighting some of her own interventions. After Cooper provided her overview, local fat activists participated in a panel discussion to consider these linkages in the context of Toronto's queer communities.

The panel had about a dozen local activists; about half presenting as white, half of colour, all there to share their stories of both fat activism and fat subjectivity. Panellists shared their experiences of fatphobia, how they came to identify as "fat" subjects, and the ways in which their activism was informed by these things. In several ways, the stories told by panellists were very similar, but there was one significant difference between them. Each panellist of colour situated their experiences of fatphobia within a broader discussion of racialization, while the white participants described fatphobia in seemingly race-neutral terms. While

Cooper's keynote offered a solid overview of the intersections between fat and queer activism, she too avoided discussing race. At an event informed by feminist theory and action, that approached fat activism from a necessarily intersectional framework, the white silences lingered uncomfortably, limiting the political possibilities we, as a community, had gathered to imagine.

This opening anecdote describes an event in Toronto, but my intention is to have it serve metonymically as an anecdote that could have taken place in many different Western metropolitan contexts. The event I describe was not only a forum to discuss the impact of fatphobia and fat activism on and in queer communities; it was the kind of event where the queer community recognized itself—filled the venue to capacity, reinvigorated its relationships, and re-encountered its limitations. To be clear, it was not for a lack of good intention that whiteness went unmentioned. There were many anti-racist statements shared throughout the evening to choruses of nodding heads. My point is that race was framed as something that happens to bodies of colour, rather than a system of power informing the lives of everyone in the room. When it came to exploring how whiteness impacted experiences of fatphobia and fat activism in queer contexts, it was clear the white folks didn't quite know what to say.

Not knowing what to say, politely not mentioning whiteness, or even not really thinking about it, are common iterations of white sociality. White silences perform the nuanced work of sustaining white supremacy while simultaneously appearing innocent and polite (Frye, 1983; Gillman, 2007; McIntosh, 2002; Ringrose, 2007; Spelman, 1988). This chapter talks back to the dynamics of white silence in fat activism by considering the terms by which it is conceptualized as queer. If fat activism is read as queer for the ways that it stimulates new ways of thinking about normative embodiment, identity, and visibility, are these disruptions also helpful in destabilizing racial logics? Isn't whiteness as invested in gender conformity as heteronormativity is? To address these tensions, I organize this chapter around the following question: how can Fat Studies scholars read whiteness into their work effectively?

I begin by highlighting how scholars have conceptualized fatness and queerness as mutually reinforcing. I then summarize ways in which fat activists use queer tactics such as camp, direct action, and public interventions to resist fatphobia. I offer a critical summary of whiteness studies and consider Daniel Coleman's notion of "white civility" as a tool for recognizing the role of whiteness in regulating social behaviour and normative gender roles. I consider recent work by Fat Studies scholars who locate the emergence of thinness as a beauty ideal in the West as part of a white colonial impulse to distinguish white bodies from black, brown, and colonized bodies. Finally, I argue for a thickened politics of white recognition within Fat Studies, so that scholars can better situate queer codes as aligned with the rejection of white civility.

Queering Fat Studies

Kathleen LeBesco (2003) argues that queer acceptance and fat acceptance share much in common, because "fatness may be read as a mere subset of queerness" (pp. 88–89). LeBesco asserts that both fat and queer studies are concerned with the politics of outing. In this, she builds upon Michael Moon and Eve Kosofsky Sedgwick's (2001) assertion that

> there *is* such a process as *coming out as a fat woman* ... like the other kind of coming out, [calling] yourself a fat woman is a way in the first place of making clear to the people around [you] that their cultural meanings will be, and will be heard as, assaultive and diminishing to the degree that they are not fat-affirmative ... it is a way of staking one's claim to insist on, and participate actively in, a renegotiation of the *representational contract* between one's body and one's world.
>
> (pp. 305–306)

Renegotiating the representational contract between one's body and one's world has been a mainstay of queer organizing for the past two and a half decades. ACT UP's reclamation of the word "queer" has been compared to fat activism's reclamation of the word "fat", particularly in studies of how fat activists have adopted a decidedly queer camp aesthetic and performative model for activism (Hill, 2009). While the parallels between fatness and queerness are inarguable, I consider LeBesco's claim to be limited in its scope. Contending that fatness is a subset of queerness suggests it is derivative or secondary as a social subjectivity. And while Sedgwick and Moon's notion of "coming out as fat" is a productive one, I think this line of argumentation may tell us more about the way hegemonic power operates than it does about the specific relationship between fatness and queerness.

Unlike queer desire, fat bodies are publicly visible. When coming out as fat, fat subjects come out as oppositional to the social expectation to engage in self-hatred and social exclusion. Coming out as fat talks back to the silent assumptions that maintain fatphobia. Queer culture works in solidarity with fat liberation by fostering an oppositional way of being in the world. Queerness and fatness are inextricably linked not because one is a subset of the other, but because both are marginalized by hegemonic gender roles. Hegemonic gender roles are predicated on white supremacy and performed through white civility. To suggest that fat bodies queer gender is, I think, a compelling and productive starting point. To that framework I add that fat bodies disrupt white hegemony as they queer gender.

Queer/fat activists subvert and resist hegemonic gender roles by staging campy, confrontational actions that make room for queer/fat culture and queer/fat bodies. In what follows, I will highlight some instances of fat activism, noting how the anti-assimilationist strategies used by activists get coded as queer in a way that sustains a tradition of white silence within the field. My point is not to deny the queerness of fat activism, but rather, to insist on reading whiteness into this field of analysis.

Fat Activist Strategies: Confrontation, Camp, and Public Space

Charlotte Cooper (2016) points to queer culture as fostering a confrontational politic that rejects the polite codes of normativity. She writes, "Queer rhymes with sneer and has an anti-normative, anti-assimilationist and punk streak to it" (p. 192). Examples of fat activists adopting an anti-normative "sneer" aesthetic include websites like www.fatpeopleflippingyouoff.tumblr.com. "Fat People Flipping You Off" was created by Substantia Jones, a fat activist photographer who also produces the celebrated www.adipositivity.com. "Fat People Flipping You Off" is a series of self-portraits of people with their middle fingers raised, embracing anger at fatphobia with confronting captions. For instance, one photograph shows a woman in a dress with her middle finger raised. The caption reads, "To the woman who called me a fat bitch for not moving off the sidewalk when she walked by" (Jones, 2018a). Of "Fat People Flipping You Off," Jones (2018b) writes, "What is FatPeople-FlippingYouOff.com? It's fat people … Fat people who're angry about sizeism, both institutional and individual … when words fail, aim it at those who're immune to logic, reject social justice, or care not about the bigotry of their words and actions." Jones positions the website's action beyond the limits of rational thinking, beyond civil dialogue and empathy. "Fat People Flipping You Off" embraces anger as a political tool and confronts fatphobia with masculinist posturing. The proud engagement in rude behaviour constitutes a rejection of white civility, as well as the codes of demure femininity. The website also serves to create a community of confrontational, angry allies, affirming each other's reactions and experiences in comments and re-posts. Fat activism creates venues for sharing experiences and building community, enabling fat activists to "perform the alchemical work of converting abjection into asset" (Cooper, 2016, p. 61), and "socially [transforming] fat … [offering] new possibilities for imagining fat" (Cooper, 2016, p. 69).

Queer camp has been associated with the alchemical work of recoding social representations of non-normative bodies and roles. Adrienne Hill (2009) points to Heather McAllister's Big Burlesque troupe, active in San Francisco from 2002–2007 as an example of fat camp. Camp allows activists to recode fat bodies within a discourse of pleasure, artifice, and sensuality in order to engage in what LeBesco (2001) calls "fat play instead of fat pathology" (p. 83). Hill (2009) argues that Big Burlesque used camp to revive a sensual performance art that is associated with a time when large bodies were eroticized within the mainstream, thereby disrupting the idea that fat has always been considered ugly or unhealthy. Importantly, the history of burlesque in Europe and North America is tied to working class mockery of upper-class norms. As cultural spaces, burlesque performances have always been venues for carnivalesque displays of boundary-breaching, role-switching, social commentary. Certainly, burlesque performance has been theorized in relation to drag performances and queer cultural production. In the context of fat activism, the code-switching potential of burlesque performers may also be made possible by the malleability of whiteness. Recoding fat pathology into fat play is achieved most easily when the bodies at stake pass as white.

Cooper has argued that "embracing fat stereotypes [enables] us to subvert them, and perhaps rob them of their power" (cited in Saguy, 2013, p. 65). In that spirit, forms of fat activism she has organized included an exhibition of "bad art" that responded directly to negative images and fatphobic discourses that circulate in the media. Cooper's Bad Art Collective was organized as part of the *Researching Feminist Futures* conference at Edinburgh University, and sought to disrupt the cliché of women as victims of media imagery by speaking back directly through a Do-It-Yourself aesthetic that proclaimed that women make their own media and can articulate their own messages about body image, desirability, fatness, and health. Similarly, "Fat of the Land: A Queer Chub Harvest Festival" went beyond polite discourses of healthy eating to celebrate food, community, queer culture, and body acceptance. These examples illustrate how queer tactics like the reclamation of public space, overt rejections of bourgeois civility and DIY cultural production have been used by queer fat activists to demonstrate that fat bodies trouble gender in queer ways.

Another way fat activists recode the fat body is by re-imagining the social spaces that traditionally limit fat social participation. Two Toronto-based (and now-defunct) performance troupes have been widely celebrated for their actions that reclaimed public spaces for fat bodies. Pretty Porky and Pissed Off, active from 1996–2005, staged campy dance parties in trendy shopping districts, passed out flyers that listed "fat facts" and asked onlookers, "Do you think I'm fat?" In another action, troupe members sang a rewritten version of the reggae song "Wide Load" while passing out peanut butter and jelly sandwiches to onlookers (Johnston and Taylor, 2008, p. 949). The Fat Femme Mafia was formed in 2005, the same year that Pretty Porky and Pissed Off disbanded. Fat Femme Mafia was a performance duo who led workshops on fat activism and danced. Both groups used tactics coded as queer in their actions: the takeover of public spaces, overt declarations that they were "out" as "fat," and emphasizing their physicality through play. As Chelsea Lichtman explained in an interview with Charlotte Cooper (2009): "The disruption of public space is something we are often invested in. We pride ourselves on shaking up people's ideas about fat bodies as well as making our bodies (and our friends' bodies) as visible as possible." Perhaps their most famous action was a bikini party in Trinity Bellwoods Park, an event that was documented in a short film circulated online and linked by many, including Rosie O'Donnell, whose endorsement of the Fat Femme Mafia raised the profile of the video significantly.

The production of cultural communities that defend each other's interests, that cultivate anger at each other's oppression, that adopt confrontational and masculinist behaviour in the face of outside attack are qualities fostered by fat activists. These characteristics have also been expressed in fat activist communities using gang symbolism, most significantly in the Chubster Gang.

The Chubsters, active from 2003–2010, were an international queer girl gang based in England with members from all over the world. The Chubsters were a loosely organized group of activists whose mission it was to tear down what they called "narrow fucks"—defined as people who "…believe fat is wrong, who hassle fatties in the street, who crow about their diets and gym memberships, and who spread lies about the horrors of obesity" ("Chubster Gang", 2013). The Chubsters had their own song, gang signs, stencils, and protocol for getting "jumped in" as a member (Cooper, 2016, p. 202). The Chubsters appeared at gatherings of NOLOSE, the semi-annual conference for fat dykes, the London Gay and Lesbian Film Festival, and for many years maintained a website featuring portraits of different Chubster members. Chubster portraits highlight decidedly "unfeminine" characteristics of gang members, including tactics for fighting back, an emphasis on physicality, and sarcastic humour. As Cooper notes, "The Chubsters want to push people's buttons with subversive situationist humour. Fat people are traditionally associated with comedy, as friendly figures of fun or passive punchlines in a joke, but The Chubsters humour is deadpan and aggressive, unsettling; Chubsters stare back" ("Chubster Gang", 2013).

The Chubsters' humourous performances use gender-bending, working class aesthetics to claim space for fat bodies, to disrupt bourgeois sensibilities, and to cultivate oppositional community in the form of a gang. The Chubsters were celebrated through public performances at feminist and fat activist events. The satirically tough image of Chubster members was read as decidedly queer, and yet the use of gang symbolism and imagery is undoubtedly racialized. Gangs are coded as racially deviant, confrontational, and anti-establishment. It would be easy to make this chapter about the misguided symbolism used by one fat activist group a decade ago. However, like my opening anecdote, I consider the Chubster Gang to again be a metonymic example of the kind of work that gets done in fat activism, wherein racialized signifiers are read as queer and subversive. How can the field of critical whiteness studies expand the conceptual tools for scholars working in Fat Studies?

The Place for Critical Whiteness in Fat Studies

Whiteness is notoriously difficult to define and has been described by critical scholars as the norm against which racism occurs (Baldwin, Cameron & Kobayashi, 2011, p. 5), an object of study "organized in tension" (Levine-Rasky, 2002, p. 2), and an enactment of power that is generated "as much through presence as absence, as much through what is said as through what remains unsaid and silenced" (Baldwin et al., 2011, p. 3). Like gender, feminists have argued that whiteness is a social construction (Frankenberg, 1993), impacting social lives in everyday ways. Studies of white privilege have elaborated on whiteness's perceived invisibility, comparing it to a metaphorical "backpack of unearned privilege" that is worn by white-skinned people as they move through the social world (McIntosh, 2002).

Beyond the more identifiable instances of white privilege or overt violence, this chapter is informed by studies of whiteness that contend with the subtle and insidious ways in which white supremacy is embedded in the careful silences, the hidden assumptions, the social norms that claim to have nothing to do with race. I approach whiteness as an identity and social phenomenon that is "only partially about skin" (Baldwin 2012, p. 173). I am informed by Daniel Coleman's (2006) contention that "race is not just bodies, but also conduct" (p. 12). In *White Civility*, Coleman argues that ideas about civility naturalize whiteness. By civility, Coleman refers to polite or gentlemanly behaviour that invokes the notion of civilization as progress. According to Coleman, civility is behaviour that can be taught, and its performance is understood as evidence of racialized superiority. The logic of civility implies that if one fails to assimilate into civilized codes of conduct, it is likely because of unchangeable racial characteristics – thereby strengthening race's mythos. Understanding whiteness-as-civility in the context of queer fat activism is a helpful framework for recognizing the ways that both queerness and fatness are coded as *un*civil.

Civility is about being proper, but its currency is embedded in its contingent relationship to its primitive correlative. Civility is proven not just by acting civil, but by acting *un*primitive, a state of being so vaguely defined it engenders a practice of constantly striving toward an unattainable goal. As Richard Dyer (1997) has illustrated, "whiteness makes a strong appeal. It flatters white people by associating them with (what they define as) the best in human beauty and virtue. The very idea of a best and of striving towards it accords with the aspirational structure of whiteness" (p. 80). Fat Studies scholars have begun to consider the aspirational drive for whiteness alongside the aspirational imperative to lose weight in the nineteenth and twentieth centuries, drawing clear connections between systemic fatphobia and related projects of white supremacy and European imperialism.

Amy Farrell's (2011) *Fat Shame* examined how advice guides for British and American women in the early twentieth century advocated weight loss because fatness was constructed as "degrading" to their "sex and civilization" (p. 64). As Farrell illustrated, male sexual desire for female thinness was considered to be a civilized form of sexuality, in opposition to beauty ideals in colonial contexts that celebrated corpulence. Similarly, Christopher Forth (2012) documented how Africa and Africans were associated with fatness in the European cultural imagination in the nineteenth century, which led directly to European women beginning to diet as a way of pursuing a beauty ideal that distinguished itself from colonial sensibilities. Many racist myths and tropes about bodies of colour emphasize excessive corpulence (for instance, Farrell points to the "Mammy" or "Jezebel" stereotypes), reinforcing the association of whiteness with thinness. These studies are reflections of a movement within Fat Studies scholarship that insist on drawing connections between racism and fatphobia (see also Ellison et al., 2016; McPhail, 2017). I want to build upon this emerging literature by considering the extent to which white civility constructs the fat body as aberrant, out of place, patholo-gized, and uncivilized. In other words: racialized.

To be clear, I am not suggesting that white subjects become racialized in the context of fatphobia. Rather, I am arguing that fat white subjects perform white civility poorly, because they are read as failing at thin aspiration. I highlight this point because, as my opening anecdote suggested, fat subjects don't necessarily articulate their failed thin aspiration as a matter related to any kind of white ideal. Similarly, the scholarship that considers experiences of fatphobia has, until recently, not mentioned white supremacy or whiteness at all. And yet, many instances of fat activism have included tactics that engage directly with acts of resistance to codes of white civility. Loud, rude, impolite actions by (often white) fat bodies reclaiming public spaces refuse to conform to the expectations of civil behaviour. Critical theorists have read the anti-assimilationist fat activist strategies as inherently queer, and of course, they *are* queer. However, the activism that queers fat bodies and spaces can also be mobilized as an agent in rejecting the imperative to assimilate into codes of white civility. I am arguing for an expanded sense of what it means to queer fat activism – recognizing the role that queer codes have played in rejecting white civility. In other words, queer is not the only word at our disposal for reading fat activist strategies that talk back to the polite silences and quiet exclusions that enable fatphobia to proliferate. It is important to foster a politics of recognition when it comes to whiteness, tracking how and where the command to "act white" constrains against movements for fat liberation.

Thickening the Politics of Recognition

The so-called invisibility of whiteness is echoed in many different instances within critical race studies, but there are two strategies I will highlight here, that I think can help pursue a politics and practice of recognition when it comes to whiteness. Bobby Noble posits that "whiteness comes into visibil-ity ... when it is articulated through class." (Noble, 2006, p. 77) Noble's argument points to the history of whiteness as a racial category that was invented in order to gain working class support for ruling class interests by encouraging white workers to think of themselves as racially superior to their neighbours of colour. This history has been documented by scholars such as David Roediger (1991), Theodore Allen (1994), and Noel Ignatiev (1995), whose historical studies trace the emergence of "white" as a racial category over the course of industrial capitalism's expansion across the North American continent in the nineteenth and twentieth centuries. The history of whiteness as a capitalist strategy informs Noble's (2006) contention that whiteness is a "class-based race: the higher up you go, the whiter you get" (p. 87). In order to recognize whiteness, scholars and activists can begin to code practices and instances of class distinction as moments of white performance and white visibility. One marker of class distinction is when activists gain credentialized entry into professional fields. In her important and comprehensive survey of fat activism, Charlotte Cooper argues that social movements can become "gentrified" when they gain access to professionalized power structures. For Cooper, changing the name of "Fat Studies" to "Critical Weight Studies" is an example of "whitewashing." Cooper (2016) argues that when professional standards gentrify otherwise radical movements what becomes erased is "a powerful fat activist voice [associated] with the impolite, the unrefined, the distasteful and the unclassy" (p. 176).

Feminist scholars read the publicly disruptive, gender troubling actions of groups like the Fat Femme Mafia, the Chubster gang, Pretty Porky and Pissed Off, and Big Burlesque as queer interventions that disrupt fatphobic discourses with campy and pleasure-based alternatives. Importantly, many of the criteria used to read these actions as queer can also be understood as interventions in the disruption of white bourgeois codes of civility. The flaunting of flesh in public spaces, the loud and disruptive use of otherwise abjected language, wearing clothes that refuse to hide curves or that are themselves "loud" colours and textures all disrupt codes of civility that manicure the boundaries of whiteness. It is precisely the interest of rejecting civility that transforms performance troupes into "gangs" within this logic. The Fat Femme Mafia and The Chubsters positioned themselves as gangs united against fatphobia. As gangs, the Fat Femme Mafia and The Chubsters celebrated a social ethic of defending each other in the face of external violence. But in so doing, they relied on iconography and language associated with groups that have been racialized throughout imperial histories as racially deviant, impure, and posing a violent threat to the health and prosperity of the nation. The fact that these tropes are coded as queer, and only queer within feminist analysis disavows the potential for a truly intersectional analysis of fat activism, while also allowing racist imagery to be celebrated as camp.

If we accept the promise that Fat Studies can thicken our models for studying embodiment, it is my hope that the contributions anti-racist scholars have made to the study of whiteness will be able to inform a decidedly anti-racist turn in the field so that queer is not the only word at our disposal that we can use to describe what it means to engage in "a renegotiation of the *representational contract* between one's body and one's world". What would it mean to engage in a queer anti-racist politic grounded in the politics of the body? One that takes seriously the contributions of queer theorists who have invited multiple considerations of how bodies read and are read, and also understands ideologies of race to be marking and unmarking bodies in fundamentally arbitrary ways? A thickened politics of recognition is needed, I think, to understand how whiteness operates and where it presents itself. The imperative to perform civility can be recoded as an imperative to act white within a thickened politics of recognition. Daniel Coleman (2006) argues that civility is "cultivated, polite behaviour … fundamental to the production and education of good citizenship" (p. 10). When activists call out the pressures to perform like "good fatties", Fat Studies scholars have an opportunity to read such a counter-discourse as a rejection of white civility. The ultimate good fatty is one endlessly committed to undermining their own fat visibility—a visibility rendered intelligible to the medical gaze, the heteronormative gaze, the male gaze. By staying fat, staying visible, white fat activists perform their whiteness poorly, and in doing so, render whiteness more recognizable and therefore rejectable.

References

Allen, T. (1994). *The Invention of the White Race*. London: Verso.

Baldwin, A. (2012). Whiteness and futurity: Towards a research agenda. *Progress in Human Geography*, 36(2), 172–187.

Baldwin, A., Cameron, L., Kobayashi, A. (2011). Introduction: Where is the Great White North? Spatializing history, historicizing whiteness. In A. Baldwin, L. Cameron, A. Kobayashi (Eds.), *Rethinking the Great White North* (pp. 1–18). Vancouver: UBC Press.

Braziel, J.E. and LeBesco, K. (2001). *Bodies Out of Bounds: Fatness and Transgression*. Berkeley: UC Press.

Chubster Gang (2013). Retrieved from Chubstergang.com. Now available at web.arch ive.org.

Coleman, D. (2006). *White Civility: The Literary Project for English Canada*. Toronto: University of Toronto Press.

Cooper, C. (2009, March 18). Interview: Fat Femme Mafia. Retrieved from http://obe sitytimebomb.blogspot.ca/2009/03/rad-fatties-fat-femme-mafia.html

Cooper, C. (2016). *Fat Activism: A Radical Social Movement*. Bristol: HammerOn Press.

Dyer, Richard. (1997). *White*. New York: Routledge.

Ellison, J., McPhail, D., and Mitchinson, W. (2016). *Obesity in Canada: Critical Perspectives*. Toronto: University of Toronto Press.

Farrell, A. E. (2011). *Fat Shame: Stigma and the Fat Body in American Culture*. New York: NYU Press.

Forth, C. (2012). Fat, desire, and disgust in the colonial imagination. *History Workshop Journal*, 73(1), 211–239.

Frankenberg, R. (1993). *White Women, Race Matters: The Social Construction of Whiteness*. Minneapolis: University of Minnesota Press.

Frye, M. (1983). *Politics of Reality: Essays in Feminist Theory*. Trumansburg, NY: Crossing Press.

Gillman, L. (2007). Beyond the shadow: Rescripting race in women's studies. *Meridians*, 7(2),117–141.

Hill, A. (2009). Spatial awareness: Queer women and the politics of fat embodiment (Master's thesis). Bowling Green State University, Bowling Green, Ohio. Retrieved at https://etd.ohiolink.edu/!etd.send_file?accession=bgsu1257110459&disposition=inline

Ignatiev, Noel. (1995). *How the Irish Became White*. New York: Routledge.

Johnston, J., Taylor, J. (2008). Feminist consumerism and fat activists: A comparative study of grassroots activism and the Dove Real Beauty Campaign. *Signs, 33*(4), 941–966.

Jones, Substantia. (2018a). Fat People Flipping You Off. Retrieved from fatpeopleflip pingyouoff.tumblr.com

Jones, Substantia. (2018b). About. Retrieved from fatpeopleflippingyouoff.tumblr.com

LeBesco, K. (2001). Queering fat bodies/politics. In J.E. Braziel and K. LeBesco (Eds.), *Bodies Out of Bounds: Fatness and Transgression* (pp. 74–90). Berkeley: UC Press.

LeBesco, K. (2003). *Revolting Bodies: The Struggle to Redefine Fat Identity.* Amherst: University of Massachusetts Press.

Levine-Rasky, C. (2002). Introduction. In C. Levine-Rasky (Ed.), *Working Through Whiteness: International Perspectives* (pp. 1–24). Albany: SUNY Press.

McIntosh, P. (2002). White privilege: Unpacking the invisible backpack. In A. Kesselman et al., *Women's Images and Realities: A Multicultural Anthology* (pp. 264–267). London, Toronto: Mayfield Publishing.

McPhail, D. (2017). *Contouring the Nation: Making Obesity and Imagining Canada 1945–1970.* Toronto: University of Toronto Press.

Moon, M., and Sedgwick, E.K. (2001). Divinity: A dossier, a performance piece, a little-understood emotion. In J.E. Braziel and K. LeBesco (Eds.), *Bodies Out of Bounds: Fatness and Transgression* (pp. 292–328). Berkeley: UC Press.

Noble, J. (2006). *Sons of the Movement: FtMs Risking Incoherence on a Post-Queer Cultural Landscape.* Toronto: Women's Press.

Ringrose, J. (2007). Rethinking white resistance: Exploring the discursive practices and psychical negotiations of 'whiteness' in feminist, anti-racist education. *Race, Ethnicity, and Education,* 10(3), 323–344.

Roediger, D. (1991). *The Wages of Whiteness: Race and the Making of the American Working Class.* London: Verso.

Saguy, A. (2013). *What's Wrong With Fat?* Oxford: Oxford University Press.

Spelman, E. (1988). *Inessential Woman: Problems of Exclusion in Feminist Thought.* Boston: Beacon Press.

Part IV

Our Gainful Failures

16 Working Towards the Affirmation of Fatness and Impairment

Ramanpreet Annie Bahra and James Overboe

The essence of this chapter is to bring forward a new way of thinking, where spasms or other impairments or fatness as simply matter can be generative and creative as expressions of life. Within Deleuzeguattarian affect, non-normative bodily capacities are understood to be innately creative and joyous. However, joy in this stance does not only refer to a positive outcome; in fact, there are various versions of joy, such as painful, confusing and disruptive joy, felt when affirming the materiality that is fatness and disability. We share a dialogue on how difference is experienced under the personal and impersonal registers as we think through affect and exposure. We offer a reconceptualization of fatness and spasms within the affective realm while questioning what can a fat and disabled body do? Thus, Affect Studies and a new materialist approach allows the exploration of the co-presence of fatness, disability, race and gender as a creative site in of offering a bodily-becoming that allows for possibilities of different forms of life and affects through exposure.

This project is an experiment for both of us as authors working towards conceptualizing a shift in register from the personal to the impersonal. The personal register is organized through a "politics of recognition" operationalized through dialectics. Hegemonic social actors make meaning of the social world. Transgressive politics are employed to transform the social world whereby people are no longer marginalized and are recognized as worthy social actors within the depth and breadth of humanity. Within the impersonal register rather than dialectic or binary thinking, singularities are how life is expressed. The impersonal singularities of fat, racialized flesh, or impairments are parts of the atomistic body and can erupt through the containment of the individual and communicate with other singularities outside the body as well as those within. This communication eschews the politics of recognition with its reliance upon naming, classifying, and ranking through judgment, in favour of the erotics of exposure, a state of communication that testifies to our striving towards a possible continuity of being beyond the prison of the self (Hardt, 2002). Drawing on Erin Manning, we ask, "When do we honour significantly different bodies and ask what they can do, instead of jumping to the conclusion that they are simply deficient?" (2016, p. 4).

We turn to Fat Studies and ask, what does it mean for fatness to be expressed on the impersonal level through exposure without transformation and a vocabulary of credit and debt?

Why Affect, Exposure, and the Impersonal

Patricia Clough (2007) suggests that there has been an "affective turn" in critical theory, meaning that burgeoning interest in affect theory is contributing to theoretical developments in various interdisciplinary fields such as Critical Disability Studies and Fat Studies. We employ affect theory because it affords us the opportunity to articulate the "agency" of impairment(s) and fatness, albeit differently from the agency of the person. In brief, our analysis of affect theory draws on Gilles Deleuze and Felix Guattari through Brian Massumi's insights about affect, coupled with Erin Manning's concept of the minor gesture, which we use to illuminate the focal point of this chapter: the impersonal register. We theorize affective forces as expressions of life from the impersonal register to argue for the agency of fat, brown, and impaired materialities. We acknowledge that our choice of theorists is limited; however, we draw on these thinkers to provide an in-depth analysis of our fleshy experiences under the personal and the impersonal, and to demonstrate how applying affective analysis affirms manifold expressions of life in capturing that which cannot be explained through self and cognition. We integrate Massumi's and Manning's theorizing of affect with Overboe's (1999, 2009, 2012) work on the impersonal register.

Massumi (2015) suggests that there is a need to think beyond the restrictive personal register—the normative "healthy" white heterosexual nondisabled man—to attune to the way different bodies move and how they affect. He urges us to investigate "what creatively exceeds the typical and refuses to be limited by resemblance to past forms" (p. 182). The "what" here hints at the impersonal which cannot be encapsulated and works to signal "the event" through its generative manner. What is this event that Massumi is speaking of? He employs Deleuze's concept of the event to imply the impersonal register. He suggests that one must will the event, allow it to come forth with no perceived notion of what becomes of that willing. This willing is not derivative of individual effort or will; on the contrary, the person allows the event to be actualized, in a sense stepping aside and allowing the event its space. Deleuze contends "the event is not what occurs (an accident), it is rather inside what occurs, the purely expressed. It signals and awaits us" (1990, p. 149). Fatness and impairment as "minor gesture[s]" under the personal register have been cast aside as abnormal, out of time, and altogether negated due to various stereotypes maintained by the personal register (Manning, 2016). Manning (2016) outlines this shift in *The Minor Gesture* as she works towards affirmation without falling into a cycle of credit and debt—a reactive form of affirmation that continues to submit to the personal register. In this project of affirmation via the impersonal there is no "credit and debt" cycle. In the relational process of the impersonal, what comes to unfold is bodily-becomings that are always in the process, changing, and emergent. The affirming part of the impersonal is not something that is reactive in nature like its counterpart, in fact it is something without a prescriptive ending, an expression of life that has yet to be determined. Seeing fatness and impairment as expressions of life that are brought forth eschews identity, self-hood, cognition, and the politics of recognition: attributes in the personal register. We recognize the split between these registers are to some extent false—parsed for convenience to help explain theoretical differences—but equally note that it is important to acknowledge that their coexistence can open life to possibilities never considered.

In a pragmatic sense, the impersonal register is informed by the concept of exposure. Rather than the reactive dialectical logic of transgression, exposure operates "on a purely positive logic of emanation. It involves casting off, or really, emptying out, all that is external to its material existence and then intensifying that materiality. What is exposed is naked flesh, absolute imma-nence, a pure affirmation" (Hardt, 2002, p. 80). Transgression always reacts to the norm and is complicit with the norm because the transgressive act is buttressing the norm by responding to it even if *that* response is negative. The transgressive dialectical act needs the norm to give it reason to transgress. Michael Hardt (2002) contends,

> exposed flesh is not transgression but scandal. ... Violation of the norm is not primary to exposure; the negation is secondary, an afterthought, an accident. ... Exposure operates in ignorance of the norm, and thus con-ducts, in the only way possible, its real destruction.
>
> (pp. 80–81)

In the social world other people will assess and pass judgement based upon the norms they follow. Whether it be the norms of the discourses of sizeism or ableism, the fat-impaired assemblage may turn its back on said norms—maybe not resulting in the destruction of norms but calling into question such norms and offering a possibility for intensifying fat and impairment as a life expressed (Hardt, 2002; Manning, 2016).

Methodology

Duoethnography, an emerging qualitative research method, is taken up to share events of the authors' life histories in relation to the differences being studied (Breault, 2016; Schultz, 2017; Zazkis & Koichu, 2015). We under-stood and approached duoethnography as polyvocal writing in a dialogical format that intertwines the life stories and theoretical frameworks being used. With our past use of autoethnography and use of our bodies as sites of research for this project, we thought doing a duoethnography would allow us to present multiple views on how our differences are taken up under the two registers. Bahra (B), the first author, shares her experience of how the personal register ensnares her in a triple bind, wherein the cultural coding of her embodied being as fat, brown, and female render her excessive, engulfing, and threatening. The second author, Overboe (O), shares his experience of being read as an ageing, white, cisgender, heterosexual, fat, and disabled man under the personal register; yet, he has never been white enough, heterosexual enough, thin enough or able-disabled enough because his impairments have spoiled these claims to identity (Goffman, 1963) and thought to not signify control, reason, or self-direction. Through narrative, both authors exemplify the ways difference as event signals lives considered sub-human or non-human under the personal register. What we urge you, the reader, to do while reading this polyvocal writing is to reflect on your narrative, how it might fit alongside or against those juxtaposed by the authors (also suggested by Schultz, 2017). We ask this to ensure our voices are made explicit throughout and to surface how our differences (and, perhaps, yours) may be negated and/or affirmed under the two registers. This process is vulnerable, but we trust that our relationship to one another and to our differences will make this narrative disruption one worth sharing.

Difference Under the Personal Register

The personal register is one that determines who is human enough through its established attributes and preoccupation with identity, representation, and ranking of bodies. Sizeist and ableist rhetoric for many marginalized people becomes a question of whether they can attain/sustain a status worthy of being invited into the realm of the human. Manning (2016) argues that the personal register, by containing only a cycle of credit and debt—what we call the reactive form of affirmation—is not affirming whatsoever because the quality of difference is pre-established. This pre-established quality of difference results in negation and the Nietzschean concept of *ressentiment*, on which Manning writes:

> Ressentiment creeps up on you. What seems active soon leads you to the same old, tired values. The worn paths become the only ones in sight, and what seemed like a taking-of-a-position now looks more like a dead end. Negation is, in the end, predictable, and this predictability tends to close in on itself.
>
> (p. 204)

Within the medical-rehabilitation industrial complex, ressentiment creeps into what initially seems to be the promise of rehabilitation, whether through weight loss or another medical fix, which becomes "the same old, tired values" of continually aspiring to a normative existence; at best this leads to attaining some form of status as an unreasonable facsimile of an ableist, sizeist prototype (Manning, 2016). Within ressentiment, fear around not achieving the expected rate of rehabilitative progress or regressing to an earlier plateau can also be found, because all that the work of overcoming difference can achieve is a dead end no matter how promising rehabilitation goals appear to be in the beginning.

The negation of the materiality of impairment and fatness is predictable, and this predictability tends to close itself as these differences are considered deficits that inhibit life. During the preliminary stages of writing this chapter, we got together to answer the following questions: What do impairment and fatness do under the personal register? How did you forfeit to the cycle of credit and debt? What events as ressentiment did impairment and fatness bring for you?

O: For me, the event was my birth with multiple impairments that began and continue to play havoc with my life within the personal register with its ableist agenda. Within the personal, the double helix of ableism and saneism pathologize my impairments and consider them as detractors from life. Whereas the personal register makes sense of life through the self with cognition, the impersonal register signals the event of difference and provides impetus for the pure essence of fatness and impairment.

B: For me, the event was my trip to India at the age of 11, when I became more aware of the ideologies being imposed on my body. I heard and felt the personal register's colonialist, racist, and sizeist discourses in interactions with my family, resulting in the devaluation of my life. The medical industrial complex continued to sustain such logic by pathologizing my "minor gestures" and placing dictates on me to normalize myself (Bahra, 2017).

O: Prior to continuing my studies at university, I spent hours swimming recreationally. In the eyes of others, I was a disabled person who, in trying to "overcome" his impairments when I swam, was an inspiration. Many people who witnessed my swimming echoed this sentiment—they made me into this disabled hero. This narrative followed the "naturalized" perspective; people must try to eradicate impairments or at least lessen their effect to grab the "brass ring of normality" and lead worthwhile lives (Overboe, 1999). As my impaired body transformed into a version of a "swimmer's body"—one that was more athletic and toned—people inferred that my goal was to "overcome" "impairment." Nothing could be further from the truth.

B: The ranking of my body and the wrath of judgement that established my proximity to the category of human worked to keep my desire for thinness and whiteness, and the utopic sense of joy I felt in striving to attain these attributes, intact. This idea of reaching the shelf of normalcy and the joy that comes with it is closely related to my makeup practices. Makeup became an act of passing as normal through camouflaging my fatness and brownness. Techniques such as highlighting and contouring became an event with its own "framed memory of ressentiment" (Manning, 2016, p. 204). This was ingrained so deep that to be happy, to gain whiteness and thinness, I needed to wear a lighter foundation. Also, I had to follow the principle of "snatching" to shave off the fatness of plump cheeks, double chin, and neck through painting shadows on my body to fulfill the trope of thinness. This was ressentiment at its finest moments. Makeup as a form of ressentiment became a part of normative time for me, its application taking on a predictability that felt nothing close to affirmation.

O: The truth is that swimming allowed me the opportunity to feel my impairments and fat giving each of them their due. My loss of weight and achieving a somewhat toned body as well as straightening my scoliosis were ancillary outcomes and not goals. When people commented on how much better I looked they missed how much the agency of both my impairments and fat were affecting the body and *a life*. Some readers might suggest that the agency in this impersonal register was my goal, but this assertion is mistaken. My intent was to feel both impairments and fat without the restrictions of the discourses of ableism and sizeism. In fact, most people complimenting me seemed surprised that I lacked enthusiasm for their observations. To embrace these compliments would necessarily disavow life expressed as impaired and fat. Politely, I accepted compliments without explaining my discomfort for two reasons: First, at the time the cultural milieu could not contemplate postulating that impairments and fat were legitimate expressions of life. Second, my time and my energy were preoccupied with creating a space for fatness and impairments as what I now call expressions of life. I had no time for justifying or explaining my position within discourses heavily weighed within normative assumptions.

Difference Under the Impersonal Register

If the cycle of credit and debt becomes something we resent due to its continuous negation and upholding of a value system, how is it that we get to the point of "affirmation without credit" (Manning, 2016)? Such affirmation exists along the impersonal register. Bodily becomings under the impersonal are tied to what Manning calls "quality-as-difference," a form without measure that is "activated in advance" or is *a priori* (p. 217). She furthers this form of quality by contending that affirmation is not predetermined, predesigned, "comfortable or comforting"; rather, it values experimentation over judgement (p. 202). Here the work of affirmation "is to invent conditions for new ways of activating the threshold of experience, new ways of experimenting. ... Affirmation is the push, the pull that ungrounds, unmoors, even as it propels" (p. 202). Following Manning, we ask: "When do we question what we mean by independence, by intelligence, by knowledge? ... When is the fat body, the immobilized body, the blind body, the deaf body, the old body, the spastic body celebrated?" (p. 4)? She goes on to provocatively question agency, claiming "this is the problem with agency: it makes the subject the subject of the action. What if the act did not fully belong to us?" (p. 16). She makes a distinction "between reflexive or automatic movements" and "directed or volitional movements" (pp. 17–18), the former of which, following Deleuze, we might code as existing within the impersonal, pre-individual, or non-human register. Deleuze asserts that these could be fruitful for reconceptualising theory and social change, writing that the "pre-individual, impersonal singularities ... are mobile, they break in, thieving and stealing away, alternating back and forth, like anarchy crowned, inhabiting a nomad space" (2004, p. 143). Taking up Manning's provocation, we ask: What do impairment and fatness do under the impersonal as singularities? What did your event(s) signal under the impersonal?

B: I would like to take up my makeup practices again in relation to the impersonal register, considering Manning's concept of *a priori* quality-as-difference, one without any value or judgement. Under the impersonal, I found that my layers of fatness and brownness were unfolding as singularities intra-acting with one another. Under the impersonal there was joy in allowing these expressions to flourish along with my makeup look, letting fatness and brownness as expressions of life have their own force without falling back into ressentiment. There was no predictability here; through the process of doing makeup, fatness and brownness were now fluid, spontaneous, and creative. Within the impersonal register these differences and make-up form an assemblage that "empties out" all judgement as well as anything external to the "pure affirmation" of the assemblage.

O: My impairments are affirmed through an expression of life within the impersonal register. Very early in life, the event of impairments and fat signalled they are part of life which needed to be expressed, not stifled. If I do not ignore or attempt to repress them, impairments and fat flourish and are affirmed. Again, the meaning of affirmation is qualified as an expression of life with no measurement value on the ledger of credit and debt. Allowing for the prominence and agency of the materiality of fat and impairments allows for *a life* moving through water without giving primacy to cognition or the self. Through the concept of exposure, the agency of fat and impairments beckon towards other life, whether animate or inanimate, ideas, and so on ... creating assemblages that are indeterminate, non-prescriptive, and vague.

The Assemblages of Fatness and Impairment

Applying Deleuzeguattarian theory, Nick Fox (2012) argues that assemblages are always about the "doing", in which "every aspect of living and our experience of the world" comprises multiple assemblages as the outcome of the interactions of these relations (p. 67). Assemblages differ under the personal and impersonal register. During a conversation between the two authors, Bahra notes that *Thickening Fat* itself is an assemblage comprised within the assemblages of Overboe and herself.

B: The different elements of my body—my fatness and wheatish brown skin—engage in the formation of assemblages with each other, and assemblages of everything around me, including the human and non-human. Through the "ecology of the body," I see the ways I engage with my environment and the relations I form with it in this process of "doing" (Fox, 2012, p. 61). For me, under the personal register, brown-ness forms one assemblage (Wheatish skin—bullying—control—bleach-ing products—cosmetic products—fairness) and fatness another (Mouth —food—bullying—fatness—food—control—diet   tactics—gym—lose weight—bullying). In taking up the impersonal, this assemblage shifted from a credit and debit accounting of difference to difference-in-itself without comparison or judgement (Wheatish + fatness—unleashed—body affirmation movements—Fat Studies—Critical Disability Studies—Critical Race Studies—Dr. Overboe—Thickening Fat—peers—confer-ences troubling the personal register—fat rejuvenated, even though it takes a lot out of me sometimes). In the impersonal assemblages exempli-fied, there is no starting or final destination for the fat body; instead the rhizomatic nature of fatness, race, and impairment all leak through and connect with one another on the same ontological field. The hyphens within these assemblages represent the "events, actions, and encounters, between bodies" (Puar, 2012, p. 58) as points and lines of movement and intensities which exert different affects each time, keeping ones bodily-becoming creative and ever-changing.

O: The agency of fat and impairments beckon to the water creating assem-blages that enhance expression of life of impairments and fat, and perhaps the water as well. The spasms and the fat fall into a rhythm of expression (sort of). Rather than being a swimmer propelling myself through water, assemblages were created within the cluster of water, impairments, and fat. These assemblages were difficult to describe because of the limits of language (thus the sort of). Assemblages often defy language and are felt, sensed, and they promote uneasiness as their expression eludes explan-ation. Over time, observers of my swimming would proclaim that I was an inspiration for overcoming my impairments. Rejecting the inspir-ational narrative, a subset of this group of observers keenly noted that I was different from other disabled people they encountered. These people could not put a finger on it but sensed something was afoot. Eventually, a fellow swimmer came up to me and said, you lead with your disability. Intrigued I admitted wanting to know my impairments and other aspects of my body including fat. We proceeded to the point that she helped me get to know my body. Or in Deleuzeguattarian terms, our assemblage with my body deepened and widened with me leading with impairments.

The Vagueness of Hardt's Exposure

In the previous sections, Michael Hardt's (2002) concept of exposure was introduced. Within the impersonal register, there is a vague life which heightens the expression of life in the assemblages being formed. By giving presence to difference through the impersonal register, difference is freely expressed through affirmation and joy, albeit with acknowledgement that these two things can be difficult, tragic and may even contradict the values stated or implied within the personal register (Deleuze, 2001; Hardt, 2002; Manning, 2016). Consequently, there is no predetermined direction, or schema, or template to give them reassurance or consolation. There is simply joy and affirmation of *a life*. *A life* is operationalized through the notion of exposure rather than the politics of recognition. Imperceptibility under exposure means two things for Hardt (2002): there is nothing to hide; nor is there a separate thing for the eyes to grasp. Exposure is a sense, but not in the sense of traditional empiricism, but more a feeling with vagueness and uncertainty that must entail a leap of faith from those that have a sense of exposure derived from "*a life*."

O: If these assemblages are deemed transgressive that is incidental as the affirmation of fat and impairments turns it back on the norm which is its greatest offence (Hardt, 2002). In turning its back on the credit and debit ledger the exposure of fat and impairments negates ressentiment and expresses *a life* that either moves beyond the restrictive human or is human and more (Manning, 2016) with its basis in experimentation. As other priorities of life took precedence my swimming declined. Able-centric and size-centric people were surprised that I had no ressentiment towards becoming fatter and more impaired. They did not realize that as Nietzsche suggests I continue to find *life expressed* through fat and impairments and subsequently continually turn my back on normality.

B: In adopting exposure to my impersonal life, I see its singularities—my fatness and brownness—do their own thing and open themselves up to the world individually and conjointly. Once again going back to the example of makeup, can it be said that in the exposure of my naked skin —a non-contoured and non-highlighted face—there is no self?

O: Yes. The self is removed and for some they would be unable to articulate what that difference entailed.

B: In the overspill of these singularities then, there is a peculiarity of these minor gestures that are no longer captured by the social world. All that is exposed is the expression of *a life* that has its own potentiality. Whether it be naked flesh or glammed-up flesh through the art of makeup, exposure here engages in no politics of recognition or dialectical manner because I let my fatness and brownness do whatever they want to, leading me down another path, one to the destruction of the personal.

O: Yes, and that is exposure's greatest offence. Turning its back on the norm and refusing to give it power.

Conclusion

In conclusion, the separation of the personal and impersonal registers has been an exercise to help explain and illustrate Deleuzian theory and affect theory as it applies to Fat Studies and Disability Studies. The impersonal and personal registers coexist and are dependent upon each other. This chapter is an attempt to give the impersonal register its due. We have provided an explication of how the agency of both fat and impairments are instrumental in social justice praxis and provide an alternative way to arrive at social change. The becoming subjectivity and assemblages are formed through exposure.

O: I have written articles that theorize the impersonal register and impairment as an expression of life without cognition and self. Each of these prior publications ground the analysis in different but interrelated areas. This chapter adds to these publications by applying the impersonal register to exercising and adds the component of fat agency to align itself more closely with this *Thickening Fat* collection.

B: In this theoretical journey of affirmation, my fatness and brownness are given presence and in doing so invent new forms of existence in and within them through the impersonal. The impersonal life is one without a self, where the politics of recognition and its homogenous mode of thinking and acting is decentralized. Fatness as impersonal singularities here goes beyond affirmation for credit to simply affirmation that allows fatness to do whatever it is going to do moment to moment without being enclosed, breaking through its movement and experimentation as entanglements of pure intensity and affects.

The exposure of fatness and impairment that are affirmed and joyous do not have a vocabulary, they are simply expressions of a life. Understanding the notion of the body in terms of the impersonal means no hierarchical order is in effect and within an affirmative light, these differences—impairment, fatness, race, and other differences—generate their own creative force to become something without limits, enabling the infinite possibilities of affective capacities to arise. The vagueness of indeterminacy of the impersonal life opens for new possibilities of expressions of life that welcomes the complexity, multiplicity, and transgressive nature of fat and impaired bodies in motion.

References

Bahra, R. A. (2017). "You can only be happy if you're thin!": Normalcy, happiness and the lacking body. *Fat Studies*, 7(2), 193–202.

Breault, R. A. (2016). Emerging issues in duoethnography. *International Journal of Qualitative Studies in Education*, 29(6), 777–794.

Clough, P. T. (2007). Introduction. In P.T. Clough & J. Halley (Eds.), *The affective turn: Theorizing the social* (pp. 1–33). Durham: Duke University Press.

Deleuze, G. (1990). *The logic of sense.* (C. V. Boundas, Ed., M. Lester & C. Stivale, Trans.) London: The Althlone Press.

Deleuze, G. (2001). *Pure immanence: Essays on a life.* New York: Zone Books.

Deleuze, G. (2004). *Desert islands and other texts, 1953–1974.* South Pasadena: Semiotext(e).

Fox, N. J. (2012). *The body.* Cambridge: Polity Press.

Goffman, E. (1963). *Stigma: Notes on the management of spoiled identity.* Englewood Cliffs: Prentice-Hall.

Hardt, M. (2002). Exposure: Pasolini in the flesh. In B. Massumi (Ed.), *A shock to thought expressions after Deleuze and Guattari,* (pp. 77–84). London: Routledge.

Manning, E. (2016). *The minor gesture.* Durham: Duke University Press.

Massumi, B. (2015). *Politics of affect.* Cambridge: Polity Press.

Overboe, J. (1999). "Difference in itself": Validating disabled people's lived experience. *Body & Society, 5*(4), 17–29.

Overboe, J. (2009). Affirming an impersonal life: A different register for Disability Studies. *Journal of Literarcy & Cultural Disability Studies, 1*(3), 241–256.

Overboe, J. (2012). Theory, impairment, and impersonal singularities: Deleuze, Guattari and Agamben. In H. D. Goodley & L. Davis (Eds.), *Disability and Social Theory: New Developments and Directions,* (pp. 112–125). Hampshire: Palgrave Macmillan.

Puar, J. K. (2012). "I would rather be a cyborg than a goddess": Becoming-intersectional in assemblage theory. *philoSOPHIA, 2*(1), 49–66.

Schultz, C. S. (2017). "Working the ruins" of collaborative feminist research. *International Journal of Qualitative Studies in Education, 30*(6), 505–518.

Zazkis, R., & Koichu, B. (2015). A fictional dialogue on infinitude of primes: Introducing virtual duoethnography. *Educational Studies in Mathematics, 88,* 163–181.

17 "Hey, Little Fat Kid"

My Impaired, Fat, Hairy, White, Male Body

Michael Gill[1]

"Hey, little fat kid." Four words that cut so deep. I am waiting to buy milk, eight or nine years old. My older, non-fat, brother with me. My mom is in the car in the parking lot. This is one of the first errands I go on. "Hey, little fat kid." Fat. Fat. Fat. It was a public recognition and reading of my body—in space and time, by a stranger. I was the little fat kid. I became the fat little kid. I am the fat little kid. Even now, I can transport myself to that moment and feel words piercing my flesh. I ran to the car after buying the milk, telling my mom what he said. I was eager to share how inappropriate—no, *ashamed*—his words made me feel. Of course, his words were not a surprise. I knew I was fat. My mom, normally reserved and non-expressive of emotion, replied, "Next time someone tells you that, Michael, you look at him in the eye and reply, I'd rather be fat than ugly." Ugly beats fatness in the competition of life? Body size pitted against attractiveness.

Anna Mollow (2015) encourages disability studies scholars to "get fat" by incorporating the perspectives and insights of Fat Studies to "reshape contemporary cultural conversations about 'obesity'" (p. 201). Mollow argues that there is fertile theoretical and political coalitional work between disability and Fat Studies. She cites Sami Schalk's (2013) claiming of crip, through her experience as a "nondisabled fat, black, queer woman" which is a type of "sideways identification," that Schalk contends is at "the heart of disability studies" (p. 200). Schalk is articulating intimacy with disability through experiences as a "personal and political connections," that is deeply informed by her own experiences in a fat-phobic, racist, ableist, and heteronormative society (2013, np). Both Mollow and Schalk articulate how bodies are read—and devalued—when nondisabled, white, gender normative ideals are upheld.

As a fat boy, teenager, and adult, I've never felt alienated from discourses of fatness. Indeed, the title of my paper comes from this experience as a young child. Unlike my intimacy with fatness, I have struggled with identifying as disabled, even while the number and severity of my impairments increased, supposedly in direct relation to fat embodiment. For example, my diagnosis of sleep apnea, according to my pulmonologist, is directly related to my fat body. I am told to lose weight and cure my apnea. In the preface to my book *Already Doing It* (2015), I describe myself as "marginally able-bodied"

(p. xii). This identification is understood through my current (fat, male, impaired) embodiment, and family histories of sickness and disability, which have hereditary elements. In this chapter, I take an autobiographical intersectional narrative approach to explore the relationship between fatness, impairment, disability, whiteness, and male cisgender identity. However, I do not seek to conflate my experiences, which are deeply framed by multiple gender, race, and ability privileges, as similar to those of Mollow, Schalk, and others. By getting fat, I come to explore the growing thick relationship between my embodiment, impairment diagnoses, and future/current/past experiences of disability.

In what follows, I examine various moments in my life which help illuminate the ways in which embodiment and identity constrict or expand discussions of impairment and disability. For example, ahead, I discuss how my body is increasingly "medical modeled" with each visit to the doctor. The ensuing diagnoses are supposedly related to my weight. Yet, I remain a white male that appears very much nondisabled. My privileges also protect me from state violence. How is my fatness connected to notions of disability and impairment, in addition to gender, racial status, and economic access? Similar to a claim of crip and the potential to destabilize boundaries of identity, I articulate my relationship to disability and impairment through my intimacy with fat embodiment. I approach crip as a capacious term that encompasses a wide range of experiences and bodily states, which may or may not be considered as diagnosable disabilities (Sandahl, 2003). I deploy crip as I do queer—to destabilize claims of identity (Kafer, 2013; McRuer, 2006). In what follows, I argue that the relationship between fatness and disability is fluid, similar to the ways in which bodies are also malleable.

Artifact 1: Husky Jeans at JC Penney

As a kid, I hated wearing jeans. My current closet has at least half a dozen pairs that I wear on rotation. But as a kid, when I bought jeans, I was constantly reminded of my fatness. My siblings could go into a store, find a pair of jeans, and try them on. When I needed a new pair of jeans, my mom would take me to the JC Penney at the mall and we would have to order them out of the catalogue. A couple weeks later my specially ordered pair of pants would arrive at home. Once unwrapped and washed, I would finally have a new pair of pants roughly two weeks after ordering them.

As I am writing these words and thinking about my experience, I can't help but notice the jeans I am currently wearing. Grey and tight, these jeans don't hide anything about the lower half of my body. My thighs and butt are tightly caressed by stretchy denim. I feel great when I wear these jeans, even —dare I say—sexy. But as a kid, I was not a fan of clothes, and certainly husky jeans were a constant reminder of my fatness. Too fat to buy regular clothes, mine were special ordered and never as stylish as my siblings or classmates; big butt, thick thighs, and wide waist.

There is a picture of my siblings and me when we were kids; my brother is probably 9, I'm 7, and my younger sister 4. We are smiling at the camera, three goofy white kids sitting on a ledge at a park. My older brother in his grey slim jeans, sporty windbreaker, and baseball cap looking like a cool kid. His arms are crossed. He is wearing a black watch. My younger sister is in the middle, wearing a crocheted jumper, her curly hair and wide smile drawing the viewer in. She is wearing jeans too, her older brothers on either side. And then there I am, smiling, seemingly very happy and carefree. My chipmunk cheeks and rounded chins, my belly partially hidden by my arm, but still the overall size well in view. And I'm wearing a pair of black husky jeans.

Husky: burly, robust, large, according to Merriam-Webster. Larger than average, a *husky* football player. I did play football for my seventh- and eighth-grade years. It was full-on tackle football and my team was terrible. I don't remember us winning a game in the two years I played. What I do remember, though, was my blue helmet. I was the only kid on the team that wore a blue helmet because my head size was too large to fit the standard issue helmets the rest of the team wore. Fat head and fat body; husky jeans and specially ordered helmet. I suppose the blue helmet helped my parents always locate me on the field. When I got to high school and the coach would approach me in the hallways telling me "a big kid like you" would be great for the team, I couldn't run my husky body fast enough to the debate team and drama club. Even though my body might signal hegemonic masculinity to others, my own experience with my husky self was (and still can be) a feeling of ambivalence.

Artifact 2: The Voicemail

"Hey, sorry I missed your call, Mom and Dad. I was spending the night at the sleep lab to address my sleep apnea."

A sleep study seems benign enough. In writing about the proliferation of studying, observing, diagnosing, and treating diverse sleep styles, Benjamin Reiss (2017) writes,

> We now have other means of taming. Over the next two centuries, the asylum doctors were displaced by an ever-proliferating array of experts and specialists who hovered over disordered sleepers: first neurologists, then physiologists, psychiatrists, pediatricians, pulmonologists – even dentists, who now treat such problems as nocturnal tooth grinding (bruxism) and pulmonary obstructions caused by overextension of the jaw.
>
> (p. 117)

The overarching ableist violence that was largely contained in the asylum is now dispersed through various medical and rehabilitative fields. Exam rooms and sleep labs become locations where biomedical diagnoses are given that determine pathways of insurance reimbursement and coverage. What appears benign can turn into a regulatory and curative maze where assumptions of normative bodies violently determine overall worth. Reiss continues that over "seventy disorders" including sleep apnea are included in the "International Classification of Sleep Disorders" (p. 117). Accordingly, "Unruly sleepers are no longer checked into asylums, but they are put under equally intense surveillance in modern sleep clinics … You can find them in universities, strip malls, hotels, and on the side of the highway" (p. 117). The sleep lab I spent two sleepless nights at was on the fourth floor of a suburban medical facility. Once I was strapped in with monitors measuring my heart rate, oxygen levels, and many other biometric measurements, I was told to sleep. A mixture of plastic, rough sheets, thin blankets, and my body tangled up, being remotely monitored by someone down the hall: the panopticon, discipline and punish, with a side of Foucault, indeed. Both times I participated in the study, I accomplished very little sleep. I mostly tossed and turned but apparently, I did sleep enough to get an official diagnosis of sleep apnea. I am an unruly sleeper and almost immediately post-diagnosis, I entered a complex medical and insurance reimbursement maze, where I ultimately was declared "non-compliant" because I am unable to use the CPAP (continuous positive airway pressure) machine.

I played the voicemail from my parents: "What is this sleep apnea business? Maybe if you lose weight, you can cure it? It will make you feel better, I'm sure." This certainly was not the first time in my life I have been told to lose weight. I have had doctors, lovers, friends encourage me to lose weight. I've been told to lose weight to lower my cholesterol and blood pressure. Supposedly losing weight would make me more desirable for a partner and less depressed. Losing weight becomes a catch-all solution for those not inside my body. I'm sure my parents meant well with their advice to lose weight as a solution to my apnea, yet their advice is not unique. The argument goes that if I could fix my body by shedding some magical amount of weight, my impairments would disappear. Should I contact the WHO to see about putting waist measurements as part of the DALY (disability adjusted life year) calculation? Might Waist x Height + Average Number of Calories Consumed Per Day/BMI = FALY (fatness adjusted life year)? Nguyen (2015) critiques DALYs as an ableist assessment mechanism and expertly argues that "disabled people assumed to have more 'disability weight' are perceived to have less value and are, thus, treated as non-deserving of public health services" (p. 76). If one DALY is considered "one lost year of healthy life," perhaps a FALY can be one year lost to endless medical testing and treatment. I'd probably have a high FALY score.

Each morning I take ten pills: a combination of prescription, probiotics, supplements, and vitamins, all directly related to the many conditions of my body. Pinks and oranges, some shades of yellow, and a white pill or two, I've gotten good at swallowing all of them in one go. It must be my large throat enabled by my fatness. At my last appointment with my pulmonologist, he once again told me to try to lose some weight because even half a pound can add ounces to my throat making my apnea worse. If I do follow his advice, what will happen to my ability to swallow my pills?

This isn't a story of pity: rather I'm narrating my story of fleshy embodiment. Underneath my tight jeans and flower-patterned shirts is a fat hairy white body. The tightness of the jeans on my thighs helps caress my body, including muscle and blood vessels, but my curves are what becomes "seen." My flesh is curvy, spotted, hairy, freckled, and marked with stretch marks and tattoos. My flesh is supposedly the sign of my fatness and, by extension, ill health, impairment, and disability. Yet, this is *my flesh*. I may have an ambivalent relationship at times with my butt, thighs, and belly, but this is the body I know. This is the body that also gives me comfort, and this is the body I take care of in ways that work for me. This is my fleshy embodiment.

As part of my body care routine, I consume pills and sleep with an oral appliance due to a host of diagnoses in my medical chart. My employment status, enabled by my white maleness, means that most of my medications are generally affordable. In addition, I could pay the high out-of-pocket deductible for the oral appliance, after being told to return the CPAP machine, by my insurance company, because of my "non-compliance." Because of my work schedule, I also have the flexibility to keep appointments with specialists all over town. It is common that one appointment can last three hours, including the many moments of waiting in lobbies and exam rooms. You would assume that I would get better and more patient of waiting, but each time, I'd rather be somewhere else, doing almost anything else. The husky white kid in jeans has grown up to be an impaired, fat, pill-taking adult.

I'm sharing a story here of the power of the medical model infused with whiteness, family pressure, and a healthy side of mainstream society disavowal. This isn't a story of overcoming. There is no inspiration here, just mundane moments on scales, exam rooms, in front of mirrors, and in changing rooms where my flesh becomes felt. And my parents, or doctors, or others tell me to lose weight to become "healthier" or less "disabled."

In these moments, my fatness is medicalized, but non-threatening. I'm the white fat man, of which there are presumably many, our individuality both hypervisible but also banal amongst the sea of large white maleness. The juncture of my identities might mean more doctor's appointments, but it also enables me to access those same medical resources of which I am weary. Yet, for many others, fatness becomes a marker of weakness, deviance, or criminality, supposedly justifying excessively violent treatment, or death.

Artifact 3: Who Is That Kid?

Part of what I have been doing in this essay has been tracing memories and experiences to consider how the current manifestation of me is influenced by my fatness, impairments, medicalization, in addition to my whiteness, maleness, access, and privilege. The little fat kid grew up into a fat man, yet there is another photograph that challenges this linear progression of baby fat to adult fat. The photograph, from over two and a half decades ago, shows "me" smirking at the camera, wearing a dark green t-shirt and an Atlanta Braves hat. My best guess is that this was from summer camp when I was 15 or 16 years old. I know this is a picture of me. I'm even wearing a nametag, but still, I don't feel like this is me. I look at this picture and feel alienated from this version of myself. This kid is smirking like a smart ass. Around this time, my good friend and I would proudly declare, "people suck" whenever we saw each other in the halls of school. We even had pencils made advertising our worldview. I can acknowledge that part of my life history, but the photographed embodiment seems very foreign. This teenager only has one chin and no belly hanging out, his shirt hangs off his average, but not fat, white body.

Today as I look at that picture I wonder: what did my body look and feel like at that moment? How did it feel to take off my shirt in public and not be immediately aware of my flesh —plump and hairy—everywhere? Did I feel particularly happy or content with my body? How soon after this moment did my belly reemerge from its hibernation to claim the spot above my waist and below my chest? I don't ever remember not feeling fat; for the most part my embodiment seemed to be confirmed by photographic and external assessments. I suppose I am wishing for some vibrant memories where my body was a sign of pleasure, for me and others. And to be honest, my response to this picture is thoroughly connected to my internalized fat phobia. It leaves me wondering: as a slimmer adult, would I find pleasure in life in more dramatic ways?

In the introduction to *Sex and Disability*, Robert McRuer and Anna Mollow (2012) highlight "the risk of reifying identity categories that might be better contested" (p. 10). They negotiate the process of "coming out" to use Ellen Samuels' (2003) phraseology: of disclosing or claiming disability status, of making visible again what might be rendered invisible. They contend that identity claims have the potential to exclude, while also being judged as not authentic (pp. 10–12). Citing Samuels, they discuss how the complicated negotiation and potential exclusions of identity can have material effects regarding accommodations, particularly for accommodations that are interpreted as being "widely unreasonable" or "impossible" (p. 12).

I've been thinking a lot about my body, in particular the relationship between my fat self and notions of disability and impairment. What does it mean to not be able to trace a moment when my body crosses over into the land of disability or ability? How can I embrace the ambiguity and ambivalence? I came to disability studies as an early-20s graduate student having most recently worked in sheltered workshops. Spending any time in medical model dominated settings, especially for folks with labels of intellectual and developmental disabilities, one major theme is reinforced: the line between the "disabled" and the "able-bodied" is assumed to be rigid and non-flexible. As I examined my own positionality, I felt increasingly unsure of how my embodiment and identities related to the social model of disability. The long list of medical conditions expanded with each year of graduate school. My lifelong life-threatening allergies to tree nuts seemed manageable next to diagnoses of irritable bowel syndrome, depression, anxiety, and sleep apnea. Tests and appointments, medical co-pays, pills and treatments; my body is deeply intertwined to the medical model of disability. I recently joked that I need to find a new primary care doctor because with each visit I get a new diagnosis added to my medical chart. I was only half joking; it is increasingly clear that I enter the exam room a fat impaired body with seemingly predictive family medical histories. As I am writing this piece, I have just returned from an appointment with my primary care doctor in which she encouraged me to lose weight once again, or risk being placed on cholesterol and blood pressure medicine in the (near) future. She told me it was not a question of *if* I would take medicine for blood pressure and cholesterol, but *when*. Supposed certainty emerges. Husky jean kid, take note: I'm becoming increasingly medical modeled. And that medical establishment is trying the hardest to get me to hate my fat body. Well played, doctor.

Artifact 4: Desiring a Disabled Fat Self?

In late February 2018, I presented earlier sections of this paper at a two-day symposium at Ryerson University connected to this collection. During the two days in Toronto and for about a week after, my body felt different. It felt freed. Nothing really changed physically but I felt a different relationship to my flesh, embodiment, fatness. Being around individuals critically engaged intersectionally with regard to body size opened something inside; a space which I could inhabit even briefly.

As I now sit to type these words some weeks later, I pay attention to my body—especially my belly. The dress shirt buttons feel tight and restrictive, and there is a heaviness in my stomach area. While quite literally my body might have changed since late February, I wonder where the opened space of comfort disappeared to, and why I have once again returned to a feeling of fatness as deficiency and negative excess, not a transgressive, or even desirable way of being. By discussing my body and its medicalization with others, the overreach of the doctor's office and some of my devaluing assessments of my body in space disappeared. Yet, once again, I am feeling medicalized, disabled by the discussion about my body by others as it pertains to high blood pressure, apnea, weight gain, and the like. Of course, this realization makes me sad, but I also recognize I have plenty of self-work to move from this place of disgust and shame, to one of desire. Instead of imagining a future skinny/less fat self, how can I desire a future self that is a continuation of my current embodiment?

I began this piece retelling the encounter as a fat boy in the market. "Hey, little fat kid." FAT piercing through my flesh. Cutting through layers of fat.

Sticks and stones bouncing off, but words wounding right through me. Anti-fatness is all around. My white maleness takes up space. This means that I am often not held accountable for the ways in which my size transgresses or violates the space of others. White + Male + a Fat Body means that I can enter a location and expect to encounter folks with bodies that look like mine. From the predominantly white institution I teach at, to the neighborhood I walk my dogs in, bodies like mine are all around. White maleness is terror, understandably, for people of color. The amount of violence and death connected to whiteness abounds and that is the history and present that I carry with me as well. As a fat white man, I have relative freedom to navigate the world without fear of state violence being enacted upon my flesh.

Anna Mollow (2017) argues, "fatphobia is routinely deployed in ways that exacerbate the problem of state-sanctioned violence against African Americans" (p. 105). Mollow traces a "racialized double bind" that connects white supremacy, slavery, and other forms of state violence including incarceration and law enforcement murder. Mollow writes:

> One side of this double bind renders violence against black people inconsequential by suggesting that fatness is the real cause of any injuries inflicted upon them, while its other side depicts violence as a necessary response to the excessive physical power that black people, especially those who are fat, are imagined to embody.
>
> (p. 105)

Mollow is articulating how fatphobia works in conjunction with white supremacy to blame those murdered by the police as "too fat" or "too big." In addition, body size is assumed to be "threatening" to the police thus supposedly warranting excessive violence. Nirmala Erevelles and Andrea Minear (2010) discuss how murder of an African American senior Eleanor Bumpurs in 1984 by New York City police when they attempted to evict her was "justified" using fatphobia and white supremacy:

> Could the perception of Eleanor Bumpurs as a dangerous, obese, irrational, black woman also have contributed to her construction as criminally "insane" (disability) because her reaction to a "mere" legal matter of eviction (class) was murderous rage? And did our socially sanctioned fears of the mentally ill and our social devaluation of disabled (arthritic and elderly) bodies of color justify the volley of shots fired almost instinctively to protect the public from the deviant, the dangerous, and the disposable? We, therefore, argue that in the violent annihilation of Eleanor Bumpurs's being, disability as it intersects with race, class, and gender served more than just a "context" or "magnifier" to analyze the oppressive conditions that caused this murder.
>
> (p. 128)

There is a long genealogy of early and violent black death in the United States. Mollow (2017) notes how Eric Garner's murder at the hands of law enforcement was explained by commentators as being a result of Garner's disabilities and fatness, a type of victim blaming, not excessive police violence (pp. 105, 107). Mollow also traces how commentators used both anti-blackness and fatphobia to justify the death of Tamir Rice. Tamir Rice was not allowed to be "a little fat boy"; instead, his black male youth was deadly for the white supremacist state. White male fatness protects from the violence of the state.

In this piece, to articulate experiences and feelings of fatness, but to ignore white maleness is to disingenuously deflect dimensions of the embodied self at these intersections. At the end of April 2018, I am only partially aware of the complex ways whiteness emerges as violation. I am fortunate that I have allies—white and non-white—who hold me accountable and signal when white privilege/violence/entitlement emerges, at times insidiously, and at other times more blatantly. This process of learning and awareness is the work that white folks need to take on—and is the work that I must take on. White supremacy is everywhere and connected to my body. White + Fat + Male all too often is violence and violation.

It seems difficult to arrive at a space where I desire my disabled fat white male body. I'm trying to articulate the necessity of critically engaging with processes and mechanisms of shame, disgust, violence, and oppression. Eli Clare (2003) writes:

> Thirty years, and now I am looking for lovers and teachers to hold all my complexities and contradictions gently, honestly, appreciatively. Looking for heroes and role models to accompany me through the world. Looking for friends and allies to counter the gawking, gaping, staring.
>
> (p. 257)

Clare is seeking guidance and support as he navigates the world of "Gawking, Gaping, and Staring." In the piece, Clare's "role models" and "teachers" include freak show performers Hiram and Barney Davis, "small, wiry men, white cognitively disabled, raised in Ohio" (p. 260) and "William Johnson – African American and cognitively disabled in the mid-1800s – [who] worked the freak show stage" (p. 257). Clare finds these examples and others helpful to contextualize his experience of body framed through ableism, transphobia, and other systemic oppressions, often experienced through others' visual and verbal assessment of his body as transgressing boundaries.

When I read this piece, I always find myself slowing down on one section. Clare writes,

> I keep looking for disabled men to nurture my queer masculinity, crip style. Looking for bodies a bit off center, a bit off balance. Looking for

guys who walk with a tremble, speak with a slur, who use wheelchairs, crutches, ventilators, braces, whose disabilities shape but don't contradict their masculinities.

(p. 260)

"Nurturing queer masculinity, crip style." I love this idea of nurturing. Certainly, the comfort I felt with my fat self in Toronto was because of the intentional care work and anticipation of my body in space with other bodies. Bodies that are marked (or might be seen as) excessive, or just generally "too much" came together to theorize intersectional fatness. This care work was once again the culmination of folks not like myself; female identified and non-binary professors and graduate students. White male fat privileges emerge again.

Clare seeks out disabled men that can nurture his "queer masculinity, crip style" (p. 260). I have never felt at home in spaces of hegemonic masculinity. I'm keenly aware of how I fail to meet masculine expectations in these spaces. I feel like a fraud. Never masculine enough. Pull back the façade and you are left with a round fat hairy body, which of course still can be the embodiment of masculinity. I am the embodiment of contradictions and stereotypes at the same time.

My ambivalence of how to continue or conclude this piece is an awareness that much of what I have written about here seems all consuming. I am medically modeled disabled. My body, my impairments are intimately connected to a system of medical doctors and specialists, co-pays, and treatments with *their goal being a skinnier me.* My fat body is too much. My privileges, especially connected to my whiteness and maleness mean I rarely move from medically modeled to socially modeled disabled.

What does my future look like? I'm not entirely sure. I know it feels urgent to move to a place of desire where my body gives me a sense of pleasure. Urgent, yet, as I enter my fourth decade of life on the earth, I fear I have comfortably settled or gotten used to my consistent feelings of disgust or alienation. I am complacent. I need to welcome my fat hairy white male body. I need models and friends. I need allies that can nurture while also prodding me along in the process of dismantling white supremacy and settler colonialism. Hey, little fat kid, put on those tight jeans.

Note

1 I sincerely appreciate May Friedman, Carla Rice, and Jen Rinaldi for their incredible editorial leadership and feedback on the multiple versions of this essay. I am also grateful to the two anonymous reviewers for their helpful suggestions for revision. Lastly, I am very appreciative to Kelsey Ioannoni for deftly keeping me on task throughout the process of this essay.

References

Clare, E. (2003). Gawking, gaping, staring. *GLQ: A Journal of Lesbian and Gay Studies, 9* (1), 257–261.

Erevelles, N., & Minear, A. (2010). Unspeakable offenses: Untangling race and disability in discourses of intersectionality. *Journal of Literary & Cultural Disability Studies, 4* (2), 127–145.

Gill, M. (2015). *Already doing it: Intellectual disability and sexual agency.* University of Minnesota Press.

Kafer, A. (2013). *Feminist, crip, queer.* Indiana University Press.

McRuer, R. (2006). *Crip Theory: Cultural Signs of Queerness and Disability.* New York University Press.

McRuer, R., & Mollow, A. (2012). *Sex and disability.* Duke University Press.

Mollow, A. (2015). Disability Studies Gets Fat. *Hypatia, 30*(1), 199–216.

Mollow, A. (2017). Unvictimizable: Toward a Fat Black Disability Studies. *African American Review, 50*(2), 105–121.

Nguyen, X. T. (2015). Genealogies of disability in global governance: A Foucauldian critique of disability and development. *Foucault Studies, 19*, 67–67.

Reiss, B. (2017). *Wild Nights: How Taming Sleep Created Our Restless World.* Basic Books.

Samuels, E. J. (2003). My body, my closet: Invisible disability and the limits of coming-out discourse. *GLQ: A Journal of Lesbian and Gay Studies, 9*(1–2), 233–255.

Sandahl, C. (2003). Queering the Crip or Cripping the Queer?: Intersections of Queer and Crip Identities in Solo Autobiographical Performance. *GLQ: A Journal of Lesbian and Gay Studies, 9*(1–2):25–56.

Schalk, S. (2013). Coming to claim crip: Disidentification with/in disability studies. *Disability Studies Quarterly, 33*(2). http://dsq-sds.org/article/view/3705/3240

18 Reading and Affirming Alternatives in the Academy

Black Fat Queer Femme Embodiment

Mary Senyonga

The fat black woman's body primarily functions in a restive and transgressive mode because her body has been the site of historic efforts to devalue black womanhood.

(Shaw, 2006, p. 14)

You are damned by your hatred of fat black women, and no part of you could ever live without them. this is why the universe (huge, black, unfolding, and expansive) shakes and shakes her head. you fools. you wasteful fools.

(Gumbs, 2017, p. 146)

In teaching and advising undergraduate students at a large public institution, I find that my agenda is at odds not only with the university's intent, but even with colleagues who think themselves at the forefront of liberatory thinking. I came into my Master's program set on studying Black fat women's and femmes' experiences of microaggressions in hopes of articulating our marginality through Critical Race Theory and the intellectual spirit of Chester Pierce. As a Black psychologist, Pierce (1970, 1995) theorized the psychological impact of racialized experiences on Black people's mental and emotional wellbeing initially as "offensive mechanisms" and later coined the daily confrontations with racialized terror as "racial microaggressions." In analyzing such experiences, Pierce described racial microaggressions as "subtle and stunning," with the "enormity" of daily confrontations with racialized terror only fully understood "when one considers that these subtle blows are delivered incessantly" (1970, p. 266). Pierce's notion of daily, subtle, and incessant racial indignations has transformed my understanding of racism. Previously conceiving of racial discrimination in the dramatic and spectacular sense, Pierce's rethinking of racism as everyday systemic, institutional, and individual acts of bias has reframed my efforts to redress racism.

My Master's project asked Black fat women and femmes about their experiences of bias at the intersection of race, gender, and body size within academic sites and as aggressed by peers, faculty, and administrators. My personal experiences with the prevalence of fatphobia inspired the project. I experienced how the world around me was structured to exclude my presence, whether through the small classroom chair and desk size (or the dreaded seat attached to desks) or the school uniforms that were never in my size. I confronted others' conceptions of my in/capacities to excel where racialized projections about my supposed intellectual inferiority compounded fatphobic assumptions of laziness. As I engaged with Black fat women on this topic, they told stories about disparaging remarks regarding their size, affronts to their intellectual capacities, and about the promises of fat affirming perspectives and spaces in which to destabilize fatphobia (Senyonga, 2017).

Coming from the field of education, I take on an interdisciplinary lens to interrogate how Black women and femmes deal with marginalization. I find that studying higher education illuminates the ideologies that undergird what we teach and practice. Specifically, I consider how the pursuit of higher education has been positioned as a means of acquiring material gain in the face of redressing racism, sexism, and other such structures of domination. The pursuit of higher education, however, mandates that individuals operate under set limitations. Bodies that are disciplined and legible as white, thin, cisgender, heterosexual, able, and other privileged positionalities are set as the standard by which we are all judged and afforded agency. I use Black Feminism and Black Queer Feminism especially to locate the work that has been done to understand how Black women and femmes have been historically sidelined in liberatory visions of racialized, gendered, and other identity-based articulations while consistently attending to the intersections of marginalization (Randolph, 2009). Through putting CRT, Black Feminism, and Fat Studies into conversation, this work explores how my position as a Black fat queer femme in academia illuminates the limits and potentials of higher education. As a graduate instructor, my body disrupts the stability of "expected" teacher while I simultaneously navigate projections regarding my work ethic, ability to contend with varying articulations of marginality, and even how I should properly "regulate" the ways that I emote.

Following the tradition and contemporary work of Black liberatory thinkers who have theorized the systemically stratifying nature of schooling, I acknowledge educational systems as violent productions of normativity that pivot on the subjugation of marginalized people (Patton, 2015). The material and discursive environment of schooling has a historical basis in oppression with institutions of higher learning predicated not only on exclusionary definitions of intellectual beings but also on the monetary substantiation of the university through slave labour and displacement (Patton, 2015; Wilder, 2013). However, I simultaneously recognize the liberatory epistemologies that I have encountered through education. Critical disciplines such as Ethnic Studies, Gender Studies, and Queer Studies have expanded my thinking of alternatives to marginalization. Here, education, not the system of schooling, has the potential to disrupt imposed subject positions. Instead of feeling indebted to the very institution(s) that bolster their endowments through the military–prison–industrial complex (Oparah, 2014), that do more to protect the interests of the university than the students in attendance, and that posture towards a radical politics while implementing restrictive governance, I aim to empower students through sharing power in the classroom. I refuse professionalization in an environment that pedestalizes "normal" bodies. I develop my pedagogy around the intention of disrupting the limits of the university in taking on a Black queer feminist, or even *femme-inist,* perspective.

As a Black fat queer *femme-inist* (Lewis, 2012), I resist the logics that insist upon knowledge as only valid when theorized from an "objective" place and thus take the pedagogical stance that my narrative and embodiment are generative tools of analysis. As Saidiya Hartman suggests:

> the 'autobiographical example,' is not a personal story that folds onto itself; it's not about navel gazing, it's really about trying to look at historical and social processes and one's own formation as a window onto social and historical processes, as an example of them.
>
> (Saunders, 2008, p. 7)

In other words, how my body is read, responded to, and appraised provides insight into academic violences, and particularly violence against those who experience intersecting marginalizations. However, my structurally disempowered position does not simply become a place of lack. Rather, I use the rich histories of resistive and liberatory texts and theorizations from women and femmes of colour broadly, and Black women and femmes in particular, to (re)imagine how I can take on teaching as resistance. Exploring the tensions that arise when teaching from a disempowered position, Moya Bailey and Shannon Miller (2015) show how, through the infusion of feminist pedagogy, the graduate classroom becomes a site for students to develop their liberatory praxis, and foster their resistance to university structures, in and outside the classroom. As Black queer women professors looking back at their graduate school experiences, both Bailey and Miller explore how they contended with isolation in the ideological and numerical sense. They consistently navigated campuses that situated them as "one of": one of x number of Black women graduate students, one of x number of queer students, and one of x number of even fewer Black queer women students. In writing about their experiences as Black queer women in academia, they complicate the heterogeneous narrative of Black women in academia that situates such experiences as straight or straight performing. Queer experience is heavily undertheorized, with few anthologies on women of colour's experiences in academia contending with queerness (Bailey & Miller, 2015).

In similar fashion, there is little written on the topic of Black *fat* queer women and femmes' experiences in academia. Fatness is a generative analytic that organizes our thinking about what is good and what is not; who is worthy and who is not. As a tool of social control, aversion to fatness has facilitated such movements as the "fight against obesity" wherein fat bodies are not only marked as abhorrent but are further designated as a public health epidemic (Wykes, 2014). Fat bodies in this climate are relegated as ill and disproportionately siphoning resources from a society that is plagued with the responsibility of providing care. With this understanding, we can interrogate the intersections of antiblackness and fatphobia to unpack how Black fat women and femmes have been positioned as the antithesis of human. As Black fat women and femmes, our genealogy of marginality traces back to Sara Baartman, a Khoikhoi woman taken from South Africa, who was used as spectacle and validation for Black fat women and femmes' bodies to be read as repugnant (Hobson, 2005; Shaw, 2006).

Our contemporary marginalization rests on the substantiation of thinness as goodness; the white supremacist project of such a position continues to operate in all arenas and, as such, figures into academic spaces. Schooling systems reproduce not only difference but marginalization based on social logics that limit who is validated and supported. Using Black Feminism and Fat Studies to approach my Black fat queer femme body provides necessary contextualization of my marginality that lives in liminality even within the margins. Kaila Story (2016) argues in defense of Black queer femme identity as an intentionally queer identity and not one as a pantomime of heterosexual femininity. Navigating the hypervisible/invisible dichotomy as a Black queer femme in academia necessitates a persistent declaration of her queerness in spaces that elide her presentation as queer. Story enters LGBTQ courses, some of which she created for the minor at her institution, to be met with shock from students and even disbelief that she can embody queerness. In the eyes of her students, her queerness is negated by her racial identity and femme gender performance. Femmeness in this way is not taken as a valid queer identity, but rather one that is seemingly performed under the influence of internalized oppression. To announce one's femme identity becomes a resistive effort to destabilize the assumption of not only what a professor looks like but one who is a queer feminist professor.

Likewise, fatness announces itself in such a fashion that engenders limiting projections. In the introduction of *Queering Fat Embodiment*, Jackie Wykes asks the question "Is fat queer?" (2014, p. 1) and contends with the trope of fat lesbians who *settle* for women because they fail to attract men. In this case, fat queerness is interpreted as a failure in heterosexuality. In writing towards a Black fat queer femme embodiment, I want to claim the intentionality of my being. My queer femme identity is inherently informed by being Black and fat. Sydney Fonteyn Lewis (2012) illuminates how she came to femme through her Black fat body. In a world that fails to acknowledge the gender agency of Black people, femme becomes a mode of articulating her defiantly queer embodiment (Lewis, 2012). Similarly, to announce myself in this manner situates my stakes in destabilizing expectations of a graduate instructor. While students may enter the classroom expecting a white, male, thin person as instructor, or even a thin person of colour, I use my body as a place of knowing to disrupt this expectation. I wear clothing that does not seek to conceal my fatness or feed into the confines of professionalization, but rather highlights my body's presence. I take my embodied experiences and identities as examples to engage my students in critical reflection. In my pedagogy, research agenda, and overall liberatory vision I aim to think critically through what it means to have an intersectional praxis and not just posture towards one.

In writing this chapter, I reflect on the history of Black fat women and femmes' marginality to illuminate the contours of our experiences, I examine my experiences as student and instructor to highlight the tensions and alternatives in teaching from a Black queer feminist pedagogical stance, and I think through possibilities that are present when we dream and work towards freer ways of being. This work seeks to articulate the nuances of Black fat queer femme embodiment, but does not aim to represent all. That is to say, I recognize the limits of my narrative. While I navigate marginality due to race, gender, sexuality, size, and other dimensions of social identity I also navigate privilege due to being able bodied, being a United States citizen, being cisgender, assumed to hold or practice Judeo-Christian ideological beliefs, and other such privileges. In attempting to bring light to Black fat queer femmes' experiences in academia, I hope that others think through this positionality and offer their own generative perspectives.

From Sara Baartman to Mammy in Perpetuity: Black Fat Femme Bodies and Constructions of the Human

Dylan Rodriguez explains, "white supremacy may be understood as a logic of social organization that produces regimented, institutionalized, and militarized conceptions of 'hierarchized' human difference" (2006, p. 11). White supremacy also organizes other sites of domination. Empire building delineates clear and proper citizens and subjected bodies. The construction of a clearly defined citizen of empire elides any consideration of Black fat women and femmes. Further, Andrea Elizabeth Shaw contends:

> the large black female body has had a significant role in the formation of both black and white identity throughout the Diaspora because it functions as an opposing identity anchor—an image that affirms "legitimate" identity as different from what that image represents.
>
> (2006, p. 19)

With white, cisgender, male, propertied individuals articulated as the paradigm of human, we can understand fatphobia as intimately tied to the project of white supremacy. The Black fat femme body becomes a visual signifier of difference in comparison to white bodies. Black fat femme bodies are deeply necessary to the substantiation of dominance.

Hortense Spillers's (1987) foundational analysis of the Black body made captive in *Mama's Baby, Papa's Maybe: An American Grammar Book* provides requisite language to approach Black fat women and femmes' specific site of marginalization. Central to this text is Spillers's argument that through the theft of the Black body and inscription of race as repugnant, Black captive bodies become "de-gendered," with the subject positions of "male" and "female" only holding weight when held in comparison to white subjectivities. In other words, Black women and femmes were subjected to the same labour and punishment as their male and masculine counterparts. However, the specific gendered violences they experienced became illegible within a "de-gendered" conception of Blackness. The imposition of meanings onto the Black body brings into relief the condition of the captive body as a tool of utility and spectacle. "Pornotroping," as used by Spillers, refers to the visual process of transforming a person into flesh under slavery wherein the flesh on display becomes spectacle for bestowing the (white) viewer with affirmation of their own autonomy. In creating a distinction between "body" and "flesh" Spillers describes the state of "total objectification" that captive bodies are subject to. In that objectification, captive bodies are appropriated for medical experimentation, freak show parades, and other such uses that define the captive body as one of use for whites.

Making body into flesh facilitates the process by which entire peoples are seen as incapable of feeling pain and are subsequently subjected to gross amounts of violence. As an illegible being, Black positionality serves as the opposite of whiteness. Spillers's concept of "pornotroping" and its facilitation of violent voyeuristic engagements with Black bodies is particularly useful as we turn to the life of Sara Baartman. As a Khoikhoi woman captured from South Africa, Sara Baartman's life, experiences with violence, and visual representation illuminate the nature of Black women and femmes' marginalization. Baartman was one of many captive Black women that were exhibited in freakshows across Europe during the nineteenth century (Hobson, 2005). In life and post mortem, Baartman's buttocks and genitalia were presented as a physiological oddity. During life, she was forced to dance in front of European audiences while nude, allowing spectators to gaze at her body which had been marked as hypersexualized and thus animalistic (Hobson, 2005; Shaw, 2006). Disparagingly referred to as the "Hottentot Venus," her moniker was no indicator of aspirational beauty, but rather a signifier of her designation as a grotesque contrast to white womanhood.

Further, Sabrina Strings (2012, 2015) reveals how fatness more generally was not always cast as a public health epidemic. Through investigating the historical construction of the ideal citizen during colonization, Strings highlights how thinness was cast in opposition to fatness at the end of the eighteenth century and the beginning of the nineteenth century (Forth 2012; Strings, 2012, 2015). The binary of white subjects as disciplined and civilized and Black people as uninhibited and primal was bolstered by racial science that purported that Black people acted upon base desires (Strings, 2015). Prior characterizations of Black people as excessive physically and emotional, lacking control, and being particularly lascivious allowed for racialized fatphobia to flourish. Colonists and racial scientists' fatphobia was not a matter of determining physiological well-being, but rather a means to differentiate "'primitive' corpulence" from "'civilized' moderation" (Forth, 2012, p. 215). This distinction is useful to note when considering the shift in how fatness was viewed as a physical manifestation of prosperity in Europe during the eighteenth century to one associated with moral ineptitude when applied to colonized peoples (Forth, 2012). Christopher Forth (2012) relays that as colonists travelled throughout Africa during the late eighteenth century and witnessed practices of deliberately fattening girls, colonial viewpoints of fatness shifted. The colonists were struck by fat girls whose skin was greased and displayed as beautiful. While European ideals of women's beauty rested on slenderness, intentional fattening practices in parts of Africa illuminated a different standard (Forth, 2012). This contrast in the colonists' minds was regarded not simply as a difference of ideals but described such standards as a "defect" (p. 219) at best, and as repulsive at worst.

Colonists shifting perspective on fatness and its racialized tones not only produced distinct categories of "primitive" and "civilized," but also prescribed an appropriate servile class. The image of the mammy further entrenches Black fat women and femmes to a subservient position that mollifies anxieties about Black women and femmes claiming agency, whether through their sexuality or disavowal of whiteness (Hill Collins, 2014; Shaw, 2006). Patricia Hill Collins (2014) argues that the mammy figure is among the oldest controlling images used to dominate Black women and femmes. As a visual signifier, the figure of the mammy represents not acquiescence but rather willful allegiance to white domination in how she happily obliges her white superiors. This image symbolically functions on multiple levels to maintain race, gender, class, ability, sexuality, and body hegemony. The image of the mammy suggests that Black women and femmes are only legible within the limits of whiteness if they care for white families as they neglect their own, lack sexual agency, and remain economically exploited in the interest of serving whiteness (Hill Collins, 2014). While the mammy has a significant impact on how all Black women and femmes are viewed and treated, the figure is especially important for Black fat women and femmes. With her large body in comparison to the paradigm of delicate, small white femininity, the mammy's size further signifies her capacity to serve—her overabundance in size is an indicator of her limitless reserve of care. Whereas Baartman's large body came to represent Black hypersexualized femme bodies, the mammy's large body is de-sexualized. Both representations serve to cast Black fat femme bodies in monstrous contrast to white femininity.

A Black Fat Queer Feminist Pedagogy: Disrupting the Neo-Liberal University

Throughout my time in graduate school, fatphobia was rarely far from view as I navigated spaces as student and instructor. The sheer lack of chairs or desks made with my body in mind amplified my discomfort. When discussions of food security led to discussions of food deserts and fat bodies, and how fat bodies of colour in particular were "evidence" of that insecurity, I felt anxious. I became nervous when announcing my research objectives. Naming the dismantling of fatphobia as intimately tied to the project of dismantling all forms of marginalization was met with seemingly polite curiosity that would often be followed by conversations about what foods were "clean" or having to exercise to "earn" the right to eat seemingly "unclean" food. I have since felt more comfortable in disrupting fatphobia and the normativity of thinness, yet it takes a daily recommitment to this struggle.

In doing this work, I needed to claim my body. I needed not only to carry my stories of marginalization as testimony, but also to recognize the power of my embodiment. Aesthetics became a space where I have pushed against the confines of how an "appropriate" academic and queer person should look. As a Black fat queer femme, my self-presentation becomes an act of reclaiming my body from entrapments that might otherwise curtail my agency. I wear colourful and exuberant clothes designed with patterns that celebrate Black culture, and short skirts, dresses, and shorts to normalize my abundant flesh in the classroom. My septum is pierced and my hairstyle changes as regularly as the quarter. Styling myself is just as much an act of remaining myself while navigating the academy as it is a chance to disrupt notions of the "appropriate" and queer. My aesthetics have been met with resistance from employers and colleagues who appraise my choice in dress, not so subtly communicating their disapproval. However, I find moments of pushing back on the expected neutral palette of graduate dress to be enjoyable.

Despite dealing with microaggressive comments or looks, I think about how my self-fashioning is a signal to students that I am an approachable instructor. Mel Michelle Lewis (2011) re-signifies her identity as a Black lesbian feminist professor as that of "sista-professor." Because she teaches in Black Women's Studies, Lewis's students are primarily Black women. She is a young professor who navigates the world in similar fashion to her students, understands the cultural references they make, receives compliments from them on her fashion choices, and builds their trust in sharing personal accounts. She crafts a learning community that calls on her students to engage fully with the material, and they, in turn, consider her to be "a very serious teacher" (p. 54). Similarly, I see myself embodying the spirit of a sista-professor. While I'm not a faculty member, my identity and role as graduate student enables me to relate to my students as I teach them about topics ranging from race and racism to how to conduct research in the social sciences and humanities. I craft spaces where students reflect on course material through lived experiences. I model critical reflection by sharing my experiences in learning about issues of marginality and my current missteps in trying to actualize liberation. Further, my students confide in me: we have conversations about topics as diverse as feeling like an impostor in the academy, struggling to come out to loved ones, dealing with mental health, sharing our astrological signs and the difficulties of navigating religious spaces. In disrupting the instructor-student hierarchy, I invite students to recognize their own validity and to resist the urge to pedestalize instructors.

Though I do not have full control over course readings, I take a Black queer feminist pedagogical stance in my instruction. As Lewis (2011) suggests, embodiment is a useful tool for instructing students on marginalization. Where course readings fail to surface how fatphobia is tied to imperialist projects, I make these connections. When students shy away from naming their internalized fatphobia, I ask them to reflect on how they read my body. When they first entered the classroom, how did they see me? Did they think I was capable of teaching? I ask these questions, not to shame students nor to subject myself to ridicule, but rather to illuminate the pervasiveness of fatphobia. It's urgent that even within courses that do not directly address fatphobia, my embodiment and my pedagogy do the work of disruption. Bryant Keith Alexander asks, "How do we not *not* teach about race and sexuality as Black LGBTQIA instructors?" (2005, p. 262). Our mere presence stands to shift the acknowledgement of the heterogeneity of Blackness. To this question, Alexander answers, "We do it not necessarily through the *material content* of the course, but through our conviction and the *material fact* of our black gay bodies in the classroom, which always already signals a teachable moment" (p. 262).

As such, my Black fat queer femme body signifies a teachable moment where we can say "fat" without it being a verbal proxy for "lazy, sloppy, uninhibited" and other such tropes. In a seminar of 20 undergraduate students, my co-instructor and I provided check-in questions to center our students' experiences as more than just academics pursuing research. In that seminar, I explained concepts from Black feminists such as Audre Lorde that explain the necessity of collectively envisioning freedom, not only as useful in our academic work, but important to how we move throughout the world. I bring in my fatness through Lorde and other texts to ask students to reflect on who we demand care from and why. I step away from being an academic mammy while still using care as a necessary facet of teaching by openly discussing my limits and need to create balance in my life. I use my Black fat queer femme body to ask students to reflect on how they can shift their understanding of knowledge production and the validity of narratives as evidence of marginalization.

Living a Black Fat Queer Feminist Life

When research is "me"-search, or we're motivated by the promise of liberation, or when we just cannot "turn off" our awareness of oppressive realities, we can encounter bias with fascination, exhaustion, determination, or even confusion. As I name the work I do, work that rests at the intersections of race, gender, sexuality, and fatness, I am met with those who think of themselves as forward-thinking. Some of these people commend the work of Fat Studies and simultaneously enact violence towards fat bodies. Within a conversation about the need to upend limiting standards of what a "good" body is, I also deal with discussions about colleagues' new diets or work out plans that will hopefully distance themselves from fatness. What does it mean to open myself up to constant disappointment? How can I prepare myself to disrupt these moments of invalidation? And what does it look like to care for myself through these experiences? Finding community with other fat people of colour who navigate the academy similarly has been an antidote to the normative fatphobic violence I confront.

With colleagues who navigate fatphobia as people of colour, I find solace from a space that consistently devalues my being. Although I feel more comfortable than I once did about announcing my research, I still feel anxious when I teach. I worry about how the outfit that made me feel confident earlier that morning will accentuate parts of my body for all students to see. I worry about how I will be compared if I am co-teaching with a thin, conventionally attractive colleague. Who will want to hear what I have to say with them standing next to me? When these anxieties come up, because fatphobia is persistent in many ways, I talk with colleagues about these feelings. I remind myself that only I can teach through my embodiment. Although I will continue to deal with the creeping moments of self-doubt, speaking these truths is a consistent act in destabilizing my own fear of fatphobia. In teaching through my embodiment I stand to do more in the pursuit of alternative realities than living in fear of how I will be read.

References

Alexander, B. K. (2005). Embracing the teachable moment: The Black gay body on the classroom as embodied text. In E. P. Johnson & M. G. Henderson, (Eds), *Black Queer Studies: A critical anthology*. Durham, NC: Duke University Press.

Bailey, M., & Miller, S. (2015). When margins become centered: Black queer women in front and outside of the classroom. *Feminist Formations, 27*(3), 168–188.

Gumbs, A.P. (2018) *M Archive: After the end of the world*. Durham, NC: Duke University Press.

Hill Collins, P. (2014). *Black feminist thought: Knowledge, consciousness, and the politics of empowerment*. New York: Routledge.

Hobson, J. (2005) *Venus in the dark: Re-presenting the Black female body*. New York: Routledge.

Forth, C. (2012). Fat, desire, and disgust in the colonial imagination. *History Workshop Journal, 73*, 211–239.

Lewis, M. M. (2011). Body of knowledge: Black queer feminist, pedagogy, praxis, and embodied text. *Journal of Lesbian Studies, 15*, 49–57.

Lewis, S. F. (2012). "Everything I know about being femme I learned from *Sula*" or Toward a Black femme-inist criticism. *Trans-Scripts, 2*, 100–125.

Oparah, J. (2014). Challenging complicity: The Neoliberal university and the prison industrial complex. In P. Chatterjee and S. Maira (Eds.), *The Imperial University: Academic Repression and Scholarly Dissent*. Minneapolis: University of Minnesota Press.

Patton, L. D. (2015). Disrupting postsecondary prose toward a critical race theory of higher education. *Urban Education, 51*, 315–342.

Pierce, C. (1970). Offensive mechanisms. In F. B. Barbour (Ed.), *The Black seventies.* Boston: Porter Sargent Publisher.

Pierce, C. (1995). Stress analogs of racism and sexism: Terrorism, torture and disaster. In C. Willie, P. Rieker, B. Kramer, & B. Brown (Eds.), *Mental health, racism, and sexism.* Pittsburgh: University of Pittsburgh Press.

Randolph, S. (2009). "Women's liberation or … Black liberation, you're fighting the same enemies": Floryence Kennedy, Black power, and feminism. In D. F. Gore, J. Theoharis, & K. Woodard (Eds.), *Want to start a revolution? Radical women in the Black freedom struggle,* (pp. 223–247). New York: New York University Press.

Rodriguez, D. (2006). *Forced passages: Imprisoned radical intellectuals and prison regimes.* Minneapolis: University of Minnesota Press.

Saunders, P. J. (2008). Fugitive dreams of diaspora: conversations with Saidiya Hartman. *Anthurium: A Caribbean Studies Journal, 6*(1), 1–16.

Shaw, A. E. (2006). *The embodiment of disobedience: Fat Black women's unruly political bodies.* Lanham: Lexington Books.

Senyonga, M. (2017). Microaggressions, marginality, and mediation at the intersections: Experiences of Black fat women in academia. *Interactions: UCLA Journal of Education and Information Studies, 13*, 1–23.

Spillers, H. (1987). Mama's baby, papa's maybe: An American grammar book. *Diacritics, 17*(2), 64–81.

Story, K. (2016). Fear of a Black femme: The existential conundrum of embodying a Black femme identity while being a professor of Black, queer, and feminist studies. *Journal of Lesbian Studies,* 1–13.

Strings, S (2012). *Thin, white, and saved: Fat stigma and the fear of the big Black body.* PhD dissertation, University of California, San Diego.

Strings, S. (2015). Obese Black women as "social dead weight": Reinventing the "diseased Black woman". *Signs,* 107–130.

Wilder, C. S. (2013). *Ebony and ivy: Race, slavery, and the troubled history of America's universities.* New York: Bloomsbury.

Wykes, J. (2014) Introduction: Why queering fat embodiment? In C. Pause, J. Wykes, & S. Murray (Eds.), *Queering fat embodiment,* (pp. 1–13). Burlington: Ashgate.

19 Fat Camp

A Conversation on YA Fiction, Fat Shame, and Queer Love

Marty Fink and Julie Hollenbach

Introduction: The Connective Shame of Fat

Fat Camp is a young adult (YA) novel in progress. The manuscript, authored by Marty Fink and imagined for a readership of preteens, responds to the challenge of femmegimp crip theorist Loree Erickson, who asks what it would mean "to create and find places where we are appreciated and celebrated for the very differences that are often used to justify our oppression" (2007, p. 42). The novel's thirteen-year-olds experience fatness not as a "site of shame" (Erickson, 2007, p. 42) but as a powerful, hungry site of adolescent desire. The novel emplaces its preteen girls in a queer, trans, kinky, D/s (dominant/submissive) dance of elementary school bullying in the world of upper-middle-class Jewish private school power negotiations.

This chapter presents a dialogue between us (Fink and Hollenbach) as queer lovers. Originally presented at the *Thickening Fat* symposium at Ryerson University (Toronto) in February 2018, this dialogue moved conversations that were unfolding privately into a public sphere, thus presenting pillow talk as a mode of theorizing central to the formation of queer intimacies and knowledges. Sharing our conversations worked to make visible a methodology that acknowledges interruption, different and evolving perspectives, tension and dissonance, and plays of control; as Lauren Berlant and Lee Edelman (2014) suggest, "conversation complicates the prestige of autonomy and the fiction of authorial sovereignty by introducing the unpredictability of moving in relation to another" (p. x).

We chose a dramaturgical format for the presentation of our intimate reflections on the power dynamics in *Fat Camp* and in our relationship, following Ann Cvetkovich's (2003) idea that "Queer performance creates publics by bringing together live bodies in space" (p. 9). Queer intimacies are never a private matter; therefore, we took theatrical dialogue as an opportunity to burst conventional boundaries of academic remove and individualism, determined that "the theatrical experience is not just about what's on stage but also about who's in the audience creating community" (p. 9). Exploding heteronormative and skinny space and time are central considerations in our discussion, and indeed anchored our decision to present our dialogue as a performance that would speak to bodies and experiences in the room, acknowledging the creation of a text as a collective unfolding utterance.

This chapter, an adaptation of our original performed script, discusses *Fat Camp*'s fictional preteens in an effort to take up Erickson's call to reimagine sites of shame through acts of queer pleasure. Our dialogue format in this chapter accepts Elsbeth Probyn's (2005) challenge to uncover shame's "hidden merits" (p. ix) and to understand shame's lessons as "interesting and important" (p. ix). As Probyn asserts, and as we discuss via *Fat Camp,* "being in love offers endless possibilities for shame" (p. ix). We animate our conversation about *Fat Camp* toward opening space for queer intimacy, curiosity, and connection, what Probyn characterizes as "our longing for communication, touch, lines of entanglement, and reciprocity" (p. ix). Probyn asks what would happen if we linger in bad feelings, reinterpreting the body's shame as that which might enable "the very possibility of love" (p. 3). We thus present a theoretical, intersectional conversation about bad feelings at *Fat Camp* to investigate how pain, failure, shame, and yearning are emotions that can bring together nonconforming bodies, including those of fat, trans, and even fictional young queers.

Our conversation engages with the ever expanding theoretical alliances between Fat Studies, Disability Studies, and Critical Race Studies. April Herndon (2002), for instance, regards Disability Studies as an opportunity to address the "pervasive and perverse *fatphobia* of our culture" (p. 124). Disability Studies also advocates for a return to the body and its limits, understanding pain as that which inspires us to engage with our own feelings, sensations, and lived experiences as vital sources of knowledge (Wendell, 2001; Mollow, 2006; Baril, 2015). Along these lines, we also acknowledge and turn to the conceptual frameworks of critical race theorists who question who has access to happiness and good feeling, and posit that people of colour often normalize pain and illness and feelings of discomfort and malady as the daily experience of race-based oppression (Romero, 2000; Ahmed, 2010; Nicolaidis et al., 2010). If, as Herndon posits and Erickson demonstrates, disabled bodies become sites of power precisely because of their differences, fatness can be understood as a way to return to the body by reimagining shame as a potential locus of using (and even sexualizing) bad feelings to generate what Cameron Awkward-Rich (2017) theorizes as a potential site of love and of "desire, that which causes us to reach for something outside of ourselves" (p. 839).

Drawing on the work of Afrofuturist theorists and black queer scholars, our dialogue further proposes that queer crip representations of fat shame can alter space and time. Fat Studies scholars have previously argued that fat bodies are queer for resisting "normative markers of time" (McFarland, Slothouber, & Taylor, 2018, p. 137; Freeman, 2010). Representing newly imagined futures, Afrofuturist theorists argue, is not about emplacing bodies in an abstract eventual moment, but about bodies "becoming present" (Eshun, 2003, p. 290) and engaging with the "depths of the subconscious and imagination" (Womack, 2013, p. 2). The Afrofuturist representation of fat flesh builds futures where fat shame opens possibilities for gender play and queer love. For example, in Kiese Laymon's Afrofuturist novel *Long Division* (2013), Citoyen "City" Coldson, the fourteen-year-old narrator, muses on his experience of "trying to eat my feelings" (p. 101). He scrutinizes his own fat image on YouTube as a site of shame for falling outside body norms: "I never thought I was super cute but I didn't realize how much my thighs rubbed together and how the back of my head was bigger than every other head in all the videos" (p. 105). City, however, locates fatness and eating as a way of countering the embodied pain of anti-black racism: "if I was eating my feelings, it felt so good while it was happening" (p. 101). City's grappling with his good and bad feelings about eating-as-coping, creates a narrative of his body's visible fatness (and queerness) as testament to the tenacity of fat, black bodies refusing to disappear.

Reading *Fat Camp* alongside these Afrofuturist YA fictional representations of fat black youth resisting state violence thus also challenges us to interrogate *Fat Camp*'s narrative function: in representing white, rich, fat bodies, how does *Fat Camp* risk creating whitewashed norms of "who fat people get to be" (Averill, 2016, p. 14). As Lindsey Averill (2016) argues, "achieving fat empowerment must walk hand in hand with the multifaceted goals of feminist empowerment, racial equality, and other movements for social and civil justice [... and] the intersectionality of oppression" (p. 29). Our conversation therefore aims to raise theoretical concerns about the process of fiction writing in order to analyze how representation, as Michele Byers (2018) asserts, might begin by "centering queerness" (p. 160) through an Afrofuturist, anti-racist framework that can reimagine preteen fat shame for the intimate connections it holds the potential to build.

Our conversation thus begins with an introduction to our writing process and to our own collaboration as lovers, before moving on to give an analysis of *Fat Camp* as a negotiation of white, Jewish fat bodies in time and space. Throughout our text we incorporate excerpts from *Fat Camp* as anchors to our discussions of character development and queer shame to reflect on the intersectional, theoretical links between embodied love and bad feelings. In doing so, we wonder what kinds of futures *Fat Camp* might bring into existence, and whether queer/trans future fatness can act backwards, bringing fat love into our own queer childhoods and into our present.

Weird Queer Love: Shame as an Opening

JULIE HOLLENBACH: Marty wrote *Fat Camp*, a young adult manuscript about fat queerdos who get sent to fat camp but rebel through friendship and the pleasure of food against the brutal strictures of "health" and "wellness" promoted by the camp's intensive diet and exercise regime. They proposed an intersectional, theoretical discussion about the manuscript in progress as a chapter for *Thickening Fat*.

MARTY FINK: Julie was looped in to collaborate on my chapter for *Thickening Fat*, but only once this reflective process was already underway.

JULIE: Well, we only met in December 2017.

MARTY: On Tinder.

JULIE: We are lovers.

MARTY: We are. And as such, we've gotten to know each other this year through a very intense long distance courtship.

JULIE: I live in Halifax, while Marty lives in Toronto.

MARTY: Yes, and the process of physical intimacy that spans centimeters and kilometers, we've been having dialogues, textual and somatic, getting to know each other, navigating bodies and space.

JULIE: And fat between us.

MARTY: Right, so, how do we identify with fatness?

JULIE: Well, I identify as fat ... do you?

MARTY: I identified as fat until maybe September of 2017? I was fat when I submitted my abstract to this book? Now I'm not fat? And what does this mean for my sense of my body via my experience of being white, Jewish, trans, queer, and disabled, I wonder? But wait, how else do you identify, Julie?

JULIE: I identify as a queer white cis femme person, who is often invisibilized into a heteronormative gender and sexuality.

When Marty invited me to collaborate on this project, they were hoping that as a cultural historian and visual artist I could bring an extra creative layer to their chapter here.

MARTY: Because of love.

JULIE: Weird queer love! What Lauren Berlant (2012) would theorize as forms of desire and attachment that prompt "a political question about the ways norms produce attachments to living through certain fantasies" (p. 7). We wanted to theorize Marty's novel through a type of desire that resists goals "like marriage and family, property relations" (Berlant, 2012, p. 7). We hope to frame *Fat Camp* as a narrative rejecting love's most normative "stock phrases and plots" (p. 7).

MARTY: Because the desires and attachments that play out between *Fat Camp*'s main characters are so unusual ... but also kind of hot? I invited Julie into conversation with me to frame these kids' weird, violent, preteen connections through our own fully consensual adult D/s kinky desires in order to transform my experience of childhood bullying into something different...

A Taste of *Fat Camp*: An Excerpt from the Novel

From the manuscript in progress:

I just turned thirteen, so I go out on weeknights now in addition to weekend nights which I already spend 100 percent downtown. Todd, who is my oldest brother, is a penis. But he is also okay because he got a Porsche Boxer for his sixteenth birthday. And every day after Toronto Hebrew Alliance he puts me in shotgun and we pick up Shaun Gill. And Shaun sits on my lap and Todd drives us downtown to Kensington Market. In Kensington, we chainsmoke packs of cigarettes. Also, we eat multiple dozens of maple glazed donuts. And, we figure out what to do about Missy Frankel.

"We need to figure out what to do about Missy Frankel," I told Shaun after school today.

Shaun and I are basically twins because we are Jews who grew up together. We go together to places where Jews go to get loaded and suntan. In summers, our families go together to resorts in Neuchâtel. In winters, our families go together to resorts in Waikiki. At Passover, our families eat together in Palm Springs at this Passover dinner thing at the Four Seasons. Last Passover Dinner, me and Shaun drank vodka on a toilet and this year we are going to Robotrip hard on cold medication because Passover is a load.

This year, at the beginning of grade 7, me and Shaun started hooking up. We go to school at Toronto Hebrew Alliance which is so filled to the brim of its vagina with straight losers that no one even noticed how me and Shaun were holding hands in the hallway and exchanging the mushiest Valentines cards and swapping our gumballs and making out in the basement bathroom by the gym for all 35 minutes of lunchtime recess; all 15 minutes of morning recess; and all 15 minutes of afternoon recess. This was the best year because I was getting so much action. At school. Three times per day. I didn't even need to go downtown to Kensington to find homos. So fun.

But then we started going on Tumblr. And Shaun got a blog and Twitter and a YouTube channel and then he said, "dude, I'm a trans fag, not a dyke anymore Leslie, we need to breakup." And I was like, "suck a bag of dicks, Shaun, where are you going to find a fag to date at Toronto Hebrew Alliance? You are going to have to fail out and transfer to alternative school like Jimmie Stein."

Then I slapped Shaun hard across the face. And I looked at him real serious for a second. And then I laughed. And then he laughed. And then we tried smoking out of Todd's bong. But we couldn't get the smoke to come out at all. And I giggled and I said, "Shaun, cheer up. Obvi Dan Silver is a full faggot. You can suck on his balls at recess. Like I even care."

Fat Camp: Who's Who, Intersectionality, and Why Write More White Queers?

JULIE: Marty, back up—maybe we should orient our readers toward these characters first by introducing them?

MARTY: Right. So, *Fat Camp's* main character is Missy Frankel. Missy is a naive twelve-year-old, who is a white, upper-middle class Jewish genderqueer kid coming of age in Toronto's early 1990s Zionist Hebrew Day School system—oops I mean, in 2018 with the Internet—and is deeply immersed in their mother's diet culture. Missy Frankel is definitely based on my own experience.

JULIE: And then there's the antagonist, Leslie Adler.

MARTY: Leslie Adler is the speaker in the above excerpt from the manuscript. She is the thirteen-year-old, white, very rich, fat Jewish dyke who loves being fat, and very brutally bullies Missy.

Missy and Leslie both go to the same school, Toronto Hebrew Alliance. Leslie and her best friend Shaun bully Missy relentlessly for being fat and weird. A lot of people don't believe Leslie Adler could be real, because she's so self-assured in her fatness. But she's based on my very real childhood bully, so I can attest that there's really nothing inauthentic about her confidence.

JULIE: For me, in this story, it is Missy who reads as an elusive character who could never be real.

MARTY: Ah yes, Julie holds all the same critiques of my manuscript as all the reviewers and peers.

JULIE: Missy occupies the center of the story, without taking the shape of the space around them, or without disrupting the space's shape. To me, they are a character who doesn't seem affected by bullying and fat shaming, and whose unperturbedness doesn't impact the experience of their tormentors or the culture of fat shaming in their home and school.

MARTY: Everyone wants me to revise significantly because the manuscript reads like Missy has no feelings.

JULIE: For me, Missy can't be real, because nothing lands. They blink into the tremendous and relentless meanness that is pointed at them. And this is tender stuff. I'm reading into this pulpy, raw narrative that reflects the childhood experience of my new lover. I'm feeling my own tender cuts and bruises from childhood. How do I hold space for myself, for Marty, and for you, my reader, in this narrative and analysis?

MARTY: I feel conflicted, too, Julie, about you holding space for my story. In fact, I feel conflicted about my own story taking up any narrative space at all: I don't know how to do effective anti-racist work when talking about my childhood, as someone who grew up benefiting from settler colonialism in Canada and in Palestine. I feel shame from my own experience of whiteness and of class privilege, and I worry that my talking about fat shame will whitewash and replace other stories. What is my objective in producing another narrative of fatness, transmasculinity, and whiteness? Is this really anti-racist work? I'm not sure if it can be, and therefore I don't know if I feel motivated to finish the project.

JULIE: I think this critique is important Marty, and I don't know how to reconcile this with your desire to publish the book or to tell your story, to narrate your trauma. I want to see you engaging intersectionally with disability theorists like Wendell, Mallow, Baril, and Awkward-Rich to reframe the conversation about pain and survival. I want you to recenter bad feelings, to address the racial injustices reflected by these very questions of whether your book should even exist.

And, I think *Fat Camp* must exist, and I insist on Missy's presence in a story in which they are the main character. Here, I am reminded of Rasheedah Phillips' (2015) theorization of Black time and space in opposition to Western linear time, as fundamentally informed by recurrence and repetition (p. 19). Recurrence offers the opportunity to change the past in the process of bringing the future into the present. Phillips draws on Henri Bergson's assertion in 1920 that "in order to advance the moving reality, you must replace yourself within it. Install yourself within change, and you grasp at once both change itself and the successive states in which it might be immobilized" (Phillips, 2015, p. 21). *Fat Camp*, as a work of autobiographical fiction, has the capacity to restructure the past and shift the future. I interpret your lack of motivation to complete *Fat Camp*, and your desire to abandon a narrative that centers whiteness and masculinity in the story's characters, spaces, and events, as the present manifestation of disembodiment brought on by shame and an unwillingness to inhabit a white, masculine-of-center corporeal reality. Finding a way into your body today, allows you to rewrite a childhood evacuated of embodiment through violent events and shame that avalanched you in the sediments of trauma, forcing you out of yourself. Opening and realizing a future where you are present and accountable to the impact of your embodiment in and on the world today transforms your past.

Embodiment? Theorizing Shame's Good/Bad Feelings through Camp

MARTY: I had a reader of the manuscript who said, "Marty, why does Missy have no embodied feelings? These are twelve-year-olds. Make their palms sweaty. Make Missy actually experience their feelings..." But Julie, how do I write from my own experience about my embodied feelings when I never had any embodied feelings about getting fat shamed or bullied to begin with?

JULIE: Marty, you have never had *embodied feelings* in response to being fat shamed or bullied?

MARTY: Julie, I guess that's why it's so easy for me to discuss my queerness via theory? Allyson Mitchell talks about fatness and the limits of theory. She writes:

One of the things that makes queer theory around fat bodies a struggle is that theory, like the media, literally can't feel me. I am not sure if there is a clear way to integrate my experiences as a fat artist, academic and activist in a clear path between the depth of my embodiment when the landscapes that I'm navigating personally and theoretically feel like a contradiction in the larger world. Working towards a tactile, corporeal, resistant, fat art that feels queerly is what the work pictured here is trying to do.

(2018, p. 157)

But for me, as someone whose experience of being fat and trans, and living with childhood trauma, creates distance between me and my feelings, theory *feels* like the perfect place through which to try to reconnect to my fatness and what it means. Or meant, I guess: my body is not fat right now, and I'm not sure yet what that *feels* like either.

JULIE: Really, Marty? You feel nothing when revisiting one of the most uncomfortable parts of the book, the scene where Dan Silver humiliatingly dumps Missy at the pool by making fun of the pubes springing free from Missy's bathing suit? And, just to clarify for our readers, this awkward exchange actually happened to you as a twelve-year-old, right?

MARTY: Yes. Verbatim. With my first love, a hot toppy tomboy mean girl at Jewish sleepaway camp.

JULIE: Can you tell us more about camp?

MARTY: Yes, camp … My Jewish summer camp had a racist name and a racist logo of Indigenous children that we wore on our white camp t-shirts to Shabbos dinner every Friday night, so the presence of the Jewish camp on stolen Indigenous land was not something unnamed, it was part of the whole camp package of settler colonial violence that of course is also the postwar project of Israel. Sandra Fox's (2018) work on Jewish sleepaway camps connects their increasing popularity since the postwar period to increasing affluence and also to a desire to create "real, authentic, or ideal Jews" (p. 157) "by taking children out of the home, the school, and away from mainstream American culture […] after the decimation of European Jewry" (p. 157). The concentration camps and their legacy, interestingly, are also identified within Heather Sykes' (2010) study of physical education as a normalizing, fatphobic space: one Jewish participant in Sykes' study discusses experiencing fatness in connection to his mother's "memories of famine during the Holocaust" (p. 56). It is interesting to think about how fatness and diet culture both reflect intergenerational trauma connected to death and displacement.

JULIE: Right. I'm reminded of Moor Mother Goddess' (2015) conception of an "Anthropology of Consciousness"; through this Black Quantum Futurist lens diet culture and Jewish fat camps can be understood as examples of how Jews today navigate the relationship between space and their bodies from moment to moment, calculating how the things and spaces in their world "affect the way we remember or forget our past and future memories" (p. 8). Moor Mother Goddess situates trauma as "cyclical," suggesting that trauma as it is remembered or forgotten in lived moments is the result of "neurological pathways set in one's brain [that] reflect the genetic trauma formed in one's genes" (p. 8). It is useful for me to extend this analysis to fat. How the fat body remembers and forgets trauma and shame on a genetic and cellular level, as the body fluctuates in its fatness; what is banished or recalled as it explodes out, what is banished or recalled through restriction and diminishment. And in *Fat Camp*, perhaps, how the Jewish fat body forgets and can come to remember trauma.

MARTY: For me, sleepaway camp involved much body shaming, and this shame could feel both bad and good. Channeling the pain and also the power of having a body that is the legacy of survival of genocide, while simultaneously being a gender non-conforming body actively erased in a society that privileges and enforces binary genders. Despite all the bullying, camp always created queer spaces for me, it was a sexy place where genderqueer Jewish kids had a lot of time and space to play with our bodies together.

JULIE: With shame, as with camp, I think it really helps to remove the "good-bad" axis. Sontag does this in relation to a camp aesthetic, which is different than "camp" as we've been discussing it, but helpful to our analysis of the disruptiveness of queer culture, and the power this culture has to erupt normative space and time. In her famous *Notes on Camp* (1999/1964), Sontag writes:

Camp taste turns its back on the good-bad axis of ordinary aesthetic judgment. Camp doesn't reverse things. It doesn't argue that the good is bad, or the bad is good. What it does is to offer for art (and life) a different—a supplementary—set of standards.

(p. 9)

MARTY: And, campy performance, as Muñoz (1999) theorizes in his queer of color critique work, uses disidentification to challenge racist and anti-queer cultural norms (Muñoz, 1999, p. 3; Richards, 2016).

JULIE: So, what can we learn from camp, Marty? Let's read the manuscript excerpt now about Missy's pubes at the swim docks. Marty, you can read as Missy.

MARTY/MISSY: "What are you laughing at, Dan Silver? Is there something wrong with you?"

JULIE/DAN SILVER: "Wrong with me? Missy, do you like spiders?"

MARTY/MISSY: "What's your problem, Dan Silver?"

JULIE/DAN SILVER: "Well, I hope you like spiders Missy, because there are spiders crawling out of your bathing suit."

JULIE: Well, did you feel anything?

MARTY: Feelings in my body? No. And not at age twelve. I wish in our collaboration, Julie, you could help me feel out what that narrative is, how to tell this story but while I actually feel it this time. To make it bring me closer to myself, closer to you.

JULIE: Marty, I'm not the fat femme here to be your fat foil. I am not here to feel your feelings for you. My role is not to allow you to deflect your vulnerabilities. The real vulnerability that presenting and sharing Missy represents as an auto-biographical gesture, nor the vulnerability of masculinity (over-represented and fraught as it may be).

Marty, think about how your relationship with me actually plays out. How there are clearly more desirable forms of gendered fatness; how fatness, along with other forms of bodily social positioning make certain gendered bodies invisible or hyper-visible as fat is more socially acceptable and desirable as a femme or feminine attribute, whereas androgenous and masculine gender presentations are troubled by fatness because of its strong cultural associations with femininity.

MARTY: And Julie, as you point out, this whole conversation essentially gives me credit for your ideas by recentering the masc subject: Missy Frankel, who is essentially me. I can now be celebrated for asking what it means for masculine people to be fat, to take up space, to disconnect emotionally from diet culture, and then to let femmes work that out. Perhaps I owe you a public apology here?

JULIE: No, Marty, I'm calling you in. And I think I'm starting to get it.

MARTY: Get what, Julie?

JULIE: The queerness of the power dynamic between Leslie Adler, age thirteen, as a bossy, bratty, mean femme top, and Missy, age twelve, but with less useful Internet access, as a clueless, soft bottom. This hot dynamic where Leslie just wants to beat the shit out of Missy, and Missy comes to long for the oblivion of … of what, Marty?

MARTY: Tell me more…

Fat Futures: Narrating Shame through Time Travel

JULIE: Marty, I'm only realizing now that what makes Leslie and Missy sexy is that this dynamic between them actually occurs outside of existing possible narrative forms. Your fat narrative will have to, in Mitchell's framework of fat queer theory, "make room for different ways of seeing fat than what has culturally been available to fat subjects" (2018, p. 148). *Fat Camp* exists in a fat place, this place of wanting where reading about the pervy, queer, D/s dynamic between these two girls made me really uncomfortable. Reading through *Fat Camp*, I could not fathom how to sexualize it because it doesn't end happily ever after. It doesn't contain wholeness or sweetness.

The dynamic between them feels coercive. Definitely non-consensual. Missy feels nothing, And Leslie seems to hold all the power –

MARTY: Exactly. And to connect this all to Queer/Fat/Disability Studies, the question of *Fat Camp*, ultimately is, as Erickson urges us to inquire: how to find power and desire through pain, in the things that bring us shame, in all the ways we long to get bullied, what happens to our bodies when we are called fat by the fat girl? What would it mean to yearn for this instead of longing for thin-ness, able-bodied health, marriage, future? What if shame really could bring us together, as good and as bad at that might feel?

JULIE: And this returns us to thinking about queer time. Sykes (2010) theorizes that "fat phobic discourses construct the fat body as out of control, out of place, and out of shape" (p. 49). And Afrofuturism reminds us that in taking control of space, the future, we must also understand fat bodies as rupturing time, of traveling through time differently. Fat time, fat scholarship teaches us, "is abundant and spacious" (Tidgwell et al., 2018, p. 115). Shame, Marty, is what holds this space for us, our love, what transforms our bodies in time for making each other "bigger" (p. 115).

MARTY: Yes! Our love exists in fat time, a time that Tidgwell et al. theorize as that which "resists containment, 'lets itself go,' and stretches boundaries. Fat time embodies a productive amplification: when a hand grabs a chunk of fat flesh, you see and feel more clearly what it is made of. Whether you squeeze it, attempt to confine it, or cover it up, fat will reveal and define itself" (p. 115).

JULIE: And what happens to our past and to our future when we read *Fat Camp* together? Marty, It wasn't until the end of the book that I even began to understand that Missy is into this torture. And Marty, this is all too terrifying to me because I haven't eroticized or fetishished meanness in this way. Or found a way to disassociate with meanness in a way that allows it to be eroticized. It's too embodied.

MARTY: But Julie, exactly! This is what allows me to return now, as a queer trans fatty who is no longer fat at the moment, to my body. This kind of meanness as play, as theory, as sex between us, pulling me back in. Making me lose myself in spite of, because of: disability, pain, past trauma. Returning to these twelve-year old moments again, pubes exposed, only to feel things this time. Through fat. And femme. With you.

Conclusion: Shame Feels Good and Bad at *Fat Camp*

I just want to kick Missy Frankel in her bony shins with my hockey skate. I want to make Missy Frankel get down on her knees and suck the salt off my Ugg boots. I want to fold up Missy Frankel's fat face and shove it into the pocket of my Canada Goose Down Jacket and then zip up the zipper and just make her just GO AWAY. Then me and Shaun can just wear our matching Versaces and just live our matching stealth lives together downtown without anyone from Toronto Hebrew Alliance

ever noticing anything that has ever gone on in the history of time anywhere south of Davenport. Missy Frankel can lick the ear gunk off my
q-tips and clean my cat's piss with her toothbrush and put this nasty
bong water into her enema and eat a big hole through my big fat lezzie
underpants.

I'm so over it.

Bibliography

Ahmed, S. (2010). *The Promise of Happiness*. Durham, NC: Duke University Press.

Averill, L. (2016). Do fat-positive representations really exist in YA? Review of fat-positive characters in young adult literature. *Fat Studies*, 5(1),14–31.

Awkward-Rich. (2017). Trans, feminism: Or, reading like a depressed transsexual. *Signs: Journal of Women in Culture and Society*, 42(4),819–841.

Baril, A. (2015). Transness as debility: Rethinking Intersections between trans and dis-abled embodiments. *Feminist Review*, 111, 59–74.

Berlant, L. (2012). *Desire/Love*. Brooklyn: Punctum.

Berlant, L., & Edelman, L. (2014). *Sex, Or The Unbearable*. Durham, NC: Duke University Press.

Byers, M. (2018). "Fats," futurity, and the contemporary Young Adult novel. *Fat Studies*, 7(2),159–169.

Cvetkovich, A. (2003). *An Archive of Feelings: Trauma, Sexuality, and Lesbian Public Cultures*. Durham, NC: Duke University Press.

Erickson, L. (2007). Revealing femmegimp: A sex-positive reflection on sites of shame as sites of resistance for people with disabilities. *Atlantis*, 31(2),42–52.

Eshun, K. (2003). Further considerations of Afrofuturism. *CR: The New Centennial Review*, 3(2),287–302.

Fox, S. F. (2018). Tisha B'Av, "Ghetto Day," and producing "authentic" Jews at post-war Jewish summer camps. *Journal of Modern Jewish Studies*, 17(2),156–172.

Freeman, Elizabeth. (2010). *Time Binds: Queer Temporalities, Queer Histories*. Durham, NC: Duke University Press.

Herndon, A. (2002). Disparate but disabled: Fat embodiment and disability studies. *NWSA Journal*, 14(3), *Feminist Disability Studies*, 120–137.

Laymon, K. (2013). *Long Division*. New York: Agate.

McFarland, J., Slothouber, V., & Taylor, A. (2018). Temporarily fat: A queer exploration of fat time. *Fat Studies*, 7(2),135–146.

Mitchell, A. (2004). Porky. In D. Kulick & A. Meneley (Eds), *Fat: The Anthropology of an Obsession*, (pp. 211–226). New York: Penguin.

Mitchell, A. (2018). Sedentary lifestyle: Fat queer craft. *Fat Studies*, 7(2),147–168.

Mollow, A. (2006). "When black women start going on Prozac": The politics of race, gender, and emotional distress in Meri Nana-Ama Danquah's *Willow Weep for Me*. *MELUS*, 31(3),67–99.

Moor Mother Goddess. (2015). Forethought. Rasheedah Phillips (Ed.), *Black Quantum Futurism: Theory & Practice*, (pp. 7–10). Vol. 1. Philadelphia: Afrofuturist Affair.

Muñoz, J. E. (1999). *Disidentifications: Queers of Color and the Performance of Politics*. Minneapolis: U Minnesota Press.

Nicolaidis, C., et. al. (2010). "You don't go tell White people nothing": African American women's perspectives on the influence of violence and race on depression and depression care. *American Journal of Public Health*, 100(8),1470–76.

Phillips, R. (2015). Black quantum futurism. R. Phillips (Ed), *Black Quantum Futurism: Theory & Practice*, (pp. 11–30). Vol. 1. Philadelphia: Afrofuturist Affair.

Probyn, E. (2005). *Blush: Faces of Shame*. Minneapolis: University of Minnesota Press.

Romero, R. E. (2000). The icon of the strong Black woman: The paradox of strength. In L. C. Jackson & B. Greene (Eds), *Psychotherapy with African American Women*, (pp. 225–238). New York, NY: Guilford Press.

Sontag, S. (1999). Notes on "Camp." In F. Cleto (Ed), *Camp: Queer Aesthetics and the Performing Subject: A Reader* (53–65). Reprinted from Sontag, S. (1964). Notes on "Camp". *Partisan Review*, 31(4),515–530.

Sykes, H. (2010). *Queer Bodies: Sexualities, Genders, and Fatness in Physical Education*. New York: Lang.

Tidgwell, T., Friedman, M., Rinaldi, J., Kotow, C., & Lind, E. R. M. (2018). Introduction. Special issue: Fatness and temporality. *Fat Studies*, 7(2),115–123.

Wendell, S. (2001). Unhealthy disabled: Treating chronic illnesses as disabilities. *Hypatia*, 16(4),17–33.

Womack, Y. L. (2013). *Afrofuturism*. Chicago: Chicago Review Press.

20 Dismantling the Empire

In Defense of Incoherence and Intersectionality

May Friedman

When I think about fat and intersectionality, I realize how much my experience of fat as an identity is as complex and layered as my physical experience of fat itself. My fat rests under my skin, covers and weaves between my muscles and bones, stretches and pulls over and around my frame, pushing out here, dripping down there.

My fat identity is similarly tangled. I can't understand my fat body without understanding my complicated pathway through race—my brown skin, my unruly hair. Fat and food do a complex dance with my sense of my gut instincts, but also my guts—my digestion, my awareness of my own metabolism, of food and ideas nourishing me. My shifts through thin and fat have kept pace with my dislinear moves toward respectability, with class and professionalism won or lost in response to my amplitude, but also my racialization, my age, maternity, and other factors beyond.

The project of articulating my own intersections and traffic jams allows me to interrogate my relationship with the theoretical models that I hold dear. I genuinely believe that I would not have survived my journey through the academic world without the scaffolding of theories of intersectionality (Yuval-Davis, 2011; Crenshaw, 1989, 1993; Keating, 2009). Likewise, Fat Studies scholarship has allowed me to understand the world around me in revolutionary and life-saving ways (Rothblum & Solovay, 2009; Harding & Kirby, 2009; LeBesco, 2004; Cooper, 2016). Thus far, however, I have felt that these two models have resisted a thorough reckoning, have failed to acknowledge one another. Nash and Warin argue: "the use of intersectionality as a concept has not yet had a significant influence or impact within Fat Studies scholarship. ... Moreover, the public face of Fat Studies is still white, middle-class, well-educated women" (2017, p. 82). At the same time, most intersectional work still ignores the ongoing impact of size oppression and its overlaps and confluences with other embodied subjectivities (van Amsterdam, 2013).

Cognizant of the many ways that attempts to clearly categorize—through BMI, race-based data collection, suppression of chosen pronouns—act as forms of violence, I reach out in my analysis here to the only topic about which I can speak authoritatively: my own experiences in my own body, and the ways that a dual focus on Fat Studies and intersectionality have simultaneously supported my internal analysis and have thus far fallen short. This chapter attempts to examine moments in my life where the lessons I have learned from intersectional scholarship and from Fat Studies have sat together—sometimes productively, sometimes uneasily, but side by side as I have explored my own identity and reality.

Limitations

To engage genuinely with Fat Studies and intersectionality is to demand something that is greater than the sum of its parts. On the one hand, the intellectual curiosity that Fat Studies offers allows us to take this new and dynamic field in multiple, fluid, supple, and exciting directions, as the chapters in this volume may attest. At the same time, some of the general trends within Fat Studies are troublesome (Cooper, 2010, 2016; Murray, 2008; van Amsterdam, 2013).

Fat Studies scholarship, for all its dynamism and sheer carnivalesque drollery, remains a space that attends to only selected diversities. Fatness has been theorized through queer theory and queer fat identities are explored amply (Pausé, Wykes & Murray, 2014). Fat experiences that speak to high fashion and confident social capital demand attention (Downing Peters, 2014) and linkages between fatness and disability are sometimes attended to (Mollow, 2015; Meleo-Erwin, 2014). At the same time, particular fat manifestations may escape the scrutiny of this scholarship. Usiekniewicz argues that "fat studies take[s] up the positioning of bodies that are white, cis gender, female, and middle-class, thus ignoring the various ways in which fatness and the war waged against it affect men, people of color, trans people, and the poor" (2016, p. 22).

Fat spaces—both in and out of the academy—remain almost exclusively white: Senyonga argues that "very few studies on fatness truly account for race" (2017, p. 2, see also Sullivan, 2013; Shaw, 2005; Mollow, 2017). Fat scholarship has privileged particular, and particularly legible, gender expressions (White, 2014), and is often uninformed by analyses of class (van Amsterdam, 2013). Samantha Murray suggests that "much fat activism reaffirms—albeit inadvertently—the very systems of power/knowledge it sets out to challenge" (2008, p. 88); perhaps echoing the inception of feminist organizing, a focus on shared identity nonetheless prioritizes more privileged experiences of oppression. Similarly, Charlotte Cooper argues that the creation of Fat Studies as an academic discipline draws on professionalizing and legitimizing discourses, which may abandon the radical potential of fat activist movements (2016). If, as Yuval-Davis attests, "The politics of belonging also include struggles around the determination of what is involved in belonging, in being a member of such a community" (2011, p. 3), then how can I find myself in a Fat Studies scholarship that does not seem to contain stories or analyses like my own?

At the same time that Fat Studies fails to consider "how body privilege is patterned by gender and race" (Kwan, 2010, p. 145), as well as other embodiments and experiences, theories of intersectionality have been accused of having increasingly limited scope. As a 21st century buzzword, intersectionality has come to stand in for limited acknowledgment of two (or occasionally more) "categories of social difference" taken together "in an additive way" (Yuval-Davis, 2011, p. 4), an understanding which is far from the term's initial devising (Keating, 2009). At other times, and even more alarmingly, "intersectionality" has simply and uncritically been thrown into analyses or actions as a shorthand for "oh and race and class, too" with no substantive engagement in anti-racist thought or anti-capitalist awareness underpinning these discourses (Rice, Harrison & Friedman, 2019).

For example: I am a brown woman. Brown + woman = heightened oppression on the basis of race and gender. Critical approaches to intersectionality aim to fill in the blanks in this equation, noting that both brownness and womanness are not merely additive criteria but rather complex and unstable markers that may interact in a range of ways (Yuval-Davis, 2011; Oprisko & Caplan, 2014). Furthermore, a truly complex approach to intersectionality clearly acknowledges that every body carries an enormous range of different markers, that "brown" and "woman" do not begin to explain me. While the best intersectional approaches take into account the ways that ultimately identity is never fixed—we both change and also are in endless dialogue with the environments around us—many approaches to intersectionality nonetheless begin with the idea of identity as concrete. Furthermore, as van Amsterdam (2013) demonstrates, spaces that grapple with intersectionality seldom genuinely engage with ideas around size. A substantively critical intersectional approach must borrow from postmodern notions of truth that abandon fixity in favour of conversation, instability, dialogue (Mollow, 2017). Such an approach must also attend to "the (im)possibilities of 'body size' as an important but neglected axis of signification in intersectional theory and practice" (van Amsterdam, 2013, p. 1).

In other words: my raced, female body is also fat, and also encompasses much more than the descriptors "raced, fat, female" can contain:

> I am in my cousin's home, a space I can only inhabit every few years, because of the expense of time and distance and money involved in getting back to the country my parents left, surrounded by dozens of family members. I am a young adult, and this is my first visit back alone, without my mom. I feel layers of tension floating off my body—everyone looks like me, talks like me. The kinky hair in the shower drain may or may not be mine. Often chided for being too loud and bombastic in Canada, here I am the quietest person in the room and I am delighting in the sheer overwhelming presence of my family, their roaring voices, their enormous energy. The meal is similarly excessive, with endless exhausting courses and frequent exhortations to keep eating. Afterward,

my cousin beckons me over and looks me up and down: "Did you get fat? I think you got fat! Or maybe it's just that dress?" All my aunties trill their laughter in response. How can I feel so secure in my excess and at the same time be policed for my large body? My working class cousins don't care about my analysis of the corrupt diet industry or my commitment to body positivity, movements that are, anyway, still years away from my suddenly ashamed young self. I shrug into myself, wrap a sweater against the objectionable dress, and realize that there are many different ways to inhabit a body that is all wrong.

In moments like this, my need for intersectional analysis is not merely intellectual, but an insistent, embodied ache. Simply put, I need a way to acknowledge the bifurcations and embeddedness of both identity and politics, a notion of intersectionality that acknowledges complexity, a Fat Studies scholarship that takes up the multitudinous and complex sphere of embodiment.

Ambiguity

My politic has always been a politic of ambiguity. Perhaps in response to my experiences in a body seen as racially ambiguous; perhaps as a confrontation to my unsteady queerness; or maybe just as a means of contending with the overall messiness of the world around me, I've resisted, in word and action, motifs of certainty (Friedman, 2017). Instead, I've worked toward an emphasis on "uncertainty as a valuable critical lens" (Friedman, 2013, p. 16). This approach to my own bodily incoherence informs my research and scholarship. The extent to which I have needed to be categorized—by strangers, by institutions, by forms and frameworks has felt, to varying degrees, like a form of violence. This violence is threaded through my history in both social and corporeal ways: through my parents' experiences as refugees when their religion positioned them as traitors to their country of origin and their brown skin made them unwelcome in the country they entered; the endless speculation about whether or not I "count" as racialized in my politicized workplace; and my own hesitation about inhabiting queer space in light of my lengthy marriage to a man.

Echoing my own liminal self-identity, the interplay between my various identities and experiences in external contexts is likewise unstable and shape-shifting—sometimes mother plus fat equals nurturing. At other times, it positions me as ignorant or irresponsible (Herndon, 2010; McNaughton, 2011); yet other times I am taken up as Mammy, presumed to be the paid caregiver for my white children (Shaw, 2005). My brown skin and my round body are sometimes honoured as delectable, while in other spaces, being a fat racialized woman just multiplies and alters the scorn (Senyonga, 2017). I do not know what will be seen, and how I will be understood; I have come to acknowledge that the vagaries of oppression and celebration are dynamic and alchemical. To acknowledge this incoherence requires that we speak of intersectionality in a different way:

I am 19 years old, barely an adult, trying to figure out who I am and how I relate to the world as a person independent of my family of origin. At this point I find the whole project of identity confusing: I'm an undergraduate from a working-class family, so I have no context for the type of leaning into respectability I'm being groomed toward—I don't know how to navigate the university and keep making what feel like humiliating mistakes. My sexuality is in flux, which is a real problem since I still live at home with my old fashioned and homophobic parents. At the same time, other markers of my identity are seemingly coming into sharp focus: I have recently tumbled from "overweight" right over to "obese", which causes me considerable anxiety. I have also begun filling in various forms that require me to clarify my ethnicity and have noted that suddenly I am no longer "Middle Eastern" but am instead "West Asian". It's not clear whether my messy, ambiguous identities or my concrete, sharp edged identities cause me more distress.

Sitting in the push/pull of my various transitions and modalities, I am reminded of the words of Eli Clare, who writes that, "The layers are so tangled: gender folds into disability, disability wraps around class, class strains against race, race snarls into sexuality, sexuality hangs onto gender, all of it finally piling into our bodies" (2003, p. 1). By contrast, the language of BMI echoes other spaces that have been medicalized, compartmentalized, empiricized, colonized. I think of the scales at the doctor's office; the boxes of the census, or the university's "self-identification" survey; I think of my children's births and the voracious need for people to know two things about them: their sex and their weight, before any of their beautiful intricacies could be explored.

In the moments when the borderlines between identity markers are shown to be laughably random, I am not sure whether I feel fear or liberation. On the one hand, we are accountable to our identities in profound ways, and are rewarded and punished based on these markers. I think about standardized risk assessments (Smith, 2011; Strega, 2009), evidence-based research (Bates, 2011)—the need to reduce the messiness and certainty and fear into a strict linear scale with distinct markers: Now we are overweight. Now we are obese. Now we are at risk. Now we will suffer and now—if we are smart and hardworking—we will thrive. Luck and privilege are erased from this analysis.

I want to offer my list of adjectives and wrap myself in certainty. I wish that I could abandon complications and intersections, go back to my childhood faith in systems and understand that I could, with a pound, move in and out of fat, move in and out of health, whiteness, respectability. I wish I could do that, but then I think about the fact that "empirical" knowledge is literally knowledge derived *from the empire*, from the colonizing forces that laid down frameworks of certainty with absolutely no regard for the complex and beautiful realities that shift and dance around us.

Impact

If intersectionality allows me to contend with the tensions between my convoluted and ambiguous identities, the best of Fat Studies opens up the notion of identity as unstable and contingent. One of the chief gifts I have received from Fat Studies is an unabashed insistence on "fat" as an ambiguous marker, a label that is as elastic as my waistband. Charlotte Cooper states that, "fat exists in context and experience; fat people know who they are and are known as fat by others" (2016, p. 1) On the one hand, Fat Studies and fat activism have dwelled in the singularity of fat identity; creating a site of identity politics necessarily requires a stripping of the intersectional or the ambiguous from the central project of fatness (Nash & Warin, 2017; Murray, 2008). On the other hand, however, thinking about fat gives me explicit permission to think about my identity—about all of my identities—in porous and context specific ways. Only I can decide that I am fat. Extrapolating from this politic gives me permission to pick my pronouns, my relationship with queerness and brownness, the room to be a working class academic mother, space to confront my contradictions.

And yet—to say that only I can decide about my own fatness is not strictly true, of course. When the car window rolls down and someone yells "Fat cow!" I suspect they are not joining me in an empowerment journey by reclaiming a reviled word. If intersectionality allows for complexity and Fat Studies honours self-authorship, both modes of scholarship have likewise acknowledged the material realities of bodies and identities. A critical feminist notion of intersectionality cannot fail to acknowledge the ways that embodied sites of oppression, such as racism, sexism, and so on, have a very real and corporeal impact (Senyonga, 2017; Shaw, 2005; Usiekniewicz, 2016). Fat Studies begins in fat activism, which serves as a rejection of the reviling of larger bodies within society (Cooper, 2010, 2016). As both Fat Studies and intersectionality scholarship well acknowledge (Wann, 2009; Crenshaw, 1989, 1993), it is impossible to consider identity from within, without acknowledging the material realities of our identities and the ways that "the meanings attributed to extraordinary bodies reside not in inherent physical flaws, but in social relationships" (Garland-Thomson, 1997, quoted in Mollow, 2015, p. 201). The extrapolation from social relationships to policy directives was made obvious for fat people in the moment in 1998 where the BMI cut-offs for overweight and obese were moved and "millions of people became fat overnight" (Wann, 2009, p. xiv). How we are perceived in society affects our ability to live authentic lives, or, in some cases, to live at all (Shaw, 2005; Mollow, 2017; Usiekniewicz, 2016). To argue that our intersectionality is unstable does not negate the extent to which we continue to function at the mercy of our social positioning—none of us can truly out-perform discrimination, stigma, violence.

Law is the birthplace of intersectionality, beginning with the integral writing of Kimberlé Crenshaw (1989, 1993), working to contest the notion that we are all equal before the law. Instead, intersectionality acknowledges the multiple and uneven ways that privilege and oppression are distributed even, or perhaps especially in the non-binary, unyielding spaces of law and institution. Legal approaches to Fat Studies elucidate these tensions clearly in exploring the myriad ways that fat people have been disqualified from human rights throughout the public and private spheres (Solovay, 2000). The tensions between institutional culture and the intersections of real life are made clear to me in one of my life's most important and mundane moments:

> I am 23 years old and I am getting married. My person is white, a man and Jewish, satisfying all of my parents' expectations/demands. It is a hopeful and happy time and I feel very lucky to have found someone with whom to build a future. We fill in our marriage license—available to us as a "straight" couple in this moment before the legalization of same-sex marriage—and I note my discomfort in listing my profession as "receptionist" while he is noted as "graduate student." Our disparate class pairing is made more evident as our parents meet and our families mesh together awkwardly. My big white wedding dress keeps needing to be let out to hide the bulges beneath, even as it hides my queerness under its capacious skirt, conceals the radical politics that will eventually stick out as much as my rolling belly. We get married; I change my name; and for the time being, in the eyes of the law and my parents, all the contradictions are resolved, or at least concealed.

Corporeality

For all the uneasiness with which Fat Studies and intersectionality co-exist, there is one place that I find unambiguous connection: the best of both fat and intersectional scholarship begins with an examination of the body. In the case of intersectionality, this examination seeks to unpack the notion of complex body knowledge (Oprisko & Caplan, 2014; Nash & Warin, 2017) by considering the ways our bodies are engaged in multiple systems of signification simultaneously. Fat Studies takes up the body in a slightly different way by providing a bridge between the enlightenment disconnect between mind and body (Murray, 2008; Kargbo, 2013). Fat Studies scholarship, in relation with other revolutionary discourses such as Critical Disability Studies (Mollow, 2015, 2017; Meleo-Erwin, 2014), offers work that is deeply corporeal and looks beyond the limits of fat itself to explore instead many of the grotesque components of our bodies that are often excised from traditional scholarship (Chalklin, 2016).

As we walk through our professional lives, our bodies are often meant to merely house our lofty brains, but ultimately our bodies and minds resist this dualism—we leave the meeting because of a bursting bladder, we cancel class because of the barfing flu, we are distracted by a sunburn, or we are overwhelmed by a migraine. Other disruptions occur, as in the following example:

> I am on maternity leave from my doctorate and teaching my first ever class as an instructor and I am fucking terrified. Barely postpartum, nothing fits and I feel overripe and bulging, all the body love of my pregnancy abruptly vanishing as I aim to perform professionalism and respectability. It doesn't help that I've left my two-month-old baby at home with the bottle she loathes and that, as I'm lecturing, my brain is ticking through a parallel pathway concerned with exactly how miserable the child is, how little milk she's keeping down and, not incidentally, how much of a pain in the ass she's being for her babysitter, my beloved sister-in-law, who didn't sign up for this shit. I think I was making some erudite point about the welfare state when I realized that the warm flush spreading across my front was actually milk leaking through my shirt and publicly puddling in front of my fascinated/horrified first year students... "Break time!"

The times my body has asserted itself have felt like moments of uncomfortable rupture, but sitting in the space between intersectionality and Fat Studies allows me to recognize that in fact, *this* is my real life. My body is not only intersected by the conversations between my race and class, queerness and family, but also in the constant engagement with my corporeal presence. This engagement is made obvious by my fat rolls, but also in the pissing, shitting, farting presence of my body. Erasing these functions from view makes me feel alone in my humiliating corporeality, but an examination of the grotesque (Chalklin, 2016), a focus on the body, reminds me that these are basic human functions and that ultimately there is connection and disruption in embracing and celebrating our bodies in the multitudes of their diversity and the similarities of their basic humanity. Furthermore, the above anecdotes reminds me that not only are our bodies and minds knit together, but that we are likewise held in complex webs of relationality: my body's dependence on the body of my child to take the milk from my breasts, my anxiety at creating discomfort for both child and babysitter, resist the liberal tropes of individuality (Chandler, 2007). Instead, I can see in this story the ways that I am held in relation to the people around me, engaging with my students and my family, with the professional and personal in messy and disorganized ways.

Conclusions

Fat Studies and intersectionality are both complex fields that contain multitudes. They cannot come under consideration without an acknowledgement of the various debates within these fields, the continuum of values and ideas that comprise the corpus, the body, of scholarships. Like our bodies, fields of scholarship are contradictory and unstable. It is perhaps unsurprising then, that reconciling Fat Studies and intersectionality feels like every meal at my house. My four children mill around, standing up to grab a book, get a glass, getting distracted by a game over here, stomping up the stairs in a snit over there. Their auntie strums a guitar. My dad, who is hard of hearing, hollers into a telephone, while a neighbour, navigating a toddler poop-mergency, dashes through to the bathroom. Trying to gather my large family around the table is an exercise in futility and at a certain point I have had to learn to let go of this ideal and instead just sit with whoever is around.

Cooper asks, rhetorically, whether "having common political goals means that theoretical differences do not matter and that diverse works can coexist harmoniously within a field?" (2010, p. 1028). I cannot yet confidently argue that common political goals are sufficient to lubricate away any friction between theoretical models; in inviting the multiple ideas, theories, beliefs, and experiences held by Fat Studies and intersectionality scholarship to sit together I must get used to the idea that no table is big enough to hold them together harmoniously. To allow them to sit separately however, requires that I bifurcate myself, ignore parts of myself in favour of others. In inviting Fat Studies and intersectionality to sit together, I must acknowledge the tensions between them, the ways that they are imperfect bedfellows—or dinner companions. In truth, however, I require them both. This chapter exists as my attempt to continue to set the table that will allow Fat Studies and intersectionality to sit together in all their extravagant, contradictory, brave and heartfelt multitudes.

References

van Amsterdam, N. (2013). Big fat inequalities, thin privilege: An intersectional perspective on "body size". *European Journal of Women's Studies*, *20*(2), 1–15.

Bates, M. (2011). Evidence based practice and anti-oppressive practice. In Donna Baines (Ed.), *Doing anti-oppressive practice: Social justice social work*, (pp. 147–159). Halifax: Fernwood Press.

Chalklin, V. (2016). Obstinate fatties: Fat activism, queer negativity, and the celebration of "obesity." *Subjectivity*, *9*(2), 107–125.

Chandler, M. (2007). Emancipated subjectivities and the subjugation of mothering practices. In Andrea O'Reilly (Ed.), *Maternal Theory: Essential Readings*, (pp. 529–541). Toronto: Demeter Press.

Clare, E. (2003). "Digging Deep: Thinking about Privilege." Unpublished paper, by permission.

Cooper, C. (2010). Fat Studies: Mapping the field. *Sociology Compass*, *4*(12), 1020–1034.

Cooper, C. (2016). *Fat activism: A radical social movement*. Bristol: HammerOn Press.

Crenshaw, K. (1989). Demarginalizing the intersection of race and sex: A Black feminist critique of antidiscrimination doctrine, feminist theory and antiracist politics. *University of Chicago Legal Forum, 1989*(1), 139–167.

Crenshaw, K. (1993). Mapping the margins: Intersectionality, identity politics, and violence against women of color. *Stanford Law Review*, *43*(6), 1241–1299.

Downing Peters, L. (2014). You are what you wear: How plus-size fashion figures into Fat identity formation. *Fashion Theory: The Journal of Dress, Body and Culture*, *18*(1), 45–71.

Friedman, M. (2013). *Mommyblogs and the changing face of motherhood*. Toronto: University of Toronto Press.

Friedman, M. (2017). Unpacking liminal identity: Lessons learned from the "other" box. In Samantha Wehbi and Henry Parada (Eds.), *Re-imagining anti-oppression social work: Reflecting on research*, (pp. 99–112). Toronto: Canadian Scholars' Press.

Harding, K., & Kirby, M. (2009). *Lessons from the fat-o-sphere: Quit dieting and declare a truce with your body*. New York: Perigee Books.

Herndon, A.M. (2010). Mommy made me do it: Mothering fat children in the midst of the obesity epidemic. *Food, Culture and Society, 13*(3), 332–349.

Kargbo, M. (2013). Toward a new relationality: Digital photography, shame and the fat subject. *Fat Studies, 2*(2), 160–172.

Keating, A. (2009). From intersections to interconnections: Lessons for transformation from "*This bridge called my back: Radical writings by women of color.*" In Michele Tracy Berger and Kathleen Guidroz (Eds.), *The intersectional approach: Transforming the academy through race, class and gender*, (pp. 81–99). Chapel Hill: University of North Carolina Press.

Kwan, S. (2010). Navigating public spaces: Gender, race, and body privilege in everyday life. *Feminist Formations, 22*(2), 144–166.

LeBesco, K. (2004). *Revolting Bodies? The Struggle to Redefine Fat Identity*. Amherst, NY: University of Massachusetts Press.

McNaughton, D. (2011). From the womb to the tomb: Obesity and maternal responsibility. *Critical Public Health, 21*(2), 179–190.

Meleo-Erwin, Z. (2014). Queering the linkages and divergences: The relationship between fatness and disability and the hope for a livable world. In Cat Pausé, Jackie Wykes and Samantha Murray (Eds.), *Queering fat embodiment*, (pp. 97–114). Farnham, UK/Burlington, VT: Ashgate.

Mollow, A. (2015). Disability studies gets fat. *Hypatia, 30*(1), 199–2016.

Mollow, A. (2017). Unvictimizable: Toward a Fat Black Disability Studies. *African American Review, 50*(2), 105–121.

Murray, S. (2008). *The "fat" female body*. New York: Palgrave.

Nash, M., and Warin, M. (2017). Squeezed between identity politics and intersectionality: A critique of "thin privilege" in Fat Studies. *Feminist Theory, 18*(1), 69–87.

Oprisko, R.L., and Caplan, J. (2014). Beyond the cake model: Critical intersectionality and the relative advantage of disadvantage. *Epiphany Journal of Transdisciplinary Studies, 7*(2), 35–54.

Pausé, C., Wykes, J., and Murray, S. (Eds.) (2014). *Queering fat embodiment*. Farnham, UK/ Burlington, VT: Ashgate.

Rice, C., Harrison, E., and Friedman, M. (2019). Doing justice to intersectionality in research. *Cultural Studies <--> Critical Methodologies*. https://doi.org/10.1177/1532708619829779

Rothblum, E., and Solovay, S. (2009). *The fat studies reader*. New York: New York University Press.

Senyonga, M. (2017). Microaggressions, marginality, and mediation at the intersections: Experiences of black fat women in academia. *InterActions: UCLA Journal of Education and Information Studies, 13*(1), 1–23.

Shaw, A. (2005). The other side of the looking glass: The marginalization of fatness and Blackness in the construction of gender identity. *Social Semiotics, 15*(2), 143–252.

Smith, K. (2011). Occupied spaces: Unmapping standardized assessments in health and social service organizations. In Donna Baines (Ed.), *Doing anti-oppressive practice: Social justice social work*, (pp. 199–213). Halifax: Fernwood Press.

Solovay, S. (2000). *Tipping the scales of justice: Fighting weight-based discrimination.* Amherst, NY: Prometheus Books.

Strega, S. (2009). Anti-oppressive approaches to assessment, risk assessment and file recording. In Susan Strega and Jeannine Carrière (Eds.), *Walking this path together: Anti-racist and anti-oppressive child welfare practice,* (pp. 142–157). Toronto: Fernwood Press.

Sullivan, M.J. (2013). Fat Mutha: Hip hop's corpulent poetics. *Palimpsest: A Journal on women, gender and the Black international, 2*(2), 200–213.

Usiekniewicz, M. (2016). Dangerous bodies: Blackness, fatness and the masculinity dividend. *Interalia: A Journal of Queer Studies, 11a*, 19–45.

Wann, M. (2009). Foreword: Fat studies: An invitation to revolution. In E. Rothblum & S. Solovay (Eds.), *The fat studies reader,* (pp. ix–xxv). New York: New York University Press.

White, F.R. (2014). Fat/Trans: Queering the activist body. *Fat Studies, 3*(2), 86–100.

Yuval-Davis, N. (2011). Power, intersectionality and the politics of belonging. FREIA Working Paper Series No.75. Feminist Research Center, Aalborg.

Contributor Biographies

Ramanpreet Annie Bahra is a PhD candidate in the Sociology department at York University, Ontario. Her research concentrates on social theory and Fat studies. Following New Materialism and Affect Studies, she explores the intersections of race, fatness and gender to offer an alternative perspective on the notion of the body.

Sarah Blanchette is a PhD candidate in the English Department at Western University, where she holds a SSHRC Doctoral Fellowship and Western's Doctoral Excellence Research Award. Her areas of research interest include: anti-psychiatric literature, narratives of embodiment and disability, feminist bioethics, medical humanities, and representations of Madness in twentieth-century American literature.

Heather Brown is a writer, editor, and researcher. In 2018, she was selected as the winner of the National Women's Studies Association Women's Centers Committee Emerging Leader Award. She may be contacted at dr.heather.a.brown@gmail.com

Rev. Dr. E-K. Daufin, former Multimedia Journalism professor and Campus National Organization for Women founding advisor at Alabama State University; (AEJMC) Commission on the Status of Women MaryAnn Yodelis-Smith Research and Minorities And Communication Division Outstanding Officer awardee, remains a National Popular Culture Association, Fat Studies scholar and private consultant

Amy Erdman Farrell is the Curley Chair of Liberal Arts and Professor of American Studies and Women's, Gender and Sexuality Studies at Dickinson College in Carlisle, Pennsylvania, USA. She is the author of *Fat Shame: Stigma and the Fat Body in American Culture* and *Yours in Sisterhood: Ms. Magazine and the Promise of Popular Feminism*. She has been interviewed in *Psychology Today* and *The Atlantic* and twice appeared on the *Colbert Report*. She is currently working on a project focusing on key moments in the history of the Girl Scouts of the USA, ones that illuminate struggles over the meanings of girlhood, feminism, racial equality, and nationalism.

Marty Fink is an Assistant Professor in the School of Professional Communication at Ryerson University. They work in archives, zines, and gay novels to bridge HIV caregiving activisms with queer crip theory. Fink's work appears in journals including *Science Fiction Studies*, *Jump Cut*, and *Journal of Fat Studies*.

May Friedman's research looks at unstable identities, including bodies that do not conform to traditional racial and national or aesthetic lines. Most recently much of May's research has focused on intersectional approaches to fat studies considering the multiple and fluid experiences of both fat oppression and fat activism. May works at Ryerson University as a faculty member in the School of Social Work and in the Ryerson/York graduate program in Communication and Culture.

Michael Gill is an associate professor of disability studies in the department of Cultural Foundations of Education at Syracuse University, USA. He is also an affiliated faculty member with Women's and Gender Studies. Gill is the author of the book *Already Doing It: Intellectual Disability and Sexual Agency* (University of Minnesota Press 2015). He also co-edited, with Cathy Schlund-Vials, *Disability, Human Rights, and the Limits of Humanitarianism* (Ashgate 2014).

April M. Herndon is a Professor in the English Department at Winona State University.

Julie Hollenbach is an Assistant Professor in the Division of Art History and Contemporary Culture at NSCAD University. Hollenbach recently curated "Unpacking the Living Room" at MSVU Art Gallery (Halifax, NS), and has published work in *Canadian Art*, *Studio*, *CRIT paper*, the *Design and Culture* journal, and *Cahiers métiers d'art ::: Craft Journal*.

Rachel Alpha Johnston Hurst is associate professor of Women's and Gender Studies at St. Francis Xavier University in Antigonish, Nova Scotia. She is author of *Surface Imaginations: Cosmetic Surgery, Photography, and Skin* (MQUP, 2015), and co-editor of *Skin, Culture, and Psychoanalysis* (Palgrave, 2013).

Karleen Pendleton Jiménez is a writer and associate professor of education at Trent University. Her books *Are You a Boy or a Girl?* and *How to Get a Girl Pregnant* were both Lambda literary finalists, and her films *Butch Coyolxauhqui* and *Tomboy* have been screened around the world.

Crystal L.M. Kotow is a PhD candidate in the department of Gender, Feminist and Women's Studies at York University. Kotow's research explores how fat women negotiate the intersections of body size, sexuality, gender and race in fat-specific social spaces. Her research interests include fat studies, queer affect theory, and feminist exploration of popular culture.

Dr. Andrea LaMarre is a lecturer in critical health psychology at Massey University. Her work spans public health, critical feminism, eating disorders, and systems approaches to mental health. She earned her doctoral degree in Family Relations and Human Development from the University of Guelph, where she was a Vanier Doctoral Scholar (CIHR) and subsequently an Ontario Women's Health Scholar.

Jade Le Grice is a Māori woman of Te Rarawa and Ngāpuhi descent, and lecturer in the School of Psychology at the University of Auckland. Broadly conceptualised, her research attends to the cultural nexus of Indigenous and western knowledge, colonising influence, response and intervention. Research spheres of interest include Māori and reproductive decisions, parenting, sexuality education, maternity, and abortion.

Emily R.M. Lind teaches Gender, Sexuality and Women's Studies at Okanagan College on the unceded territory of the Sylix (Okanagan) Peoples in Kelowna, British Columbia. Her research examines the intersections between identity, materiality, power, and knowledge production in interdisciplinary contexts.

Deborah McPhail is an Associate Professor in Community Health Sciences at the University of Manitoba. Her work centres around the marginalization of fatness within and by the Canadian healthcare system. Deborah's latest book, *Contours of the Nation* (2017), is the first critical feminist history of the emergence of "obesity" in Canada.

Lindsey Mazur is a Registered Dietitian and MSc Candidate at the University of Manitoba. Her research will address weight stigma in perinatal care, seeking perspectives of fat women and dietitians. In 2016, she founded Manitobans Against Weight Stigma to advocate for a human rights code amendment for protections based on weight.

Sonia Meerai is a full-time PhD student within the Gender, Feminist, and Women Studies Program at York University, Ontario, Canada. Her commitment within her professional and personal work is dismantling oppressive, colonial practices within mental health and health care systems through her social work practice and in her research.

James Overboe is an associate professor in the department of Sociology at Wilfrid Laurier University, Ontario. His current research offers an alternative view of life as an impersonal expression rather than being restricted by the human registry.

George Parker is a Pākehā person, a doctoral candidate in the School of Social Sciences, and lectures in the medical humanities programme at the Faculty of Medical and Health Sciences at the University of Auckland. A registered midwife, George's research interests include the politics of women's health; gender, queer, and intersectional perspectives on health and embodiment; fatness and reproductive justice.

Cat Pausé is a white USian expat and the lead editor of *Queering Fat Embodiment*. A Senior Lecturer in Human Development and Fat Studies Researcher at Massey University in New Zealand, her research focuses on the effects of spoiled identities on the health and well-being of fat individuals. Her work appears in scholarly journals such as *Feminist Review* and *Narrative Inquiries in Bioethics*, as well as online in *The Huffington Post* and *The Conversation*, among others.

Dr. Carla Rice is an award-winning Professor and Canada Research Chair at the University of Guelph specializing in embodiment studies, arts-based and creative methodologies, non-normative cultures, and accessibility and inclusion. She founded *Re•Vision: The Centre for Art and Social Justice* as an arts-informed research centre with a mandate to foster inclusive communities, social well-being, equity, and justice. More information about the *Re•Vision Centre* can be found at: https://projectrevision.ca/.

Dr. Jen Rinaldi is an Assistant Professor in the Legal Studies program at Ontario Tech University. She earned a doctoral degree in Critical Disability Studies at York University, and a master's degree in Philosophy at the University of Guelph. Currently she engages with narrative and arts-based methodologies to deconstruct eating disorder recovery, and to re-imagine recovery in relation to queer community. She also works in collaboration with Recounting Huronia, an arts-based collective that explores and stories traumatic histories of institutionalization.

Margaret Robinson is a fat, vegan, feminist scholar from Eskikewa'kik Nova Scotia and a member of the Lennox Island First Nation. She is an Assistant Professor of Indigenous Studies at Dalhousie University and an Affiliate Scientist at the Centre for Addiction & Mental Health in Toronto.

Sucharita Sarkar, PhD, is an Associate Professor of English at D.T.S.S College of Commerce, Mumbai, India. Her doctoral thesis investigated mothering narratives in contemporary India. Her research focuses on intersections of mothering, gender, writing, religion, body, family, media, diaspora, culture, food, and fat, especially in the context of South Asia.

Mary Senyonga is a doctoral candidate in the Social Sciences and Comparative Education division in the Race and Ethnic Studies sub-specialization of the Education department at UCLA. Her work explores the resistive and healing projects Black women and femmes employ as they attend what she argues are Traditionally Oppressive Institutions.

Francis Ray White (pronouns: they/them) is a senior lecturer in sociology at the University of Westminster, London. Their research exploring fat, queer and (trans)gender theories and embodiment has been published in journals including *Somatechnics*, *Fat Studies*, and *Sexualities*.

Index